NORTHERN IRELAND'S '68

Simon Prince is a Senior Lecturer in Canterbury Christ Church University's School of Humanities. His research is concerned with how relations between the local, national, and transnational-shaped protest movements and the production of violence, with civil breakdown in democracies, and with narratives of the Troubles. His publications include *Belfast and Derry in Revolt: A New History of the Start of the Troubles* (co-authored with Geoffrey Warner, 2011).

NORTHERN IRELAND'S '68

Civil Rights, Global Revolt and the Origins of The Troubles

Simon Prince

IRISH ACADEMIC PRESS

First published in 2007 by
Irish Academic Press
10 George's Street
Newbridge
Co. Kildare
Ireland
www.iap.ie

This Revised Edition © 2018, Irish Academic Press

9781788550369 (Paper)
9781788550376 (Kindle)
9781788550383 (Epub)
9781788550390 (PDF)

British Library Cataloguing in Publication Data
An entry can be found on request

Library of Congress Cataloging in Publication Data
An entry can be found on request

Interior design by www.jminfotechindia.com
Typeset in Classical Garamond BT 11/15 pt

Cover design by www.phoenix-graphicdesign.com

Contents

Acknowledgements

I should begin by thanking Robert Tombs and Paul Bew as without their help this book would not have been written. From the very beginning, they have given me their time, their advice, and their support. The debt that I owe to them cannot be calculated. I was also fortunate enough to be one of the last students to be supervised by Peter Clarke. Like all the others that came before me, I benefited enormously from the experience.

Brendan Simms, George Boyce, Vincent Comerford, Tony Judt, Geoffrey Warner, Bob Purdie and Roy Foster all took the trouble to read early versions of some of the chapters. I am deeply grateful for their incisive and invaluable comments – all of which resulted in improvements to the text. Eugenio Biagini, Chris Clark, Mike Broers, Richard Drayton, Ray Ryan and John Bew gave me much-needed help and advice – I am glad to have this chance to thank them for their efforts on my behalf.

Although I have consciously tried to rely upon printed sources, this was not always possible. Fortunately, Roy Johnston, Anthony Coughlan and Kevin Boyle graciously allowed me to draw upon their memories and private papers. Their kindness kept me from making some costly errors and brought to my attention many things that I had overlooked.

The staffs of many research institutions have offered great assistance and I would like to thank everyone who has helped me at the Public Record Office of Northern Ireland in Belfast, the National Archives at Kew, the British Library Newspaper Library at Colindale, the Linen Hall Library in Belfast, and the University Library in Cambridge. St John's College, Cambridge, and Lady Margaret Hall, Oxford, have been incredibly generous with the support that they gave me while I was writing and researching this book. At Irish Academic Press, Lisa Hyde and Kay Hyman deserve special thanks. Lisa has guided me through every stage of the process with sensitivity and professionalism.

Kay carefully read through the typescript spotting problems and finding solutions.

My friends and family have always believed in me – even when I had stopped – and it is to them that this book is dedicated.

Dramatis Personae

Ken Bloomfield: Terence O'Neill's closest civil service adviser and his speechwriter.

Kevin Boyle: A popular young lecturer at Queen's University who was elected onto the Faceless Committee of People's Democracy.

Sir Basil Brooke (Viscount Brookeborough): Prime Minister of Northern Ireland from 1943 to 1963.

Paddy Byrne: Secretary of the Campaign for Democracy in Ulster.

Stokley Carmichael: American civil rights activist and Chair of the Student Non-violent Co-ordinating Committee.

Daniel Cohn-Bendit: The star of France's '68.

Ivan Cooper: Chair of the Derry Citizens' Action Committee.

Anthony Coughlan: Independent thinker who built upon C. Desmond Greaves's ideas to construct the Republican movement's civil rights strategy.

Bill Craig: Unionist politician who was initially a close ally of Terence O'Neill, but later became one of his chief rivals.

Sir James Craig (Viscount Craigavon): Northern Ireland's first Prime Minister (1921–40).

Austin Currie: Nationalist MP for East Tyrone from 1964 to 1972 and one of the organisers of the first civil rights march.

Bernadette Devlin: Queen's University student who was elected onto the Faceless Committee of People's Democracy and became the star of the civil rights movement.

Finbar Doherty: One of the Derry radicals. After the 5 October 1968 march, which he helped to organise, he agreed to join the Derry Citizens' Action Committee.

James Doherty: Nationalist councillor on Londonderry Corporation and Eddie McAteer's chief lieutenant.

Paddy Doherty: One of the leaders of Derry's self-help movement and the man in charge of stewarding protests in the city during the civil rights crisis.

Rudi Dutschke: The public face of West Germany's Extra- Parliamentary Opposition.

Michael Farrell: One of Northern Ireland's leading leftists and a hugely influential figure within People's Democracy.

Brian Faulkner: The second man in Terence O'Neill's government – but he entertained hopes that the premiership would soon be his.

Gerry Fitt: Republican Labour politician who was elected to both Stormont and Westminster during the 1960s. As the civil rights campaign developed, he began to challenge for the political leadership of the minority population.

Frank Gogarty: A key member of the Belfast Wolfe Tone Society and of the Northern Ireland Civil Rights Association.

Cathal Goulding: The Irish Republican Army's Chief of Staff from 1962.

C. Desmond Greaves: The Communist Party of Great Britain's Irish expert and the dominant figure within the Connolly Association – which pioneered many of the tactics used in the civil rights campaign.

Cahir Healy: Veteran Nationalist politician.

John Hume: Community activist and Vice-Chair of the Derry Citizens' Action Committee.

Roy Johnston: Socialist intellectual who searched for a political home first in the Communist Party, then in the Connolly Association, and finally in the Republican movement.

Séan Lemass: Veteran of the Irish Revolution and Taoiseach from 1959.

Eddie McAteer: Nationalist MP for Derry's Foyle constituency from 1953 to 1969 and party leader from 1964.

Eamonn McCann: One of Northern Ireland's leading leftists and organiser of Derry's first civil rights march.

Conn and Patricia McCluskey: Civil Rights activists who helped to lead the Homeless Citizens' League, the Campaign for Social Justice, and the Northern Ireland Civil Rights Association.

Eamon Melaugh: One of the Derry radicals. Following the 5 October 1968 march, he too became a member of the Derry Citizens' Action Committee.

Séan MacStiofain: Traditionalist Republican who opposed Cathal Goulding's turn to the left.

Terence O'Neill: Prime Minister of Northern Ireland from 1963 to 1969.

Ian Paisley: Pastor and politician who strongly resisted any liberalisation of the Protestant Churches and the Northern Irish state.

Betty Sinclair: Veteran Communist and Chair of the Northern Ireland Civil Rights Association.

Cyril Toman: A close comrade of Eamonn McCann and Michael Farrell.

Eamon de Valera: The most important politician in the history of modern Ireland. De Valera served for long spells as both Taoiseach (1932–48, 1951–4 and 1957–9) and President (1959–73).

Foreword

Controversy is the lifeblood of history. If Burke taught us that truth has a certain economy of expression, John Stuart Mill taught us that truth also has a necessary vitality. In history, at least, ideas which are not challenged tend to atrophy and harden into dogmas. Modern Irish history in recent years has been marked by many serious and important debates, which tend to spill out of the academic forum to engage wider public interest. Was the 1798 rebellion inspired by the modernising ideas of the French Revolution, or was it essentially a sectarian jacquerie? Were the victims of the Great Irish Famine of 1845–9 sacrificed to a narrow vision of political economy, or did the British governments of the time do the best that could have been done under the circumstances? Who were the real victors of the Irish Land War – the Irish peasantry as a whole, or simply a privileged rural bourgeoisie? One event alone in the war of independence – the Kilmichael ambush – has produced a growing literature, involving significant numbers of locally based historians as well as professional academics, about whether Crown forces staged a 'false surrender' to lure Republican ambushers into the open and were rightly refused quarter thereafter, or whether this is a story to justify the deliberate killing of disarmed prisoners.

All these controversies, even the more tedious and embittered ones, are in principle to be welcomed. The willingness to question and debate is one of the most striking and attractive features of modern Irish historiography. There is one great exception to this rule – the historical treatment of the Civil Rights crisis of 1968. Here the iron hand of consensus rules. This is not without good reason. Northern Ireland in 1968 was characterised by a dead weight of Unionist–Nationalist antagonism which expressed itself in the denial of equal citizenship to the Catholic and Nationalist minority. The most striking example of this denial was the gerrymander of the province's second city to ensure that the control of local government remained in the hands of the Unionist minority – but there were other significant injustices, not only in electoral arrangements but in the allocation of jobs and housing. In this sense, then, a moral case definitely existed in support of the civil rights movement.

The strength of this moral case has, however, led to the suppression of all the more normal forms of historical enquiry. For example, what were the real motivations of the 68ers – in '68, and not as reconstructed in later years? What was the relationship between the radical leadership of the movement and its support base on the street? What was its real international context? Here lies the importance of Simon Prince's book. It applies all the techniques of historical questioning and research methodology one would expect from one of the most gifted young Cambridge historians (now teaching in Oxford) of his generation. Prince pushes aside the cobwebs and gives us a fresh look at one of the most important moments of modern Irish history. His book will provoke debate – and some disagreement – but it will shake up the subject and thus perform a great service.

Paul Bew Professor of Irish Politics Queen's University, Belfast

May 2007

Preface to the New Edition

Young men throwing petrol bombs at police officers. This image has defined the summer of 2018 in Derry – just as it became visual shorthand for revolt during the early years of the Troubles.[1] For modern historians, the temptation is always there to see the past in the present and to view things through a national lens.[2] But *Northern Ireland's '68* set out instead to look sideways, finding the global interconnectedness in the local story of the start of the Troubles. Eamonn McCann, who organised the first Civil Rights march in Derry, recalled coming home convinced that he 'could sweep up the local, parochial politics ... by introducing an international dimension'.[3] He succeeded, transforming forever the contexts in which everyone in Northern Ireland thought and acted. Since the book's publication over a decade ago, I have become even more convinced of the need for historians to write the long '68 into the history of Northern Ireland, and Northern Ireland into the history of the long '68.[4] Where the account offered here has activists on the Celtic fringe adopting and adapting ideas from the north American and western European core, I would now argue that Northern Ireland was central as well as peripheral. Myriad networks of people, objects, and ideas linked together disparate points around the western world in these years – and for some of these networks the central nodes lay in Northern Ireland. During 1970, for example, militants from the United States and France took direct inspiration *from* their Northern Irish comrades, who they believed had successfully bridged the gulf between western youth and Third World guerrilla fighters.[5] The confrontations of the long '68 – in places like Chicago, Paris, and Derry – were characterised by individuals drawing on the ideological positions of the time in an effort to mobilise support. At the start of the Troubles, the assorted forms of street politics and the variety of reactions they brought from the authorities produced dynamic processes which carried Northern Ireland in unanticipated directions and away from what was originally in dispute. The conflict should be viewed as a series of interrelated phases rather than as a seamless whole. So, while the images of petrol bombers from half a century apart may look similar, they represent very different struggles.

The Derry violence weakly echoes the early Troubles; another news story from the summer of 2018 is explicitly about this history and about how to deal with it. Starting in May, the United Kingdom government has been consulting on the best way to address Northern Ireland's past. The proposals have elicited emotional responses from Cabinet minsters and other public figures as much as from victims and their families.[6] Past events are still very much present politics. I did not fully appreciate this was the case until after I had finished writing *Northern Ireland's '68*, however. During the fortieth-anniversary commemorations, I witnessed political groups furiously battling to take control over the narrative. The Derry-born Republican Martin McGuinness claimed 'we marched along Duke Street and along many other roads and country lanes across the northern state, as we demanded change'. Irishmen and women were subsequently forced to take up arms and fight to make the British treat with them as equals. But, throughout the long war, the 'march for civil rights and national rights' always remained the same.[7] The Social Democratic and Labour Party pushed back against this reading of events, insisting that 'Civil Rights are part of our DNA'. Republican violence was not only unnecessary, it had also held up 'a journey that took a community from grievance to governance'.[8] McCann founded 'Reclaim the Spirit of '68' to challenge both these narratives. According to this group's press release, the Civil Rights movement was about 'the struggle of working class people for economic and social rights'.[9]

What all the interventions in the 'memory wars' have in common are neat frames which do not fit with the messy pictures I found in the archives and presented in this book. The narratives, though, are much more robust than I had originally thought them to be. They resist evidence that contradict them and play more of a role than precise, qualitative information does in how individuals make sense of things.[10] Significantly, these things help the men and women whose actions – whether directly or indirectly – produced violence live more easily with the choices they made. Outsiders are not in a position to understand, let alone to judge. 'He sees it from his side,' explained one bomb victim of the view taken by the Irish Republican Army (IRA) volunteer who planted it.[11]

The main reason for the primacy of narrative in public debates on the past in Northern Ireland is because they have endings as well as beginnings and middles: real evidence cannot refute imagined futures. While the Republican narrative promises a future free from Britain, the Unionist one envisages an endless siege, with enemies outside the walls and traitors inside them. One more push could bring victory; one more compromise could bring defeat. The two principal narratives, then, are simply impossible to bridge, spiraling around each other without ever touching. This problem is not just about historical events being read in radically different ways. Even supposing that a consensus could be reached on a factual account of, say, the long march undertaken by the People's Democracy from Belfast to Derry in January 1969, the narratives would arrive at this shared site from different starting points in the past and would head off in different directions towards the present and on to their respective imagined futures.[12]

Unsurprisingly, then, previous attempts to deal with the past in a systematic manner have failed to gain enough public support to go ahead. The main stumbling block has typically been the differences which exist in Northern Ireland over the legitimacy of the paramilitary campaigns. Historians cannot resolve those disagreements – and no document discovery or fresh analysis will change that state of affairs. Attitudes to Republican and Loyalist violence are, in turn, shaped by differences over to what extent Northern Ireland in 1968 was the 'Orange State'. Yet again, it is difficult to see how these narratives of democracy subverted or of tyranny overthrown can be either proved or disproved by historical research. The people of Northern Ireland are divided not so much over questions of fact and interpretation as over moral issues: the ultimate responsibility for the violence, the underlying motives of the principal actors to the conflict, and the fundamental meaning of victimhood.

When I was writing *Northern Ireland's '68*, I did not properly understand just how passionately my dispassionate account could be read. Historians have to work with concepts that have a political dimension and I also made the choice to use, wherever possible, the language of the time. An unintended consequence of writing this way was to give certain readers the false impression I was making firm moral judgements. Looking back, I regret not explaining those decisions more carefully. For example, the word 'provoked' – which appears in the very first line of the book – has implications for the issue of responsibility for the violence of the start of the Troubles. I used the term because contemporary activists throughout the western world often employed it. The leader of an American anti-war group said in September 1967 that its aim was to 'provoke confrontation', West German leftists said the 'protest violence' of the Easter 1968 marches was a way of 'provoking the state', and an article in the *New Left Review* that summer urged student radicals to behave 'provocatively'.[13] What I should have made clear in *Northern Ireland's '68* was exactly how these activists were employing this term. The protest repertoire of the late 1960s was a radicalised version of the one showcased a few years earlier in Birmingham, Alabama, during Project 'C' for Confrontation. As Martin Luther King explained in the midst of the campaign to 'the white moderate who is more devoted to "order" than to justice', 'we who engage in non-violent direct action are not the creators of tension. We merely bring to the surface the hidden tension that is already alive.'[14] So, McCann's 'provocation' on 5 October 1968 was about seeking to reveal the violence – broadly defined – that he believed lay behind the Northern Irish Prime Minister's liberal mask. '[Terrence] O'Neill talked about progress but,' McCann predicted, 'he would go back to the old Unionist background of open suppression.'[15]

Suspending 'one's own perceptions long enough to enter sympathetically into ... alien and possibly repugnant perspectives,' writes Thomas Haskell, is what separates a historical narrative from a political one.[16] Indeed, a historical approach to understanding the past can incorporate *multiple* conflicting viewpoints. A historical narrative can also move between different scales of space and time, from subjective individual experiences to the local, the national, and the transnational and from fleeting moments to days, weeks, months, years, and decades. These are all things that *Northern Ireland's '68* sets out to do. As a result, the book asked new questions, identified overlooked patterns, processes, and trajectories, and highlighted the complexities and contradictions of the time. But, will this (still) fresh account unsettle the political narratives during the fiftieth-anniversary commemorations? I fear a more consensual version of the past will become tolerable only after the combatants in the memory wars seek détente.

Unlike a political narrative, *Northern Ireland's '68* presents itself as personal and provisional rather than truthful and definitive. To quote Mary Fulbrook's 'basic code of historical practice', historians are committed to 'accepting the possibility of revision of particular interpretations in the light of further evidence'.[17] As I have explained already in this preface, I have subsequently changed my mind about how the transnational diffusion of ideas worked and about the importance of narrative to how people thought and acted. I have also had my mind changed on other matters by the excellent scholarship that has been produced over the last decade. For instance, Richard Bourke has persuasively argued against the Troubles being viewed as an ethnic conflict; Marianne Elliott has highlighted how religious divisions in Belfast neighbourhoods did not stop close-knit communities developing; Brian Hanley and Scott Millar have seen evidence that the pre-split IRA remained committed to armed struggle; and Maggie Scull has brought into sharper focus the roles played by the different parts of the Catholic Church.[18] Writing history is very much a collective effort. Indeed, what has made me cringe the most about revisiting my earliest work is that I did not acknowledge in the introduction the debt I owed to the many well-grounded and valuable histories of modern Ireland. The person who had the most right to be offended was Bob Purdie, author of the first book-length history of the Civil Right movement, but he instead showed me great kindness during his final years. I hope I will one day prove worthy of it.

Introduction

5 OCTOBER 1968

The protesters provoked the police; the police attacked the protesters. This pattern was repeated in cities throughout the world during 1968. On 5 October 1968, it was Derry's turn to stage what had become a familiar drama for the world's television viewers. The protesters who gathered at the city's railway station for a civil rights march on that Saturday afternoon represented, according to a later commission of inquiry, 'most of the elements in opposition to the Northern Ireland Government'.[1] This was what brought them together, but the marchers were also engaged in a number of other struggles – some of which were with each other.

The march was for civil rights, not Irish unity. It was part of a loose campaign to overthrow the sectarian system that relegated the Catholic minority to the status of second-class citizens. The authorities, however, insisted upon treating the march as a traditional Republican/Nationalist parade and banned it from entering the walled city – the Protestant citadel that had resisted Catholic armies in the past.[2] Republicans and Nationalists were indeed well represented among those who assembled at the railway station.[3] The disastrous Irish Republican Army (IRA) campaign of 1956–62 appeared to have marked the end of the armed struggle. Republican modernisers were instead hoping to unite Catholic and Protestant workers in a non-violent struggle for a socialist Ireland. Civil rights were seen as a stepping stone to this ultimate goal, a way of allowing the working class to recognise its common interests. The architects of this new departure, Roy Johnston and Anthony Coughlan, were there to witness their theories being tested. Johnston had joined the IRA; Coughlan had kept his distance from it. They were nonetheless both close to the IRA's Chief of Staff, Cathal Goulding, and had expected him to join them on the march – as had the Special Branch detectives who spied upon the movement. But Goulding's car had broken down on the road to Derry.[4] The leader of the Nationalist Party, Eddie McAteer, had encountered no such problems making his way to the outskirts of his home town. McAteer had spent his life campaigning against the partition of his country and to improve the lot of the Catholic community. In the last few years, however, his party's main battle had been against political extinction. McAteer had recently warned those with 'public voices' to guard against having their words 'enlarged into hideous actions', yet he could not ignore the shift to street politics.[5] He therefore lined up alongside his rivals against his better judgement.

The young community activist tipped to replace McAteer as the leader of constitutional nationalism, John Hume, also preferred working within the system to direct action and had helped to set up a credit union as well as a housing association in Derry. However, the Northern Ireland government's heavy-handed decision to ban the march from the city centre had pushed him onto the streets.[6] The Republican Labour MP Gerry Fitt, another one of McAteer's challengers, was more enthusiastic about the march, seeing it as an opportunity to advance the cause of civil rights – and his own political career. Fitt had arrived from the Labour Party Conference in Blackpool with three British MPs in tow to act as independent observers. They belonged to a ginger group that was struggling to persuade the Prime Minister, Harold Wilson, to impose reform upon the devolved government in Belfast.[7]

One of the Labour MPs, Russell Kerr, had already witnessed another of '68's big set-pieces: he had been in Chicago when the anti- war movement had confronted the politicians at the Democratic Convention. Kerr was later to tell the General Secretary of the Connolly Association, the Irish emigrant organisation that had first suggested the idea of a civil rights campaign, that the two police forces 'both play in the same league'.[8] This was what the youthful radicals who had staged the march were counting on – indeed, their entire plan depended upon it. American activists believed that they had found a short cut out of the political margins: 'You create disturbances, you keep pushing the system. You keep drawing up the contradictions until they have to hit back.'[9] Northern Ireland's activists adopted an almost identical approach. As the principal organiser of the march, Eamonn McCann, noted in his memoirs, the 'strategy was to provoke the police into overreaction'.[10] Another leading leftist, Michael Farrell, remembered the Derry protest as 'our Chicago', but it was also 'our Paris, our Prague'. 'One world, One struggle' – that was the motto of '68 according to McCann.[11]

The leftists saw themselves as part of a global revolt against imperialism, capitalism and bureaucracy. At the local level, this meant that they were opposed to the 'Green Tories' – the Nationalists in the North and Fianna Fáil in the South – as well to the 'Orange Tories' who controlled the state.[12] It also meant that they were opposed to the bureaucratic socialism of the Old Left. A year earlier, McCann's newspaper had denounced the Republican modernisers as 'Stalinist fakers'.[13] At a march from Coalisland to Dungannon held as the Soviets were suppressing the Prague Spring, leftists from Belfast and Derry had greeted the Communist Chair of the Northern Ireland Civil Rights Association (NICRA), Betty Sinclair, with shouts of 'Russia' and 'jackboot'.[14]

The leftists had tried to provoke the police at this protest too, but had been restrained by the stewards. The Communists, Republicans and Nationalists who sat on the NICRA executive felt that violence would wreck the civil rights campaign and had worked hard to ensure that the Coalisland–Dungannon march passed off without incident.[15] However, NICRA was only acting as the sponsor of the Derry march – the city's leftists had taken over responsibility for organising it. But this did not ensure that everything went the way that the young radicals wanted. Although an impressive number of politicians and activists had turned up at the railway station, the overall attendance fell far short of the planning committee's prediction of 'in the region of 5,000 people'.[16] The *Derry Journal* estimated that only somewhere between 350 and 400 people assembled for the start of the march – five times fewer than the number that had paraded from Coalisland to Dungannon.[17] Like so many other innovative challenges to the Northern state before it, the civil rights campaign seemed to be marching into obscurity.

In the years since Derry's last street protests, however, the new medium of television had acquired a mass audience. As veteran anchorman Walter Kronkite later explained, a demonstration now needed 'only enough people to fill the frame of a television camera' to be a success.[18] Indeed, the publicity for the march was aimed as much at inducing the BBC, Ulster Television and Telefís Éireann to send camera crews as at bringing out the citizens of Derry.[19] All the leftists had to do to have their protest covered by the network news programmes at home and abroad was to provide the drama demanded by television.

Several clashes involving policemen and protesters occurred soon after the march got under way. These violent incidents were partly the result of the confusion over tactics that both sides were experiencing. The original route had been spontaneously abandoned and an unguarded road taken instead – forcing the Royal Ulster Constabulary (RUC) to move a reserve unit hurriedly into place.[20] The first rank of marchers, which at the insistence of the organisers mainly consisted of MPs, had been pushed into the hastily assembled police line. Although no explicit order was given to draw batons, certain officers appear to have reacted by striking McAteer and Fitt.[21] The latter was then arrested for disorderly behaviour and taken to the hospital via the police station.[22] The RUC later claimed that a placard wielded by one of the marchers rather than a police baton had cut Fitt's head. The explanation given for McAteer's injuries was even weaker. The police report devoted an entire paragraph to an analysis of the 'bruised area below the right groin' before concluding that there was 'nothing which would give any indication as to the exact nature of the blow causing the contusion'.[23]

Following the initial scuffles, however, both sides backed away from each other.[24] In the absence of anything else to do, Sinclair began to improvise a meeting. Her hope was that the same tactics that had kept the peace in Dungannon would work again in Derry. The police also adopted a conciliatory stance, providing Sinclair with a chair and making no attempt to disperse what was an illegal assembly. The NICRA Chair's plea for the right of non-violent procession to be properly respected was echoed by McAteer.[25] McCann's speech was more ambivalent regarding the use of force.[26] As McCann later testified in court, he had told his audience that he was 'not advising anyone to rush the police cordon' nor – being a 'private individual' – was he going to 'stop anyone'.[27] Indeed, given that the leftists were responsible for the marshals, anyone who wanted to attack the RUC was probably not going to be stopped. The stewarding was not completely reckless: they had succeeded in moving the marchers back from the police line before the meeting and the chief marshal had called for the crowd to depart at its conclusion. But the stewards lacked the numbers, the training and the inclination needed to contain any trouble in a crowd that had swollen to almost 1,000 people.[28] Consequently, when the Belfast leftists started to insult the police and hurl placards at the cordon, their bid to provoke the RUC was not checked by the marshals as it had been in Dungannon.[29] The police officer in charge later gave sworn testimony that he had ordered his men not to react. After about five minutes of being subjected to 'Sieg Heil' taunts and a fusillade of missiles, they were told to draw batons and 'clear the mob'.[30] The commission of inquiry found that 'nothing resembling a baton charge took place but that the police broke ranks and used their batons indiscriminately on people'.[31] The strategy of provoking the police into an overreaction had succeeded.

The ensuing violence was made worse by an earlier decision to move a party of police from the original route to the opposite end of the street. The RUC later claimed that the officers had been sent to guard a 'demolished building, containing more than ample ammunition for violent demonstration'. However, the unintended consequence of stationing men here was that the marchers were effectively trapped. This 'tactical error on the field', to employ the term used by headquarters, was compounded by another: the party was not informed that the crowd was being dispersed nor given orders to allow people through.[32] As the commission of inquiry observed, 'when a number of marchers hurried towards them some violence was almost inevitable'.[33] With the demonstrators seemingly reluctant to leave, the RUC called in water cannons to clear the area. The water wagon, which was making its first appearance in Derry, sprayed people indiscriminately.[34] As well as sweeping both sides of the street, the water cannons also sprayed Saturday afternoon shoppers on the bridge leading to the city centre.[35]

The water wagon directed a jet through an open window on the first floor of the house where the Ulster Television camera crew was stationed.[36] The BBC team's filming was also impaired.[37] The Telefís Éireann cameraman, however, managed to record several hundred feet of film. A former BBC employee living in Derry contacted the current affairs department about this footage. Since the Irish Television Service's launch in 1961, the two national broadcasters had co-operated extensively. The BBC was therefore allowed to screen the dramatic Telefís Éireann film of the march on its regional and network news bulletins.[38] The television coverage transformed the political situation. When one of the Unionist MPs at Westminster described the RUC as 'probably the finest police force in the world' during Prime Minister's Questions, Wilson referred him to the BBC's reporting. 'Up to now we have perhaps had to rely on the statement of himself and others on these matters,' he explained. 'Since then we have had British television.'[39] Events in Northern Ireland were to remain on British television screens into the next century.

John Hume, the community activist, had been a writer and performer on BBC Northern Ireland's answer to 'That Was The Week That Was'. The British show's satirical assault on the establishment had made it a hit with critics and viewers alike. But Northern Ireland's attempt to build up a domestic satire industry proved a failure.[40] It was difficult to deliver topical comedy in a political culture where the topics never seemed to change. Four decades later, this is still a problem for people seeking to satirise Northern Irish politics. Newton Emerson, editor of the spoof *Portadown News* website, mined the hypocrisy of the peace process for material. However, he eventually decided to 'decommission' the website as he feared that he was on the verge of repeating himself. Emerson had been able to get away with attacking men who were normally intolerant of criticism for the simple reason that he was funny. Northerners on both sides of the communal divide pride themselves on their sense of humour. In 2006, the Cambridge University Ireland Society held a forum on 'Humour in Northern Irish Politics'. Most of the panel and the audience members had come to praise Northerners for learning to laugh in the face of adversity. Emerson, by contrast, rubbished this cliché. He recalled how when he had lived in England he had not found that the natives lacked a sense of humour – and suggested to the students that they had probably made the same discovery. Northerners had not forged a unique brand of comedy that set them apart from the rest of humanity.[41]

The central theme of this book is that Northern Ireland was different, but not exceptional. Thirty years of virtual war while the rest of the continent experienced a period of uneasy peace has encouraged some people to forget that Northern Ireland has always been part of Europe. Fleets of tugs did not spew forth from Harland and Woolf's great shipyards to tow the six counties to a new mooring off the Atlantic coast of Africa. Northern Ireland should be compared to France and West Germany, not to apartheid-era South Africa and Israel-Palestine. This does not lead to the injustices of the Unionist regime being ignored. Western Europe in these years was a place where former Nazis held high office, the police invoked laws from the fascist era, and a counter-insurgency war was fought in one of its greatest cities.[42] Northern Ireland under the Unionists was not outside the mainstream in this Europe.

The civil rights movement was part of the rising tide of radicalism that swept the continent during the 1960s. This, however, has often been obscured in accounts of both the global revolt of 1968 and the origins of the Troubles. In 1988, the street protests of twenty years earlier were commemorated in Western Europe as the post-war generation's coming of age.[43] When they reached maturity, the baby boomers had supposedly found themselves in conflict with an adult world where conservative values and institutions had not kept pace with economic modernisation.[44] '68 was presented as the beginning of a cultural revolution that had delivered personal freedom. This view was championed by the handful of former activists who had established themselves as spokesmen for the '68 generation.[45] By contrast, Northern Ireland was regarded as having a civil rights generation. Roy Foster's history of modern Ireland warns against making 'analogies with student movements' of the late 1960s. The 'absence of a distinct youth culture in Ulster society' has led Foster and others to conclude that Northern Ireland was not part of the international festival of liberation and therefore not part of '68.[46]

The intensity of the Northern Irish conflict suggested that the Troubles must have been an inevitable product of the sectarian divide. The creation of a Protestant-dominated state with a sizeable Catholic minority in the years following the First World War did not solve the Irish question so much as rephrase the problem. For decades, Northern Ireland apparently remained the 'static society'.[47] Unionists presided over an unjust system and both Nationalism and Republicanism failed to challenge it. According to the official story, this only changed when the first generation of Catholics to benefit from the education reforms of the mid-1940s came of age in the late 1960s. The minority population then began to protest in the streets against the crimes of the Protestant supremacist state – and was met with police batons.[48] This time, however, the traditional hardline response split the Unionist Party rather than binding it together, led to condemnation not support from Britain and, instead of crushing the movement, brought more Catholics into the streets.[49]

By the thirtieth anniversary of '68 and the start of the Troubles, historians had begun to challenge these dominant narratives. The media's favourite '68ers had retrospectively claimed that the movement's leftist rhetoric should be ignored. Activists had supposedly resorted to outdated Marxist terminology to describe the fledgling struggle for individual autonomy as nothing else was available to them at that time. Historians have preferred, however, to research the political language of '68 for themselves rather than rely upon the self-appointed translators.[50] As the fortieth anniversary nears, this approach has resulted in what is becoming the new consensus on '68. Examining the flood of words spouted out in the late 1960s, it becomes obvious that political change mattered more than experimenting with new lifestyles. Sixty-eighters were not turning away from politics in the pursuit of pleasure; isolated individuals were finding fulfilment in collective action. They believed that they were part of a global struggle to free humanity from imperialism, capitalism and bureaucracy, not the individual from old-fashioned ways of living. Instead of a fleeting festival of liberation, '68 emerges as the climax of post-war radicalism. There was a 'long '68' dating back to at least the 1950s and continuing into the 1970s.

This political interpretation allows events in Northern Ireland to be written back into the story of '68; it also allows the events of '68 to be written back into the story of Northern Ireland. The region's leftists had believed that by initiating an escalating cycle of provocation and repression the dictatorial face of the Unionist government would be unmasked. The divided working class would then unite in opposition to the 'Orange Tories' and in pursuit of a socialist vision that transcended those offered by the Labour and Communist parties. Like the nineteenth-century French revolutionary Auguste Blanqui, Northern Ireland's '68ers had thought, 'Why discuss what it is like on the other side of the river? Let us cross over and see.'[51] When they marched over the River Foyle into the centre of Derry, they hoped to discover a society polarising along class lines. Instead, they soon found that sectarianism was gaining in strength. Sixty-eight was a global revolt, but across the world it took place in national and local contexts. The Troubles is perhaps the most tragic outcome of this coming together of international trends and historic divisions.

Northern Ireland lends itself well to a case study of the global revolt. Thousands and thousands of pages would be required to do proper justice to the 'long '68' in France or the Federal Republic of Germany – to look at the shape of the state; the way mainstream political parties struggled to adapt to a changing world; the attempts made by the extremes of Right and Left to escape the political margins; the rise and fall of social movements; activism at a local level; the impact of international politics and intellectual fashions; and the bewildering array of marches, riots, occupations, meetings, speeches, negotiations, sit-downs, and strikes that made up the revolt itself.

Examining these developments in Northern Ireland is an altogether more manageable task. It is also just as worthwhile. Northern Ireland might have been seen as a provincial backwater, but it was home to no fewer than three of the world's greatest contemporary poets: Derek Mahon, Seamus Heaney and Michael Longley.[52] Similarly, Northern Ireland's leading activists should be counted among the star '68ers. Telling the story of the 'long '68' in Northern Ireland and tying it in with recent research on other Western countries is therefore one way of trying to pin down this 'elusive revolution'.[53] As the nineteenth-century French traveler Gustave de Beaumont observed, 'Ireland is a small country where the greatest questions of politics, morality and humanity are fought out.'[54]

CHAPTER ONE

Unionism and its State

BUILDING A PROTESTANT STATE

Sir Basil Brooke sat underneath an oak tree on his family's estate of Colebrooke, Fermanagh, one night a week for much of 1920 and 1921.[1] Brooke began his vigil after accompanying his pregnant wife to Dublin, which he found had been transformed in the four years since the Easter Rising. Sinn Féin, which had won a majority of Irish seats in the 1918 Westminster election, was striving to bring into being the republic that had been proclaimed during the insurrection. The struggle to end British rule was spearheaded by the movement's military wing, the Irish Republican Army (IRA). During Lady Brooke's confinement, from March to May 1920, the IRA scored a significant victory: Dublin Castle capitulated to Republican hunger strikers and released hundreds of prisoners. Brooke returned from the capital determined to stop the lawlessness that he had seen there from spreading to his part of Ireland. With a dozen other local men, Brooke formed an illegal vigilante force. He had spent the previous decade in the British army – defending the Empire in India and South Africa, at Ypres, Suvla, Vimy, Cambrai and Arras.[2] In 1920, the same 'loyalty and devotion to empire' required Brooke to 'fight the agents of murder, anarchy, and terrorism' in the place of his birth.[3]

Across Europe, hundreds of thousands of soldiers returned to their homes after the First World War to fight similar battles against revolutionary change. Frenchmen formed the Union Civique, Italians the Organizzazione Civile and Germans the Freikorps and the Einwohnerwehr. In rural, conservative and Catholic Bavaria, war weariness allowed a left-wing Jewish journalist from Berlin to transform a massive peace demonstration into a revolution. Between November 1918 and April 1919, this unlikely revolution regressed into an absurd attempt to erect a dictatorship of the proletariat.

Munich's rag-tag 'Red Army' was easily defeated by regular German troops and Bavarian Freikorps units. The brutal suppression of the Räterepublik and the vengeance visited upon its leaders failed to exorcise the fear of revolution. Bavaria's small farmers and middle classes believed that when the next insurrection came the police and the army would be no match for the Bolsheviks. Concerned citizens reacted by organising themselves into 'civil guards', the Einwohnerwehr. By the start of 1920, around 357,000 men had volunteered to serve in the Einwohnerwehr. The Allied governments saw these paramilitary forces as a way for Germany to get round the commitment it had made to reduce its army to 100,000 men. At the Spa disarmament conference in July 1920, Germany agreed to disband the Einwohnerwehr after the Allies had threatened to occupy the Ruhr. David Lloyd George, the British Prime Minister, had admitted to the conference that if millions of guns were in the hands of English civilians he would not be able to sleep at night.[4]

During that same month, Lloyd George agreed to consider enrolling vigilante forces in the North of Ireland into the service of the state. Brooke was one of the men lobbying for official recognition: he told the top British general in Ireland that 'If the government will help [the people] they will do all they can to help the government.'[5] With the war in the South against the IRA escalating, the overstretched British state welcomed the idea of letting loyalists defend the North. In return, Westminster consented to bear the huge costs of arming, equipping and maintaining a Special Constabulary. For leading Ulster Unionists and the British government, this arrangement also had the benefit of calming Protestant fears that they had been left unprotected. Brooke was not alone in worrying that the more extreme loyalists might otherwise have taken matters into their own hands, sparking an accelerating cycle of attack and reprisal.[6] Serious sectarian violence did occur – men wearing Special Constabulary uniforms did murder Catholics. But the battle for the North did not degenerate into a full-scale communal conflict. Indeed, it was the new Southern state that descended into civil war following the IRA split over the Anglo-Irish Treaty of December 1921, which had established the Irish Free State. Both factions, however, remained allies in the North. Brooke, County Commandant of the Fermanagh Special

Constabulary, led an unsuccessful amphibious assault on the village of Belleek, which had been occupied by IRA irregulars with the help of pro-Treaty forces at the end of May 1922. Although the Belfast government had to turn to the British army to recover the village for the empire, the IRA's Northern campaign was ultimately defeated by the resistance of the Special Constabulary. When the new Irish Free State army moved against the anti-Treaty IRA in June 1922, incursions across the border ended and Northern volunteers flocked south to fight.[7] The immediate threat to the existence of Northern Ireland faded away.

The Special Constabulary not only guarded against the irredentist South, but also against perfidious Albion. With Britain desperately searching for a way out of the Irish bog, Ulster started to lose its friends. The Special Constabulary reduced the North's dependence upon its doubtful ally. However, the formation of the force did not make the Protestant community master of its own fate. Self-determination required self-government – something that the Unionist population lacked as the crisis came to a head. During the Anglo- Irish truce, which began in July 1921, the British had the Special Constabulary stand down. The IRA's observance of the truce was not so strict.[8] In Fermanagh, volunteers drilled, enforced the economic boycott of Belfast, carried out kidnappings, and attacked police barracks.[9] For the British, securing a deal with Sinn Féin mattered more than the security of Northern Ireland. The Unionists therefore were relieved to assume responsibility for law and order under the terms of the Government of Ireland Act at the end of 1921 – just before the IRA's spring offensive. The Act established the devolved institutions of government, the division of responsibilities between the British and Northern Irish parliaments, the legal requirement for the regime to exercise its legislative and executive powers free from discrimination, and Westminster's supreme authority. Despite its beginnings as a movement that defended direct rule from Westminster, Unionism had come to embrace devolution as a defence against being abandoned by London. As Sir Edward Carson, the Unionist leader at the time, explained in the House of Commons debate on the legislation, 'you cannot knock Parliaments up and down as you do a ball, and, once you have planted them there, you cannot get rid of them.'[10] By the summer of 1922, Northern Ireland had become a political fact.

Northern Ireland's difficult birth marked the state and its inhabitants. A senior British civil servant who was assigned to Belfast in June 1922 was reminded of a previous posting to the Baltic states: 'The Protestant community of the North feels that it is an outpost of civilisation set precariously on the frontiers of Bolshevism.' The victorious but embattled unionists believed that they had been 'misunderstood' and 'betrayed' by Britain.[11] The long-standing alliance between Ulster Unionism and the British Conservative Party had faltered, while the cross-class alliance of Protestants had held firm. In March 1922, under pressure from London and under attack from Dublin, the Northern Irish government had agreed that Belfast's mixed districts should be policed by a force made up of equal numbers of Protestants and Catholics. As the South turned in on itself and Britain turned away from Ireland, the need to build a non-sectarian state disappeared. Without allies to please and enemies to appease, the Unionist leadership was left only with supporters to indulge. The power compromise between the party elite and its grass-roots was continually being renegotiated. Extreme Protestants successfully pushed for the law to be strictly enforced against Catholic offenders and to be applied with discretion when loyalists were accused of criminal acts.[12] Plans to establish a secular public education system fell foul of the Churches. Integration gave way to segregation: Protestants attended state schools while Catholics were catered for by the voluntary sector. Unionist associations campaigned for changes to the structure of local government that would allow them to take control of councils previously held by Irish Nationalists.[13] In Fermanagh, the abolition of proportional representation and the redrawing of boundaries ensured that when the 1924 local elections were held a county with a Catholic majority returned a Unionist council. Brooke represented the new ward of Brookeborough.[14] The safeguards for minorities contained in the Government of Ireland Act proved no more effective than similar provisions in the treaties of recognition concluded between the Allies and the new states of central Europe. Britain had more pressing concerns than protecting minorities.[15]

By pandering to Protestants, the Northern Irish government further alienated Catholics from the new state. But peace could never have brought reconciliation. The two communities could not forget the riots, the shipyard expulsions, the burning houses, the bombings, the kidnappings and the assassinations. As the violence receded, the conflict mindset persisted in the form of conspiracy theories. They described a society marked by a binary divide between patriots and a diverse – often incongruous – collection of traitors.[16]

In Bavaria, the Right portrayed the short-lived Soviet as a Jewish–Bolshevik conspiracy that had stabbed the Germany army in the back and unleashed a reign of red terror. This myth was embraced by a Bohemian corporal serving with the Munich garrison: Adolf Hitler.[17]

In Northern Ireland the unionist population believed that the global conspiracy was being orchestrated by the Vatican, not the Kremlin. A Catholic civil servant 'learned' that his Protestant colleagues were convinced that he was 'subject to malevolent direction by black-robed priests to whom Rome had entrusted its master plan for world domination'.[18]

Conspiracy theories disfigured Northern life. They even gripped the mind of the otherwise phlegmatic Brooke. On 12 July 1933, the anniversary of the Protestant William of Orange's victory over the Catholic James II at the Battle of the Boyne, Brooke warned that Northern Ireland was being undermined by its enemies. The new MP for Linaskea explained: 'There was a definite plot to overpower the vote of unionists in the north. He would appeal to loyalists, therefore, wherever possible, to employ protestant lads and lassies … catholics … had got too many appointments for men who were really out to cut their throats if opportunity arose.'[19] Brooke was never allowed to forget these comments. When he claimed that 'his own view was that a man's religion was his own affair' during a 1967 television interview, the *Derry Journal* reminded its readers that this was the man who had once boasted that 'he had not a Roman Catholic about his place'.[20] But Brooke's plot was not a figment of a rabidly sectarian imagination. In June 1933, the Unionists had lost the previously safe council ward of Linaskea to an independent farmers' candidate. Brooke blamed the defeat upon the way that the rural depression was being exploited to weaken Unionism's cross-class alliance and upon the 'peaceful penetration' of Southern workers. There was no doubt in his mind that the new government in Dublin was behind both these threats. Eamon de Valera, one of the leaders of the Irish revolution, and Fianna Fáil, the successor to the Sinn Féin faction that had rejected the Treaty, had taken office in 1932 promising to end partition. A slight increase in Catholic numbers and the defection of part of the Protestant vote to independent candidates would deliver Fermanagh to de Valera. Brooke's speech was warning the unionist people to stand firm and remain vigilant against Irish nationalism.[21]

Conspiracy theories, therefore, were not irrational: they constituted the dark reflection of competing visions of the future. Conspiracy theories gave expression to anxieties and reduced them to order. This was implicitly acknowledged by Sir James Craig, Northern Ireland's first Prime Minister, when he declared that the devolved Parliament should contain 'men who are for the Union on the one hand or who are against it and want to go into a Dublin Parliament on the other'.[22] Unionists had no illusions about what the reunification of the island would bring. The Southern state's 1937 constitution paradoxically reflected a Catholic worldview while purporting to speak for a thirty-two-county Ireland that included two million Protestants.[23] 'One person's Utopia usually means another person's hell,' a former IRA volunteer later observed.[24]

The unending struggle over the existence of the Northern Irish state deeply affected those charged with running it: the civil servants. When Sir Earnest Clark, a former tax inspector, arrived in Belfast in September 1920 to set up the new administration, the city had nightly gunfights but no institutions of government. There was no parliament, no high court, no departments, no senior officials, and no plan. Displaying the discipline, diligence, and determination upon which bureaucrats pride themselves, Clark helped to conjure a state out of thin air. He organised the elections to the new devolved Parliament; he devised a comprehensive scheme setting out the new Ministries and the staff needed to operate them; he ensured that the four British principles of anonymity, confidentiality, impartiality, and incorruptibility were adopted; and he found – mainly in London and in Dublin – the experienced personnel required to work the new machinery of government.[25] In 1924, Clark told the first annual dinner of the new civil service that the 'Government of Ulster is the child of its people, and if the Ministers and their Parliamentary Secretaries are its Godfathers and Godmothers, we are certainly its nurses'.[26] As Northern Ireland grew into adolescence, the civil service nursed its ward through the Great Depression. In the words of one official, it carried on 'an administration as good, as liberal, and as humane as political conditions allowed'.[27] Those final four words are telling – the Unionist godfathers never allowed their civil servants to do anything that could jeopardise their party's control.

Clark's successor as head of the Northern Ireland civil service was a man whose many enthusiasms included the German constitution.[28] This attempt to reconcile liberal parliamentarianism with mass democracy excited people across Europe. The keenest student of the new Weimar order was the German legal theorist Carl Schmitt. Liberal constitutionalism, he argued, was trying to hide the fact that politics lies behind the law. As the chaos that followed the First World War demonstrated, it was impossible to write a constitution that could foresee and foreclose every crisis. 'In the exception,' Schmitt contended, 'the power of real life breaks through the crust of a mechanism that has become torpid by repetition.'[29] The strong rule that Schmitt advocated could no longer be justified by the divine right of kings, so he turned instead to the people as a source of legitimacy. For Schmitt, 'the political' was the most intense and extreme antagonism between friend and enemy.[30] An authoritarian state was justified by the need to preserve the political unity of the people and defend them against the enemy within and without.

The development of Northern Ireland seemed to support Schmitt's ideas: the liberalism of the Government of Ireland Act had given way to a 'Protestant state'.[31] At the start of the Anglo-Irish truce, Brooke hoped that 'within the next few days the healing process will begin whereby all Irishmen can unite for the good of their country'.[32] By the early 1930s, at the very latest, he had concluded that the hostility that existed between the two communities could not be overcome. As Brooke explained to Parliament, 'There is a catholic political party which ... ranges from benevolent nationalism to the extreme of the extreme ... but the one plank in their platform is the destruction of Ulster.'[33] To defend the state against this ever-present danger, the Special Powers Act authorised the government to 'take all steps and issue all such orders as may be necessary for preserving the peace and maintaining order'.[34] But Northern Ireland fell short of Schmitt's stipulation that the state should have a monopoly on the political. While the German jurist wanted interest groups excluded from the political sphere, Stormont – the seat of the Northern Ireland government from 1932 onwards – received an endless stream of delegations.[35] Schmitt's beliefs brought him into the service of the Nazis; the unionist people's beliefs brought them into conflict with the Third Reich.[36] Indeed, Brooke was prepared to accept reunification as the price for the South entering the Second World War. He instead had to make a much greater sacrifice to defend the empire: two of his sons were killed.[37]

POST-WAR APPEASEMENT

On the night of 15–16 April 1941, the Luftwaffe dropped incendiaries, bombs and landmines on Belfast. In Brian Moore's novel *The Emperor of Ice Cream*, Freddy Hargreaves cheers on the destruction of the city: 'Blow up ... Stormont Castle and Lord Carson's statue and the Houses of bloody Parliament.'[38] These buildings survived the Belfast blitz, but the government of John Andrews was dealt a major blow. The smooth succession of the sixty-nine-year-old Andrews to the premiership after Sir James Craig's death in November 1940 betrayed the Unionist leadership's growing complacency. The German bombers had attacked the least prepared city in the United Kingdom and inflicted the highest casualty rate – over 900 people were killed – for any single night's raid outside London. Belfast's working-class districts were the worst hit, revealing the city's hidden poverty and the need for urgent social reform.[39] From 1941 onwards, increasing labour unrest provided a constant reminder of the government's unpopularity and incompetence. A rebellion of junior ministers and Unionist backbenchers finally deposed Andrews in April 1943. Brooke, the only Unionist leader who was having a 'good war', was installed as the new Prime Minister.[40]

Although he harboured doubts about the expense of post-war reconstruction and had pushed for a stronger approach to industrial relations, Brooke recognised that Northern Ireland would have to change.[41] The civil service was eager to start work on reform. Some officials had taken a part-time course in social studies at Queen's University Belfast in 1941–2 and afterwards had kept together as a reading group. The circle's sacred text was the Beveridge Report.[42] Drawing upon the experience of three decades in social administration, Sir William Beveridge brought together and expanded existing welfare schemes into a comprehensive system of national insurance. He also recommended the creation of a national health service and an end to mass unemployment. Surveys found that nine out of every ten people in the United Kingdom backed Beveridge's crusade to slay the giants of poverty, ignorance, want, squalor, idleness, and disease.[43] A return to the failed *laissez-faire* order of the 1930s was out of the question; a better new world had to be built.

The Beveridge Report reasoned that: 'A revolutionary moment in the world's history is a time for revolutions.'[44] Brooke might appear to have been an odd revolutionary: he was fifty-seven years old when the 1945 Northern Ireland general election was held and had been involved in politics for over a quarter of a century. However, the welfare states of post-war Europe were all built by men from similar backgrounds. Clement Attlee, the British Prime Minister, and Konrad Adenauer, West Germany's first Chancellor, were even older and more seasoned than Brooke. The exhausted populations of Western Europe desired social and economic reform, but they also wanted political stability. Brooke and his generation of statesmen provided a living link to the old Europe that had perished in 1914. After the ideological conflict between communism and fascism during the inter-war years, they offered the voters pragmatic, consensus politics. Like Germany's Christian Democrats, Brooke piloted a middle course between the extremes of *laissez-faire* and socialism.[45] Although there was substantial support within the party for low taxation and limited public spending, Brooke stood firm. 'The backbone of Unionism is the Unionist Labour Party,' he reminded a rally in 1947. 'Are those men going to be satisfied if we reject the social services and other benefits we have had by going step by step with Britain?'[46]

Unionist opponents of the welfare state objected not only to the high rates of taxation demanded by the system, but also to the beneficiaries of the redistribution of resources. The welfare state was universal: Catholics as well as Protestants would receive benefits. 'These people who are protected under our laws are turning around and biting the hand that feeds them,' one MP indignantly remarked.[47] Brooke reacted to this criticism. To allay fears that the welfare state would attract Southern migrants, eligibility for benefits was made dependent upon the fulfilment of a five-year residence requirement. Such tactical manoeuvring, however, did not head off the growing rebellion over the apparent concessions being made to the minority. The confrontation between the leadership and the dissidents came over the issue of education. The Brooke government was proposing to increase capital grants to Catholic schools, yet was refusing to ensure that local authorities were represented on their management committees.[48] The internal discussions on the legislation involved a February 1951 meeting of the party at which the wider unease with 'appeasement' was voiced. Brooke recalled that he had recently been forced by the Orange Order to defend the new Northern Ireland Housing Trust (NIHT). This public body had the power to build and to manage housing estates – allocating tenancies without any regard to religion. The Prime Minister explained that he had 'finished by saying that if they … thought we were not handling the Socialist government right and wanted a government which would discriminate against Roman Catholics they could do so [but] I would not take on the job'.[49] Brooke pointed to the European Convention on Human Rights: minorities would now be better protected. The post- war trend towards internationalism would expose Stormont to much greater scrutiny. When Unionists thought of the defence of Northern Ireland, they had to think about Strasbourg and New York as well as the borderlands of Fermanagh and Tyrone.

The Unionist leadership was not merely seeking to present a positive image of Northern Ireland. Brooke and his liberal allies believed that the welfare state could serve as the foundation for a rapprochement with the Catholic community. Given that social and economic conditions were far superior to those in the South, the assumption grew that the minority population was starting to accept partition. By softening Stormont's sectarianism, liberal Unionists hoped to aid this process. The dominant position of Protestants in Northern Ireland would be left untouched by this strategy. Catholics would receive a fairer share of public appointments, but the important posts would still be reserved for Protestants.[50] Nevertheless, key features of the regime that had developed during the inter-war years would have been dismantled. Home Affairs Minister Brian Maginess, the most prominent moderniser, recommended the repeal of the Special Powers Act.[51]

The Brooke government's liberal policies towards the minority made many Protestants uneasy. The complexities of the leadership's stance had proved too sophisticated; the simplicity of the claim made by its critics that this was appeasement had won the argument. The rebellion over this issue proved much more difficult to contain than the earlier one over building the welfare state. With Northern Ireland threatened by a reinvigorated Irish nationalism and the election of the Labour government in Britain, Brooke had been able to emphasise the need for unity. In the intervening years, the danger to the state's continued existence had receded. Following the South's unilateral decision to leave the Commonwealth, Westminster had made reunification conditional upon the consent of Stormont. After this crisis, a more prudent government had taken office in Dublin and the Conservatives had returned to power in London. Protestants felt free to vote against official Unionist candidates without weakening partition.

Eight Independent Unionists contested the 1953 parliamentary election on an anti-appeasement platform. Maginess' less partisan approach to law-and-order matters came under the fiercest attack. During the celebrations to mark Elizabeth II's coronation, the Home Affairs Minister and the police had clamped down on provocative displays of the Union flag. The Independents portrayed this sensible desire to keep the peace as a capitulation to Republicanism. Their campaign helped to reduce the official Unionist vote by about 37,000 in contested constituencies. At the beginning of 1954, the Independents pressed home their advantage by organising a massive loyalist meeting. This gathering passed a symbolic vote of no confidence in the government and its appeasement policies. Showing his customary pragmatism, the Prime Minister, who had been made Viscount Brookeborough in 1952, opted to regain his lost support and to retreat from a more inclusive Unionism. The government passed the 1954 Flags and Emblems Act, requiring the police to protect the display of the Union flag in all circumstances and to remove the Irish tricolour when it threatened a breach of the peace.[52]

The Act has frequently been cited as evidence that Northern Ireland was a police state.[53] However, an almost identical law had been added to West Germany's penal code a few years earlier.[54] Indeed, the Federal Republic shared many of Stormont's supposedly undemocratic features – justified by the threat posed by the other half of the country.[55] The Christian Democratic Union (CDU) remained in sole power from the creation of West Germany until 1966; Unionism's political hegemony lasted from partition until 1972.[56] To their enemies, Northern Ireland was the 'Orange state' and the Federal Republic was the 'CDU state'.[57] Admittedly, the Christian Democratic stranglehold on the Bundestag was tempered by West Germany's federal structure. With the Social Democratic Party holding office in several *Länder*, their voters did not feel the same estrangement from the state that Northern Ireland's Catholics did. Nevertheless, at a federal level, the CDU's position appeared impregnable: in 1957, more than half of all the votes cast went to the party.[58] Such 'dominant party systems' were so common in Western Europe at this time that Raymond Aron lectured on the phenomenon at the University of Paris. 'It is not a one-party system,' he explained. 'Opposition parties exist, and intellectual and personal freedoms are respected. But one party has an overwhelming majority, and the opposition parties are so divided that no-one can see any possibility of the majority party being replaced in power.'[59] Following the advent of the Cold War, the French Communist Party, which enjoyed the allegiance of nearly one-quarter of the electorate, had been actively excluded from government. This was hardly surprising as the Communists were committed to the revolutionary transformation of France – albeit after taking power through the ballot box instead of armed insurrection.[60] Moreover, as the veteran Socialist Léon Blum recognised, the Communists were a 'foreign nationalist party'.[61] Their ultimate allegiance was to the Soviet Union, not France. Northern Ireland's Catholic parties occupied a comparable position: effectively barred from power, supported by a substantial minority of the population, pledged to overthrow the constitution, and loyal to a political entity beyond the territorial boundaries of the state.[62]

CHANGING THE FACE OF ULSTER

In August 1962, more than 10,000 workers marched through the streets of Belfast in protest at plans to shut down the city's aircraft factory. At the head of the march were Stormont MPs from the Northern Ireland Labour Party (NILP) and the Nationalist Party. Unionism's fears had seemingly been made flesh: part of the Protestant proletariat had made common cause with its Catholic counterpart.[63] Previously, when the problem of unemployment had started to undermine Unionist control, Stormont had turned to Westminster for aid. As Northern Ireland's strategic importance and the IRA threat diminished, however, such appeals lost their potency. By the beginning of the 1960s, Whitehall civil servants had come to regard the septuagenarian Brookeborough as an anachronism.[64] In October 1962, a working party of Northern Irish and British officials published a report that favoured a different economic policy.[65] The *Derry Journal* delighted in outlining the political implications of this assessment: 'the report amounts to a total rejection by the British Government of the requests for assistance made by Lord Brookeborough on his many futile visits to London'. 'In any other democracy,' the editorial concluded, 'the Government's resignation would already have been tendered.'[66] Within six months, Brookeborough had indeed left office – diplomatically citing ill health rather than the personal humiliation of the working party's findings. According to Lord Wakehurst, Northern Ireland's Governor, Brookeborough said that 'he could step down without loss of face'.[67]

During the final years of the Brookeborough premiership, the Northern Irish civil service became frustrated at the failure to build upon the success of post-war reconstruction. When a protracted dispute with Belfast Corporation over whether or not to extend the city's boundary offered an opportunity to regain lost momentum, the Stormont administration eagerly grasped its chance. In March 1960, the Ministry of Health and Local Government invited Sir Robert Matthew, Edinburgh University's first Professor of Architecture, to select a few sites outside the city on which housing estates could be built. Matthew instead agreed to draw up a development plan – originally for the greater Belfast region, but ultimately for the whole of Northern Ireland. His report recommended that suburban sprawl should be halted by surrounding Belfast with 'Greenscape', creating a 'substantial new Regional Centre', designating a number of 'centres for development', and improving the transport network.[68] The Belfast Regional Plan was published four months after the working party on unemployment had rejected Brookeborough's policies. The Matthew Report mapped out a different road for Northern Ireland: what a senior official at the ministry later described as 'the path of a positive, activist approach to the physical and economic problems of the province'.[69] Britain was already travelling along the road of regional planning – away from the over-heating south-east of England to the North, Scotland, and Wales. By adopting and adapting the new Whitehall vogue, the Stormont civil service hoped that this road and the resources it would bring would come to Northern Ireland.[70]

The political benefits of Stormont's conversion to planning were reaped by Brookeborough's successor, Terence O'Neill. As Finance Minister since 1956, he had stressed that Northern Ireland's future prosperity should be based upon the people's own resourcefulness. In May 1962, O'Neill lamented that 'Northern Ireland has become too sorry for itself'. He proposed that the country should take as its motto 'similar responsibilities for similar opportunities'.[71] The rhetoric of self-help was the ideal language in which to present the new economic policy devised by the administration. Matthew himself had called for 'a replacement of the general attitude that the best thing that can be done is not to get too far behind the rest of Britain, by a determination to go straight ahead'.[72] O'Neill had already cultivated close relations with a group of rising civil servants in Belfast and with the mandarins at the Treasury. This was partly the result of his rift with the Permanent Secretary at the

Ministry of Finance, which had encouraged the Minister to seek out the advice of other officials and to deal directly with Whitehall. O'Neill persuaded the Treasury to include him in the United Kingdom delegation to World Bank conferences – allowing him to network and come into contact with the latest ideas.[73] He was therefore well placed to negotiate the planning world. O'Neill would secure resources from London by framing requests in the new language of economic modernisation rather than by repeating traditional calls for stopgap subsidies.[74]

Northern Ireland's new Prime Minister was not elected; he 'emerged' in the fashion of Conservative leaders until Ted Heath. Brookeborough and Wakehurst discussed 'the best man for The Governor to send for'. 'Two or three possibilities were mentioned,' London was told, 'but it was clear that The Governor and Lord Brookeborough were of one mind.' O'Neill's standing in Parliament and with the public had been on 'the increase for some time'. However, it was only in the immediate aftermath of the Matthew Report's publication that he had become 'the obvious choice'.[75] O'Neill therefore was not an elegant anachronism, but his aristocratic and military background may still have made a crucial difference. The O'Neill family were substantial landowners and descendants of the High Kings of Ireland. O'Neill's father was the first Westminster MP to die on the Western Front, while his maternal grandfather was a Lord Lieutenant of Ireland. After leaving Eton, O'Neill eventually joined the Irish Guards and was wounded during Operation Market Garden.[76] These impeccable credentials probably account for why the Governor contacted O'Neill ahead of his rivals. This gave O'Neill and the Chief Whip, his close ally Bill Craig, the chance to develop an irresistible momentum for his candidacy.[77] Craig had served in the Royal Air Force as a Lancaster bomber rear-gunner and had risen rapidly through the ranks of the Unionist Party. However, his boyish charm and youthful enthusiasm barely masked his inexperience, impatience, and irritability. Craig shared O'Neill's technocratic approach, but he preferred to steamroller through reform rather than secure it through more subtle arts.[78]

Brian Faulkner was the opposite: an inveterate intriguer and – in 1963 at least – a traditional Unionist. In July 1960, as Minister of Home Affairs, Faulkner had allowed 10,000 Orangemen to parade through the Catholic village of Dungiven. Two days of rioting had, predictably, followed.[79] With a background in the region's shirt-making industry, Faulkner became the spokesman for the interests of local factory owners.

This put him at a disadvantage in the struggle to succeed Brookeborough: he was identified with the old man's failed economic policy. A further obstacle was that he had spent the Second World War running his father's factory in Northern Ireland, not fighting in Europe.[80] John Andrews, O'Neill's principal challenger and the son of Northern Ireland's second Prime Minister, did possess the necessary qualifications of status and service. The difference between the contenders was O'Neill's 'constructive ruthlessness'.[81] The new premier displayed this characteristic again a year later when dispatching Andrews to the safety of the Senate. O'Neill also benefited from the premature deaths of Maynard Sinclair and William Morrison May – both potential successors to Brookeborough.[82]

On the day after he became Prime Minister, O'Neill telephoned his former Private Secretary in America. 'I want and need you at home,' he told Ken Bloomfield.[83] O'Neill's patronage speeded Bloomfield's inexorable rise. But the political master also owed much to his favourite civil servant. Although the term O'Neillism implies a personal leadership style, the Prime Minister heavily relied upon his advisers. Policy emerged not from Cabinet meetings, but from the long discussions that O'Neill regularly had with this reform-minded clique. According to Bloomfield, who served as 'assistant and later deputy secretary to the cabinet', this 'team' consisted of himself, 'the cabinet secretary (at first Cecil Bateman and from 1965 Harold Black), [and] the prime minister's private secretary Jim Malley'. Bloomfield's 'role was to be the word-spinner and ideas man', which entailed 'preparing the prime minister's public utterances'. As this was the era of John F. Kennedy, the team were dubbed 'the presidential aides'.[84] It was also the age of Charles de Gaulle. At the beginning of the 1960s, in both France and Northern Ireland, a tiny elite of politicians and bureaucrats was pursuing economic and social modernisation.[85]

ANNIHILATING THE NORTHERN IRELAND LABOUR PARTY

In June 1963, over a century after his eight great-grandparents had left its shores, President Kennedy came to Ireland. When he arrived in Wexford town, a choir began singing a ballad celebrating the 1798 rebellion. The President joined the schoolboys for the second chorus and reduced even cynical journalists to tears.[86] This may well have been sentimental, but Kennedy's once-removed Irish patriotism had a political impact. As an up-and-coming Senator, he had supported a congressional resolution supporting Irish reunification. Nevertheless, O'Neill had hoped that the leader of the free world would find time to open the Giant's Causeway Park. The invitation – made through the British government – was politely but firmly turned down.[87] Despite this public snub, O'Neill continued to idolise Kennedy. He undertook a pilgrimage to Washington in March 1964 and offered his condolences to Jackie Kennedy – they then went on to discuss eighteenth-century Whig politics.[88] O'Neill found inspiration in Kennedy's teachings. At Yale in 1962, the President had told the students that 'The fact of the matter is that most of the problems ... that we now face are technical problems, are administrative problems ... that do not lend themselves to the great sort of passionate movements which have stirred this country so often in the past.'[89] Six years later, the Prime Minister echoed this sentiment: 'Democracy – let us face the fact – is better attuned to broad simple issues than to complex and highly technical decisions.'[90]

O'Neill was not the first Northern Irish politician to advocate a technocratic approach to the region's economic problems. The NILP had been winning over Protestant working-class voters with the claim that it would succeed in cutting unemployment where the gentlemen amateurs of Brookeborough's Cabinet had failed. On the other side of the Irish Sea, a similar campaign swept Labour into power. Harold Wilson, the Leader of the Opposition, had mocked Sir Alec Douglas-Home's emergence: 'In this ruthlessly competitive, scientific, technical, industrial age, a week of intrigues has produced a result based on family and hereditary connections.'[91] Wilson, the grammar-school boy who had gone on to lecture at Oxford and to work as Beveridge's research assistant, portrayed himself as a meritocratic, technocratic manager with a plan to get the country going again. Staking his claim to the political legacy of the martyred President, he called upon 'the youth of Britain to storm the frontiers of knowledge, to bring back to Britain that surging adventurous self-confidence and sturdy self-respect which the Tories have almost submerged with their apathy and cynicism'. Nineteen sixty-four presented a 'chance to change the face and future of Britain'.[92] Nine months before, O'Neill had declared that his 'task will be literally to transform the face of Ulster'.[93] This Old Etonian's mastery of the new language of politics rivalled that of Wirral Grammar School's former head boy. O'Neill had stolen the NILP's thunder.[94]

For O'Neill, planning was more about politics than economics. In late 1963, Tom Wilson, who had succeeded Harold Wilson as the economics fellow at University College, Oxford, was invited to prepare an economic plan for Northern Ireland. The Belfast-born professor may actually have invited himself.[95] When the Prime Minister belatedly informed his Cabinet that Wilson had started work, economics was far from his thoughts. O'Neill instead stressed that Stormont 'must not only be active, but be seen to be active'; the likely 'improvement of confidence [as] had clearly resulted from the Whitaker Plan in the Republic [of Ireland]'; and the importance of 'the Treasury, in considering the well documented claims of other areas, [taking] into account a similar survey for Northern Ireland'.[96] Moreover, when Matthew and Wilson's blueprint for Ulster's new face threatened Unionism's delicate electoral position, sectarianism prevailed over modernisation. Geoffrey Copcutt, an Englishman responsible for implementing part of the Matthew Report, resigned in protest. He told the British press that the 'situation of the Roman Catholics in Northern Ireland was very similar to that of the Negro in the United States'.[97]

O'Neill's economic plans may have been flawed, but his political plans appeared flawless. The *Derry Journal* grumbled that the 1965 Stormont general election was 'thrust on a jaded public, in the dead of winter, eighteen months before it is due, and on what grounds is anyone's guess'.[98] It was called on the grounds that O'Neill wanted to exploit communal divisions within the NILP and it succeeded in repulsing the party's advance into Unionist territory. The NILP lost half its seats and saw its share of the vote fall by a third. 'The unfortunate Labour Party', O'Neill gleefully recalled, 'was in fact practically annihilated.'[99] The Prime Minister had not always been such a committed enemy of the NILP. 'In an interview given to the *New Statesman*, in 1958,' the party's main strategist remembered, '[O'Neill] came as close as any Unionist politician could do to welcoming the advent of Northern Ireland Labour as a constitutional opposition'.[100] However, as the *New Statesman* interviewer acknowledged in a later article, the then Deputy Prime Minister's endorsement of the NILP had 'got him into serious trouble with his party'.[101] It was widely believed that losing working-class votes to the NILP – whose support for the Union was far from certain – was the beginning of a process that would lead to the end of partition. Similarly, the West German Christian Democrats viewed their Social Democratic opponents as the party that would let in the Communists.[102] Historians have tended to regard O'Neill's subsequent attack on the NILP and its gradualist, parliamentary approach to civil rights reform as a 'classic misjudgement'.[103] O'Neill though had recognised that his survival as Unionist leader depended upon driving the NILP to the edge of political extinction.

THE ARCH TRAITOR

O'Neill's self-appointed task may have been to 'transform the face of Ulster', but he later defined this ambition rather narrowly.[104] In an October 1963 television interview, which was reported in the *Derry Journal*, O'Neill 'explained that "what he really had in mind" in that statement was simply the promotion of better industrial relations and enterprise with a view to economic recovery'. O'Neill, the newspaper regretfully concluded, 'implied that his objective as Premier had nothing to do at all with ... co-operation ... between the two sections of the Six County community'.[105] Although he was an interventionist when it came to the economy, the new Prime Minister preferred to entrust the problem of community relations to the free play of forces. Protestants should content themselves with playing good neighbours to Catholics until the ecumenical movement, the welfare state, and all the trends associated with modernisation finally delivered communal harmony. Conceiving of the British link as a source of economic benefits and privileged access to the international community, O'Neill hoped that 'those who are now in opposition' would be convinced 'that their own ultimate best interests' lay with the Union.[106]

O'Neill's reluctance to intervene disappointed liberal Unionists. Jack Sayers, the editor of the influential *Belfast Telegraph*, marked O'Neill down in this area when he delivered his end-of-year report. '[O]n the subject of political evolution, of communal relations,' Sayers observed in his radio broadcast, 'the Prime Minister's statements and those of his ministers have been ... muted'. He concluded 'that the Unionist leadership has done little or nothing to come to terms with [the] feeling for tolerance and ... freedom of expression among a great many people on both sides of the politico-religious fence'.[107] O'Neill could not ignore this disenchantment: Faulkner had not given up on his leadership ambitions and his plotting was forcing the Prime Minister to seek liberal support.[108] Shortly after Sayers's negative review, O'Neill took what he later described as his 'first step in the direction of improving community relations'.[109] On 24 April 1964, he became the first Northern Ireland Prime Minister to visit a Catholic school. O'Neill listened to the school choir, attended a hurling match, and had his photograph taken with some nuns.[110]

This focus upon symbolism rather than substantive reform climaxed the following year with the invitation of Seán Lemass, the Southern Prime Minister, to Stormont. Lemass was a veteran of the Easter Rising, but economic modernisation mattered more to him than traditional Irish nationalist concerns. Like O'Neill, he was confident that economic and social change would bring an end to the island's ancient animosities. Unlike O'Neill, he believed that a modernised Ireland would be a united Ireland.[111] The Northern Prime Minister was effectively forced into responding to the overtures from the South: Lemass was planning to speak at Queen's University, the media were calling for a meeting, liberal Unionist pressure was growing, and Faulkner was apparently considering a similar initiative.[112] Nevertheless, when Lemass arrived in Belfast on 14 January 1965, it came as a surprise to politicians as well as to the general public.[113] O'Neill's Cabinet was informed only on the morning of the meeting – just a few hours before the news was released to the press. Standing in 'the rather spacious loo at Stormont', the Southern Prime Minister confided to his Northern counterpart that he was going to 'get into terrible trouble for this'. 'No, Mr Lemass,' came the reply, 'it is I who will get into trouble for this.'[114] O'Neill was right.

The blaze of publicity surrounding O'Neill's bridge-building gestures was soon to be eclipsed by the dark fears that they raised. Lemass's invitation to Stormont brought an unwelcome guest to the seat of government: Ian Paisley. The Moderator of the Free Presbyterian Church, an evangelical Protestant sect that he had helped to found, came to accuse O'Neill of treachery.[115] For Paisley, there was no halfway house between truth and error, good and evil, Christ and Antichrist. The Protestant conspiracy theory had undoubtedly found its most eloquent and most inventive spokesman. Paisley invoked an IRA–Vatican plot marked by darkness, secrecy, violence, and sexual perversity. The *Protestant Telegraph*, Paisley's weekly newspaper, contained articles with headlines such as 'Love Affairs of the Vatican', 'Jesuit Plots Unmasked', and 'Papal Conspiracy'.[116]

Paisley believed that Christ had sent him forth as a sheep in the midst of these black-robed wolves. As a gifted Bible scholar, he understood that God's instruments were expected to be as wise as serpents. For the Unionist leadership at least, however, Paisley was not as harmless as a dove. When, in June 1963, Belfast City Hall flew the Union flag at half-mast to mark the death of Pope John XXIII, Paisley explained that he would not tolerate such actions because he 'remembered … men like [the sixteenth-century Reformers] Calvin, Knox, Cranmer, Ridley and Latimer broke rather than bent for the Gospel and liberty'.[117] The post-war ecumenical movement was attempting to forge closer links between the world's Churches. But Paisley and other Protestant fundamentalists, such as the American Baptist preacher Bob Jones Jr., remained at war with Rome.[118] Since the 1950s, Paisley had been at the forefront of protests against the Protestant Churches and the Unionist government's supposed appeasement of Catholics. As religious and political ministers started to build bridges in the 1960s, Paisley stepped up his campaign against those he saw as the 'Iscariots of Ulster' crossing over to the other side.[119]

Although his language echoed seventeenth-century sermons, Paisley's message still resonated with a twentieth-century audience. During a period of rapid change, he reaffirmed unionism's traditional values. But Paisleyism was not simply a regressive phenomenon, retarding O'Neill's efforts to modernise Northern Ireland. Like the New Catholicism of the late nineteenth century, the Protestant preacher criticised liberalism while embracing many contemporary developments.[120] He set up a newspaper, founded voluntary associations, organised mass demonstrations, travelled regularly to Continental Europe and North America, and forged links with like- minded foreigners. These were the means that Paisley used to reach those unionists who had benefited from post-war social and economic reforms but nevertheless wanted Northern Ireland to remain a Protestant state. This was a small but growing constituency. Beginning in 1965, the Orange Order and frontier Unionists came together to oppose further concessions being made to Catholics.[121] At a rally held that year to commemorate the Battle of the Boyne, the Grand Master of the Orange Order was heckled into silence for supporting O'Neill.[122] In 1966, the Order passed resolutions condemning ecumenism and calling for a return to the fundamental principles of the Protestant faith. By pandering to Paisley's views, the Orange leadership was hoping to isolate Paisley the man. Indeed, the Grand Master urged the Order to bar Paisley from speaking at its events.[123]

The Unionist government also followed the risky strategy of co-option and condemnation. When Paisley threatened to march into the heart of Catholic Belfast in September 1964 to remove the Irish tricolour from Sinn Féin's election headquarters, the police were sent in before he could act. Home Affairs Minister Faulkner vainly tried to balance out this decision by banning Paisley from entering the Catholic Falls Road district. Paisley instead held a meeting in the city centre, but a hostile crowd gathered in the Falls in case he defied the ban. These protesters clashed with the police, thus provoking the worst rioting that Belfast had witnessed in decades.

The Irish flag was again placed in the window of the Sinn Féin office and was again removed by the Royal Ulster Constabulary (RUC). Barricades were built, petrol bombs were thrown, police Land Rovers were sent in, and water cannons were used.[124] O'Neill blamed Paisley for the disturbances and warned against a return to the sectarian violence of the past.[125] However, the heightened tensions helped to deliver to the Unionists the marginal Westminster seat for West Belfast. As one Nationalist politician observed, the party leaders believed that they had exploited Paisley for their own ends and, in turn, he was certain that he had used them to score a notable victory.[126]

The political calculations upon which O'Neill's triangulation strategy rested were upset by the events of 1966. The fiftieth anniversary of the Easter Rising presented the Unionist government once again with a choice between keeping public order and maintaining party unity. On this occasion, fears that the IRA intended to renew the armed struggle led O'Neill and his ministers to prioritise security over sectarianism. Stormont warned Westminster that the Republicans were planning to provoke sectarian violence and bring the army onto the streets. Harold Wilson was told that the 'IRA campaign would then be publicised as a people's uprising against the excesses of the Crown forces'.[127] The Northern Ireland government therefore decided – with a few exceptions to appease loyalists – to allow the parades to go ahead and the Irish tricolour to be flown. The *Derry Journal* praised Stormont's restraint, which had 'paid off handsomely in the unruffled peace and calm throughout the community that has prevailed at this commemoration'.[128] Although Northern Ireland escaped serious disturbance, the government would have been prepared for it. In the week running up to the anniversary, the press were briefed that 'police and other security forces have been placed on a footing of instant readiness to meet any unlawful activity which may be mounted by the IRA'.[129] The Nationalist Party accused Stormont of indulging in 'scaremanship of the worst type'. Indeed, O'Neill appears to have hoped that the massive display of state power would placate Protestant extremists. It did not. At a huge Ulster Hall rally, O'Neill was denounced as an 'arch traitor'.[130]

The fiftieth anniversary of the Easter Rising was celebrated in stanzas as well as in the streets. Seamus Heaney's *Requiem for the Croppies* linked the risings of 1916 and 1798. The poem's theme is resurrection. The eighteenth-century rebels, the 'Croppies', marched with 'pockets ... full of barley'. The Croppies were defeated by the British army, vainly 'shaking scythes at cannon', and their dead were buried – 'without shroud or coffin' – in mass graves. 'And in August the barley grew out of the grave.'[131] For Heaney, 1916 was the political harvest of the seeds sown in 1798. In 1966, the Republican crop competed for light with Unionist flowers. During and after the First World War, poppies grew on the battlefields where Irishmen died in their tens of thousands. To mark the fiftieth anniversary of the Battle of the Somme and the sacrifice of the Ulster Division, O'Neill travelled to France. Many of the men who served with the division had previously belonged to the Ulster Volunteer Force (UVF), a paramilitary organisation that had been founded in 1913 to resist Home Rule. Half a century later, a small group of militant loyalists decided to resurrect the UVF name. The new UVF saw itself as part of a long tradition of defending Protestant Ulster from its enemies; everyone else saw it as a murder gang that killed Catholics in cold blood. In the early hours of 26 June 1966, three Catholic barmen leaving a pub in a Protestant area of west Belfast were shot by UVF gunmen.[132] One of the men, eighteen-year-old Peter Ward, was killed and his companions were wounded.[133] O'Neill, who had flown back from France to deal with the crisis, highlighted to the Stormont Parliament the contrast between men who had willingly laid down their lives fighting on the Somme and men who had senselessly taken life in the back streets of Belfast.[134]

One of the UVF killers supposedly said in police custody, 'I am terribly sorry I ever heard of that man Paisley or decided to follow him.' He later denied in court having made this statement.[135] O'Neill – encouraged by reports from the RUC – also believed that the UVF was part of the wider 'Paisleyite Movement'.[136] Paisley himself had immediately condemned the murder and called upon the government to use the full rigour of the law against the guilty men.[137] He apparently felt no need to ask himself, 'Did that sermon of mine send out certain men that shot Peter Ward?' While there was categorically no direct connection, Paisley's words and indeed his actions undoubtedly fuelled the fears of militant loyalists. At the beginning of June 1966, Paisley and his Church had marched on the Irish Presbyterian General Assembly along a route that passed close to a Catholic area of Belfast. The Protestant marchers were met by stone-throwing Catholic youths. The Free Presbyterians had provoked the violence, but they were protected by the police. As the RUC battled with the rioters, the marchers continued on to the city centre. Trouble flared up again when they reached the assembly: the Paisleyites shouted anti-ecumenical slogans at the Irish Presbyterian leadership and abused Northern Ireland's Governor. With moderate opinion outraged at Paisley's conduct, O'Neill felt confident enough to draw analogies with the 1930s: 'The contempt for established authority; the crude and unthinking intolerance; the emphasis upon monster processions and rallies; the appeal to a perverted form of patriotism: each and every one of these things has its parallel in the rise of the Nazis'.[138] The counter-attack continued with Paisley being charged with public order offences. Having been found guilty, the Protestant preacher decided not to pay his fine but instead embrace the martyrdom of a prison sentence.[139] The blood on Belfast's streets had not made Paisley less sanguine. During late July 1966, the loyalist vigils held outside the city's Crumlin Road gaol degenerated into riots. The Cabinet accepted the Home Affairs Minister's proposal to use his powers to impose a three-month-long ban on all marches and meetings within a fifteen-mile radius of city hall.[140] The ministerial order transferred the crisis from the streets into the Unionist Party.

Six years later, O'Neill claimed that the 'seeds of 1966, germinating in 1968, unfortunately have now bloomed into violence'.[141] Throughout the Western world, the radical Right played an important supporting role in the political street theatre of '68. Comparisons can be made between Northern Ireland and the American South: protests against the half-heartedness of efforts to dismantle the old order and prevent murders motivated by hate.[142] But drawing parallels with Continental developments is perhaps more revealing. In 1964, the same year as the riots in the Falls district of Belfast, the extreme right-wing Nationaldemokratische Partei

Deutschlands was founded in West Germany. The party's successes in the 1966 *Land* elections prompted considerable concern.[143] Theodor Adorno, one of the country's most important philosophers and social critics, warned that many West Germans had not yet let go of the reactionary beliefs of the last century. He feared that 'so-called national renewal movements in an age in which nationalism is outdated are especially susceptible to forming sadistic practices'.[144] Across the border in France, the rabidly nationalist group Occident had already been seduced by violence. From 1964 onwards, drilled commando units armed with iron bars launched a series of attacks in Paris on left-wing students as well as on Jews, Africans, and Arabs.[145] When leftists in Western Europe took to the streets to provoke confrontations, they found that the radical Right was only too willing to oblige.

O'NEILLISM

In his autobiography, O'Neill 'face[d] up to the difficulty of saying a word about my predecessor, Lord Brookeborough':

> A man of limited intelligence, his strong suits were shooting and fishing in Fermanagh and when he came up on Monday night or Tuesday morning it was difficult to shake him from some of his more idiotic ideas. In short, it would have been quite impossible, even with his immense charm, for him to have been a minister in London.[146]

What O'Neill failed to grasp was that the qualities needed to run a big Whitehall department were not necessarily those needed to govern Northern Ireland and lead the Unionist Party. When the future viscount began to become involved in politics, he claimed that he knew 'what is being thought by the people here'.[147] As the head of a government and a party that had to be responsive to the popular mood, Brookeborough's common touch proved invaluable. By contrast, as a senior civil servant later observed, O'Neill 'liked politics as an art' and 'didn't find it easy to meet the ordinary middle-class people'.[148] With the bloody and battered year of 1966 limping into the autumn, this weakness would almost cost him the premiership.

During September 1966, backbenchers were asked to sign a document calling for O'Neill's resignation.[149] Paisley had weakened the Prime

Minister's position, but the Moderator of the Free Presbyterian Church was one concern among many in the party. O'Neill's modernisation strategy had stripped local authorities of some of their jealously guarded functions. This loss of patronage had damaged the clientelism upon which Northern Irish politics was largely based.[150] Unionists from the West of the province were unhappy that development had been concentrated in the greater Belfast region. Liberals were disappointed by the absence of ambitious reform. Traditionalists were dismayed by the North–South summit and the Easter Rising commemorations. What united this disparate discontent was a vague feeling of dissatisfaction with O'Neill's detached, presidential style.[151]

The Prime Minister made clear to the rebels that this would not be a bloodless coup. He counter-attacked in the media as well as in meetings of the parliamentary party and local associations. He disingenuously associated the rebellion with Paisley and exploited internal party divisions. Faulkner calculated that the moment was not right and declined to offer himself as an alternative leader. The revolt subsequently lost all momentum. Having overwhelmingly won a vote of confidence, O'Neill recognised the need to appease his critics. Bill Craig, who headed the Ministry of Development that had removed responsibilities from local government and neglected the West, was demoted to Home Affairs.[152] A high-level civil servant maintained: 'That's when Craig first got the idea that he could be a rebel himself.' 'In fact, [Chief Whip] Jimmy Chichester-Clark ... found Bill drunk. And Bill said, "Well, if Faulkner can be a rebel I'll get to the right of Faulkner, so".'[153] The internal revolt and the loss of a key ally darkened further O'Neill's pessimistic disposition. Assessing the dying year in a letter to Bloomfield, he observed that at the end of September he could not fully appreciate his supposedly much stronger position after the Stormont election. 'My forecast for 1967', he concluded, 'is that it will be much worse than 1966.'[154]

The rebellion persuaded O'Neill to start to base his premiership upon appeals to a public opinion that he believed was substantially more liberal than official Unionism. O'Neill had declared in response to 1966's loyalist violence and Republican triumphalism that 'Those who seek by word or deed to incite hatred and widen divisions in the community can be crushed by the universal disapprobation and distaste of decent people'. With his references to 'the steady ground-swell of moderation' and the 'dignified expression of moderate opinion', O'Neill appeared to embrace Sayers' contention that there was an expanding middle ground.[155] Following the party revolt, the Prime Minister actively sought to cultivate this emerging moderate consensus.[156] This became the 'Programme to Enlist the People' (PEP): an attempt to 'get away from jargon and bureaucratic complications, and to tell the average Ulsterman what "building the new Ulster" actually means'.[157] O'Neill outlined his full ambitions for PEP to the North Antrim Unionist Association:

> Our work is not a dreary effort of plans and blue-prints and statistics. Forget jargon words like 'infrastructure' or 'community relations'. Rather keep before your eyes a vision of an Ulster which – if we will and work for it – can be ... An Ulster in which our economic growth will keep pace with a growing population, providing satisfying and useful work for all ... an Ulster in which these material benefits will create such a spirit that our constitutional position will cease to be an issue in politics.[158]

As well as helping to bridge the gulf between 'us', the people, and 'them', the government, PEP was seen as a way of providing a space in which the two communities could co-operate to achieve shared goals.[159] O'Neill hoped that PEP would encourage 'youth organisations', 'Chambers of Commerce', 'Rotary Clubs', and 'the Churches' to 'consider working together in some field of public benefit'.[160] 'Is it, for instance, too visionary', he asked the Belfast Irish Association, 'to look forward to Protestant young people helping to re-decorate a Youth Club in Andersontown, or a young Catholic reading to a bed-ridden old lady on the Shankill Road? The firmest links can only be forged at the basic level of ordinary, warm, human contact.'[161] PEP was not, therefore, a complete retreat from O'Neill's *laissez-faire* approach to community relations: he was seeking to build a structure that would support pre-existing trends.[162]

O'Neill offered the most coherent analysis of the thinking behind PEP at a June 1968 conference on community work. In the opening speech, he claimed that the complexity of the modern state 'accounts for much of the detachment, the "couldn't care less" approach ... which we see here and everywhere else'. 'Alienation of government from the governed,' continued the Prime Minister, 'of town from country, of employer from working people – these are some of the chief ills of our age.'[163] This instant analysis of the causes of the global revolt of 1968 bears comparison with those offered by some of Europe's greatest minds. Within a few short months, however, O'Neill would no longer be in a position to deliver lectures on how the Western world could overcome alienation.

Narrowing his focus to Northern Ireland, O'Neill highlighted the specific difficulties rapid change posed in a society of 'very fixed sympathies' and in a political system 'accustomed to saying "We are attacked; we must defend ourselves."' In its 'modest' attempt 'to tackle some of those problems', PEP based itself in the 'local community, which people could know and understand', and 'sought to involve as many diverse interests as possible in some form of active work in the interests of the community'. For O'Neill, 'civic spirit' constituted the 'building blocks out of which some wider sense of loyalty and involvement might one day be constructed'.[164] Catholics would gradually be assimilated, a process that would in turn encourage Protestants to abandon their mistrust. Nationalism, as well as what O'Neill regarded as the coarser aspects of Unionism, would wither away to reveal a society comparable with Britain or Canada. While visiting North America in the spring of 1968, he was surprised to discover that the Grand Master of the Newfoundland Orange Order regularly took sick Catholics to mass. 'I have often thought,' O'Neill wrote in his autobiography, 'that if only the Order in Ulster had developed in the same way as the Order in Newfoundland then today's troubles might never have taken place.'[165]

PEP was supplemented by efforts to redress some substantive Catholic grievances. This was a gradual process that never went further than what the parliamentary party and the wider Unionist movement would accept. O'Neill had no intention of provoking another rebellion against his leadership. Indeed, the Prime Minister and key members of the Cabinet agreed in March 1967 that 'there would be further consultations with representatives of the Orange Institution before final decisions were made'.[166]

'Of all the proven injustices that exist in the Six Counties,' commented the *Derry Journal* in May 1963, 'none is more glaring than the manner in which the Mater Hospital is treated by the Stormont Government.'[167] At the hospital's 1966 prize-giving ceremony, the Bishop of Down and Connor noted the O'Neill administration's professed good intentions towards the Catholic community and suggested that the Mater was 'the place where it should be easy to begin to do something'.[168] Protestant opinion, which was probably more influential with the Prime Minister, similarly favoured state aid for this hospital, which had opted out of the National Health Service. A *Belfast Telegraph* poll conducted in December 1967 found that 81 per cent of Unionist voters backed such a move. This perhaps reflected the substantial number of Protestants treated by the Mater.[169] Progress on the issue was impeded by backbench opposition – championed in the Cabinet by Faulkner – to public funding for a Catholic institution. In January 1967, following much manoeuvring, the party conceded in principle state aid for the hospital. This was conditional upon the government reaching an agreement with the hierarchy of the Catholic Church about protection for the Mater's religious character.[170] Mutual suspicion, however, ensured that almost two years later these negotiations had yet to be concluded.[171]

The bishops appear to have entertained even greater doubts about the motives underlying Stormont's October 1967 White Paper on education. The Bill offered Catholic schools 'maintained' status: increased grants in exchange for Local Education Authority (LEA) nominees sitting on the management committee. The Bishop of Down and Connor almost immediately accused the government of 'taking advantage of our grave financial need' to 'introduce representatives' of bodies whose 'attitude' to 'Catholic interests [in many cases] is so notorious that we can only regard with dismay their direct involvement'. At a later stage, 'a mere alteration in the proportion of representation could turn the position into one of complete control by non-Catholic and indeed anti-Catholic forces'. By contrast, the Nationalist Party and the teaching unions cautiously welcomed the proposals.[172] Such feelings proved sufficiently wide-spread within the community to encourage the hierarchy to seek a compromise. In May 1968, the bishops agreed to a model scheme whereby teachers would be appointed by the school committee subject to the requirements of the Ministry. Other staff would be employed by the LEA after consultation.[173] During the Bill's second reading, the Education Minister had reassured the hierarchy that 'this was not a deep-laid plot to take over the voluntary schools'.[174] In the privacy of the Cabinet, however, he described 'what he proposed … as a useful first step towards breaking clerical control'.[175]

The government's response to a paper on citizens' rights presented by the NILP and the trade unions also confirms the Catholic conspiracy theory. This memorandum stated that 'the time is overdue ... for the Prime Minister ... to give an earnest of his liberalism and enlightenment by the acceptance of the basic principle that equal citizenship should confer equal civic rights in every part of the United Kingdom'. In practice, this entailed bringing electoral law into line with Britain, fair representation for minority groups on public bodies, measures to diminish discrimination in employment and in the allocation of public housing, the appointment of an ombudsman, and reform of the existing trade union legislation.[176] A few years later, this would have been a moderate reform package. In October 1966, however, the Unionist Cabinet regarded most of the proposed changes as a threat to the party's dominance.

Attorney-General Teddy Jones, who had long acted as a lobbyist for the interests of Londonderry Unionism, made a comprehensive attack on the Labour memorandum.[177] Jones asked rhetorically,

> what equity is there for a Government, which represents the majority in Northern Ireland, to be subjected to influence to alter laws which suit the Province and are the basis of, and essential to, its constitutional existence and have been duly passed and accepted by the superior government and which have no way infringed the safeguards laid down in the Government of Ireland Act?

According to the Attorney-General, the constitution had been enacted to avoid a united Ireland – for which the 'Nationalist opposition' were still contending. The 'minority groups' were therefore 'seeking, in the name of progress, to force the government here to change to procedures which they feel will suit them better when, in fact, what is sought to be changed is the very basis on which the constitutional structure of Northern Ireland was established'. The 'day' had 'not yet been reached' when 'Catholic citizens, in general, would look on political issues as open questions'.[178] In the heart of Stormont Castle, the Protestant conspiracy theory was being advocated as government policy.

The influence of the conspiracist mentality was less obvious in the subsequent Cabinet discussions. Nevertheless, ministers were uniformly hostile towards the assumptions underlying the Labour memorandum. It was 'generally agreed' that it 'would be wise' to accept only those changes that 'would have no marked political effect'. Consequently, the business vote would be ended, the university seats abolished, and an independent boundary commission for Stormont elections established. To avoid the appearance of being forced to make concessions, the Cabinet opted to announce these changes in Parliament rather than to the Labour delegation. The accusations of discrimination that had been made in the NILP/trade union paper were dismissed without debate. Addressing the question of the local government electoral franchise was postponed until the review of the entire system had been completed. Indeed, it was suggested that the eventual restructuring would probably strengthen the case for a property franchise. The issue of reforming the trade union laws was also deferred – in this case pending the report of a royal commission.[179]

O'Neill looked upon political concessions as both risky and unnecessary. Given the vulnerability of his position as party leader, O'Neill could ill afford to have his critics accusing him of appeasement. Faulkner and Craig may have been compromised by their involvement with the modernisation strategy, but they still remained close to the traditionalist position in their attitude towards the minority. The problems that would be created within the party would not be offset, O'Neill calculated, by a rise in Catholic support. He assumed that civil rights only mattered to a small number of political activists and that the majority of Catholics were interested in houses, jobs, and public services. The Union's 'economic and social advantages' would eventually convince the minority population to abandon Irish nationalism.[180] While waiting for economic and social change to transform political allegiances, the O'Neill government offered Catholics increased funding for their community's institutions and the PEP.[181] Pressure from outside Northern Ireland, however, pushed him into at least giving the appearance of wanting to do more. From 1967 at the latest, O'Neill reluctantly found himself in danger of provoking another rebellion within the party.

BUYING TIME FROM THE BRITISH

Harold Wilson used to joke that more Irish Catholics cast their vote for him than for any Irish politician. But his once-removed Irish nationalism was not solely motivated by electoral calculation. Wilson's spin doctor later recalled that his former boss 'had the traditional attitude of the Left that Ireland should be united under Dublin'.[182] During the 1964 general election campaign, Wilson promised to tackle discrimination in Northern

Ireland. In a well-publicised reply to a letter from a Catholic pressure group, he stated that 'a Labour Government would do everything in its power to see that the infringements of justice to which you are so rightly drawing attention are effectively dealt with'.[183] Wilson failed to fulfil this promise when he came to office. Nevertheless, O'Neill still found himself under greater pressure than any of his predecessors to treat the minority fairly. Westminster had considered vetoing the 1922 Local Government Bill, but had backtracked after the Unionist Cabinet had threatened to resign and fight an election on the issue. The British government had no desire to provoke a constitutional crisis.[184] By the 1960s, however, London could impose its will upon Belfast without testing the limits of the Government of Ireland Act. The post-war expansion of the state had been funded by the Treasury, which made Stormont susceptible to financial blackmail. O'Neill had to tread softly.

Even before Wilson moved into Downing Street, O'Neill found himself struggling against separatist tendencies within his party. A constant theme of his premiership was that Northern Ireland and by extension – the Unionist regime were 'utterly dependent' upon continued British goodwill.[185] 'There can be no room in Unionist philosophy', O'Neill warned a local association, 'for a kind of loyalist Sinn Féin which would turn its back upon British opinion.' He instead proposed to demonstrate to 'the ordinary, decent Englishman, Welshman, or Scot' 'that behind all the talk about "discrimination" ' was a 'warm and genuine community spirit'. This strategy was designed to ensure that 'the voices of criticism' would 'fall increasingly upon deaf ears'.[186] At the 1967 annual meeting of Unionism's governing body, O'Neill formalised this approach by launching the largely ineffective Campaign for Truth about Ulster.[187] As part of this endeavour, the Prime Minister told the party conference that detractors should have 'the humility to appreciate that we in Northern Ireland live in a complex social and historical setting and can best be left to work out our own social problems for ourselves'.[188]

The British civil service was inclined to agree with O'Neill. Whitehall's mandarins shrewdly recognised, however, that they had to indulge their political master's Irish obsessions. When he came to power, Wilson received a letter from the Nationalists requesting that he intervene to stop discrimination in the allocation of public housing. The 'Prime Minister', according to the inter-departmental correspondence, 'asked that the Home Secretary should advise him how to deal with it not simply as an isolated letter but in the context of the new relations with Northern Ireland.'[189] In light of 'the interest taken in this matter by the Prime Minister', the higher reaches of the civil service decided that it was 'undesirable merely to follow without any modification' the previous practice of simply 'defining the constitutional position'.[190]

The rather limited research conducted by both the state and party bureaucracies emphasised the NILP's reading of the situation.[191] They studied a series of *Guardian* articles written by the party's Charles Brett during early 1964. In these pieces, the NILP's leading theoretician adopted a 'plague on both your houses' attitude. According to Brett, the allegations that both Unionist and Nationalist councils were allocating public housing to their respective supporters were 'justified'. 'In general,' he concluded, 'it appears that there is less deliberate discrimination on the part of the Unionist Government than the Nationalists allege; but in the sphere of local government, and in the private sphere, there is far more discrimination than the Unionists will admit.' Brett detected that 'Many Catholics and many Protestants are coming to regard the old deadlock with repugnance.' However, the 'Nationalists and Unionists are now under the control of their own extremists'.[192] The implication was that there was an emerging moderate constituency – which would be increasingly drawn to the NILP's centrist approach. With the party confident of advancing under the existing system, the leaders wanted their British counterparts to stay out of Northern Irish politics.[193]

The civil service's report on the constitutional relationship between Belfast and London was also against intervention. It was noted that 'successive Governments have taken the view that ... it would be quite wrong for the United Kingdom Government to interfere in matters for which responsibility has been delegated to the Northern Ireland Government'. As regards discrimination, the report recognised that the Nationalist accusations usually involved matters that had been transferred to Stormont. Indeed, the Home Office's existing procedure for dealing with letters alleging discrimination was 'to outline the Northern Ireland Government's constitutional responsibilities and to decline to comment further'. Similarly, if 'the subject is raised directly in the United Kingdom Parliament, it runs the risk of being ruled out of order'. The report concluded that it would be 'difficult to see how any departure from this view could be reconciled with the existence of the Parliament and Government of Northern Ireland'.[194]

Relatively early in this process, Home Secretary Sir Frank Soskice informed his civil servants that 'the United Kingdom Parliament is still supreme and it may be the time has come to intervene in matters of this kind'.[195] Less than two weeks later, however, the rudimentary analysis conducted within Whitehall had convinced Soskice that such a policy was impractical. In a letter to Wilson, he presented his 'reluctant' conclusion that 'it would be constitutionally wrong, and most unwise in practice,' for the government to 'offer any comment upon or attempt directly to intervene in matters which clearly fall within the field of responsibility of the Government and Parliament of Northern Ireland'.[196] Wilson dutifully dispatched to the Nationalists the reply that had been prepared by the Home Office civil servants: he stressed that the issue fell within the responsibility of the Stormont regime.[197]

A Westminster intervention would have seriously drained the Wilson premiership's limited reserves of time, energy and authority. As Roy Jenkins – Soskice's successor at the Home Office and H.H. Asquith's biographer – warned his colleagues, embroilment in Irish affairs had derailed other reforming ministries.[198] Labour had more politically pressing matters to attend to than Northern Ireland. The first Wilson government was defined by the balance of payments deficit, with which almost every crisis was inextricably bound up. American requests for Britain to support the Vietnam War, the seamen's strike, the end of the military presence east of Suez, the 1966 wage freeze, and, the following year, devaluation were all linked to the unrelenting pressure on sterling. Jenkins's time at the Home Office was dominated by the task of laying the legislative foundation for what he termed the 'civilised society'. He would later admit that Northern Ireland 'was about 12th on my agenda'.[199] The next Home Secretary, Jim Callaghan, reached the same conclusion as his predecessors: 'theoretically and logically we could have taken action, [but in] practice it was not ... politically possible to do so'. It was therefore unsurprising that British policy was 'to use O'Neill to put the reforms through and not in any circumstances to get our fingers burned'.[200]

Consequently, O'Neill made the pleasing discovery that his fears about Wilson's intentions had been exaggerated. Following a courtesy visit soon after the election, O'Neill met Wilson on 19 May 1965 'to get down to realities'.[201] The British Prime Minister's recollection was that he had only been 'anxious that the ... Unionist Government under ...

O'Neill should be encouraged to press on with their programme of ending discrimination'.[202] Acknowledging the Stormont premier's achievements and suggesting rather than demanding further reform became the established pattern for later meetings. On 5 August 1966, Wilson and Jenkins 'expressed understanding of [O'Neill's] position [but] explored serious lines along which further progress might be achieved'.[203] The British ministers raised the possibility of appointing an ombudsman to examine claims of discrimination in the allocation of public housing, the current state of electoral reform, and the feasibility of Stormont passing a religious relations bill. The debate, however, was perfunctory. This enabled O'Neill to wriggle out of making specific commitments. Indeed, he was able to convince the British that it was 'politically impossible to make further moves at present'. Jenkins simply insisted that 'any pause should be of short duration' and warned that 'a return to unenlightened policies could mean Westminster "taking over"'.[204]

O'Neill's success in claiming that the rise in extremist activity demanded a temporary halt to his reform programme reflected the recent IRA scare. In December 1965, O'Neill had alerted Soskice that he had 'been advised by the R.U.C. that preparations are on foot for an early assumption of I.R.A. activities in Northern Ireland'. He stressed that the intelligence that had been acquired included 'refer-ences to the perpetration of I.R.A. outrages in England'.[205] As the fiftieth anniversary of the Easter Rising approached, Soskice became increasingly nervous. 'Information received from both Scotland Yard and the Northern Ireland Government', he told Wilson in early April 1966, 'shows that the threat is a real one.' The British government responded by sending over 'an additional infantry battalion ostensibly for training'.[206] Violence did follow in the wake of the Easter Rising commemoration, but it was perpetrated by loyalists rather than Republicans. Westminster was therefore reluctant to weaken O'Neill's position still further and risk this perceived reformer being replaced by a reactionary. A memorandum written in preparation for the talks outlined London's thinking:

O'Neill has pursued a markedly more liberal line than his predecessors ... there is no doubt that ... O'Neill is running some political risk ... Any action taken by the Westminster Government that implied that the present Northern Ireland Government did not enjoy its confidence would encourage the extremist elements which are opposed to the existence of Northern Ireland as part of the United Kingdom. It would also have an effect on the Unionist Party itself and would probably bring more extreme elements there also.[207]

The Stormont premier, however, confessed to his Cabinet that by playing to Westminster's sympathy for his difficulties he had merely 'bought time'.[208]

Following the September 1966 revolt, O'Neill recognised that he had to protect himself against the criticism that he was selling out Ulster to the Labour government. Northern Ireland's Prime Minister therefore arrived at Downing Street in January 1967 with his rivals, Faulkner and Craig. Wilson and Jenkins were joined by Alice Bacon, the Home Office Minister responsible for Northern Ireland. Greater familiarity with the region on the British side – limited though that still was – coupled with the presence of Stormont's most chauvinistic ministers led to a fractious exchange. According to O'Neill, the sniping actually began as they filed into the Cabinet room:

> 'Have you got no vices?' the Prime Minister enquired [of Faulkner]. 'I see you drank nothing at lunch.' 'I'm not against smoking and drinking,' Brian replied. 'It is just that my father gave me £100 not to drink till I was 21.' 'Oh, I see,' said Wilson, 'you're earning the next £100 now.' It was some time before Brian regained his composure.[209]

Bacon opened her assault by discussing how the Unionist government had responded to the memorandum on citizens' rights. She stated that the Stormont Cabinet 'had seemed convinced of the merits of the present [local government electoral] system' and that Craig 'was reported to have defended the principle of tying the franchise to a property qualification'. Craig countered that the question of universal adult suffrage should be addressed only after the review of local government had been completed. He nevertheless indicated that following the restructuring his preference would still be for a property based franchise. This clumsy admission led Wilson to 'enquire ... whether the present system would still be thought right if it produced a different political result'.[210]

O'Neill might have calculated that his rivals would relax their resistance to his strategy after personally witnessing Labour ministers pushing for reform. Indeed, O'Neill's reluctance to confront opposition within the Cabinet and the wider party encouraged him to exploit British pressure as justification for change. During the subsequent Cabinet meeting, Faulkner acknowledged that 'Wilson had clearly threatened', while Craig noted that 'pressure on the local government franchise would continue'. The pair, however, remained convinced that warnings about a possible intervention were hollow and that serious concessions were thus unnecessary. Faulkner's 'own impression' was that 'if the critics of Northern Ireland could be satisfied about alleged discrimination in housing and employment', Westminster 'might press less hard' for universal adult suffrage. Craig – even after the mauling he had received at Downing Street – continued to hope that the existing franchise 'could be defended by reference to the process of local government reorganisation'.[211] Although their reasoning lacked sophistication, O'Neill's rivals probably assessed Britain's willingness to intervene more accurately than he did. Ironically, O'Neill's liberal image had allowed Faulkner and Craig to obstruct reform without fear of sanctions. If a Faulkner or Craig premiership had been equally recalcitrant, Wilson might well have resorted to financial blackmail.

At one stage, the British Prime Minister had admittedly threatened that 'within a period of about three years' 'Parliament would insist on interfering more and more with the internal affairs of Northern Ireland'. This menace, however, was not intended to speed up reform. Instead, it was designed to promote 'an arrangement' 'whereby the British Parliament and Government would refrain from interfering at all ... provided that Northern Irish members of ... Westminster ... observed the same discretion on voting on matters appertaining to Britain'.[212] Wilson had not forgotten how the twelve Unionist MPs had conducted themselves during the first seventeen months of the Labour government. With an overall majority of only three, the ministry's survival was made still more precarious by the Unionists voting with the Conservatives on exclusively British questions. In early 1965, Wilson had even consulted the Attorney-General about the possibility of restricting their voting rights.[213] Following the August 1966 meeting, the Stormont Cabinet had responded to the 'considerable resentment on the Labour side' by agreeing to exercise 'more control over the activities of Ulster Unionist Members'.[214]

The 'greatest surprise' of the January 1967 summit had therefore been 'Wilson's reiteration of the theme of the Ulster Members'.[215] The Labour leader was so obsessed with this precursor to the West Lothian question that it was mentioned in his memoir of the 1964–70 government.[216] At the January 1967 talks, O'Neill reminded Wilson that devolution had been reflected in Northern Ireland's reduced Westminster representation. If 'full rights of debate and voting' were to be withdrawn, then 'a larger number' of MPs – proportionate to the area's population – would be required. While acknowledging that he was 'aware of this', Wilson nevertheless cautioned that 'if the Westminster Parliament reverted to a marginal balance of the Parties, the position of the Ulster members could create a first class political crisis'.[217] This showed the extent to which British party political concerns shaped Wilson's thinking on Northern Ireland. Given that Labour and the Conservatives were neck and neck in the opinion polls, the Prime Minister's primary objective was to retain his parliamentary majority beyond the next general election.[218]

When Bacon's successor, Lord Stonham, visited the province in June 1968, he declared that the British government had 'no wish to meddle'. With relations between the two governments 'so harmonious' and the 'old differences in Ulster ... being put aside', Stonham had 'faith in the future of Northern Ireland'.[219] The civil service briefed their Minister to convey Westminster's desire for reform of the Special Powers Act and the local government franchise – but not to exert any significant pressure. The Home Office offered no objections to Stormont's plan to complete the restructuring of local government before studying the suitability of universal adult suffrage. Indeed, London was still more concerned with Northern Ireland's economic problems than with civil rights.[220] O'Neill had successfully persuaded Westminster to work through him rather than impose reform upon Stormont. In the process, however, right-wing Unionists had increasingly come to regard him as compromised. A report on discussions with grassroots members in September 1968 found that the 'ordinary loyalist no longer believes that the Unionist Party is an effective influence on the course of events'.[221]

REFORMING A PROTESTANT STATE

O'Neill was a reformer. His conception of reform, however, differed from that of the British government and the various groups campaigning for civil rights. Stormont was not trying to meet the minority population half-way but pursuing a Catholic capitulation. O'Neill was adamant 'that the constitutional position of Northern Ireland is not a matter on which there can be any compromise, now or in the future, and I must say, too, that I believe we have a right to call upon all our citizens to support the Constitution'.[222] Economic and social modernisation, he assumed, would strengthen the Union and weaken its opponents. Catholics would eventually recognise that their material interests were best served by accepting partition.[223] As Irish nationalism headed towards the dustbin of history, Protestant extremism would lose its justification and also fade away. With the expansion of the political centre ground, Stormont could finish dismantling the sectarian and authoritarian aspects of the regime.[224] Partition would no longer need to be protected by discrimination and oppression. In stark contrast, the overwhelming majority of Stormont's opponents saw civil rights reform as a stepping stone to reunification, not something to be delivered in full only after partition became permanent. Differences over reform, rather than its absence, brought politics into the streets at the end of the 1960s.

CHAPTER TWO

Nationalism and its Discontents

CATHOLIC LOYALTIES

Eamonn McCann and Kevin Boyle went on a month-long holiday to Donegal at the end of the 1950s. The schoolboys had travelled over the border to the Gaeltacht to learn Irish under the watchful eye of Catholic priests. This was what generations of Irish nationalists had been struggling to achieve: the youth of Ireland leaving behind the corruption of the towns and cities to seek their true language and culture among simple rural folk. McCann and Boyle, however, were Western teenagers as well as Irish Catholic schoolboys; they had no intention of devoting their leisure to things of the spirit. Late one night, McCann and Boyle went swimming with some girls. The party was discovered by the priests, who forgave the girls and punished the boys. For their sins, McCann and Boyle were cast out of the Irish nationalist paradise of the Gaeltacht. Fearing what his mother would do if she found out, Boyle took up McCann's offer to stay with him in Derry rather than head straight home to Newry. The two teenagers enjoyed a carefree couple of days in the city. They ran around shouting their heads off and leaping up aiming to hit street signs with their hands. When a policeman put a stop to their antics, Boyle followed McCann's lead and gave a false name. The highlight of Boyle's visit was a trip to the cinema to see Victor Mature in a 'sword and sandal' movie – a genre that was at the peak of its international popularity.[1]

McCann and Boyle were far from the only members of Northern Ireland's Catholic community to possess complicated and contradictory identities. An attitude survey conducted on the eve of the Troubles found that three-quarters of Catholics described their nationality as 'Irish'. This did not mean, however, that they embraced a Dublin-designed identity and abandoned all others.[2] The minority population was made up of Republicans, citizens of Derry, members of the working class, Roman Catholics, and so on.[3] Moreover, what was understood by 'Irish' might differ for each individual. For the dominant figure of twentieth-century nationalism, Eamon de Valera, God had ordained that the island of Ireland should be one nation. This sacred land must once again be filled by a frugal, Gaelic, Catholic peasantry. De Valera's 1937 constitution committed the Southern state to this goal. In turn, many Northern nationalists committed themselves to Dublin. Londonderry Corporation's Nationalist councillors refused to attend a Battle of Britain commemoration service because 'Our Government in Dublin declared its neutrality'.[4] De Valera, however, was a consummate politician. By presenting Fianna Fáil as a national movement that transcended social divisions, he pushed mere political parties to the margins of public life. But when de Valera said Ireland, he meant only the South. Indeed, almost all politicians did.[5] The Nationalist Party repeatedly asked for the right to be seated in the Dáil and the major parties repeatedly refused.[6] Such experiences provoked a prominent Nationalist to remark that Northern Catholics were 'the bastard children of the Republic ... sometimes they needs must acknowledge us, but generally speaking they try to keep their distance'.[7] By the end of 1967, opinion polls were finding that the great majority of these children were hoping that London and Dublin would finally agree to share custody: a united Ireland with a link 'of some sort' with Britain. In the space of four decades, 'Ourselves Alone' had become Ireland should not be 'going it alone'.[8]

Léon Gambetta, the nineteenth-century French republican leader who had escaped from Paris by balloon during the Franco-Prussian War, said of the loss of Alsace-Lorraine to the new German Empire, 'Let us think of it always; let us speak of it never'. Instead, the recovery of the lost provinces became something for French nationalism to rally behind and something that no government ever thought of fighting a war to achieve. A wit reversed Gambetta's maxim: 'speak of it always, think of it never'.[9] In post-war Europe, Southern Irish parties were not alone in following this injunction. The idea that Germany would one day be reunified was the *Lebenslüge*, 'life-lie', of the Federal Republic. Almost half of the West German population during the 1950s and 1960s felt that reunification was the most important political issue, while almost all of West Germany's politicians felt that reunification was neither possible nor desirable.[10] Dublin and Bonn were not prepared to risk the hard-won political and social stability of their states by embarking upon foolhardy nationalist adventures.

An independent Dungannon councillor sadly concluded in 1964 that 'the official attitude down South is … that they no longer want us'.[11] Rejected by Dublin as well as Belfast, Northern Ireland's Catholics were given a home by Rome. The Church hierarchy had been convinced during the early 1920s that either the new Northern state would collapse, London and Dublin would force Belfast to treat the minority fairly or Catholic territory would be transferred to the South. When all these hopes had failed, the Church set about providing the faithful with a state within a state.[12] Since the 1850s, Rome had battled against the Kingdom of Italy, the French Republic, and the German Empire. The One, Holy, Catholic, and Apostolic Church had no intention of capitulating to the Northern Ireland statelet.

The nineteenth-century 'culture wars' had not been fought in Ireland. British governments had accepted the dominant position of the Irish Catholic Church and had tried to avoid provoking a conflict with it.[13] Readers of *The Tablet*, however, were able to follow in detail the struggles of their co-religionists on the Continent as the 'two Europes' – Catholic Europe and liberal Europe – clashed. The Holy See believed that it was fighting the 'criminal machinations of the evil ones' who 'set about devouring the foundation of the Catholic religion and of civil society'.[14] By contrast, Gambetta observed that 'bad times for our country are always good times for the Jesuits'.[15] The Society of Jesus and other religious orders were supposedly standing in the way of progress. They were teaching children to be superstitious, submissive and, above all, unpatriotic – a grievous crime in the era of nation-building. Through schools, armies, railways, bureaucracies, and newspapers, the states of Europe were turning peasants into Frenchmen, Italians, and Germans.[16] Although the Catholic Church was seen as a major obstacle to these transformations, it was also undergoing a process of modernisation. Like the other great capitals of Europe, the Vatican was centralising power and imposing uniformity in its realm. Both sides in the culture wars sought to rally the masses to their respective banners. The resulting mobilisation and polarisation led to the formation of parallel societies: Catholic versus liberal, Protestant, or anti-clerical.[17] While the rise of socialist parties at the end of the century pushed liberals and Catholics into a coalition of convenience, these divisions persisted into the inter-war period.[18]

As the German army swept towards Paris, a state schoolteacher and a Catholic priest met in a small Alpine village. 'So, this is it then,' the *instituteur* remarked to the *curé*. 'Well, we're friends, we only hate the invader now.'[19] In Ireland, however, the First World War brought an end to the Act of Union rather than a *union sacrée*. Throughout nineteenth-century Europe, culture wars had flared up after significant constitutional changes had taken place. Both sides recognised that an expansion of the franchise or the creation of new institutions presented opportunities and threats.[20] Partition and devolution sparked a similar struggle in Northern Ireland. London had appeased the Catholic Church; now it was believed that Dublin would defer to it and Belfast would persecute it. In the 'Swiss Ireland', the Bernese Jura, clerics who endorsed the dogma of infallibility agreed at the Vatican Council of 1870 were driven from their offices and replaced by priests loyal to the state. Catholic parishes that resisted the Protestant canton came under military occupation.[21] The culture wars in Northern Ireland were not as fierce: Protestants wanted to control the state, not for the state to control the Catholic Church. Nevertheless, the result was the same: a Protestant state and a Catholic counter-society – although the lines that separated them were never clearly defined.

Schools were one of the main battlegrounds in Europe's culture wars. In Northern Ireland, the Church was able to remain responsible for educating Catholic children. However, voluntary Catholic schools received less financial support from Stormont than they had received from Dublin Castle. The Church periodically campaigned for increased state funding – with some degree of success.[22] Nevertheless, the consensus within the Catholic community was that the spiritual reward of having its children raised in the traditions of the Church was worth the material sacrifice required to support the schools. As well as receiving religious instruction, Catholic children played Gaelic games and were taught 'Irish' history. A civil rights activist observed that pupils in Northern Ireland's state and voluntary sectors 'were all learning the same things, the same events, the same periods of time, but the interpretations ... given were very different'.[23] This was what the 1968 attitude survey had found: half of all the Catholics interviewed remembered having teachers with explicitly nationalist views.[24] One such teacher later described how the

Church, 'being greater than Northern Ireland, part of the whole island, of Europe and the world', 'lent an ability to think outside the immediate context'.[25] This mental world was reflected by the Catholic community's newspapers. For example, the *Derry Journal* reported upon the city, the north-west of the island, Catholic organisations and societies, Southern politics, and the latest occurrences at the Vatican.[26] Newspapers helped their readers to bring together all the different threads that made up the Catholic counter-society – within which their whole spiritual, social, and cultural lives took place.

What marked Northern Ireland out from the rest of Europe was not the stand-off between a Protestant state and a Catholic counter-society. When Stormont's Education Minister spoke of 'breaking clerical control' and the Bishop of Down and Connor warned of the threat posed by 'anti-Catholic forces' to Church schools, they were echoing their counterparts in the Europe of a previous generation.[27] Neither did Northern Ireland's minority problem set it apart. Over the centuries, Europe had developed into a maddening mosaic of religious and ethnic groups. Beginning in 1914, however, the pieces that made up the old Europe were removed and rearranged. Three decades that witnessed total war, brutal occupations, the fall of empires, the emergence of new states, the constant redrawing of borders, the forced relocation of entire peoples, and murder on an industrial scale simplified the patterns on the map.[28] Northern Ireland was a product of this process, but it had escaped the final and worst phase. Elsewhere in Europe, Hitler and Stalin had found inhuman solutions to human problems. What therefore marked Northern Ireland out from the rest of Europe was that these problems survived into the post-war era.

WE ARE VERY MUCH ON OUR OWN HERE

In 1936, the Royal Ulster Constabulary (RUC) raided the Derry home of the McAteer family. The police officers found weapons hidden in the house and arrested the male members of the family on arms charges. Hugh McAteer, one of the sons, confessed to the crime. He received a heavy prison sentence, but his father and two brothers were set free. Hugh McAteer would subsequently rise to the highest ranks of the Irish Republican Army (IRA). Although Eddie McAteer always respected his brother and shared his commitment to Irish unity, he never believed that the armed struggle would end partition.[29] Eddie McAteer chose constitutional nationalism over militant nationalism. The many disappointments he endured in the course of his long political career made him cynical, yet he never came to regret this decision.

At the 1968 Nationalist Party conference, McAteer used the leader's speech to outline his pragmatic Irish nationalism. He implored delegates to 'be realistic': 'try to remember that we are entrapped minority' and that 'there is not much good in looking for help from overseas, from America, or indeed, I regret to say, from our own fellow countrymen.' 'My feeling', the leader confided to the party faithful, 'is that we are very much on our own here in the North of Ireland.' Consequently, in McAteer's opinion, 'the greatest problem that lies before us at the present moment is the problem of ourselves'. Nationalism suffered from 'too many splits', which encouraged loose co-operation rather than a disciplined party structure. The party was at times divided and directionless because it had been condemned to permanent opposition. Unionist domination ensured that reforms – if they were to come at all – would have to be conceded by Stormont. McAteer, however, feared that the desired changes would not come. He suspected that 'the way to power and advancement in the Unionist Party is by kicking the Nationalist people'.[30]

This lecture on Nationalism's inherent weaknesses was directed at the 'impatient ones' inside the conference hall. McAteer was speaking from personal experience: he, too, had once been a young man in a hurry. On the eve of the D-Day landings, Seán Mac Entee, a leading figure within the de Valera government, had attacked the Nationalist Party for condemning its supporters to 'political futility for 22 years'.[31] As war slowly gave way to peace, Europeans were determined to avoid repeating the mistakes of the 1920s and, above all, the 1930s. They wanted to build a new and better world in the post-war era. McAteer was among those Nationalists who believed that the moment had come to revitalise the party and reunify Ireland. Labour's election victory had fuelled these hopes. Nationalists told themselves that the British Labour movement had sympathised with their cause in the past. Indeed, a number of backbench Labour MPs headed by Geoffrey Bing had honoured that tradition, in November 1945, by forming a pressure group called the Friends of Ireland. The ascendancy of America was also regarded as an opportunity. Nationalists deluded themselves that the Irish diaspora could be mobilised and Washington made to right English wrongs.[32] With imperialism in retreat, Nationalists became convinced that the world was going their way. McAteer invoked 'the mighty spirit of the late Mahatma' when he proposed a 'new campaign' of 'non-cooperation, no violence'. In his *Irish Action* pamphlet, McAteer sketched out ways to make 'local misgovernment' 'impossible': these ranged from delaying tax payments to occupying public buildings.[33] The Catholic community, however, was not yet ready to embrace civil disobedience.

The ten MPs returned to the Northern Irish Parliament in 1945 decided to set up the Anti-Partition League (APL). It sought to unite all Nationalists around a common platform, fight winnable Stormont and Westminster seats, and make the party more accountable to its supporters. In 1947, the APL co-operated with the Friends of Ireland's fruitless efforts to stop the passage of legislation that relaxed some of the restrictions imposed upon Stormont by the Government of Ireland Act. The parliamentary debate, however, did provide a rare opportunity to criticise the Unionist regime.[34] The APL also publicised perceived injustices through a series of pamphlets. The most notable of these, *Mutilation of a Nation*, was written by Cahir Healy, who entered politics as a founding member of Sinn Féin and ended up as a Nationalist MP. These efforts to attack partition in print were supported and supplemented by the Southern political parties. In 1949, they came together to create the Mansion House Committee to support Nationalist candidates in the Stormont election.[35] Its publications became the raw material for *The Indivisible Island*. As well as powerfully restating the traditional Irish nationalist reading of history, this book presented exposures of gerrymandering and of discrimination in public employment.[36] But all these labours were in vain.

As frustration at the APL's lack of success mounted, McAteer's branch chose to march through Derry in defiance of Stormont's bans. Conflicts over the right to march through areas identified with the other community had marked the region since the nineteenth century. When McAteer had discussed in *Irish Action* the possibility of marching through Protestant territory, he had maintained that the 'important thing' would be to 'be seen by foreign observers'.[37] On St Patrick's Day 1951, McAteer and a small number of APL members attempted to parade with the Irish tricolour through the walled city. Although the march itself was legal, the organisers had consciously violated the law by publicly displaying the Republican flag. The marchers succeeded in provoking the police, which encouraged the local APL branch to plan a larger protest for the following year. This demonstration was banned and baton-charged. In the opinion of many who were present on both occasions, the violence that ensued was comparable to that unleashed on 5 October 1968. The difference between the two marches was that one was seen by foreign observers on television and the other was not.[38]

This was one of the last in a sequence of disappointments that fatally undermined the APL. In September 1951, the American House of Representatives voted against a resolution calling for an all-Ireland plebiscite on partition.[39] At the height of the Cold War, the American political establishment was reluctant to damage its alliance with Britain. Strategic concerns also superseded Labour's sympathy with Irish nationalism. The North's commitment during the Second World War – in sharp contrast to Southern neutrality – had transformed the attitude of many Labour ministers. Herbert Morrison, while limited to influence rather than direct involvement, was the champion of the Unionist cause.[40] In 1946, Morrison produced a memorandum for the Cabinet based upon private visits to both Irish states. He recommended that partition should be maintained.[41] The Friends of Ireland not only proved impotent when confronted with the opposition of the party leadership, but also disagreed with the APL over the solution to the Irish question. The Friends of Ireland looked at the other island through British eyes. The 1950 *Tribune* pamphlet, *John Bull's Other Island*, assumed that class rather than communal divisions lay behind discrimination in Northern Ireland. The best way of achieving unity, therefore, was for the different Irish Labour parties to take office on both sides of the border.[42]

Domestic politics similarly dominated the calculations of the Southern parties. Following a long period of Fianna Fáil rule, politics had become more competitive. The parties sought to gain an advantage over their rivals by parading their respective republican credentials. This climaxed in September 1948 when the interparty government declared the Republic. The wider consequences of this action were apparently overlooked. It brought an immediate British guarantee that reunification would require the consent of the Stormont Parliament: the Ireland Act of 1949. The Unionists quickly called an election to exploit their stronger constitutional position and the South's republican rhetoric. For the APL, the South's withdrawal from the Commonwealth and the passage of the Ireland Act ended the hopes of progress that had inspired the new departure. Support for the APL declined, divisions within Nationalism re-emerged, and Republicans exploited the polarised political climate to reassert themselves.[43] McAteer had witnessed at first hand confidence give way to collapse; the experience was to leave its mark upon him.

THE PROBLEM OF OURSELVES

In December 1956, the IRA began 'Operation Harvest'. McAteer lamented the failure of constitutionalism and the pointless waste of life. 'The present outbreak would be quelled for a time,' he told the Department of External Affairs, 'only to recur again in five or ten years.' McAteer feared that Catholic politics had become trapped in a endlessly repeating cycle: the IRA campaign would be abandoned; a peaceful approach to the Northern Ireland problem would be developed; expectations of change would be raised to unrealistic levels; enthusiasm would fade away as the failure of the strategy became obvious; the resulting disenchantment would be exploited by Republicanism to renew the armed struggle. McAteer, however, found some comfort in rumours that certain leading Unionists had reached the same wearied conclusion. These Unionists had supposedly recognised that IRA violence was a product of the 'secondary aspects of partition' – anti-Catholic discrimination. McAteer recommended that the matter should be raised with the British. Instead, the proposal was merely absorbed into Dublin's wider policy reappraisal.[44]

Although McAteer pictured a gloomy future for Nationalism, he was not prepared to give up on the party. He battled against a return to the ineffectiveness that had stamped the period before the APL. As a statement of intent, McAteer attacked Derry's Nationalist MP – a symbol of the old order. He represented the Catholics of the second city, yet he usually abstained from attending Parliament and remained aloof from his constituents. McAteer challenged for the seat in the 1953 election, promising to use Stormont as a platform to expose Unionist abuses. Fighting alongside McAteer was James Doherty, his electoral agent. The Derry businessmen and Londonderry Corporation councillor had worked closely with McAteer in the APL.[45] At an election rally, Doherty urged the crowd to support 'the vigorous policy carried out by McAteer and his colleagues'.[46] Derry duly elected McAteer to represent the Foyle division at Stormont.

At times, however, McAteer seemed to have joined the old guard of the party. Following the 1956 Stormont election he successfully blocked an attempt to bring together all the Catholic parliamentarians. He would not unite with Belfast's various Labour groupings, nor would he support this new party becoming the Official Opposition. Three years later, McAteer again rebuffed agitation for Nationalism to adopt this status. He was not ready to recognise the legitimacy of the Northern state. In 1958, McAteer similarly resisted pressure from the Catholic Social Study conference for greater engagement with Stormont.[47] McAteer, writing in the *Sunday Independent*, pleaded with readers to 'spare a little pity for an uncouth Northern Nationalist so far removed from the genteel tinkling of intellectual coffee cups in the purified air of Garron Tower'.[48]

McAteer was himself opposed in the Stormont elections of 1958 and 1962 by a candidate who urged Derry's Catholics to break with the past. The Independent Labour challenger claimed that the Nationalist MP's 'policy throughout his public life had produced nothing in the way of improvement of standards of living'. It was 'one of negative denunciation without constructive effort'.[49] The most glaring example of this was the Nationalist Party's decision to welcome the closure of the local naval base in 1958: Doherty had announced that 'any Irishman who said he was sorry to see "occupying forces" leave would be a renegade'. There were many loyal Irishmen, however, who were angry that their representatives were welcoming the loss of almost 4,000 jobs.[50] For Northern Catholics, economic and social issues mattered as much as political principles. Nationalism had failed to recognise how aspirations and concerns had changed since 1945.

West Germany's Social Democrats found themselves in the same position during the 1950s. In the first years of peace, the party naively believed that the occupying powers would allow a united and neutral Germany to be built on the ruins of the Third Reich. The Social Democrats were confident that they would be the natural party of government in the new Germany. The first Federal Republic elections in 1949 were fought on a platform of nationalisation, unification, and neutrality. The party lost.

The years that followed saw the 'economic miracle', the start of European integration, and West Germany joining the North Atlantic Treaty Organisation (NATO). While everything around them had changed, the Social Democrats had stayed the same – with predictable results in the elections of 1953 and 1957. At the Bad Godesberg congress of 1959, the party finally accepted that it would be forever condemned to opposition unless it accommodated itself to the post-war world. Henceforth, the Social Democratic Party would be a *Volkspartei* – a 'people's party' – rather than an exclusively working-class party. Dropping the formal commitment to Marxism was the symbol of this transformation.[51]

Nationalists, however, could only follow the Social Democrats part way along this road. Social Democrats could win West German voters away from the Christian Democrats; Nationalists could not win Protestant voters away from the Unionists. Each election in Northern Ireland was effectively two parallel elections. Nationalists campaigned to increase their share of the Catholic vote while Unionists campaigned to increase their share of the Protestant vote. Nationalists needed to adapt to the post-war era not to defeat the Unionists, but to remain the political leaders of the Catholic community.

During the same year that West German socialists recognised the new political realities, similar voices were heard within Northern Ireland's Catholic community. Michael McKeown wrote a *Hibernia* article in 1959 suggesting that 'nationally-minded people' should organise themselves into a more professional and pragmatic political party. They then 'might hope to secure some reforms within the Northern system'. Among those intrigued by what McKeown called this 'appallingly ingenuous' appeal was James Scott, a lecturer at Queen's University. As a convert, Scott understood Catholicism and Irish nationalism differently from people 'nurtured in those cradles'. He felt that Northern Catholics needed to get involved in public life as a first step towards persuading Protestants that their future lay with a united Ireland. Scott's house became the meeting place for a wide array of politically active individuals. This circle developed into National Unity, which can probably be best described as a part-time Irish nationalist think-tank.[52] The Special Branch investigation into the new organisation highlighted National Unity's commitment to achieving unity through consent, to co-operating with 'all elected representatives of the National people', to reassuring Protestants, and to non-violent methods. The RUC concluded that 'there would not appear to be anything of a subversive nature attached to it'.[53]

From a Nationalist perspective, however, the group was subversive. Scott attempted to reassure McAteer that it merely wished to serve 'as a link between all people who believe in a united Ireland'. But the Nationalist MP paid rather more attention to National Unity's attacks on his party made at a meeting in Derry and its move into electoral politics.[54] Fears that the group intended to assume the political leadership of the minority community were to reach their peak in April 1964. National Unity invited all Catholic politicians and other interested parties to a convention in Maghery to discuss forming an umbrella body to co-ordinate future political activity. The result was the National Political Front. A spokesman for the independent candidates in the Dungannon local elections described it as the 'something new' that was 'needed' to take the 'place' of the 'dying' Nationalist Party.[55] McAteer was therefore not too disappointed when splits – a familiar problem for Irish nationalist organisations – led to the Front's rapid demise.[56] He told the press that Nationalist MPs had 'found it impossible to abdicate our position as elected representatives in favour of people who have no claim to representation whatsoever'.[57]

McAteer was undermining attempts to unite all the 'nationally-minded people' and to build democratic structures, yet he had previously pushed for such changes. This apparent contradiction between the progressive and the reactionary can be resolved. McAteer had to fill the conflicting roles of statesman, *de facto* party leader, and local party boss. He generally pursued the policies that he felt were in the best interests of Northern Catholics. But McAteer occasionally had to make tactical deviations to protect the party against potential rivals and to defend his Derry fastness. However, he was also able to exploit the challenge posed by the National Unity critique to help justify change to the old guard.

The decision to embark upon a major shift in strategy was finally taken during mid-1962. The timing was influenced by a combination of international, national, and local developments: the Second Vatican Council, London and Dublin's joint application for membership of the European Economic Community (EEC), the formal end of the IRA's failed campaign, and Nationalist successes in the Stormont election. Doherty later recalled that Nationalists felt that this would be an opportune moment to offer the Unionists the 'hand of friend- ship' in the hope of winning concessions – to adopt a policy of normalisation.[58] Senator James Lennon explained the party's position at a rally staged in Omagh by the Ancient Order of Hibernians, the Orange Order's Catholic counterpart: 'faced with the present terrible unemployment conditions in this area and the unknown consequences of the advent of the Common Market we owe it to our country as a whole to make every effort within the framework of our National aspirations to find … solutions'.[59]

European integration required states to surrender some of their sovereignty. Britain's initial reluctance to join was based upon fears as to where the loss of national control would eventually lead. For Northern Catholics, the prospect of Britain and Ireland pooling sovereignty – four decades after they had gone to war over that same issue – raised the possibility of new solutions to the old problem. At a March 1963 debate held in Dublin, McAteer argued that the 'border in this small island' was becoming 'more and more an anachronism in the world of today in which nations were merging with each other'.[60] In the short term, however, the EEC was a source of inspiration rather than a potential *deus ex machina*. As McAteer told a meeting of the Derry party in July 1962, our wondering eyes behold such traditional enemies as the French and Germans working in harmony for their mutual good, and it gives rise in my mind to this perhaps startling suggestion … Why can we not meet leaders of Orange and Protestant opinion across the table to examine whether means – even gradual means – can be found to afford our people their just status and to ensure that a man's religion is not an insurmountable barrier in obtaining a job, a house, a civic position?

McAteer concluded by reminding his audience that set next to the challenges facing Northern Ireland the dispute between the two communities was a trivial one: 'we are as two furiously battling mice in the path of a steamroller heedless of the doom that is overtaking both of us'.[61]

Londonderry Unionists welcomed McAteer's suggestion of discussions, but not 'on the basis of the implication that a man's religion presents a barrier to him obtaining a job, house, or a civic position'.[62] This established the twin themes for what became known as 'the Orange and Green talks': support for improving community relations coupled with reluctance to acknowledge the other side's interpretation. The megaphone diplomacy continued the following month with Lennon's declaration that he was 'prepared, publicly or privately, to meet Senator George Clarke, the Grand Master of the Orange Order in Ireland'.[63] Clarke agreed, leading to private conversations that were adjudged sufficiently successful to be raised to a more formal level.[64] The Orange Order, however, insisted that the Nationalists had to recognise the constitution before allegations of discrimination could be discussed. Having smoked 'a pipe-full of tobacco on the information received', McAteer declined the offer. It was 'simply unconditional surrender by another name'.[65] Indeed, capitulation was what Unionism constantly demanded of Nationalism.

THERE IS NOT MUCH GOOD IN LOOKING FOR HELP

On 15 January 1965, McAteer travelled to Dublin for clandestine discussions with Seán Lemass.[66] This was the day after the historic North–South summit – an initiative that had sidelined the leader of the 'oppressed Irish minority in the Six Counties'.[67] McAteer believed that the Nationalists had been left with no choice but to accept the role of Official Opposition, to recognise the legitimacy of Northern Ireland. Nevertheless, he wanted to discuss the matter with the Taoiseach. Lemass, however, understood little and cared even less about the Nationalist position. He argued that reunification would most likely take the form of Westminster transferring its powers under the Government of Ireland Act to the Dáil. The survival of Stormont, which the Taoiseach thought would be needed to reassure Protestant opinion, was simply out of the question for the Nationalist leader.[68] The contempt with which Lemass regarded the Nationalists became public after his retirement.[69] In October 1967, he told the New Ireland Society at Queen's University that Nationalism was partly responsible for sectarianism and discrimination. An enraged *Derry Journal* rejoined that what 'Lemass and any other politician in the Republic who takes a similarly rarefied view of the conditions with which the Nationalist Party is faced in this area needs to do is to take up residence herein'.[70]

Lemass's attitude to the Nationalist Party was shared by other Fianna Fáil statesmen. A fortnight after the McAteer meeting, the External Affairs Minister, Frank Aiken, warned Lemass to limit any future co-operation with the Nationalists: 'no Government wishes another Government with which it is negotiating to be in regular formal consultation with its own Opposition'. He also suggested that the Nationalist Party's local branches 'might concentrate on securing social justice in such matters as housing [and] employment'.[71] If the Minister had bothered to conduct even a cursory investigation, he would have found that the Nationalists had been trying to do so for years. In 1962, for example, three Nationalist councillors in Derry looked into the allocation of municipal jobs. The survey revealed that Protestants occupied 80 per cent of the administrative posts and that there was not a single Catholic cleaner at the Guildhall.[72] McAteer presented these findings to Stormont. The 'disclosures' were also publicised in Britain, where they attracted the unexpected attention of the *Sunday Express*. Right-wing columnist John Gordon, according to the *Derry Journal*, 'quoted some of the figures and added: "Intolerance or just the luck of life, call it what you like, I think it is a shaming state of things".'[73]

McAteer recalled leaving the South with 'the conviction that as far Sean Lemass was concerned, the Northern Irish were very much on their own'.[74] Dublin wanted the Catholic minority to make its peace with Stormont. Partition was no longer seen as the work of perfidious Albion but instead as the result of divisions among the Irish. Reunification, Lemass reasoned, would come through economic and social modernisation rather than political agitation. Irredentism had to give way to cross-border co-operation; the dialectic of polarisation for one of conciliation.

To borrow the phrase used by the architect of West Germany's *Ostpolitik*, Dublin was aiming for 'Wandel durch Annäherung' – 'change through rapprochement'. During Konrad Adenauer's reign as Chancellor, the Federal Republic had steadfastly refused to recognise East Germany. As the 1960s progressed, however, it became clear that America and the other Western powers had accepted the stalemate in Central Europe. Germans would have to try to solve the German problem by themselves. With a Social Democrat in the Chancellery from 1969 onwards, Bonn reached out to Pankow. Communication, it was believed, would expose the East to Western ideas and encourage change. *Ostpolitik* therefore entailed developing a range of contacts between the two German states.[75] Similarly, Dublin's *Nordpolitik* involved offering the hand of friendship to Belfast. Recognition of the status quo in Ireland was regarded as the first step towards overcoming it.

Viscount Brookeborough had not been prepared to shake hands with one of the men who in 1916 had stabbed the British army in the back. By contrast, Terence O'Neill seemed to be more open to Southern overtures. Lemass believed that he had finally found someone on the Unionist side with which he could do business. For both Dublin and Bonn, starting a dialogue with their neighbouring state required the subtle use of language. In July 1963, Lemass gave a speech at a Fianna Fáil dinner in Tralee, County Kerry, that questioned many Irish nationalist dogmas: Stormont existed with 'the support of a majority in the Six County area'; 'the solution ... to partition' was 'one to be found in Ireland by Irishmen'; and 'an extension of contacts at every level of activity' was needed.[76] Despite its guarded language, this speech was a significant step in the direction of improved North–South relations. Just three months later, however, Lemass appeared to have returned to an orthodox position. He gave a series of addresses in America in which he called for a British intervention to end partition. Through newspaper reports and back-channel communications, the Southern Prime Minister learned that his Northern counterpart was astonished and disappointed by this rapid reversal. Lemass's secret go-between concluded his report by criticising this inconsistency: 'As you said in Tralee the problem of partition can only be settled in Ireland by Irishmen. To appeal to the British is, therefore, merely an aggravation and a waste of time and purpose.'[77]

Lemass was giving the impression of being pulled in two different directions because that was what was happening. The Taoiseach was piloting the ship of state away from economic disaster. The only safe harbour for the economy, however, was Britain. On 14 December 1965, the Anglo-Irish Free Trade Agreement was signed. The more extreme Irish nationalists denounced this agreement as a new Act of Union.[78] Many Fianna Fáil politicians and supporters sympathised with the accusation that the Irish Revolution had been betrayed. To appease his party, Lemass resorted to traditional anti-partitionist rhetoric.[79] The contradictory messages coming from Dublin slowed and weakened the North–South détente. They also damaged Northern Ireland's two main parties. Liberal Unionists and the British government pointed to Lemass's conciliatory statements and pressed O'Neill to give more ground; traditional Unionists and Ian Paisley pointed to Lemass's combative statements and portrayed O'Neill as a traitor. Southern posturing helped to cast doubt on the Nationalist Party's claims that its policy of normalisation – which had been adopted partly as a response to Dublin's *Nordpolitik* – marked a genuine shift rather than a mere stratagem in the crusade for unity.

As well as being disappointed by Dublin, Nationalists were frustrated by O'Neill's failure to fulfil the hopes that the Catholic population had of him. Many within the minority community attached excessive significance to his efforts to project a modern image. In May 1962, when O'Neill was at the Finance Ministry, he gave a speech on the subject of 'self-help' that attracted the *Derry Journal*'s attention. The newspaper focused upon the phrase 'similar responsibilities for similar opportunities'. O'Neill was referring to the relationship between Belfast and London. But the newspaper applied the concept to Stormont's treatment of the Catholics.[80] This tendency to interpret O'Neill's rhetoric as a willingness to address discrimination became more pronounced after he became Prime Minister. The *Derry Journal* was encouraged to speculate the next day that O'Neill would have 'sufficient political and moral courage and sense of statesmanship to march with the times and in so doing break with that bigotry which has been the bane of this area'.[81] Disillusionment, however, rapidly developed inside the Catholic community. As early as August 1963, the *Derry Journal* declared that 'the succession to Lord Brookeborough has brought only a change of names and a less dour countenance in that office but otherwise the image is unchanged'.[82] After the Belfast riots of 1964, the newspaper angrily reacted to O'Neill's claim to have been striving for improved community relations. 'Where', asked the *Derry Journal*,

> did his contribution to the bridge building between the two traditions … come in? Was it in the test-case of the Mater Hospital, for example? Or of dealing with the discrimination scandal? Or the relentless policy of Unionist controlled local authorities even where Catholics are a majority in the community? … Can Mr O'Neill point to a single case where he has intervened by exhortation, representation or otherwise, in favour of a new and fairer deal for those of the Catholic and Nationalist tradition … ?[83]

O'Neill had no intention of delivering change along the lines that the minority population desired. Nevertheless, the misreadings of his words and actions by Catholics continued to encourage them not to despair – not yet anyway.

SELDOM PRAISED AND OFTEN CRITICISED

On 2 February 1965, McAteer announced to the press that the Nationalist Party had 'reviewed the whole political landscape [and] reached the following conclusions':

> Stormont must be seen as a federated or regional Irish Parliament to continue in existence until fears of an all-Ireland Parliament are finally resolved. There must be co-operation to ensure that the Stormont Parliament makes good on better laws for the benefit of all the people, thus promoting better harmony. It is essential to enter into Official Opposition at Stormont to ensure that the existing Parliamentary machinery operates for the common good. For all practical purposes this will mean little change ... Our fidelity to the united Ireland ideal remains unaltered by this decision. Pursuit of this aim is an entirely lawful political object in no way inconsistent with full community status. Co-operation will not and cannot be carried beyond the brink of national principle.[84]

The statement hedged it round with evasions, qualifications, and justifications, but the party had nevertheless abandoned one of its articles of faith. Nationalism had recognised the legitimacy of Northern Ireland.

Almost all of Western Europe's opposition parties had been confronted with a similar dilemma around this time. West Germany's Social Democrats had distanced themselves from their Marxist past. In 1960, one year after the Bad Godesberg congress, the British Labour Party voted on whether or not to abandon its commitment to bringing the means of production into common ownership. The leadership maintained that to recover from three successive election defeats the party needed to rebrand itself 'New Labour'. This argument failed to carry the day and Clause IV was retained.[85] Three decades later, Tony Blair and Gordon Brown triumphed where their predecessors had been defeated. New Labour went on to win the 1997 election by a landslide and send the Conservative Party into opposition for the first time in eighteen years.

McAteer's 'Clause IV moment', however, did not mark the beginning of his rise to power. In Northern Ireland's sectarian political system, this was never a possibility. Nevertheless, the new status did bring McAteer's party some benefits. The Nationalists discovered that it gave them access to British ministers. The policy of normalisation had elevated the question of partition to the level of negotiation between Dublin and London. This shift freed the party to take 'complaints about discrimination' to the 'higher tribunal' of Westminster. In January 1964, letters were sent to the leaders of the main British political parties requesting 'a substantial measure of immediate relief from ... planned discrimination'.[86] The Prime Minister and the Leader of the Opposition refused to meet the Nationalists. Only politicians who would never have the responsibility of power invited them to Westminster.[87] McAteer brought a delegation and a dossier on alleged discrimination to meetings with the Liberal leader and former Friends of Ireland.[88] The decision to accept the role of Official Opposition a year later opened doors that had previously been shut. McAteer was granted several interviews with Roy Jenkins and Lord Stonham.[89] These trips to London became regular events, reflecting his growing frustration with Stormont's attitude to reform.[90] 'If we are not satisfied that there is sincerity on the Unionist side,' McAteer told the party in September 1965, 'the conference may wish to consider bringing our troubles to Westminster again.'[91]

The influence that these Nationalist interviews had on British strategy was admittedly minimal. Nevertheless, the party still enjoyed greater access to the powerful than those who, in the words of the *Derry Journal*, 'seldom praised and often criticised' it.[92] Such groups fantasised about involving the United Nations, but McAteer actually met the Secretary-General on two separate occasions.[93] As the titular spokesman for the Catholic community, McAteer was also asked for comment by the media more often than other public figures.[94] Nevertheless, McAteer recognised that some of the accusations levelled against Nationalism were justified. He acknowledged that change was needed if only to counter the 'appall[ing]' 'public image' 'shown to friends as well as enemies'. Writing to Healy after the party's 'inevitable severance from the so-called National Political Front', McAteer stressed that 'each of us is under an urgent obligation to establish or improve constituency organisation'.[95] Nationalism therefore introduced a manifesto – the '39-Points'. As well as outlining 'national, social, economic and political policy', the document also spoke of the need for party conferences, the development of constituency organisations, and greater co-operation among the community's elected representatives.[96] The 39-Points in themselves were partly a fulfilment of this last commitment: they had been produced by a committee of Irish nationalist political groups.[97] McAteer attempted to build upon this by proposing the idea of a single party to the leaders of the various Catholic labourite factions and the new National Democratic Party – the political heir to National Unity.[98] By the end of 1964, however, irreconcilable differences brought an end to this proposed marriage.[99]

The policy of normalisation brought some gains for the Nationalist Party and the Catholic community. The passage of the 1968 Education Act, which increased government funding for voluntary schools, was a qualified success for the policy. Indeed, during the second reading debate, McAteer observed that 'the fact that they could discuss so important an issue in a calm atmosphere showed how far they had come'.[100] Fifteen Derry voluntary schools lodged applications for maintained status during the remainder of the year. For the Londonderry Education Office, this indicated 'a measure of mature co-operation ... between the voluntary and statutory education authorities'.[101]

The new approach's inherent weakness was that it depended upon the Unionist government granting political concessions at a time when Stormont conceived of reforms in socio-economic terms. McAteer frequently pleaded with O'Neill to respond to the Nationalist peace moves. A *Derry Journal* editorial from 1965 noted that the 'Nationalist leader, for his part, has made it plain that he is prepared to meet with Captain O'Neill and co-operate with him, up to a point of principle, in any and every progressive approach to the problems of community life'.[102] At the 1968 party conference, McAteer revealed that he had secured a private interview with the Stormont premier. 'It is thought in Nationalist circles', disclosed the *Derry Journal*, 'that Mr. McAteer will "lay it on the line" to the Prime Minister, that unless something is done quickly to alleviate the grievances of the minority, frustration is bound to grow.'[103] O'Neill listened to the Nationalist leader's concerns, but chose not to change his government's policy. McAteer recommended to the 1968 conference that the party should practise on-going patience. The cautionary tale of the APL haunted his thoughts. McAteer warned his fellow Nationalists against being 'goaded into precipitate action which could only set the clock back a very considerable time and which indeed might not be fully supported by the body of our people'. The conference delegates were reminded of the political realities of their position: Northern Catholics could not count on foreign support, Unionism pandered to loyalists, and the party's biggest problem was splits. Against the advice of their leader, some Nationalists continued to advocate different approaches. Austin Currie, the MP for East Tyrone, echoed the young McAteer and called for a policy of non-violent civil disobedience. 'Are we prepared to wait forever to get justice?' Currie asked. 'I suggest that if we cannot obtain justice through normal channels then we should do so through the only effective means at our disposal.'[104]

McAteer warned those 'amongst us who are thinking about going home and taking up their pikes' that this was 'a very dangerous time in politics throughout the world'. On 5 June 1968, a few weeks before the conference started, Robert F. Kennedy was celebrating his victory in the California presidential primary. As he was leaving the party, the Senator was shot by Sirhan Sirhan, a Palestinian Arab. McAteer asked the delegates to picture this 'young man ... bleeding and dying in America'. In 1968, 'those who had public voices must be very careful that their words were not enlarged into hideous action'.[105] Nevertheless, intentionally or recklessly provoking the state into a violent reaction was the only obvious way to wrest the political initiative from the Unionists. While Nationalism under McAteer was not prepared to take the gamble, other bodies existed that seemed less concerned about the probable risks. As West Germany's Social Democrats were also discovering, the move to the centre ground meant surrendering political territory to other opposition groups.[106]

HOUSEWIVES DECLARE WAR

In early 1963, three Dungannon housewives, Mrs T. Dunlop, Mrs Susan Dinsmore and Mrs Angela McCrystal, went to the offices of the local nationalist newspaper to complain about their housing problems. Dinsmore lived with her child and eight other people in her mother's house, while her husband was forced to reside with an aunt in an old people's home. The other two women had similar stories to tell. They were therefore angry that the Unionist-controlled council was rumoured to be moving only Protestant families into the new housing estate. The *Dungannon Observer* was persuaded to carry out an investigation into the local housing situation. It found that segregation and overcrowding were endemic to the area.[107]

However, an academic study conducted on the eve of the Troubles 'acquit[ted] the Unionist regime of blanket charges of discrimination in public housing'. The figures demonstrated that 'in aggregate Catholics are more likely than Protestants to be living in council houses'.[108] But an assessment as to whether or not discrimination existed cannot be based on aggregate data alone: the bias of one provider could have been balanced out by another. The Northern Ireland Housing Trust (NIHT) was foremost among the public agencies that had constructed a quarter of all the houses built since the Second World War. It seems not to have consciously discriminated against Catholics. Protestants benefited more than Catholics because the NIHT tended to select its tenants on the basis of ability to pay the rent.[109] Local authorities undertook the bulk of post-war house building. But here, too, the 1968 study uncovered 'no evidence of systematic discrimination against Catholics'. In Unionist-controlled Belfast, Derry City, Armagh, and Tyrone, 'a majority of respondents in public housing were … Catholics'. A housing policy that was free of discrimination, though, would not merely have entailed the distribution of tenancies in a way that was proportionate to the size of the Protestant and Catholic populations. It would also have been weighted heavily in favour of those in need. Assessing need on the basis of income and family size, the 1968 study found that this was indeed the case in Northern Ireland.[110] This was confirmed by the 1971 census: while 26.1 per cent of all households were Catholic, 30.7 per cent of local authority households were Catholic.[111] Establishing the absence of wholesale discrimination is not the same as proving that there was no discrimination. The large number of complaints certainly implies that there were individual instances.[112] The Nationalist Party often protested not that Catholics were refused tenancies, but that they were not considered for houses in Protestant wards. As ever in Northern Ireland, it came down to the Unionist Party's determination to remain in control. Criticism therefore tended to be directed at those councils where the Nationalist-Unionist electoral rivalry was especially fierce – places like Dungannon.[113]

'In Omagh and Dungannon Urban Districts,' reported the independent inquiry into the civil rights crisis, 'Catholics have been allocated houses virtually in the West Wards alone. Conversely, Protestants have been rehoused in Unionist wards where they would not disturb the electoral balance.' Although the 'principal criterion' was 'not actual need but maintenance of the current political preponderance', the commission noted that 'the total numbers allocated were in rough correspondence to the proportion of Protestants and Catholics in the community'. The other major difference between the way that Protestants and Catholics were treated was in the type of people awarded tenancies. In 'Dungannon Urban District', 'houses allocated to Catholics tended ... to go to rehouse slum dwellers, whereas Protestant allocations tended to go more frequently to new families'.[114] The number of Catholic families with more than six children was five times greater than the number of Protestant families. The Catholic community was therefore more affected by the problems that came with overcrowding.[115] A Dungannon resident later recalled that 'newly-weds were compelled to move in with in-laws', which brought mounting 'family tensions' when 'the second child arrived'.[116] Slum clearance often made the situation worse as regulations prevented new families from remaining with their rehoused relatives.[117]

The strain of supporting their families in such circumstances sent Dunlop, Dinsmore, and McCrystal into the streets to protest. They found themselves heading up a group of 'forty young housewives' who had 'declared war on the local Urban Council'. 'If the Council will do nothing for us,' the women told the *Dungannon Observer*, 'then we will see ... our M.P., and if he refuses to help then there is always the Prime Minister to appeal to.'[118] Dunlop, Dinsmore, and McCrystal started their campaign by picketing the May meeting of the council. In front of the television cameras, the women presented their 'declaration of independence' to the councillors. 'No provision has been made in the Urban Council's housing schemes for any of the young married couples in the town,' the statement read. 'This leaves them with no alternative except to squat in the condemned houses.' The women asked what was to become of young families after the relatives that they lived with were moved to new estates as part of the slum clearance programme, whether provision would be made in future developments and when a points system would be adopted.[119]

At the picket, the women carried placards bearing such slogans as 'Racial Discrimination in Alabama Hits Dungannon' and 'If Our Religion Is Against Us Ship Us to Little Rock'.[120] In the weeks leading up to the protest, the American civil rights movement had once again become headline news around the world. Martin Luther King had come to Birmingham, Alabama, in dire need of a victory. On 3 April 1963, he launched 'Project C – for Confrontation'. Marches were held, sit-ins were staged, boycotts were imposed, and King got himself sent to jail – but the media remained uninterested. Out of desperation, King was reduced to sending schoolchildren into the fray. On 2 May 1963, groups of children – most were teenagers, but some were as young as six years old – marched towards the city centre. Within a couple of hours, the police had arrested almost a thousand children for marching without a permit and for failing to disperse when ordered. The following day, yet more children set out to reach the heart of Birmingham. As the jails were already full, the Police Commissioner chose to defend downtown with firehoses that shot streams of water powerful enough to break bones. Police dogs were also used to push the marchers back from the city centre. The television news that night showed pictures of children knocked down by jets of water and menaced by snarling German Shepherds. The media had got their story; King had got his victory.[121]

The American civil rights movement inspired Catholic activists throughout the 1960s. However, the complexity of adopting ideas from across the Atlantic and adapting them to Northern Ireland conditions ensured that the process was slow and far from smooth.[122] In the first stages, the African-American struggle influenced only the rhetoric. Comparing their condition to that of the black population from the Deep South was useful propaganda for the Dungannon housewives. For similar reasons, Nationalists identified Northern Catholics with whatever occupied nation was currently in the news. In the aftermath of the Second World War, it was with wartime France; in 1968, it was with the Czechs.[123] But the African-American analogy was different. It focused upon reform within the system, not resistance. It suggested new tactics: publicity-seeking civil disobedience and non-violent mass protests. Indeed, as the Dungannon and American campaigns progressed, the black struggle became more than a metaphor. Correspondents to the *Dungannon Observer* even advocated a Northern Irish version of the March on Washington.[124]

At a public meeting held a few days after the picket, the housewives created the Homeless Citizens' League (HCL). Dunlop, Dinsmore, and McCrystal were appointed onto the committee of the new group. But

Patricia McCluskey, who had only just got involved in the protest and who was not even affected by the housing problem, became Chair of the HCL.[125] She laid out her qualifications for leadership in an interview with the unionist *Tyrone Courier and Dungannon News*: she had worked to rehouse people who had been bombed out during the war, she had been a teacher, she had visited German refugee camps, and she had travelled extensively in the Middle East.[126] Patricia McCluskey had also attended National Unity meetings.[127] She had neglected to mention this to the reporter as the HCL was eager to present itself as non-political. A socially conscious, politically engaged, middle-aged doctor's wife had pushed herself forward; a group of young, working-class women had let her take charge. Deference was far from dead in Dungannon during the 1960s.

Despite the change of leadership and organisation, almost everything else stayed the same. The goal was still to secure local authority housing for young families forced to share with relatives or to rent overpriced, substandard flats.[128] The *Dungannon Observer* remained supportive. It covered HCL activities, printed Patricia McCluskey's views, and criticised the intransigence of the local Unionists.[129] The HCL maintained the strategy of working within the system, petitioning the council to change and applying further pressure through appeals to Stormont.[130] The comparison with the black struggle for equality was further developed. Slogans inspired by the civil rights movement appeared on an increasing number of placards, the *Dungannon Observer* carried articles that highlighted similarities, and one letter writer declared that the 'Catholic people' were 'white negroes'.[131] The African-American influence also contributed to the HCL's decision to start marching. 'There were no bands, no sashes and no fuss,' commented the *Dungannon Observer* on the first parade, 'just a group of well-dressed and attractive young women ... their prams [and] their older children.'[132]

The council's final decision to allocate 142 tenancies on the new estate to people who already had homes pushed the HCL into direct action. The housewives, from the very beginning of their protest, had warned the local Unionists that as a last resort they would squat in the vacated properties earmarked for demolition. Many members of the HCL now felt that the council had left them with no other option. 'One family moved into [the prefabs at] Fairmount Park,' reported the *Dungannon Observer*, 'then another. Soon the "squatters" came in a stream. The dam had burst.'[133] This was a spontaneous action by the HCL's rank and file taken against Patricia McCluskey's express wishes. She was anxious about stepping outside the law; the working-class families were anxious about having somewhere to live.[134] The *Dungannon Observer* noted that the HCL's leadership almost immediately 'issued instructions that no more families are to squat'.[135] Patricia McCluskey, however, appropriated the incident with her subsequent actions. Indeed, she was one of the authors of a 1969 pamphlet that described the episode under the heading 'How the Civil Rights Movement Began'.[136]

The council switched off the electricity supply, removed access to running water (until this action proved illegal) and contemplated proceedings to eject the squatters. This overreaction was typical of the inflexible attitude of the local Unionists. Moderate Protestant opinion, which had possessed doubts about the behaviour of the Unionist councillors from the start, was outraged. 'The Dungannon Council's post-war housing record', commented the *Belfast Telegraph*, 'is not one of signal achievement. In these circumstances it is negative to assert that the squatters "will not be considered" when houses become available.' The editorial suggested that 'Stormont should adopt a tougher line with those local authorities whose building programmes fall short of requirements.'[137]

This opinion piece appeared on the same day that Joseph Stewart, the titular Nationalist leader, presented a HCL delegation to the Minister of Health and Local Government. Conn McCluskey, Patricia's husband, brought to the meeting what he later described as a 'carefully researched dossier'.[138] The memorandum detailed how since 1945 the council had failed to allocate any of the 194 houses built for normal letting to Catholics. It had, however, assigned 102 of the 128 rehousing schemes to Catholics. The squatters, most of whom were young married couples and families, were listed alongside a short description of the unsatisfactory accommodation where they had previously been living. The HCL proposed that the 'Council should regularise the position of the "squatters" ' – who 'have in fact collected the rent to date'. The deputation felt that the squatters 'could be moved to' the Ballygawley Road estate following the completion of the '60 houses' due within the next year'.[139]

The compromise settlement reached was a commitment to extend the Ballygawley Road estate, which was being built in the Nationalist ward, and to consider the squatters for rehousing there after they had ended their protest. The Minister of Health and Local Government wrote to Stewart that the 'result is, I think, a happy one and should ensure that the families in Dungannon who are most in need of housing will receive houses fairly quickly'. A year later, however, Conn McCluskey was complaining about the gap between this aspiration and the inadequate delivery. 'Of the ninety-six houses promised by you,' he berated the Minister, 'forty-eight have been completed for normal letting but eighteen of these have turned out to be Old People's Bungalows.' Other problems had also emerged which had meant that 'four families [still] had to be housed'.[140]

This was a qualified success but that still meant it was a success – particularly for a community that had become accustomed to defeat. Several hundred Dungannon residents were moved to present Patricia McCluskey with 'a silver tea service "For Services Rendered"'. The guest of honour informed the victory party that she 'intended retiring from public view'.[141] But she soon changed her mind: 'I could not have lived with myself had I not done something to help the downtrodden people.'[142] The following April, Patricia McCluskey announced that she would 'lead a group of candidates' in the forthcoming local election.[143] These independents benefited not only from her popularity but also from widespread anger at the abstentionist tactics of the local Nationalists. At the convention to select candidates for the town's Catholic ward, Patricia McCluskey's group secured all seven nominations.[144] The Nationalists refused to accept this verdict and decided to fight the election. During the campaign, superior experience meant that two Nationalists topped the poll. 'Obviously they [the Patricia McCluskey group] were prepared for a nice, quiet, well-conducted debate in a calm, cool atmosphere', commented the *Dungannon Observer*, 'and found themselves floundering helplessly out of their depth.' Nevertheless, Patricia McCluskey and three other independents were elected, which made her the leader of the largest Catholic group on the council.[145] The housewife-general was having a 'good war'.

THE CAMPAIGN FOR SOCIAL JUSTICE

On 17 January 1964, Conn and Patricia McCluskey launched the Campaign for Social Justice (CSJ). 'It was housing which brought us into this,' Patricia told reporters, 'but then the jobs situation came with housing and the whole picture is really frightening.'[146] The approach adopted by the HCL was to be extended to other aspects of alleged discrimination and to every part of Northern Ireland. The couple recognised that they could develop the tactic of appealing to a higher authority to bring pressure upon a subordinate body. As Sir Basil Brooke had feared, a Catholic political group was seeking to attack Unionist rule by taking to the international stage. Indeed, the forums that the couple targeted were those that the former Prime Minister had indicated: the British and American publics, the United Nations, and the Council of Europe.[147] The McCluskeys felt that the vehicle for this campaign should have an elite membership. The CSJ was therefore drawn from the couple's Dungannon associates as well as people who had also been 'leading isolated battles against bigoted councils in various towns in the North'.[148] The HCL's more relaxed attitude to membership and organisation was rejected, Conn McCluskey later claimed, 'because large groups of Irish people are prone to discuss matters too fully without making final decisions, and eventually split up'. The couple was eager to retain the initiative entirely in their own hands after their problems with the HCL.[149] The African-American model of a mass movement engaging in acts of civil disobedience had been abandoned in favour of a civil liberties pressure group.

Space had opened up for the CSJ as a result of the Nationalist Party's stuttering efforts to move to the middle ground. Across Western Europe, new actors were appearing alongside traditional parties on the political stage. This process began with the anti-nuclear campaigns of the 1950s and climaxed with the explosion of 'single- issue' groups in the 1970s. Ideologies were giving way to issues. The new groups were therefore able to search out and indeed find a contradictory collection of supporters and allies. West Germany's *Bürgerinitiativen* ('citizens' initiative' groups) often brought together conservatives, leftists, and people who had no clear set of political beliefs.[150] Similarly, CSJ members held a range of opinions and adapted their message to different audiences. Conn McCluskey declared that he was a 'sincere Socialist', but later maintained that 'my kind of Catholic would never dream of offering a discourtesy to the Queen'.[151] Patricia McCluskey was working for 'equality', yet felt that Northern Ireland was a 'police state' and that the 'abolition of ...

partition' was an 'important' 'matter'.[152] The one constant was that CSJ members were dignified, concerned citizens. The memorandum Conn McCluskey presented to the Minister of Health and Local Government stressed that the HCL delegates were 'not politicians or members of any political party' but rather were 'aware of, and disturbed by, housing injustices'.[153] When deciding who should join the CSJ, Conn McCluskey recalled that the couple opted for 'people whom we judged to be entirely reputable'. They included an architect, an ear, nose and throat surgeon, a dentist, a wealthy businessman, and a science professor.[154] The CSJ was to make great play of this respectability in its pamphlets.[155]

The CSJ was composed of professionals, but its approach was far from professional. Conn and Patricia McCluskey's correspondence with politicians suggests that they were rather naive. In a 1967 letter to Prime Minister Harold Wilson about discrimination, the CSJ claimed 'that a word from you would reverse the position overnight'.[156] A year earlier, the CSJ had attempted to solicit legal advice from the Home Secretary, Roy Jenkins.[157] The CSJ may have been feigning innocence for tactical reasons. The requests to harness the Home Office's legal expertise were a chance to highlight the problems of seeking redress through the courts.[158] But the subtlety was lost on Labour politicians and their staff, whose replies were politely didactic.[159] On one occasion, Roy Jenkins's Private Secretary informed the CSJ that the 'provision of legal aid in Northern Ireland is, I am afraid, a matter solely for the Northern Ireland authorities'.[160] The CSJ's attempts to fight discrimination through the courts show the group at its most dilettantish. During Prime Minister Alec Douglas-Home's visit to Northern Ireland in March 1964, he had indicated that the rights of Catholics could be protected by recourse to law under the terms of the Government of Ireland Act. This was not merely a standard brush-off – it was sound advice. An act of parliament is the highest form of law within the British constitutional structure. The devolution of legislative power to Northern Ireland did not alter the essentials of parliamentary sovereignty. The authority of legislation enacted by Stormont was derived entirely from the Government of Ireland Act. This expressly preserved the Westminster Parliament's power to make laws for the region and placed restrictions upon the devolved Parliament's competence. Legislation that directly or indirectly conferred an advantage or a disadvantage due to religious belief was outside Stormont's competence and hence void.[161] Nevertheless, the CSJ was told by 'Senior and Junior Counsel' that 'the discrimination practiced [*sic*] by Local Authorities is not capable of review by the courts under the terms of the Government of Ireland Act, 1920, or any other Statutory Provisions'.[162]

Harry Calvert, an academic lawyer at Queen's University and a prominent member of the Northern Ireland Labour Party (NILP) during the 1960s, found this to be 'superficially a plausible interpretation of the constitution'. But, he continued, 'there are a number of reasons for preferring the view that the limitations on legislative action cannot be avoided by executive discretion'. Calvert referred to the principle that constitutional safeguards should not be circumvented. He also supported his argument by reference to legal authority. Lord MacDermott L.C.J., in the 1959 case of *O.D. Cars Ltd.* v. *Belfast Corporation*, ruled that a 'constitutional provision cannot be side-stepped by empowering a government department or an official to do something or to come to some determination which could not validly be done or determined on the face of the enabling statute'.[163] The discrimination practised by local authorities was unconstitutional and could have been challenged in the courts.

In 1968, before the civil rights marches began, Calvert presented his reading of the constitution in person to the CSJ. His audience was left unconvinced. 'The Unionists sent a kind of spy, Calvert ... to our private Campaign meeting,' Conn McCluskey wrote. 'He was pathetically insistent that we ... continue our local litigation against the Council – which they can manipulate, I feel sure. But nothing doing. We insulted him well.'[164]

Northern Ireland's leading authority on constitutional and public law was held in higher esteem by the Unionist government. Two Attorney-Generals shared Calvert's opinion that discrimination by local authorities could be questioned in the courts by virtue of the safeguards in the Government of Ireland Act. 'If such a case were brought,' Teddy Jones told the Stormont Cabinet in April 1965, 'he would not – appearing on behalf of the Government – argue before a Northern Ireland Court that there was no remedy.'[165] In late October 1968, his successor presented a memorandum to the Cabinet that endorsed Jones's reasoning:

A local authority is a statutory body and it exercises its powers under the authority of a statute, or rather a number of statutes.

> If ... the statute may not be discriminatory then, in my opinion, a discriminatory exercise of the powers conferred by statute may not be effected and if such discrimination in the exercise of statutory powers were to be effected, such exercise would be bad and could, in my opinion, be challenged successfully.[166]

The CSJ had therefore received poor legal advice. But the group believed that it had received a propaganda gift. Patricia McCluskey sent letters to Douglas-Home, enquiring – in light of contrary legal advice – how redress against alleged discrimination could be pursued under the Government of Ireland Act. Downing Street informed the CSJ about the sections that prohibited religious discrimination. The correspondence was reproduced in a pamphlet entitled *Why Justice Cannot Be Done*. It concluded that legal redress was impossible and that the British Prime Minister was unwilling for Westminster to exercise its ultimate political authority.[167]

The CSJ's efforts to seek either a private law or prerogative remedy followed the same pattern. According to the traditional *ultra vires* model of judicial review, the courts preserve the legislative monopoly of Parliament by ensuring that public authorities remain within the powers that the legislature has granted them. If the court finds that the power has been exercised illegally, irrationally, or through unfair procedures, the action might be condemned as unlawful. Consequently, the inherent supervisory jurisdiction of the courts provided the CSJ with a chance to overturn the discrimination practised by local authorities. Indeed, the group was associated with a 1971 legal challenge to Dungannon Rural District Council's allocation of housing that produced a qualified victory.[168] The Government of Ireland Act prohibited the Governor's executive powers being used in a way that led to discrimination. A proven case of bias against Catholics in the allocation of public housing might therefore have been ruled illegal.[169] If it was established that a public ppointment had been made exclusively on religious grounds, then the court could have regarded such a decision as irrational. As councillors allocated public housing, the court might have ruled that giving tenancies to political supporters constituted a violation of the rule against bias.[170]

The law of remedies, however, was disfigured by ambiguities and anomalies. These problems prevented many cases that had merit from being argued fully in court. Having developed substantially out of private law, administrative law includes restrictive rules about which litigants have the right to be granted standing before the court. At this time, there were different tests of standing for all three prerogative remedies and within each particular one. For the CSJ's test case against Dungannon Urban District Council, the litigant alleged that discrimination in housing allocation had forced him into mediocre accommodation outside the area. Given the case law on standing, the CSJ's barrister advised that a ratepayer should bring the action instead. Such a litigant would have rights capable of being enforced against the council. The CSJ had only crossed one of the hurdles placed in the way of someone seeking judicial review; it still had to decide which particular remedy should be sought.[171] *Certiorari* could apply to every type of error and had interim relief available. On the other hand, the remedy's time limit was six months, an action for damages could not be combined with it and disputed issues of fact presented problems because evidence was taken on affidavit. Indeed, this last problem contributed to the failure of a 1971 action against Dungannon Urban District Council in which the CSJ was involved.[172] The declaration, by contrast, had considerably longer time limits, allowed a claim for damages to be joined with it and generally permitted discovery of documents and cross-examination of witnesses. It also had disadvantages, though. In particular, it was not available as a matter of right and there were doubts about whether it could be used to challenge executive discretion.[173]

The complications that could have ensued from choosing to seek an unsuitable remedy were not given a chance to arise. The denial of Legal Aid led the CSJ to abandon the action. Although the Legal Aid scheme had been established in Britain by the post-war Labour government, it was not implemented in Northern Ireland until 1965.[174] Indeed, the interest aroused by its introduction had encouraged the CSJ to embark upon its test case. The CSJ's application for Legal Aid was declined by the Law Society of Northern Ireland. The reason given was that 'the proceedings to which the application is related are not proceedings for which Legal Aid may be given'. This refusal was subsequently upheld on appeal to the Society's Legal Aid Committee.[175] The Attorney-General later told the Cabinet that the rejection was 'a straightforward exercise of statutory powers which have their exact counterpart in Great Britain'. He could find 'no suggestion of pressure or influence from any quarter being brought to bear'. 'Despite this refusal,' the Attorney-General continued, 'one would have thought that if the case had been well founded no difficulty would have been experienced in finding other means of bringing it to trial.'[176]

The CSJ was told that it would cost an estimated £20,000 to pursue a private law or prerogative remedy to the House of Lords. The group decided that this figure was beyond its means and gave up on fighting discrimination in the courts.[177] The episode was cannibalised for propaganda material: a pamphlet entitled *Legal Aid to Oppose Discrimination – Not Likely!* The possibilities of securing the financing necessary to fight the test case or of acting as litigants in person were not properly considered by the CSJ. Instead, the group had returned to seeking its favoured option of a Westminster intervention.[178] It is understandable that the opaqueness of the law encouraged the CSJ to concentrate upon a political approach. This was an arena in which they were more comfortable. Nevertheless, the failure to explore fully the potential of the legal process tarnishes the CSJ's professional image. It also contradicts the claim made by Patricia McCluskey at a meeting held in Westminster that 'We have tried to take legal action. It is impossible.'[179] Civil rights could have been pursued through the courts instead of in the streets.

VERY LITTLE, IF ANY, INTEREST

In 1963, Conn and Patricia McCluskey were watching their 'very small little television set'. A Nationalist MP and a Unionist MP were taking part in a televised debate on the issue of discrimination.

Patricia McCluskey remembered that the Nationalist 'made such a poor showing' that she was reduced to tears.[180] At the CSJ's press launch, Patricia McCluskey stressed that the group's 'first objective' would be to 'collect comprehensive and accurate data on all injustices done [and] to bring them to the attention of as many socially minded people as possible'. The group assumed that 'the presentation of the unvarnished truth will be sufficient'.[181] Once the British people knew what was happening in Northern Ireland, it was hoped that their sense of fair play would be outraged and calls for change would come. As the *What the Papers Say* pamphlet put it, 'Pressure of British opinion, properly directed ... could ensure the removal of any bias against Nationalists and Catholics because of their political or religious convictions.'[182]

The culmination of the CSJ's investigations was *The Plain Truth*. This pamphlet's statistical breakdown of job appointments and housing allocation in Derry and Dungannon developed further the approach of the HCL memorandum. This was also the direction taken by APL propaganda. *The Indivisible Island*, for example, presented comparative tables of Protestant and Catholic appointments.[183] But the CSJ's literature did differ from the Nationalist tradition in the extent to which it tailored its message to a British audience. Conn McCluskey recalled that while 'fervent nationalists' objected 'to our use of the word "Londonderry" instead of "Derry"', the CSJ 'had no wish to confuse' 'foreign readers' by referring to a name absent from most maps. The space devoted to the Special Powers Act and policing was minimal. Northern Ireland was being portrayed as a region of the United Kingdom where British citizens were denied their rights rather than as an occupied country.[184]

The CSJ's propaganda improved upon that produced by the APL. But the CSJ was aspiring to do more than this; it wanted to prove that systematic discrimination was being practised in Northern Ireland. Conn McCluskey proudly boasted of the CSJ's professional approach: 'in only one case, in the reams of documentation we supplied, did we make an error'.[185] The problem, however, was not so much with the data itself but with the way in which it had been interpreted. CSJ pamphlets failed to consider that anything other than conscious discrimination could account for the disparity between the number of houses and jobs going to Protestants and Catholics.[186] The Omagh investigation merely stated that Catholics made up 61.2 per cent of the local population but Protestants had the majority of the houses and jobs doled out by the council.[187] The five short paragraphs devoted to housing detailed how certain local authorities provided Catholics with houses only in electoral wards where they would not threaten Unionist majorities.[188]

The academic research conducted into charges of discrimination has suggested a number of other factors that may have contributed to the imbalances found by the CSJ. To take the example of public appointments, a 1962 study suggested that the Catholic community's lower standards of education played a role – particularly when it came to the higher posts.[189] An American sociologist working in the 1980s took this argument a stage further. On the eve of the Troubles, 9 per cent of Protestants had a higher education as compared to 5 per cent of Catholics. This difference was identified as the reason for the minority population's lower occupational status.[190] The reason for the lower standards of education in the first place was laid at the door of the Church. Catholics throughout the English-speaking world supposedly placed less emphasis upon education than Protestants did. This therefore accounted for 'the similarity between the position of Catholics in Northern Ireland and other countries'.[191] Some of the Catholics who had the necessary qualifications might have been reluctant to work for their oppressors. One of the few Catholics to rise to the top of a Stormont department remembered 'that some Catholics, and especially those in Belfast where, I have been told, the Bishop had advised them against seeking Government employment, looked with suspicion on Catholic civil servants'. However, he also recalled that his headmaster had abandoned the Northern Ireland Civil Service entrance examinations after two outstanding pupils had been rejected at the interview stage.[192] This headmaster was not the only Catholic to think that it was not worth applying for posts that had – it was suspected – been reserved for Protestants. Although technically a justification for discrimination rather than an explanation for the imbalance between the two communities, many writers have pointed out that politicians were expected to look after their own supporters.[193] Indeed, less than 2 per cent of the workers employed by Nationalist-controlled Newry Urban District Council were Protestants, even though Protestants made up 25 per cent of the local population.[194]

CSJ pamphlets therefore had more in common with propaganda than academic studies. But it was propaganda that was failing to make a significant impact. As a senior civil servant at the Department of External Affairs observed, 'very little, if any, interest in the problems of the Northern Ireland minority is taken outside Ireland'.[195] The CSJ did enjoy some small successes. In 1964, Wilson had promised Patricia McCluskey that a future Labour government would do 'everything in its power' to find a solution to the problem of discrimination. Although the CSJ made great play of this commitment, Wilson's reply had used weasel words. The Labour leader had made intervention conditional upon the NILP somehow securing an electoral breakthrough.[196] Anyway, Wilson hardly needed to have Patricia McCluskey playing the role of the agent provocateur to get him making unguarded comments about Irish affairs. Indeed, the Unionists were concerned about his exact intentions even before he put pen to paper to reply to her letter.[197] Another small success savoured by the CSJ was a 1966 *Sunday Times* article headlined 'John Bull's Political Slum'. The writer, Northern Irish-born Cal McCrystal, 'obtained' the 'background' for the piece during 'an interesting evening with three of [the] committee'.[198] The CSJ's influence on the article was clear from the way that it detailed the 'pattern of prejudice' and suggested that 'real liberalisation of the Ulster regime will only come after vigorous prodding from Westminster'.[199] McCrystal, however, later recalled that his editor had despatched him across the Irish Sea in response to 1966's disturbances rather than a CSJ letter.[200] Violence was what attracted the media's attention.

THE BRITISH PEOPLE KNOW LITTLE AND CARE LESS

The CSJ had not been writing letters just to the Labour leadership. Conn McCluskey wrote in his memoirs that he and Patricia 'had been steadily plying the Labour Party backbenchers with documenation [and the] result was the formation of an important new group called the Campaign for Democracy in Ulster' (CDU).[201] Paul Rose MP, the Chair of the CDU, also recollected being 'inspired by the [CSJ] led by Dr and Mrs McCluskey who attended our first meeting in the House of Commons'.[202] On 2 July 1965, just over two years after the meeting of Dungannon housewives had made her their leader, Patricia McCluskey addressed a meeting of MPs and peers of the realm. This grand occasion, however, was the CDU's christening, not its birth. CDU Secretary Paddy Byrne traced the organisation's origins to a meeting held early in 1965 at a Streatham pub under the auspices of the local Labour Party. These activists, many of whom were of Irish origin, approached Rose after he had spoken out at Westminster against discrimination. Rose consented to become Chair and helped to interest 101 other parliamentarians in becoming sponsors for the body.[203]

Although the CDU set out to 'pursue an independent policy', it still built up links with many groups from Northern Ireland, the Irish emigrant community, and the Labour movement.[204] In April 1967, Rose headed up a CDU fact-finding mission to Northern Ireland. The short tour ended in Derry, where the British MPs met local Nationalists, NILP members, the city's Liberals, and other groups.[205] Rose wrote in the *CDU Newsletter* that the visit had 'rocked the Unionist establishment on its heels'. 'The enthusiasm which greeted us demonstrated that in spite of many disappointments Irishmen have a touching faith in the ability of Westminster to bring discrimination, gerrymandering, and economic neglect to an end.'[206]

Byrne's trip to Ireland later that year led him to arrive at a somewhat different evaluation. The NILP executive gave Byrne 'the impression that they considered CDU to be a damn nuisance'. There was broad agreement that outside attacks united Protestants behind the Unionist government and that Rose had aligned himself too closely with the Nationalists during his tour. The NILP executive suggested that the CDU should push for achievable goals. Reform of the local government franchise, they argued, was more likely and would have more of an impact than a royal commission being appointed to investigate allegations of discrimination.[207] By contrast, the CSJ shared the CDU's commitment to a Westminster intervention. Parliament could press Stormont into reform or – if the first approach failed – pass legislation itself to end discrimination. Consequently Byrne had a more comfortable time in Dungannon with his 'true friends', the McCluskeys.[208]

The Government of Ireland Act clearly stated that Westminster remained supreme. The issue of discrimination, however, came under the responsibilities that the Act had devolved to Stormont. By convention, the matter could therefore not be debated at Westminster. The CDU MPs had to resort to skillful manipulation of Commons procedure to present their case. In May 1966, Rose exploited an adjournment debate on the Race Relations Act to propose 'legislation in this regard to Northern Ireland'. Although the Speaker prevented him from continuing, Rose's intervention led Alice Bacon, the Home Office Minister, to note that the Act neglected 'a number of important fields where discrimination does occur'.[209] According to a junior minister in the first Wilson government, 'there's no doubt that they [the CDU MPs] deserve a page in history for the persistence with which they pressed [their] case'.[210]

The election of Gerry Fitt strengthened the CDU's efforts to break the convention. The new MP was a 'corner boy' politician and put his street smarts to good use in the House of Commons. Although he came from Northern Ireland's minority population, Fitt did not regard himself as 'an Irish nationalist, as such, or an Irish Catholic, as such'. Instead, he saw himself as 'a Labour man, a socialist, who thought of rising above nationalisms'. Fitt's socialist convictions had not come from reading books – he found Marx 'heavy going' – but from living in working-class Belfast. 'I have clear memories of the Thirties,' Fitt told an interviewer, 'everyone was hungry.' During the Second World War, the teenage Fitt served on the Merchant Navy ships that sailed in the Atlantic and Murmansk convoys.

In peacetime Belfast, Fitt fought elections for a variety of anti-partition Labour groupings. As he later explained, 'In Northern Ireland it is very difficult to be a socialist without being labelled a Unionist socialist or an anti-partition socialist.' Standing as the Republican Labour candidate, he won the West Belfast seat in March 1966.[211] When he arrived at Westminster, Fitt cannily used the convention that a maiden speech can be on any subject and will not be interrupted to denounce the Stormont regime.[212] From that moment on, he never let up the pressure.

However, the labours of Fitt and the CDU went largely unr warded. Rose remembered that Roy Jenkins 'listened with great sympathy', but 'wasn't going to get himself involved in a topic that might bring about his downfall'.[213] A quarter of a century later, Jim Callaghan sat down with former members of the CDU to explain the Wilson government's indifference:

> There was a group that was interested in Northern Ireland consistently from the ... middle 1940s ... That group was always interested, just as there is always a group interested in relations with Namibia or with South Africa, or with any other part of the Commonwealth ... there was as much interest and detachment as that ... the government very sensibly said, 'We are not going to get involved in this when we are not welcomed by the Northern Ireland government ... we have a majority of only three ... We want to use Northern Ireland ministers as far as we can in order to introduce the reforms.'[214]

Outside Parliament, the CDU was also failing. In June 1968, Byrne wrote a confidential memorandum for the CDU's central committee that concluded that the group's 'efforts appear to be in vain'. Only three resolutions on Northern Ireland had made the agenda for the next Labour Party conference. Only three constituency Labour Parties had voted to affiliate themselves to the CDU. Byrne bitterly complained that the letters he had repeatedly sent to the Labour leadership had been 'treated with contempt'. Indeed, Wilson's Personal Secretary had misaddressed one of the Prime Minister's negative replies to 'Miss Patricia Byrne'.[215] 'In short,' Byrne summarised,

> no mass movement has developed and there is no indication that one will. In the present situation in the Labour movement,

the people most likely to aid our cause, the British Left, are far too concerned to save socialism from extinction than to bother about Northern Ireland about which the mass of the British people know little and care less.[216]

REPEATING MISTAKES

'It must be a great feeling to look down from such a high vantage point,' McAteer wrote to Healy in late 1967, 'on the repeating mistakes of newcomers.'[217] The CSJ spent its first four years gradually and painfully acquainting itself with the constraints upon Catholic political action. Dublin declined to co-operate with the CSJ and the CDU. The Southern state feared that getting involved in the discrimination controversy would weaken its *Nordpolitik*.[218] The British government was worried about being lured into the quagmire of Northern Ireland politics. Backbenchers at Westminster showed enthusiasm for the cause, but lacked the power to change the leadership's stance. Stormont regarded the CSJ as a minor irritation. O'Neill dismissed an investigation by *The Times* into accusations of discrimination as 'a mere repetition of the stock in trade of the so-called Campaign for Social Justice'. Although the article contained no reference to the group, he went on to denounce the CSJ's 'publications' as 'highly tendentious and often inaccurate'.[219]

The CSJ was able to provoke such intemperate comments from Unionist politicians and the occasional pause for thought – but no change of policy.[220] This shortage of success contributed to the 'apathy' that the CSJ – like the Nationalists and the Republicans – encountered within the minority population. The group was also frustrated by the opposition it faced from other Catholic politicians, who were anxious to defend their own positions. Conn McCluskey complained to Byrne about how Derry Nationalists had 'whined away, McAteer included'.[221] Illustrating the ambiguity that was typical of relations between Catholic activists, it was to McAteer that Conn McCluskey wrote 'longingly of a wish to get back to [his] sculpture' after the disappointments of politics.[222]

Even if the CSJ had somehow managed to secure the desired Westminster intervention, this would not have brought a peaceful solution to the problem of discrimination. On 5 August 1966, O'Neill warned Wilson and Jenkins that it would be 'disastrous if Westminster were to intervene': 'to do so would be to invite a revival of the spirit and policies of 1912'. The Home Secretary, who had carried out research on the Home Rule crisis, 'disputed the historical analogy'. But the Northern Irish Prime Minister was adamant that the 'crux in each case was coercion of the loyal Ulster population'.[223] O'Neill was right; Ulster would fight. In the first half of 1974, popular Protestant opposition and paralysing industrial action defeated British efforts to introduce a power-sharing executive.[224]

The British intervention followed the outbreak of civil disorder rather than acting as its catalyst. As Callaghan observed, it 'needed a crisis to enable us to take the action that was necessary'.[225] In a mirror image of the CSJ's original strategy, it was at this stage that their literature attracted the attention of those in power. For British politicians and civil servants who were unfamiliar with Northern Ireland, the CSJ's material acted as a primer.[226] 'I should be glad', Lord Stonham wrote to the McCluskeys, 'if you would kindly let me have ten more copies of "The Plain Truth".'[227] The CSJ's pamphlets also served as source material for Fleet Street journalists after the 'paper wall' had fallen.[228] A supply of CSJ literature was even acquired by Dublin, which used it in an international propaganda campaign. Conn McCluskey estimated that 'over 100,000 copies' of the second edition of *The Plain Truth* 'were produced and circulated'.[229] This was merely compensation for the failure of the CSJ's new approach to the old problems.

CHAPTER THREE

Republicanism and Socialism

THE CONNOLLY ASSOCIATION

The English port of Liverpool, so the old joke went, was the capital city of both Ireland and Wales. For most of the twentieth century, elections in the city's Netherfield and St Domingo wards were contests between Irish Protestant and Catholic candidates – the immigrants had brought their politics with them. Militants within the Loyal Orange Order of England and the Knights of St Columba battled each other in the streets of Liverpool. As late as the 1950s, the Catholic Archbishop could spark a riot merely by visiting those members of his flock living in the marches of Protestant territory. In March 1958, mounted police were called upon to free him from a house that had been besieged by hundreds of stone-throwing Protestants.[1]

Birkenhead – part of the greater Liverpool area – was perhaps an appropriate birthplace for the man acknowledged as 'the intellectual progenitor of the civil rights movement', C. Desmond Greaves. Like his city, Greaves was a mixture of English, Irish, and Welsh influences. Unlike most of the people who marched for civil rights in the 1960s, Greaves was a middle-class Protestant. However, he cast this identity aside during his youth – joining the Communist Party in the early 1930s. Europe was taking sides and the choice was not so much between democracy and dictatorship but rather a question of fascism or communism. Britain was not immune to the problems caused by the First World War, the Russian Revolution, the Great Depression, and the Spanish Civil War. Yet the body politic was not at risk from the British Union of Fascists nor from the Communist Party of Great Britain (CPGB). The electorate seemed to agree with Stanley Baldwin, the Conservative leader, that 'we do not want masses. We want Englishmen.'[2] Only in the universities and among the intelligentsia were there mass conversions to the extremes of

Right and Left. When Greaves left Liverpool for London in 1937, he became friends with some of the leading lights of metropolitan Marxism. Greaves was particularly close to Thomas Alfred Jackson, an English historian of Ireland. The orthodox Communist position on Ireland was that the end of English imperialism was in the interests of both the British and Irish working classes. James Connolly, the Marxist martyr of the 1916 insurrection, had argued that only as a free, independent nation state could a country come to socialism.[3] Jackson had known Connolly; Greaves later claimed that he was a link in the apostolic succession of socialist republicanism.[4]

In 1941, Greaves joined what was then known as the 'Connolly Club' – the heir to the left-wing Irish emigrant groups of the 1920s and 1930s. The club aimed to work for the complete freedom of the Irish people, to show solidarity with oppressed nations throughout the world, and to propagate Connolly's teachings. The club's membership was divided about how to interpret its constitution and Connolly's legacy. Was the goal socialism first and foremost or should a united Irish republic come before such a transformation? This question went unanswered for more than a decade.[5]

As the Second World War gave way to the Cold War, Greaves became the editor of the Connolly Association's newspaper, the *Irish Democrat*, and the effective leader of the group. He also began work on his biographies of Connolly and Liam Mellows – which together formed a history of the Irish Revolution. Greaves had given up a well-paid job in private industry for what he thought was the public good.[6] The sacrifice was all the greater as it coincided with a decline in the fortunes of the Communist Party. The Red Army had liberated Eastern Europe and broken the Nazi war machine. The Soviet model seemed to have triumphed; Stalin's crimes appeared to have been justified. But the Red Army had become an army of occupation and imposing the Soviet model on Eastern Europe had required coups, purges, anti-Semitism, show trials, and terror. Some of the British faithful began to doubt the Kremlin's infallibility. One of the characters in Doris Lessing's novel *The Golden Notebook* recalls 'spending a lot of time fighting inside the Party [during the early 1950s] – a naive lot we were, trying to persuade people it was much better to admit that things stank in Russia than to deny it'.[7]

Stalin's successors arrived at a similar conclusion: to save the system it was necessary to sacrifice the reputation of the man who had built it. At the 20th Party Congress in February 1956, First Secretary Nikita Khrushchev detailed the mistakes that had been made and placed the blame for them upon Stalin's monstrous personality. The Soviet leadership wanted to control the process of de-Stalinisation, but Khrushchev's 'secret speech' could not be kept secret. When the news reached Britain, Communist intellectuals E.P. Thompson and John Saville led a campaign for open debate within the party. The pair belonged to the Communist Party Historians' Group and enjoyed a degree of intellectual freedom. Thompson and Saville now wanted the party to concede a degree of political freedom. Greaves had some sympathy for the editors of *The Reasoner*. He wrote in his diary on 19 October 1956 that

> E.P. Thompson ... is the brother of Frank Thompson who died in Yugoslavia, became a hero, and then after the Cominform was started was denounced as a villain and is now I suppose rehabilitated again. It is probably this which renders him so obdurate about his *Reasoner* though how any political party could encourage the production of an unofficial paper dealing with its affairs is difficult to see. Still, it shows the way past errors return to plague us. If only we knew how to avoid them.[8]

Moscow was in the middle of making one of its more serious 'errors' as Greaves was writing these words. In Eastern Europe, Khrushchev's speech was misinterpreted as the most important sign yet that Moscow was relaxing its control over the satellite states. Hungary had been staggering in the direction of reform since Stalin's death. From October 1956 onwards, however, the country was in revolt against its Soviet masters. The Hungarian government was able to guarantee the support of the workers' councils by withdrawing from the Warsaw Pact; it was a decision that also guaranteed that the Red Army would invade. As Hungarian students battled Soviet tanks on the streets of Budapest, the prospect of renewing Communism from within the party disappeared for many British members. Thompson and Saville were among those who resigned; Greaves was not.[9] His principal interests lay in the West not the East and the party remained an implacable opponent of British imperialism in Ireland.

In *The Golden Notebook*, Paul 'got drunk ... and said he was sick and disgusted with the Party, but he joined it in 1935, and if he left it, he'd be leaving his whole life'.[10] Greaves, too, had dedicated his life to the cause. He believed that becoming a revolutionary required two decisions: the first was made in the innocence of youth, the second after bitter experience. Nevertheless, Anthony Coughlan, a member of the Connolly Association between 1958 and 1961, later claimed that his friend of thirty years should not be dismissed as a 'Stalinist'. 'One could scarcely meet a less dogmatic person,' he remembered, 'or a mind more open to alternative explanations of events'.[11] Roy Johnston, another friend of Greaves, similarly recalled that the leader of the Connolly Association had come to the conclusion that 'the simplistic "class struggle" formulations of the CP in Britain were quite remote from the Irish reality'.[12]

Greaves, however, was able to hold on to both his doubts about certain aspects of Communism and to his party membership. When the Kremlin sent out an encyclical on some aspects of Communist doctrine, CPGB inquisitors dutifully enforced the new orthodoxy. In 1948, Mendelian genetics was denounced as 'reactionary' and those scientists who subscribed to this theory were condemned as 'enemies of the Soviet people'. The CPGB required its members to endorse the bogus belief that acquired characteristics could be inherited by the next generation. Professor J.B.S. Haldane, a leading geneticist and eccentric who had thoroughly enjoyed the First World War, struggled to reconcile his science with his politics. Haldane's intelligence eventually won out over his intransigence and he resigned from the party in 1950.[13] Unlike 'Old Haldane', Greaves – a former research chemist – chose Stalin instead of science.[14] As the Politburo had neglected to endorse a particular line on how Irish emigrants in Britain should work to build a thirty-two-county socialist republic, Greaves faced no such dilemma. He was therefore able to pursue his own agenda without breaking with the party. Indeed, Greaves was able to lay down the party line on Ireland. He recalled in 1966:

> It took several years in the 1950s to work out the right policy for the Connolly Association. The ultra-lefts wanted it to purvey socialism in green paint, to be a transmission belt for the Irish emigrants into British left-wing organisations. I fought for it to be an independent organisation of the Irish and their friends in Britain. It would champion the interests of Irish people there while at the same time seek to influence British Government policy on Ireland. Preaching socialism was none of its business.[15]

Greaves believed that conservative Ireland needed to be brought slowly to socialism and that nationalism was the surest road to success. In 1955, the Connolly Association's annual conference ratified a new constitution that endorsed the Greaves line. Two years later, the socialists in green warpaint counterattacked and the decisive battle began. As many people on both sides were also members of the CPGB, the struggle was also fought out within the party. When the matter came before the CPGB's Irish Committee, Greaves lost his temper and threatened to split the party. The Communist leadership was scared into helping to enforce a compromise solution. The rebels could remain within the Connolly Association if they were prepared to accept the 1955 constitution. Given that the rebels had no intention of doing any such thing, this was really a victory for Greaves.[16]

The Connolly Association promoted a 'three-pronged attack against British imperialism, in the twenty-six counties, in Six Counties, and in Britain'. The association, however, restricted its activities to the British sphere. Although the other spheres would be left to other groups, each campaign would not only bolster the others but would also be interdependent.[17] Following Connolly, the group maintained that the Unionists were kept in power by Northern Ireland's sectarian political system. Religious and ethnic divisions were used by the regime to divide the working class and to strangle socialism. The association consequently believed that if full civil rights could be secured, Catholic and Protestant 'would learn to respect each other'. The coming together of the Protestant and Catholic working classes would almost inevitably lead to the election of 'an anti-Unionist Government'.[18] Civil rights were a stepping stone to a united Ireland.

Britain, where power ultimately rested, would attempt 'to enforce imperialism' in Ireland.[19] 'The keystone of the Connolly Association plan', stated the *Irish Democrat*, 'is therefore to enlist the services of British democracy in the struggle for Irish freedom.' Among the British working class and 'those whose thoughts and interests run the same way', an 'anti-imperialist upsurge' was detected.[20] The association consequently set out to show that oppression and discrimination were not just African and Asian problems. The hope was that the British Labour movement could be convinced of the need for civil rights reform in Northern Ireland. The Unionist government would then be forced to concede previously denied civil liberties and hasten its own demise.[21] When a progressive coalition was voted into power at Stormont, the support of the British Labour movement would be the deciding factor in this fledgling government's struggle against British imperialism.[22]

The Connolly Association's strategy also assumed that the progressive coalition in Belfast could look for help from an anti-imperialist government in Dublin. The group argued that Fianna Fáil's attempt to replace economic nationalism with freer trade could be defeated. Progressive forces could take power in the South, too, and cast off the restraints imposed by British finance capitalists. London banks would then no longer control the land and lives of the Irish people. The common interest of North and South would eventually bring about unification.[23]

A united, independent, democratic, Irish republic – this was what every member of the Connolly Association wanted. Connolly himself wanted this too, and also something more. As the *Irish Democrat* acknowledged,

> Connolly distinguished two stages of Irish freedom. The first was national democracy in which private enterprise would be permitted provided it did not endanger the interests of the nation as a whole. Coming after it he envisaged a second stage of freedom in which private interests would be merged and subordinated in the best development of the whole. He was quite clear in his mind that before the Irish people can have socialism, and he passionately wanted them to have socialism, they must have a country to have it in.[24]

Like Marx, Greaves had a strict rule against utopian speculation. The Connolly Association had no blueprint set down for how Ireland should develop after unification was achieved. Like Marx, Greaves bent his strict rule and hinted at what dreams may come. This was the case even in an article that rubbished the 'old slander about [the Connolly Association] having ulterior motives going beyond the freedom of Ireland'. The Connolly Association had a 'Plan to End Partition', but Greaves believed that the 'fight against imperialism will not end when partition is abolished'. 'For what must take place then is what the great patriot James Connolly called "the reconquest of Ireland by the Irish people".'[25]

Greaves never prescribed Connolly's second stage; he simply assumed it would happen after unification. At the *Irish Democrat*'s '21st Birthday Party', he spoke of how a united Irish Republic would contain a completely different balance of forces. It would be nothing like, and could be nothing like, the present partition arrangement where one reaction bolsters up another. It would free the rails for progress. It would be the decisive step, and whether you liked it or not, the Irish people would themselves demand the reconstruction of the country and that Ireland should enter the path of social progress with the willing consent of the majority of her citizens. That is the revolution that is needed in Ireland, the concrete defeat of the most reactionary class, not some abstraction passing under the name of 'socialism' for lack of a better label. This is the meaning of James Connolly.[26]

Socialism was not just an unhelpful label: for the Connolly Association it was a harmful one. In the era of the Cold War, it would have fuelled the false accusation that the association was Communist. Greaves preferred instead to write about an Ireland that had 'a native government to plan and direct the whole economic life of the country, to control investments, prevent money flowing abroad, and check all attempts from outside to undertake the old imperialist robbery under new and concealed forms'.[27] 'Although such a programme does not spell socialism,' the *Irish Democrat* claimed in February 1960, 'its direction is as unmistakeable as [Fidel] Castro's Cuba.'[28]

A CHALLENGE TO DEMOCRATIC BRITAIN

In June 1961, Shadow Home Secretary Patrick Gordon Walker received a delegation headed by Greaves. This was two-and-a-half years before the CSJ even wrote to the Labour leadership. Gordon Walker, reported the *Irish Democrat*, 'promised to facilitate a debate in the House on the questions of Unemployment and Civil Liberties'. At the request of the Shadow Minister and with the help of its solicitors, the Connolly Association prepared a memorandum on the Government of Ireland Act. Having established that Article 75 protected Westminster's 'supreme authority', the submission claimed that 'Parliament therefore has the power to intervene; what has up to now been lacking is the will'. The paper concluded with a call for 'a rigid insistence on similar standards of democracy in Northern Ireland as the British people rightly demand for themselves'.[29] Twelve years after the Labour government had passed the Ireland Act, the party's spokesman on matters relating to Northern Ireland promised to have Parliament debate the question of civil rights under Stormont. This was a significant turnaround in attitudes and it owed a great deal to the work of the Connolly Association.

The Irish Republican Army's (IRA) decision to launch 'Operation Harvest' in 1956 had created problems for the Connolly Association, but it had also given them an opportunity. By renewing the armed struggle, the IRA forced Stormont to reveal its authoritarian character. In August 1957, a sergeant in the RUC was lured to an empty house in Dungannon, where he was murdered by a booby-trap bomb. The following summer, two young Republicans from the local area, Kevin Mallon and Francis Talbot, were put on trial for the crime. There were charged with murder on the basis that they had confessed to making the telephone call that had brought the policeman to the house. As the trial progressed, it became increasingly obvious that these statements had been extracted by force. The Connolly Association had sent an experienced lawyer to observe the proceedings.[30] His reports encouraged the Labour-leaning press – the *Guardian* and the *New Statesman* – to take an interest in the case. The Connolly Association also organised a petition that was signed by left-wing luminaries like Doris Lessing, Victor Gollancz, and Freda Laski.[31]

The all-Protestant jury found Mallon and Talbot innocent, but the damage had been done to Stormont's reputation.[32] At the beginning of 1959, the Connolly Association held a conference on civil liberties in Northern Ireland and the British government's responsibility. A number of constituency Labour parties and trade union branches sent delegates.[33] The momentum was building. The Connolly Association highlighted how some of the Republicans interned without trial were trade unionists and that Labour MPs could not discuss their plight in the House of Commons. The campaign to free the prisoners appealed to the British Labour movement's sense of fair play. In July 1960, the *Irish Democrat* directed its readers to

> Look at the amazing Trade Union movement against the Belfast internments, decided upon at conferences called by the Connolly Association, carried through by members of the Association in their own branches, till conviction of their fellow trade unionists was won, and action ensued. Look at the series of Parliamentary lobbies,

communications with Westminster, supply of information all over the world.[34]

By the spring of 1961, the newspaper could proudly proclaim that 'The Belfast Government Has At Last Climbed Down. There Are Now No Internees Left.'[35]

The Connolly Association continued and expanded its lobbying of the Labour Party. During the first half of 1962, twenty-four MPs put their names to a petition that demanded 'a public enquiry be held into the working of the Government of Ireland Act, in view of the widespread allegations of the denial of human rights'. Among the signatories was Fenner Brockway, the so-called 'member for the colonies', who was to become an important ally.[36] Brockway's Movement for Colonial Freedom voted to accept a resolution proposed on behalf of the Connolly Association calling for the 'complete overhaul of the system of administration of justice in the Six Counties'.[37] The Connolly Association's Manchester branch also established links with local Labour MPs – including Paul Rose and Stan Orme.[38] Branch members were active in the city's Labour Party and managed to include six resolutions about Ireland on the agenda of the 1965 national conference. Connolly Association General Secretary Sean Redmond attended the conference as well, making 'available to delegates … expert information on Irish affairs'.[39]

The Connolly Association's activities were not just limited to the Labour movement. Each year, the body organised a march through London to Trafalgar Square, where a political rally was then held. Sympathetic Labour parliamentarians as well as Northern Irish politicians joined leading association members on the platform.[40] During 1961 and 1962, some youthful Connolly Association supporters undertook marches from London to Birmingham and Liverpool respectively.[41] 'Strictly speaking,' Coughlan recalled, 'these were the first Irish civil rights marches.'[42]

At the beginning of 1962, the association sent a three-man delegation to Northern Ireland to investigate allegations of discrimination. In Derry, they found that gerrymandering, the householder franchise, and the company vote ensured that a city with a two-to-one Catholic majority had a Unionist-controlled council.[43] This was several years before the CSJ conducted a similar investigation into the abuses perpetrated by Londonderry Corporation.

The *Irish Democrat* team's analysis of electoral manipulation was based upon information provided by, among others, Councillor James Doherty. Nationalists acted as guides during the team's tour of Northern Ireland.[44] Given Nationalism's links with Catholicism and the Connolly Association's alleged connections with Communism, such co-operation seems surprising. In a February 1960 letter to Cahir Healy, Greaves recollected that the pair had 'crossed swords in the now somewhat distant past'. Nevertheless, he continued, the Connolly Association 'distinguish clearly between friends who want the same object as we do, who disagree with us on certain aspects of tactics, and enemies whose purpose is the reverse of others. We have never regarded you as an enemy.'[45] This rapprochement reflected the more constructive thinking within Nationalist circles and the relative decline in anti-Communist feeling. When a Nationalist delegation came to Westminster in January 1964, the Connolly Association returned the hospitality that it had been shown by putting the Nationalists in contact with Brockway.[46]

The Connolly Association also forged links with other opposition groups from Northern Ireland. In May 1965, Greaves was at a meeting arranged by the Belfast Trades Council that aimed to unite 'Catholic and Protestant workers ... in a campaign for democratic rights for everybody'. The gathering's organiser, Betty Sinclair, later attended the Manchester branch's 1965 conference.[47] As a senior member of the Communist Party of Northern Ireland (CPNI), Sinclair was on familiar terms with Greaves. She too had become a Communist during the 1930s – and had gone on to study at the International Lenin School in Moscow. This institution had been created to 'Bolshevise' the international movement and many of its graduates went on to lead their parties. Sinclair's status as the Secretary of the Belfast Trades Council and her commitment to civil rights led to her being commissioned to write a series of articles for the *Irish Democrat*.[48] A special edition of the newspaper was devoted to Fitt's maiden speech in the House of Commons. His denunciation of the Stormont regime was published in its entirety.[49] The *Irish Democrat* reprinted the CSJ's first pamphlet in full and produced a summary of *Legal Aid to Oppose Discrimination – Not Likely!*[50] The group invited both Fitt and Patricia McCluskey onto the platform at the annual Trafalgar Square rallies.[51]

The Connolly Association was at the centre of the network of connections between the Northern Irish opposition groups and the British Labour movement. So it is not surprising that the group was deeply involved in the development of the Campaign for Democracy in Ulster (CDU). Indeed, the *Irish Democrat* proclaimed that 'the Connolly Association's long arduous campaign to interest British Labour in the Irish Question bore important fruit on June 2nd [1965] when the "Campaign for Democracy in Ulster" was formally launched'. The founding Secretary of the CDU had previously been the Treasurer of the Connolly Association's South London branch. Brockway, who had been elevated to the peerage after losing his seat in 1964, was awarded a senior position in the new organisation. Orme, one of the first MPs to commit to the ginger group, immediately recommended that 'the Connolly Association and the "Campaign for Democracy in Ulster" should work together'.[52]

Rose, Orme's fellow Mancunian MP, had attracted the attention of Paddy Byrne and his colleagues by speaking out against discrimination.[53] According to his memoirs, Rose traced his concern for Northern Irish matters back to 'a talk on civil liberties to an Irish group in Manchester, in 1962'.[54] This group was the Connolly Association. During 1962, it held meetings in Britain's big cities about the denial of human rights under the Stormont regime.[55] Whatever the exact role played by the Connolly Association in inspiring Rose's initial interest, subsequent contact undoubtedly encouraged it to deepen. In his seminal speech at Westminster, Rose commented upon having received 'evidence' 'week by week' that 'points to a manifestation of discrimination in jobs and housing' as well as having dedicated an evening of his election campaign to the issue. Shortly after this parliamentary intervention, the Manchester branch had its annual general meeting. The committee described the 'commitment' of Rose and the city's other Labour MPs to 'Irish National demands' as a 'notable feature' of its 'work'.[56]

The pages of the *Irish Democrat* contained extensive coverage of the CDU's activities both inside and outside Westminster.[57] In February 1967, Byrne attended a forum arranged by the *Irish Democrat* on 'The Irish Question – a challenge to Democratic Britain'.[58] In turn, the Connolly Association sent two delegates and an observer to the January 1968 CDU conference.[59] Byrne contributed an article entitled 'CDU and the Tasks Ahead' to the March 1968 issue of the *Irish Democrat*.[60] Greaves received a letter from the CDU Secretary thanking him 'for giving it such a good show'. He was also asked if he would 'very kindly agree' to attend the April meeting of the 'London Area Committee of the CDU' as the 'Guest Speaker'.[61] Greaves accepted the offer and delivered a paper on 'the origin, content, and significance of the Government of Ireland Act'.[62]

While the CSJ exerted a greater influence upon the CDU than the Connolly Association, the reverse applied to the National Council for Civil Liberties (NCCL). Redmond even succeeded in getting himself elected onto the NCCL's executive committee in 1966. He boasted that it 'took the Connolly Association' to convince the NCCL that Westminster was ultimately responsible for Northern Ireland.[63] This was an exaggeration: the NCCL had sponsored a commission of inquiry into the Special Powers Act during the 1930s and in 1948 described the human rights situation there as 'very grave'.[64] The Connolly Association reawakened this interest in Northern Ireland. At the 1959 NCCL conference, Coughlan tabled a resolution calling upon 'the British Government to institute an impartial enquiry into the conduct of the Royal Ulster Constabulary [RUC]'. The executive council initially expressed doubts about the association's arguments. However, after seeking legal advice, the objections were withdrawn and the resolution was passed unanimously.[65] The Connolly Association then worked to secure a provisional commitment from the NCCL that it would launch an investigation into civil rights abuses in Northern Ireland.[66] During September 1962, the NCCL sent its General Secretary across the Irish Sea to hold consultations with interested parties. McAteer advised against holding an inquiry while the Orange and Green talks seemed to be progressing. He told the *Derry Journal* that at this delicate moment 'such an investigation, for which I myself have often pleaded, would be inadvisable'.[67] The short-lived Northern Ireland Council for Civil Liberties – a group that mainly campaigned for the release of interned Republicans – was more enthusiastic about the proposal.[68] Nevertheless, the executive council opted to abandon plans for an inquiry.[69] Rumours began to circulate among Ireland's radical Left that this was at the request of the Labour leadership.[70]

The Connolly Association continued to press the NCCL to act and in March 1965 a conference on Northern Ireland was called.[71] Delegates were sent to London from the Unionist Party, the Liberal Party of Northern Ireland, the NILP, the Belfast Trades Council, the CSJ, and the Republican movement. The association had observers at the conference and the *Irish Democrat*'s coverage filled most of the April 1965 issue.[72] Although this forum was the high-water mark of the NCCL's concern, the

Connolly Association still made use of the links between the two groups to promote its cause. At the 1967 Labour Party conference, Redmond organised a NCCL fringe meeting on Northern Ireland.[73]

By this stage, the failure of the Wilson government to intervene had led to disillusionment within the emigrant community. The Connolly Association, though, had learned to be patient after years of political activism without serious reward.[74] This long-term perspective enabled the association to appreciate the limited gains that had been made since the mid-1950s. The *Irish Democrat* claimed that there were signs by 1964 that the three-pronged strategy was working: the Southern economy was growing; rising unemployment in the North was weakening working-class support for Unionism; militant Republicanism had given way to a more constructive constitutionalism; and the British Labour movement was becoming concerned about discrimination.[75] When Greaves met Gordon Walker in June 1961, the Shadow Home Secretary 'agreed to try and find a young MP who would take Geoffrey Bing's place'.[76] Within the space of a few years, however, the Labour benches in the House of Commons again seated numerous friends of Ireland.[77]

In addition to this relative success, the Connolly Association was sustained by a conviction that history was on its side. This led the association to underestimate the strength of sectarian feeling. In a November 1962 editorial on discontent within the Protestant working class, the *Irish Democrat* claimed 'we are now witnessing the preliminary stages of the inevitable return of the North to the proud position it occupied in 1798, when the mists leave the eyes of the people, and they see Unionism, the miserable tool of British imperialism, as the charlatanry and humbug that it is'.[78] Even when O'Neillism was winning back its lost Protestant proletarian support, the Connolly Association remained convinced that a 'rapprochement of workers of the two religions is inevitable and only a matter of time'.[79]

One of the few Northern Protestants who did hark back to the United Irishmen Rising of 1798 was John Hewitt. During the late 1930s, he had been the *Irish Democrat*'s newspaper's literary editor. Almost three decades later, 'when, on the fringes of an open-air meeting in an English city, a young man with a thick brogue invites me to buy a copy, I always experience a momentary thrill of emotion for those far away days of the Left Book Club, The Popular Front, Aid for Spain ... and take my copy'. But this 'momentary thrill' then gave way to 'rage at the betrayal of our dream': 'It seems to me now an altogether deplorable production, its pages well padded with the words of sentimental Irish songs ... Wildly wrong in its interpretation of Irish affairs, foolishly supporting the reactionary IRA, lacking in frankness, blatantly opportunist, it has nothing to do with what we intended.'[80] Bringing together Protestants and Catholics was not inevitable and was not only a matter of time.

THE FIRST NEW LEFT

The cafés of St Germain where Parisian intellectuals mused on history were a world away from the pubs of Camden Town where members of the Connolly Association sold the *Irish Democrat*. But some – by no means all – of the regulars in these two places had something in common: the grand illusion of Communism. The French Revolution had bequeathed *la grande nation* an apocalyptic political culture. Utopias were founded upon bloodshed and terror.[81] Communism, to quote Marx's famous phrase, was 'the solution to the riddle of history'; realising this vision not only excused violence, it required it.[82] However, some of France's greatest thinkers were beginning to question the revolutionary catechism. Albert Camus, the Algerian outsider who fought for France during the war and thought for her after the Liberation, was the most influential dissenter. Like Jean Tarrou in *The Plague*, he felt that 'on this earth there are pestilences and there are victims – and as far as possible one must refuse to be on the side of the pestilence'.[83] Camus hoped, though, that there was a way he could remain loyal to his Left Bank friends and to himself. There was not. In 1951, Camus published *The Rebel*: a condemnation of Communism and revolutionary violence.[84] The essay marked his final break with Jean-Paul Sartre.

The dominant existentialist thinkers – although Camus was uncomfortable with this characterisation – had taken the philosophy in very different directions. Sartre believed that there was no God and that humanity was condemned to freedom from all authority. Life was without meaning; each individual had to give meaning to meaninglessness him or herself. In the shadow of war, Sartre argued that this action and commitment needed to be political and revolutionary. He therefore moved increasingly closer to the Communists – while refraining from joining the party. Sartre's evolution into a fellow-traveller drew criticism not only from Camus, but also from Raymond Aron and Claude Lefort. For Aron, his former friend had failed to recognise that the Communist states were crimes against humanity and that the Communist ideology was an escape from the political realities of the post-war world.[85] Lefort attacked Sartre from the Left. Along with another ex-Trotskyist, Cornelius Castoriadis, Lefort produced the journal *Socialisme ou barbarie*. They maintained that a socialist society would be run by the proletariat through a system of self-management termed *autogestion*. This vision of future freedom was contrasted with the Soviet Union's perverted present. According to Castoriadis and Lefort's critique, Stalin had erected a state in which the bourgeoisie's role as the exploiters of the working class had been taken over by the bureaucracy.[86]

Socialisme ou barbarie's interpretation of Soviet Communism gained influence only after 1956. The Red Army's tanks crushed the Hungarian revolt and many of the political illusions held by Western intellectuals. Lefort embarked upon a tour of the Eastern European upheavals accompanied by Edgar Morin. As an act of romantic rebellion during the Second World War, Morin had joined the Communist Party. He was always more interested in cultural change in the Western world than in Soviet politics and the French economy. In 1951, the party finally cast out the heretic. When Morin returned to France from Eastern Europe, he came together with recent refugees from Communism to found the journal *Arguments*. Their plan was to create a forum for open Marxist debate along the lines of the Italian journal *Argomenti* or Thompson and Saville's *New Reasoner*. Although the editors of *Arguments* had rejected both the party and Stalinism, their work still referenced the Communist canon. But greater attention was paid to Western Marxists like Georg Lukács and Karl Korsch than to the Eastern Marxist ideologues of Soviet Communism.[87]

The claim that the Western Marxist tradition was the true faith was supported by the resurrection of the young Marx. The Marxist-Leninist orthodoxy that the Kremlin had imposed was based upon Marx's later writings. The mature Marx was an economist and social scientist: a positivist who had developed a supposedly scientific theory of economics and society. Just as Sir Isaac Newton had discovered the laws that governed the natural world, the mature Marx had discovered the laws that governed human history. He predicted that capitalism would collapse to be replaced by communism. Lenin's party was the agent of history and as such was justified in taking any action – however ruthless

– that brought communism closer. The young Marx was a philosopher; a former follower of Hegelian idealism who was using a transformation of the master's philosophy to criticise politics and society. While living in Paris under the July Monarchy, the young Marx had written notes on political economy and Hegelianism that were to remain unpublished during his lifetime. These *Paris Manuscripts* only became available in the French capital on the eve of the Second World War; it was not until after the Liberation that this early work began to attract attention. The young Marx and post-war French intellectuals were concerned with a similar problem: alienation.[88]

The young Marx adopted and adapted the Hegelian concept of alienation. Georg Hegel believed that humans were driven by the need to take control of their lives, to stop being the playthings of external forces. The outside physical world had to be transformed into an expression of the internal mental world. Instead of freedom from, Hegel was advocating freedom through. Alienation was a stage in this process: when humans had developed the power to change their environment in some way but were not yet in complete command of this power. Something that originated with humanity and should therefore be regarded as part of it had instead become a separate, hostile power that was exercising control over it. For the young Marx, philosophy after Hegel was about uncovering deeper and deeper levels of alienation: from religion through politics to labour.[89]

Alienation in the sphere of labour – the act of self-creation – was presented as the most fundamental form from which all the others followed. Private ownership of the means of production alienated humans from themselves: the worker was unable to see the product or the process of his labours as an expression of himself. It also alienated humans from each other, forcing workers to compete with each other for scarce jobs and capitalists to compete with each other for scarce profits.[90] In *The Holy Family*, which was written a year after the *Paris Manuscripts*, the young Marx presented private property and the proletariat as two sides of a Hegelian contradiction. The maintenance of private property required a supply of labourers to work in the factories. In turn, the proletariat would eventually be driven to dissolve itself on account of its miserable existence. Such a change would demand that the proletariat rise up in a revolution that would abolish private property: 'The proletariat executes the sentence that private property pronounced on itself by begetting the proletariat, just as it carries out the sentence that wage-labour pronounced on itself by bringing forth wealth for others and misery for itself'. Private property and the proletariat would disappear in a new synthesis that would resolve the contradiction.[91]

In his later writings, the mature Marx attacked capitalism as a system of exploitation in which surplus value was extracted from the labour of the workers. But the concept of alienation was not repudiated. This made it possible to argue that there was continuity in Marx's thought. The young Marx had laid down the basic principles of Marxism; the mature Marx had worked out the economics that underpinned the philosophy. This was a stone cast at the clay feet of the Communist colossus. Marxism was transformed from a science that was to be applied unquestioningly into a collection of ideas that could be adopted and adapted. The Kremlin had lost its monopoly on truth: the sacred texts of Marxism were open to interpretation by anyone.

The *Paris Manuscripts* were brought over to Oxford from France in 1958. A circle of dissident Communists and independent socialists had formed at the university around G.D.H. Cole – professor of political theory, leading member of the Fabian Society and author of such detective novels as *Poison in the Garden Suburbs*. Members of this Oxford group had travelled to Paris for a conference called to debate setting up an 'International Socialist Society'. While in the French capital, the Oxford delegation met the independent Marxist Claude Bourdet. Morin's decision to publish an article in Bourdet's newspaper, *L'Observateur*, was what finally forced the Communist Party to expel him.[92] Bourdet was seeking to define a *nouvelle gauche* – a term that the Oxford contingent adopted for its own political project.[93] Its *Universities and Left Review* – the first issue of which featured contributions from both Cole and Bourdet – came together with Thompson and Saville's *New Reasoner* to form the British New Left.[94]

Among the students who were encouraged by Cole to think critically about left-wing politics and theories was Roy Johnston. Cole and Joe Johnston, Roy's father, had moved in the same radical Liberal circles at Oxford University in the years before the First World War. When Cole visited his old friend in Ireland during the 1940s, he impressed the young Roy Johnston with his insider's knowledge of the post-war Labour government.[95] At school and then at Trinity College Dublin, Johnston belonged to a 'Marxist think-tank' called the Promethean Society. Looking back on this period, Johnston judged that the Promethean view 'was similar to that of the young Marx' and 'a long way from the centralising Stalinist pathology'. Nevertheless, the society had links with Greaves and other British Communists. The Trinity students went to summer schools in Britain and encountered Eric Hobsbawm, a colleague of Thompson and Saville in the Communist Party Historians' Group. Johnston was uncomfortable with the emphasis that the Communists placed upon the Soviet Union. He searched out contacts among Dublin's Fabians and among former Republican internees who wanted to move to the Left. Johnston was instrumental in bringing together Communists, Republicans and the student Left in the Irish Workers' League (IWL). The new group's 1949 manifesto concluded that post-war Europe was falling to the Left and called for the development of a strong Irish Labour movement in the tradition of Connolly.[96]

Johnston agreed with Connolly that the 'struggle for Irish freedom has two aspects: it is national and it is social'.[97] For Johnston, the great weakness of Stalinism was that it sought to impose itself upon countries whose political, social and economic histories were very different from Russia's. By contrast, Connolly stood for a specifically Irish Marxism. He also stood for the Marxism of the Second International, which had collapsed under the strain of the First World War and the Russian Revolution. As the post-war period progressed, growing numbers of left-wing intellectuals in Europe reached back beyond 1917 to reconnect with a Marxist tradition that had not been corrupted by the theory and practice of the Soviet state. Lost Marxist leaders such as Rosa Luxemburg had their reputations restored. A Polish Jew who had belonged to the radical wing of Germany's Social Democratic Party, Luxemburg had been thrown out of the Marxist pantheon by the Kremlin for criticising Lenin. Her claim that the October Revolution was a betrayal of orthodox Marxism now became a reason to admire her, not to admonish her. Connolly was not so much a forgotten leader as a misunderstood one. To reverse the condemned Connolly's complaint: Irish nationalists did not understand why he took part in the Easter Rising – they had forgotten that he was a socialist.

Johnston's hopes that the IWL would take its inspiration from Kilmainham Gaol rather than from the Kremlin were crushed by the Cold War. The first issues of the IWL's *Education Bulletin* were devoted to understanding and defending the Soviet Union. There was a review of Lenin's *What Is to Be Done?*, a summary of 'Stalin on the National Question,' and a 'Salute to Stalin'. As the IWL evolved into what was effectively the Communist Party of Southern Ireland, Johnston's involvement declined and he began to search for a more appropriate vehicle for his politics – a quest that would take more than a decade.[98] During the early 1960s, Johnston was working as a research scientist for Guinness in London. Although he attended meetings of the local branch of the CPGB, this was merely to confirm that orthodoxy was exhausted of ideas. Johnston instead dedicated most of the time that he could spare for politics to the Connolly Association.[99] Greaves was critical of Communism and had developed a practical political strategy for freeing Ireland from British imperialism. This was close to what Johnston had been initially trying to achieve with the IWL. By this stage, however, his thinking had gone beyond where Greaves was willing to venture. While Johnston was preparing to return to Dublin in the autumn of 1963 to take up a post with Aer Lingus, Greaves was despairing for his friend's future. He wrote in his diary that Johnston 'wants to talk to everybody about his "role" there. But he is incapable of pursuing single-mindedly a political course of action, let alone originating one. So I made no suggestions. And in any conflict between his duty and his interests or convenience, his interests or convenience are bound to win. Still he is not the worst.'[100]

In September 1963, Johnston drove to Fishguard in his Morris Minor car to take the Rosslare boat back to Ireland. Once on board, he retired to the saloon to gather his thoughts together. He wrote what he was later to describe as 'some notes on how I saw the movement for Irish national unity and liberation of the Irish working people might be developed'.[101] Johnston had read himself into Marxism as a schoolboy and he had continued to read everything he could. While he was at the École Polytechnique physics laboratory in the early 1950s, Johnston had been 'just about aware of Sartre'. Afterwards, however, he took a greater interest in the Paris intellectuals and 'became aware of most of the others'.[102] Sartre was a contributor to the *Monthly Review* – an independent socialist magazine published in America that was read throughout the Western world by left-wing intellectuals like Johnston. Cole and Thompson were also among the European contributors to its pages. As Johnston sat on the ferry sketching out his Irish revolution, it was the *Monthly Review*'s special issue on Cuba that informed his thinking. The editors had visited the island in 1960 and concluded that a socialist revolution was taking place.[103] Johnston had found a model to adopt and adapt: 'a broad-based movement of politicised working people, rural as well as urban, in the country as a whole, had subsumed, upstaged ... a narrow doctrinaire urban "workerist" party based on the orthodoxy of the Communist international movement'.[104]

Castro and his small band of guerrillas had landed in Cuba just a few weeks after the Red Army had invaded Hungary.[105] At the moment that Western intellectuals were having their illusions about Soviet Union dispelled, they were provided with the chance to develop new ones about the Third World. The survivors from the Soviet shipwreck could swim south as well as back into Europe's past. The national liberation struggles offered not only new forms of Marxist theory and practice, but also romance. Young freedom fighters battling against the status quo exuded more revolutionary glamour than the elderly *apparatchiks* who ruled Eastern Europe. In *The Golden Notebook*, an American writer who has come to Britain to escape the Communist witch-hunts half-jokingly regrets not having 'gone to Cuba ... and joined Castro, and been killed'.[106]

Johnston did not feel the need to go to Cuba; he believed that the Third World could be brought to Ireland. In a draft paper that he wrote shortly after his return, Johnston argued that 'There are two camps today in the world: the rich nations and the poor nations. By tradition and inclination Ireland is the senior member of the latter.' Fianna Fáil was carrying the country closer to Continental Europe. Johnston instead wanted the Irish people to 'throw in our lot with Africa and jointly to achieve independence from imperialism'.[107] They needed, he thought, to take inspiration from Frantz Fanon – a French-trained psychiatrist from Martinique who became the theorist of the Algerian national liberation struggle. In *The Wretched of the Earth*, Fanon claimed that Europe was heading towards the abyss and that the Third World was starting a new history of humanity. This revolution would come from the countryside, where imperialism was at its most oppressive and least rewarding.[108] Greaves dismissed these ideas as 'nonsense'.[109] He clung to the orthodox line that change would come only through the 'working-class movement': the Labour parties, the trade unions, and the Communists.[110] Johnston, however, wanted to launch a national liberation movement. He arrived back in Ireland to find that he was not alone.

REVOLUTIONARY POTENTIAL

On 25 July 1953, Cathal Goulding and Séan Mac Stíofáin raided the armoury of a public school in Essex. The IRA volunteers captured an impressive haul of rifles, machine guns, and mortars, but were arrested soon afterwards by the police. The two men came from different backgrounds and would follow different paths from the prison gates. Mac Stíofáin was born John Stephenson to an English father and a mother of Protestant-Irish descent. He was nevertheless baptised and raised a Catholic. After National Service, Mac Stíofáin became involved with Irish emigrant groups and ultimately joined the IRA.[111] Goulding, by contrast, was born into the Republican movement: his grandfather was a Fenian and his father had taken part in the Easter Rising. By the time he reached his early twenties, the working-class Dubliner had already been interned and imprisoned in the South for his IRA activities. Goulding's five years in an English gaol coincided with the disastrous start to Operation Harvest.[112] The strategy of driving the security forces out of parts of Northern Ireland and then establishing 'liberated zones' in those areas was fundamentally flawed. The Northern security apparatus possessed an overwhelming superiority over the IRA units and the campaign lacked the support of the Catholic community.[113] On 26 February 1962, the IRA Army Council reluctantly conceded defeat. The Fianna Fáil government concluded that the internees should be released as they posed no threat: the prisoners were men of limited ability and their movement had no public backing.[114] Goulding, who had not been marked by the failure of Operation Harvest, was given the task of resurrecting Republicanism.

The new IRA Chief of Staff's diagnosis was that the movement was suffering from a pathological obsession with armed struggle. Republicans were shooting without thinking; they needed to think without shooting. At a time when Fianna Fáil and the Irish Labour Party were abandoning principles for pragmatism, Goulding saw an opening on the radical Left of Southern politics. The movement therefore needed to reacquaint itself with the socialist republican tradition. In the mid-1930s, a substantial minority of IRA volunteers had argued that physical force alone would not deliver the republic. This group accepted Connolly's assumption that the working people were in their hearts social radicals as well as Irish patriots. Republicanism thus had to be a movement that would escape Ireland's sectarian and conservative past; a movement that would unite the Protestant and Catholic working classes. The resulting Republican Congress, however, swiftly succumbed to splits.[115] Under Goulding, two of its leaders – Peadar O'Donnell and George Gilmore – were again to have an intellectual influence on Republican politics. But the IRA also recognised that it had to look beyond the ranks of its own veterans for inspiration.[116]

1963 was the 200th anniversary of the birth of Theobald Wolfe Tone – the founding father of Irish Republicanism. Goulding hoped 'to use the Tone Bicentenary as a launching point from which the doctrine of Republicanism could be taught anew so that Tone's aim of a free, united Ireland, in which Catholic and Dissenter would work together in harmony and liberty, would be soon achieved'.[117] The organisations – the Wolfe Tone Directories – that were created to stage the commemorative events brought together IRA men and Republican sympathisers. When the anniversary year drew to a close, the directories were developed into a Republican think-tank. The Wolfe Tone Societies – as the directories were renamed in 1964 – made contact with individuals and groups that had socialist and nationalist backgrounds.[118] The Belfast Wolfe Tone Society worked with the CPNI, the Queen's University Labour Group, and National Unity.[119] In Dublin, Johnston and Coughlan, who had returned home to Ireland in 1961, became involved in Wolfe Tone activities: they had finally found the right vehicle for their politics.[120] Their different interests – Johnston's in economic organisation and Coughlan's in democracy – were to shape the transformation of the Republican movement.

The notes that Johnston had sketched out on the ferry from Fishguard were expanded into a strategy of 'economic resistance'. This new departure was discussed within Republicanism and eventually became the official line. In the April 1965 issue of the *Irish Democrat*, Johnston reported that 'the Republican Movement now recognised the fact that partition has divided the Irish question into a number of distinct areas'. As a 'significant step [between] the present situation and the goal', Republicanism was aiming to become the head of 'a 26 County "liberated area" government'. One of the main goals of this future administration would be the reunification of Ireland. The government would pass laws for the whole island, exploit every available means to enforce them in the North and appeal for aid from 'the anti-imperialist element in the United Nations'. Johnston stressed that this policy would be different from the 'economic war' that Fianna Fáil had waged against Britain during the 1930s. His government 'would put national interest before the interests of large property (whether native collaboratist or alien) and would look to the Labour Movement for support'. The Republicans were seeking to lead 'a national social-economic movement of resistance to the economic forces of imperialism'. Johnston claimed that Republicanism would be joined in this struggle by the rural co-operative movement and the trade unions. By forging together social radicalism and Irish nationalism, this resistance movement would possess a 'powerful revolutionary potential'. Johnston hoped that this second stage of the Irish Revolution would not only deliver reunification. He envisaged the capitalist economy giving way to 'municipal or co-operative social ownership' and the state to 'a federation of people's organisations'.[121]

At the same time that Johnston was writing this article, he was beginning to take his message directly to IRA volunteers. Unlike Coughlan, Johnston chose to join both the IRA and Sinn Féin. On 7 March 1965, Johnston, as Goulding's new Political Education Officer, met with members of the Dublin Brigade. He told them that the IRA needed to 'survey the battlefield': they had to go to the people, to make the people's economic and social struggles their own struggle.[122] When he spoke to the Cork Brigade, Johnston encouraged the volunteers to get involved in the campaign against the sale to developers of the local town of Midleton. Since 1960, this unit had been under the command of Mac Stíofáin, who felt the Political Education Officer's contribution was pointless: 'I said, "Look Roy, we know instinctively that we must do something about Midleton. We don't need you to tell us."'[123] He thought it would be good, from time to time, to 'take out' a landowner or a speculator, *pour encour-ager les autres*. Mac Stíofáin was dour and devout; he was strongly opposed to Johnston's efforts to take both the gun and God out of Republican politics. Mac Stíofáin was suspended for refusing to sell the issue of the *United Irishman*, the Republican movement's newspaper, which contained Johnston's criticism of the custom of reciting rosaries at political commemorations.[124]

At the Sinn Féin Ard Fheis held in late 1965, Mac Stíofáin counter-attacked. Motion 46 condemned Communism, opposed working with Communist organisations and called for the expulsion from the movement of any Republican known to have connections with Communism.[125] This motion was not considered at the conference: the attempt to remove

Johnston had failed. Goulding had resisted this traditionalist assault on his Political Education Officer as he knew that Johnston's ideas owed more to Connolly than to Communism.[126] Greaves later complained to his diary that Johnston 'draws our Marxist ideas without acknowledgement, and retails them to the republicans opportunistically tailored to suit their prejudices'.[127]

Mac Stíofáin and Johnston could occasionally be civil to each other. The two men found some common ground when they discussed Pier Paolo Pasolini's film *The Gospel According to St Matthew*. In magnificent monochrome, amateur actors retold the story of Christ in the Italian countryside. Jesus was played by a Spanish student, Judas by a truck driver from Rome, and Mary by Mamma Pasolini.[128] Christ was shown as a revolutionary driven by anger at the injustice that he saw all around him. The director's ambivalent Catholicism and ambivalent Marxism were briefly and brilliantly reconciled. Mac Stíofáin's Catholicism and Johnston's Marxism, however, could not be reconciled in the Republican movement.[129]

Goulding was aware that he had to make some concessions to the traditionalists. The Republican Congress had made the mistake of breaking with the IRA; Goulding was anxious not to repeat it.[130] Taking Flann O'Brien's advice, he decided that he had to keep the wolf from the door to prevent him getting out. Mac Stíofáin was kept occupied planning a military campaign in the North that the Chief of Staff had no intention of fighting. An early version of this plan was captured by the Southern police at the start of 1966. Terror and assassination were to be the order of the day. References were made to Cyprus, where the National Organisation of Cypriot Fighters (EOKA) had waged war against British rule in the second half of the 1950s. Mac Stíofáin had come into contact with EOKA prisoners while in gaol for the arms raid and had been impressed by their guerrilla tactics. No reference was made in the plan to the minority Turkish population. In his mind, Cyprus was 'British-occupied Greece' just as the North was 'British-occupied Ireland'.[131]

As early as December 1965, Johnston had to assure Greaves that 'there is no truth in the six-county rumour that a further disturbance is to be expected'. He was certain that the RUC was exaggerating the extent of the Republican threat for political purposes: 'if the IRA didn't exist, the six-county government would have to invent it'.[132] The police, however, clearly had serious doubts about whether Republicanism really was moving away from the armed struggle. 'When the IRA think the time is ripe,' the Inspector-General of the RUC told Stormont in June 1966, 'they will step in and open another campaign of violence in Northern Ireland.'[133] Goulding's strategy of appeasing the traditionalists merely served to reinforce the RUC's scepticism.

Coughlan was not a member of either the IRA or Sinn Féin, so he was not involved in this struggle. As Johnston would later observe, his friend preferred 'to act as an independent source of political ideas'.[134] Coughlan was convinced that 'There is nothing stronger than an idea whose time has come': 'It will ... root itself in the minds of the people, burgeon into fruitful action, change the old ways of looking at social reality, act as an organising force. Superior ideas are more effective than armies.' The divide in the wider Republican movement was not between 'intellectuals' and 'practical men'; it was between dead and living ideas. According to Coughlan, the minds of the physical force men were 'rag-bags, stuffed with dead men's theories, old saws, conventional wisdom, scraps of opinion, and prejudice'.[135]

In the August 1966 issue of *Tuairisc*, the Wolfe Tone Society's newsletter, Coughlan mapped out the road to 'an All-Ireland Republic – politically and economically – in control of its own destiny, the home of a nation of free and educated citizens, in which the exploitation of man by man has been abolished'. Coughlan agreed with Johnston that Republicans should seek to lead a revolutionary coalition that would also include a politicised co-operative movement and militant trade unions. Coughlan, however, recognised that a different strategy was needed in the North where the 'iceberg of political life ... seemingly frozen solid for half a century, is beginning to melt and to drift into new and strange waters'.[136]

Following the Connolly Association line, Coughlan argued that British imperialism would never willingly abandon its dominion over the whole of island of Ireland. Instead, it was abandoning the strategy that it had been pursuing since 1920: 'In the North British troops plus discrimination to divide the people – in the South economic pressure, [to] prevent the development or the success of radical policies designed to loosen the ties of dependence with Britain'. Under Séan Lemass's premiership, however, the Southern political and business classes had come to accept the 'ignominious role of local managers for imperialism'.

The 'far-seeing leaders of British imperialism' were hoping to 'snare Lemass back into the United Kingdom' with the Free Trade Agreement. For this 'trick' to succeed, the 'old fashioned Unionist intransigence which served Britain so well in the past' had to change. Consequently, 'O'Neill has been given his orders to play down discrimination and brush the corruption of his regime under the carpet'.[137]

Coughlan calculated that the 'unfreezing of political life in the Six Counties' was to the advantage of 'republicans, nationalists, and genuine labour men' as well as imperialists. 'If things change too much the Orange worker may see that he can get by alright without dominating his Catholic neighbour,' Coughlan suggested. 'How can Unionism possibly survive when Protestant and Catholic are no longer at one another's throats, when discrimination has been dealt a body-blow?' Yet again, it was assumed that sectarianism rested on nothing more than political and social discrimination. Once this was removed, the 'Orange masses' could be 'enlighten[ed]': they could be shown the 'real nature of Britain's imperialist policy towards Ireland' and become part of the 'movement for independence'. The Republican movement's task was therefore to push for the reform process in Northern Ireland to go faster and further than the Unionist leadership wanted. Stormont 'should be squeezed by popular demands from the disenfranchised, the gerrymandered, the discriminated against, the oppressed Catholic and nationalist minority within the North itself, demands for reforms, for civil rights, for genuine democracy and opportunities of free political expression'.[138] The Republicans needed to launch and lead a civil rights movement in Northern Ireland.

Coughlan advocated that the 'whole gamut of civil resistance' should be used in this struggle: meetings, petitions, sit-ins, and hunger strikes. But he was adamant that the IRA had to stop short of returning to violence. Such 'irresponsible adventures' could only slow the break up of the Unionist cross-class alliance. 'Let us choose our own battlegrounds and not be provoked,' Coughlan advised. 'At the present time the strength of the Catholic and national forces in the North lie in their political discipline and restraint. Let the Unionists expose themselves and rend one another asunder.' Coughlan warned that the success of the civil rights strategy required Republicans to abandon outdated practices. There was no longer a place for rosaries and revolvers in the IRA. The Protestant working people could only be reached by 'a movement which is completely divorced from any elements of Catholic sectarianism ...

by a movement animated by the non-sectarianism and democracy of the traditional republican movement, in other words'.[139]

Johnston was slow to grasp the significance of Coughlan's plan. In September 1966, the Dublin Wolfe Tone Society discussed setting up working groups for a number of 'special areas'. These included language, literature and drama, music and dancing, science and technology, the co-operative movement, and the trade unions. At the bottom of the list, 'civil rights – Tony Coughlan' had been added in pen. For Johnston, this indicated a lack of interest.[140] For Coughlan, it indicated that the issue of civil rights was so important that it was taken for granted.[141]

On 26 July 1966, members of all the Wolfe Tone Societies met in Maghera, County Londonderry, to consider 'civil rights and discrimination' and 'trade unions and unity'. Coughlan was absent due to the death of his father, so Johnston represented the Dublin Wolfe Tone Society in his place. As Johnston's stammer inhibited him from reading aloud from a script, a fringe member of the Dublin group read Coughlan's *Tuairisc* article. It was agreed that a seminar on civil rights should be held in Belfast and other interested groups should be invited to take part.[142] In his article, Coughlan argued that 'full attention should be paid to securing the maximum and broadest unity of action'. This meant that 'Old feuds' had to be forgotten and that Republicans had to 'give way to others for the sake of unity where that is necessary'.[143] Giving way to others, however, involved giving away many of the central points of Coughlan's strategy.

CHAPTER FOUR

The Civil Rights Campaign

THE NORTHERN IRELAND CIVIL RIGHTS ASSOCIATION

In May 1965, the Belfast Trades Council hosted a conference on discrimination. The Trades Council's Secretary, Betty Sinclair, and other Northern Irish Communists accepted C. Desmond Greaves's arguments that discrimination was the main barrier to an anti- Unionist coalition from taking power at Stormont. It was assumed that when new Communist-led governments in both Belfast and Dublin began to adopt state capitalist policies, working people on both sides of the border would recognise the advantages and inevitability of Ireland becoming one country once again. The conference was regarded as a first step towards implementing this strategy. The event was attended by delegates from fifteen trade unions as well as by representatives from the Northern Ireland Labour Party (NILP), the Campaign for Social Justice (CSJ), and the Republican movement. The keynote speech was delivered by a law lecturer at Queen's University who had once been a card-carrying member of the Communist Party of Northern Ireland (CPNI). He told his audience about the inequities of Northern Irish electoral law – a subject that he had spoken about at the National Council for Civil Liberties (NCCL) conference earlier in the year. It was repeatedly stressed that the absence of universal suffrage disenfranchised more Protestants than it did Catholics. 'In a resolution which was passed unanimously,' the *Irish Democrat* reported, 'the meeting decided to go for "one man, one vote, one value"'.[1] In the slightly revised form of one-man-one-vote, this became the slogan of the civil rights movement.

The emphasis that the conference placed upon electoral reform reflected the CPNI's concern that the issue of civil rights would become one of Catholic rights. The party had no desire to alienate the Protestant workers who dominated the ranks of the trade unions by highlighting only the injustices that affected the minority population. In January 1965, the CPNI leadership claimed that 'closer examination of the anti-democratic laws reveals that they are aimed at the Catholic population, to some extent, in the main they are aimed against the interests of the working class'.[2] Sinclair informed the NCCL conference that trade unions and workers suffered the most under Stormont. Supposedly sectarian measures such as the Special Powers Act and the restrictions upon Southern migrants were revealed to be 'in fact, anti-working class'. She concluded with a plea 'for nothing more than an equal opportunity with the workers in Great Britain for democratic practices'.[3]

Greaves published a copy of Sinclair's statement in the *Irish Democrat* and was an observer at the Belfast Trades Council conference. He hoped that this was the beginning of the civil rights struggle that he had been advocating for over a decade. It was not to be: the NILP stopped the trade unions from becoming fully involved and too few CPNI members were prepared to back the plan. Anthony Coughlan and the Republicans would instead take the lead in organising the civil rights campaign. The first Maghera meeting was followed up by a second in October 1966 and by a civil rights seminar in November 1966. The second Maghera meeting was called to persuade the Republican grassroots to support the civil rights strategy.[4] The subsequent civil rights seminar was held at the British Legion's War Memorial Hall. Among the large audience that attended were leading Republicans as well as representatives from the CPNI, the Nationalist Party, the National Democrats, the trade unions, the NILP, and the Liberals. Papers were delivered on the African-American struggle for equality and on civil liberties in both Irish states. The seminar ended with the decision to create an *ad hoc* committee to develop the ideas that had been discussed.[5]

On 29 January 1967, members of every political party in Northern Ireland, as well as key figures from the CSJ, the Wolfe Tone Societies, the Belfast Trades Council, and the trade union movement, gathered at Belfast's International Hotel. They had come together to found the Northern Ireland Civil Rights Association (NICRA). A steering committee was elected to draft a constitution and produce a provisional programme. No Nationalist or Unionist could be found to serve on this committee – although a Young Unionist was later co-opted. With the exception of the CSJ's Conn McCluskey, NICRA's executive officers belonged to either the CPNI or the Belfast Wolfe Tone Society.[6] These committee members unsurprisingly used the press launch to push their respective party lines. Sinclair claimed that NICRA would not only be concerned with alleged discrimination against Catholics. She listed other 'matters' that would require NICRA's attention: 'the civil rights of the mentally ill, of the unemployed, the behaviour of officials at the employment exchanges, securing equal access to education for [children from the Protestant working-class district of] Sandy Row'. Jack Bennett, who had once belonged to the Connolly Association and was now a member of the Wolfe Tone Society, stressed that the new body should 'seek to build a broadly-based movement'.[7]

Although Republicans and Communists dominated the committee, the civil rights campaign failed to unfold as they had planned. The Communist position was weakened by the failure of a single trade union to affiliate to NICRA. Instead of securing a crusade for democracy led by the Labour movement, the CPNI found itself struggling to stop the emergence of a campaign for Catholic rights. NICRA's first public action was to join the protests against Stormont's proscription of the Republican Clubs – the guise under which Sinn Féin operated in the North. In March 1967, Sinclair was a reluctant observer at an illegal gathering of the Republican Clubs. She was aware that her attendance could be misconstrued by members of the Belfast Trades Council – the majority of whom were firm opponents of the Irish Republican Army (IRA). She appears to have sought to limit the potential damage by weakly asserting at the rally that the ban threatened the Orange Order as well.[8] When Sinclair wanted to speak at Republican events, she discovered that many members of the movement had doubts about involving her. In April 1967, Sinclair confided to Greaves that she had been blocked from speaking at the biggest rally commemorating the fiftieth anniversary of the Easter Rising.[9]

NICRA's support for the Republican Club protests fulfilled one of Roy Johnston and Coughlan's initial hopes for the civil rights campaign. Southern concerns, however, remained a higher priority for the Republican leadership. In the summer of 1967, IRA volunteer Mick Ryan was asked to tour the country in his Austin Metro meeting the people who sold the *United Irishman*. The trip began in County Kildare, where Ryan was told over a cup of tea that the state of the movement was 'dire'. The story was the same in Counties Wexford, Waterford, Kilkenny, Connaught, Donegal, Londonderry, Tyrone, Armagh, Down, and Louth.

Ryan returned to Dublin with the impression that 'the few members we had were in the main disheartened and demoralised and without much hope in a future for the republican ideal'. When he reported that there was 'no real functioning organisation', the Republican leadership was shocked.[10]

Cathal Goulding believed that the solution to the movement's problems was for his reforms to go further, faster. Indeed, IRA numbers had doubled to just over 1,000 since the Chief of Staff had embarked upon his new departure.[11] The Republican movement had become involved in popular campaigns to keep ground rents down in Dublin, to save the West of Ireland, to preserve Georgian Dublin, to revive the Irish language, to abandon the Anglo-Irish Free Trade Agreement, and many others. Politicisation appeared to be having some success. By the end of the year, the IRA Convention and the Sinn Féin Ard Fheis had officially declared that the movement's 'aim' was 'the establishment of a democratic Socialist Republic'.[12] Consultations were started on the possibility of dropping abstentionism in favour of 'revolutionary parliamentary action'. As the leadership edged towards abandoning another article of faith, rumours circulated that a break with the traditionalists was coming.[13] Talk of a split, however, failed to hinder the campaign of socio-economic agitation in the South. The Dublin Housing Action Committee was created to bring together Republicans, members of the Connolly Youth movement, and the Southern Communists to take direct action in relation to the city's housing crisis.[14]

The Republican Clubs were growing increasingly restless. Their frustration centred upon NICRA's failure to deal with civil rights issues in their areas. On 28 June 1967, Johnston was pressed to raise the matter with Sinclair. He also passed on the warning that there was a danger of 'a return to the mental ghetto on the part of the dispossessed'. Sinclair made the excuse that she had just come back from the People's Republic of Hungary and was still trying to re-acquaint herself with the civil rights campaign. She complained that NICRA had 'not been able to attract the right kind of people' and had 'too much in the way of groups'. In short, the association could not 'do its job properly'.[15]

During its first eighteen months, NICRA operated along similar lines to the CSJ and the NCCL – which had sent observers to the International Hotel launch.[16] According to the authorised history, NICRA's 'main activity was writing letters to the Government … complaining about harassment of political and social dissidents ranging from Republicans to itinerants'. Stormont responded as it had done to every other accusation of discrimination levelled against it over the years: a reply was sent 'denying that a particular abuse had occurred and suggesting that even if the NICRA allegation was true, there was probably a very good reason for the abuse'.[17] NICRA had failed to solve the problem of permanent opposition; Unionism still held the political initiative.

DEAD-END STREET POLITICS

On 20 June 1968, Austin Currie and his pregnant wife, Annita, drove in their Volkswagen Beetle to Caledon, County Tyrone. The Honourable Member for East Tyrone then proceeded to break into No. 9 Kinnaird Park. Together with two other men, he used whatever came to hand to barricade the front and back doors. Afterwards, the three of them settled down to wait anxiously for the arrival of the police – and the journalists that Annita had gone to fetch. Within a few hours, a crowd of television crews, press photographers and policemen was gathered outside the house. But still nothing had happened: the officers explained that this was a civil matter and that they were only present in case of a breach of the peace. The expectant audience was finally treated to some action when the tenant's brother made his entrance. Having been informed that Currie and his companions were staging a non-violent protest, the brother went away to find a sledgehammer. The door was smashed down, Currie was escorted from the property and the media had their story.[18]

Dungannon Rural District Council had given the tenancy of No. 9 to Miss Emily Beattie – a Protestant teenager who worked for a Unionist parliamentary candidate. Currie recalled saying at the time that 'if I live to be a hundred I'll never get a better case to symbolise the situation in Northern Ireland'.[19] The allocation of the house to Beattie was not as blatant an abuse as it seemed. The village of Caledon was mainly Protestant, Beattie was engaged to be married, her fiancé was ineligible to register in his own name as he was from the South, her family home was overcrowded, and her brother was intending to live with her. Nevertheless, as the independent commission of inquiry subsequently found, Beattie was by 'no stretch of the imagination ... a priority tenant'.[20] Anyway, Currie was interested only in how things would appear to the media. The Caledon 'sit-in' was all about attracting publicity and it succeeded in doing this.[21]

Currie had long been urging the civil rights campaign to adopt direct action tactics. He had studied the history of the United States at Queen's University and had paid close attention to the media coverage of the African-American civil rights movement.[22] With both the Nationalist Party and NICRA struggling to make an impact, Currie felt that Northern Ireland needed to learn from the American example. In October 1967, the Nationalist MP declared that 'he foresaw a growing militancy, with more squatting, more acts of civil disobedience, and less emphasis on traditional parliamentary methods'.[23] Most Nationalists were unconvinced, so Currie had to look elsewhere for allies. The Dungannon police reported that it was 'increasingly clear' that Currie had 'aligned himself with noted Republicans in this area'. Beginning in October 1967, Currie, the Republicans and two local councillors from Patricia McCluskey's group staged a series of squatting incidents. Four years after the Homeless Citizens' League (HCL), direct action tactics were again being used in the Dungannon area. Like Patricia McCluskey, Currie was eager to reach what the police described as 'amicable settlement[s]'. He also recognised the importance of attracting the attention of the media. But the Nationalist MP wanted his actions to reach a wider audience than the HCL's campaign had and he did not share its Chairwoman's doubts about civil disobedience. In the opinion of the local police, Currie 'believes ... that he is the saviour of the downtrodden in Northern Ireland'.[24] Caledon was merely his first act of martyrdom.

'I will not be dissuaded from doing my public duty by sentences, fines or threats,' Currie told a rally on 22 June 1968. 'There will be other Caledons.' He was joined on the platform by Eddie McAteer, Gerry Fitt, Patricia McCluskey, and Kevin Agnew (the last had hosted the Maghera meetings in 1966).[25] Currie's success could not be ignored. The Nationalist Party decided to undertake 'a detailed examination of the implications that would arise from the adoption of a policy of civil disobedience'.[26] NICRA, too, had to afford Currie's opinions greater weight. He later recalled contacting Conn McCluskey to suggest that NICRA should hold a protest to capitalise upon the Caledon incident's favourable publicity: 'I put the proposal that it was time to get away from just disseminating facts and figures, time to get away from the

civil liberties groups in Britain ... and to take it to the streets'.[27] Conn
McCluskey requested a meeting of the executive committee and Agnew
again opened his home. On 27 July 1968, Currie travelled to Maghera in
a Hillman Minx to argue for Northern Ireland's first civil rights march.[28]

NICRA was open to Currie's idea. As the Wolfe Tone Society's
Frank Gogarty explained in a speech given at Trinity College Dublin
on 17 April 1969, he and other NICRA activists had been distant but
interested observers of the Poor People's March on Washington.[29] Martin
Luther King felt that the struggle for racial equality needed to enter its
next phase, where the struggle against political injustice in the South
would give way to a struggle against economic injustice in the whole
of America.[30] What interested those watching on their televisions in
Northern Ireland was not why King embarked upon his last campaign but
how he and his successors planned to gain mass support and the interest
of the media. Fred Heatley, one of the Wolfe Tone Society members on
the committee of NICRA, recalled that 'the tactics of Martin Luther
King in America had been absorbed inasmuch that it was felt by some
that only public marches could draw wide attention to what we were
trying to achieve'.[31] NICRA therefore agreed to sponsor a march from
Coalisland to Dungannon on 24 August 1968. 'The politics of the matter
are not our concern,' the committee asserted in the press statement
announcing the march. 'It is the incredible refusal to concede even the
slightest infringement of Human Rights which we consider should now
be challenged by more vigorous action than Parliamentary questions and
newspaper controversy.'[32]

The police initially offered no objections in principle to the planned
march going ahead. The attitude of the Royal Ulster Constabulary (RUC)
changed, however, when a counter-demonstration was threatened.
Loyalists were determined to prevent what they regarded as a Catholic
march entering the Protestant enclave of the town centre – 'The Square'.[33]
Forcing the authorities to intervene in the interests of public order had
long been used as a means of halting Catholic parades. Local police
accordingly met with the local organisers on 21 August 1968 and tried
without success to persuade them to reroute the march. Later that same
day, representatives from all levels of the RUC and the upper reaches
of the Ministry of Home Affairs attended a conference at Bill Craig's
Belfast home. The decision was taken to impose an alternative route
upon the organisers. On the eve of the protest, the Distinct Inspector

officially notified Currie: 'I told him that the police would prevent, as far as possible, any attempt to enter The Square, purely in the interests of preserving the peace.' Currie's compromise of allowing 'the march to enter The Square with possible prosecutions afterwards' was rejected out of hand. In turn, the MP could not assure the District Inspector that marchers 'would use no physical resistance to the police enforcing the order'.[34] The discussion was ended by a telephone call: a nurse informed Currie that there were serious complications with Annita's pregnancy. A second telephone call came later that night congratulating Currie on the birth of his first child and reassuring him that mother and daughter were both fine.[35]

On the following evening, the march was finally led off after a delay by the Coalisland Silver Band. Behind the band came the first ranks of marchers: Currie, McAteer, and five other Nationalist parliamentarians; Sinclair, Conn McCluskey, Gogarty, Heatley, Agnew, and other members of NICRA; and politicians from the NILP, the Republican Labour Party, the National Democrats, and Patricia McCluskey's group on the local council. Conn McCluskey recalled that the first civil rights marchers were serious, sober, and overwhelmingly well behaved.[36] However, the accounts offered by both the local police and a Catholic student who took part suggest a more chaotic protest. The student claimed that the demonstration had a 'carnival feeling'. 'Most of the people on the march hadn't really thought about civil rights,' she concluded. After the NICRA leadership denounced the ban on entering The Square in Dungannon, local marchers, who were '90% Republican', were left to sing 'rebel songs till midnight'.[37] The RUC was also 'satisfied that the protest march was a Republican one'. A 'great number of noted Republicans' were present and IRA volunteers were responsible for the stewarding. At the end of the protest, Agnew was 'leading 'part of the crowd' 'in the singing of "The Soldier's Song"'.[38]

Among the estimated 2,000 people facing the police barrier that was separating the marchers from a crowd of about 1,500 loyalist counter-demonstrators were Johnston and Coughlan. The latter had written a statement entitled 'Declaration … Dungannon August 24 1968' to mark the first step on the path to liberation first mapped out by Greaves. It began 'To our fellow-countrymen, to the people of Britain and to all democrats and democratic governments everywhere'. It listed at some length the grievances that the civil rights campaign wanted addressed. It called upon Westminster to pass a Bill of Rights for Northern Ireland. It was not read out at the march: Heatley had objected on the grounds that the statement had not been agreed in advance.[39] Coughlan had lost what little influence he had over the civil rights campaign.

Sinclair, the godmother of the civil rights campaign and the chair of NICRA since February 1968, received only slightly better treatment than its godfather.[40] She clambered on to the back of the lorry to chair the meeting. This had been postponed for close to an hour while the loudspeakers were repaired. Even with amplification, however, it was difficult to hear her calls for civil rights reform over the shouts of 'Czechoslovakia'.[41] On 21 August 1968, 500,000 soldiers from the Soviet Union and other Warsaw Pact states had marched into Czechoslovakia to apply the principles of Marxism-Leninism.[42] The violent suppression of reform on the Vltava was a better story for the British and international media than a peaceful march in Dungannon calling for reform. Currie's careful calculations had been upset. 'When criticism was levelled at [NICRA] on the basis that communists like Betty Sinclair were on the executive,' he remembered with some bitterness, 'I often retorted that if the communist influence had been as great as was alleged, the Russians should have told us of their intentions.'[43]

Currie delivered rather than received insults during his speech: he referred to 'the Orange bigots' controlling the Unionist government and compared the police line to the Berlin Wall. In another fiery speech, Fitt branded the senior RUC officers charged with policing the march 'a pair of black bastards'.[44] The civil rights campaign had been reduced to shouting empty threats at the state that was successfully ignoring even the least of its demands.

NO MOVEMENT

On the evening of 21 August 1968, St Patrick's Hall in Coalisland had been packed with people. The meeting had largely been called to organise the stewarding for the civil rights march. The reason why the attendance was so high was because Fr. Austin Eustace, the senior curate in the Dungannon parish, had been speaking. He had tended to more than just the spiritual needs of his flock: he had helped to set up a co-operative, a housing association, and a credit union. Fr. Eustace gave his blessing to the march.[45] Another large meeting was held in St Patrick's Hall two days after the march. The local Catholic community had again come to hear Fr. Eustace's opinion. According to the police report, he 'expressed the view that the march was a failure and castigated ... Currie and Fitt for their violent speeches'. 'The meeting endorsed these views.'[46]

The civil rights campaign was marching along the same road to obscurity that the Anti-Partition League (APL) had taken a decade- and-a-half before. The shift to a marching strategy had found NICRA few supporters outside those who were already politically active. Claims made by the organisers that in excess of 20,000 people would join their march from Coalisland to Dungannon had proved to be ridiculously optimistic.[47] NICRA had failed to interest the Catholic community in the civil rights campaign, let alone the Protestant working class, Westminster, or the world's media. O'Neill remembered how pleased he was to read the *Sunday Times* 'from cover to cover' and find 'not a word about it'.[48]

The new approach promised by the civil rights campaign had culminated in a traditional political protest: an Irish nationalist parade. NICRA began as an attempt to cultivate virgin political soil but the opposition groups found themselves ploughing the same old furrow. Many Unionists therefore concluded that they were facing their old enemy. NICRA appeared to be the Protestant conspiracy theory made flesh: Republicans and Communists had joined forces to destroy Ulster. For fundamentalists, an unholy alliance had been concluded between the Vatican and the Kremlin. The more sober *Belfast Telegraph* reported that the civil rights campaign was a Republican idea and that the IRA had been infiltrated by the Communists.[49] Admittedly, this view failed to acknowledge that discrimination was a serious problem, that other groups were involved, and that the campaign was committed to non-violence.[50] Nevertheless, the conspiracy theory was a shadowy reflection of the Republican-Communist partnership's utopian ambitions. These two groups hoped that the civil rights campaign would split Unionism's cross-class alliance and bring a progressive coalition to power at Stormont. When anti-imperialist governments held office in Belfast and Dublin, their common interests would inevitably lead to the end of partition. The unification of Ireland would be achieved by constitutional or at the very least semi-constitutional means, not through armed insurrection. This subtle distinction mattered little to Unionists. They were still facing a challenge to Northern Ireland's very existence. Indeed, even some of the moderate civil rights activists were convinced that the end of discrimination would bring the end of partition closer.

By adopting provocative tactics, the American civil rights movement had achieved its political goals – this was where NICRA had failed. When Martin Luther King led a peaceful march through Albany, he too had been ignored by the television news and by politicians in the capital. In Birmingham, the civil rights leader had resorted to whatever was needed to provoke the authorities into carrying out the desired outrages. The savage scenes were what the American movement needed to attract media attention and thus secure a federal intervention.[51] No one who belonged to Northern Ireland's civil rights coalition was this cynical. Five years after the HCL had taken inspiration from the black struggle for equality, key lessons from across the Atlantic still had to be learned.

Although Currie and Fitt were becoming increasingly militant, neither man sought to provoke violence.[52] In his autobiography, Currie recalled that he had felt 'proud' that the Coalisland– Dungannon march had been 'non-violent'.[53] The Republican and Communist leaderships were both determined to make a bloodless revolution. Sinclair had told the crowd at Dungannon that 'the parade was a peaceful one'.[54] The NICRA Chair's caution was the legacy of her early political experiences. At the beginning of the 1930s, the Marxist Revolutionary Workers' Group had taken to the streets in pursuit of working-class unity. In 1932, unemployed Protestant and Catholic workers rioted together against Belfast's parsimonious system of outdoor relief. For loyalists, however, militant sectarianism was the only appropriate reaction to the problems that the Great Depression had brought. Rising tensions in the city reached a climax during the Orange Order's July 1935 processions. The resulting sectarian violence left ten dead, hundreds forced from their homes, and Communism in serious decline.[55] The Republicans were also anxious not to risk anything that could tip the civil rights campaign into communal conflict. Republican marshals repeatedly stopped marchers from attacking the police in Dungannon.[56] Indeed, Tomás Mac Giolla, the then President of Sinn Féin, later remembered 'an actual fistfight between our people – the ones saying "No, this is a peaceful march, this is the civil rights march, we're not here to fight the police" and the ones saying "Get the bastards!"'.[57]

In January 1968, Paul Rose told Currie that: 'Unless you and others like you can create a situation where [the Labour] government will be forced to intervene in Northern Ireland nothing will happen and the position will remain unchanged.'[58] The peaceful Coalisland– Dungannon march failed to generate the required crisis. Television pictures of police attacking protesters were what were needed. These would attract extensive media coverage, inspire previously passive people to take to the streets, and force those in power to act.

Lobbying Westminster, publicising allegations of discrimination, and staging demonstrations were tactics that had failed for the APL. They were now failing for the civil rights campaign. While Northern Ireland remained free of disturbances, Unionism remained in control.

There was, however, one political group that was prepared to adopt the necessary strategy of provocation: the leftists.[59] Indeed, they were responsible for many of the unsuccessful attempts to spark serious disorder during the first civil rights march. Currie remembered that this group was 'prevented by the stewards from engaging in confrontation with the police'.[60] One of the leftists addressed the crowd from the platform – his name was Eamonn McCann.[61] The next civil rights march would be held in Derry and he would be responsible for organising it.[62] On 5 October 1968, there would be no one standing between the protesters and the police, between the leftists and a violent confrontation with the state.

CHAPTER FIVE

Paris, London, Rome, Berlin, Derry

'We Shall Fight, We Shall Win: Paris, London, Rome, Berlin'

– Black Dwarf, May 1968

CAPITAL CITY OF INJUSTICE

Mrs Ellen McDonnell and her three children were expecting their new landlords to evict them from their home in Harvey Street, Derry, on 7 October 1966. The night before the bailiffs were due to arrive, however, the city's Republicans intervened. Members of the Young Republican Association arrived at the house, barricaded themselves in, and promised to guard the door night and day. In the morning, a picket was mounted outside the McDonnell home for the benefit of the local newspaper. The front page of the *Derry Journal* carried a photograph of a man holding a placard that read 'Stop unjust evictions'.[1] The Young Republican Association did indeed succeed in stopping this unjust eviction. The McDonnell family were allowed to remain in their home for another year.[2] As one of the Republican protesters later recalled, 'The younger generation had totally embraced the finer points of the new social and economic objectives of the post-1962 era.'[3]

The 'capital city of injustice' was an ideal battlefield for the struggle being waged by Cathal Goulding's Irish Republican Army (IRA).[4] A Nationalist councillor told the last Corporation meeting of the 1950s that 'Derry City as far as housing is concerned is probably the blackest spot in Ireland.' The McDonnell family had been on the housing waiting list for eighteen years. Thousands of people were in a similar position. The Corporation operated a points system, but this did not mean that houses went to those most in need. As the Housing Manager explained in 1958, factors such as 'number of children in family, sex, age, length of time on waiting list, period of residence in city, and ... housing need' were awarded 'consideration' rather than points. The Unionist Mayor was therefore effectively free to allocate tenancies as he wished.[5] He used this power to maintain his party's control over the city.[6]

Londonderry's citizens had withstood siege by the Catholic James II in 1689. The defiance of their forefathers had produced what Seamus Heaney described as 'an emotional charge in the Orange mind for centuries'.[7] Unionism would not willingly surrender the city to its enemies. In November 1968, the veteran MP Edmund Warnock confessed to Terence O'Neill the role he had played in the Londonderry gerrymander. During Northern Ireland's difficult first years, the 'manipulation of the ward boundaries for the sole purpose of retaining Unionist control' was 'defensible on the basis that the safety of the state is the supreme law'. Stormont, however, had consented to this 'temporary measure' becoming permanent.[8] By the beginning of the 1960s, the Catholic Registration Association calculated that because of the gerrymander an electorate with a Catholic majority of 8,056 was returning a Unionist Corporation.[9] Derry, to quote the Anti-Partition League's chief propagandist, was 'the example par excellence of the art of gerrymander'.[10]

The Catholic Registration Association's figures for 1961 showed that the South Ward contained more voters than the other two combined. This ward was overwhelmingly Catholic: 70 per cent of the total Catholic electorate and 16 per cent of all Protestant voters.[11] The Mayor with almost no exceptions awarded tenancies in the other two wards to Protestants. The claims of more deserving Catholic families were cynically ignored. A fairer system was followed by the Northern Ireland Housing Trust (NIHT) – the public body charged with supplementing private and local authority house building. The NIHT, though, could only build when and where it received an invitation from a council. In Derry, the Corporation limited most of the NIHT's activities to the South Ward.[12] The gerrymander was therefore preserved – but at a cost. By 1966, the NIHT was giving notice that there was 'virtually no land left for housing within the city boundary'. The Corporation's housing policy had made Derry one of the most overcrowded cities in the whole of Britain and Ireland.[13]

Unionism's dogged defence of the gerrymander was also dragging down the city's economy. As was the case throughout the region, the second city's suffering stemmed from the long-term decline of the staple industries of shipbuilding and linen.[14] The shipyard had briefly reopened after the Second World War only to close for good soon afterwards. Shirt manufacturers were losing markets to their Asian competitors.[15] Like many other Derrymen and women, Ellen McDonnell's sister had been forced to leave for England in search of work.[16] The Corporation was pleased to see people depart from its city – and terrified that this trend might be reversed. Senior members of the Londonderry Unionist Party feared that new industries would attract too many Catholic workers from other parts of the North and even the South. Teddy Jones, who represented Londonderry City at Stormont, was charged with bringing the worries of frontier Unionism to the attention of the leadership. In 1956, Jones asked Viscount Brookeborough to ensure that the American multinational DuPont gave the job of personnel officer at its new Derry venture to a Unionist. The MP warned that if the position went to anyone else, it would lead to the loss of Londonderry. Brookeborough was, as ever, responsive to the concerns of party hardliners and secured the appointment. The Prime Minister, however, had his limits. When Jones came to him in 1958 to oppose any more factories coming to the city, Brookeborough was appalled.[17] 'No government', he wrote in his diary, 'can stand idly by and allow possible industries not to develop.'[18]

Brookeborough's and, later, Terence O'Neill's various efforts to attract foreign investment fell foul of geography as well as the gerrymander. Many companies wanted to locate to the industrial heartland of the greater Belfast area and nowhere else. O'Neill's plan to 'transform the face of Ulster' made a political virtue out of an economic necessity.[19] However, creating jobs in the Protestant East and neglecting the Catholic West also gave fuel to the conspiracy theorists. In February 1964, the *Derry Journal* suggested that there was 'a deep political motive behind the Belfast government's eagerness to implement' 'the grandiose project of a brand new ... city in North Armagh'. 'It seems significant that the new city, a lesser Belfast, so to speak, is to be planted ... where there is the most solid support for the Unionist Government.'[20] These suspicions were supported by the resignation of Geoffrey Copcutt, the Englishman heading the design team for the new city. In August 1964, he informed the press that the project was 'basically unwise' and that Derry should be developed instead.[21] For the *Derry Journal*, the statement was 'both an indictment of and a challenge to [the] glaring indifference to the future of Derry' shown by Stormont and 'the kept Corporation'.[22]

THE MASTERPLAN

The Unionist government was finally forced to plan for Derry's future the following year – when Protestants joined with Catholics to protest about their city being abandoned by Belfast. At the end of 1964, rumours began to circulate that the second city would not be chosen as the site for Northern Ireland's second university.[23] A group of 'business and professional men' – as they were described in the local newspaper – responded by forming the University for Derry Committee. Church leaders from the city's four main denominations were persuaded to back the campaign. In early February 1965, they issued a statement to the press that welcomed the 'beginning [of] a period of greater co-operation among all the citizens for the educational, social, and industrial development of their city'.[24]

As a symbol of the new mood of co-operation apparently abroad in Derry, representatives from the city's biggest political parties spoke at a public meeting held by the committee. Nationalist, Liberal, and Labour MPs as well as the Unionist Mayor addressed an audience in excess of 1,500 people.[25] The drive to unite the city behind the university issue climaxed on 18 February 1965 with a vast motorised parade to Stormont. 'Clergy of all denominations', reported the *Derry Journal*, 'joined with business and professional men, factory workers, dockers, school teachers, and students in a motorcade which varied from the stately limousine to furniture vans, coal lorries, and bread vans.' The front-page photograph was of the leaders of Nationalism and Unionism in the city standing together on the steps of Stormont in front of a sizeable crowd.[26]

This unusual display of civic pride, however, quickly gave way to the more familiar sectarian politics. As early as March 1965, Jones was publicly warning the Londonderry Unionist Party that its 'political opponents' were 'rubbing their hands' at the prospect that the campaign would 'split' 'the Unionist ranks'.[27] This was the justification Jones gave for voting with the Unionist government to site the second university in Coleraine rather than in his own constituency.[28] One of the rebel MPs, Robert Nixon, whispered that there was a hidden agenda. Local party grandees, he claimed, were determined to prevent the new university being located in a 'Papist city'. Nixon's 'nameless, faceless men' and the loss of the university were weaved into the conspiracy theory that Derry was being deliberately done down.[29]

The chief critic of this supposed plot was the man who had headed the University for Derry Committee, John Hume. Although he had been born in the Bogside, the 1947 Education Act had provided him with a way – via grammar school and the seminary at Maynooth – out of poverty and into the professions. But Hume wanted to be more than just a respected member of the community; he wanted to lead his whole community out of poverty.[30] Hume was instrumental in founding the Derry branch of the Credit Union. In a February 1961 article for the *Derry Journal*, he described it as more than a means of promoting 'thrift' and providing 'a source of credit'. Here was something that would bring 'men together to co-operate'.[31] Hume's faith in the self-help approach had been vindicated by the end of the decade. When the branch moved into its new headquarters, there were 6,200 members and around £1 million had been loaned.[32]

In his article on the Credit Union, Hume had been confident that 'the same spirit ... if brought to bear on other and larger problems at the local level, would soon solve them'.[33] It had not, however, solved the problem of how to bring the second university to Derry. In October 1965, a disillusioned Hume spoke about his city's suffering at a symposium entitled 'The West's Asleep':

> When one understands the great demoralisation of the individual and the community that takes places as a result of continual unemployment and emigration, is it any wonder that there is complaint? Is it any wonder that the images of places like Derry ... are those of anger and frustration? Add to this the whole sorry tale of the new city, the accusations of Copcutt and Nixon ... and is it any wonder that there is a feeling of bitterness and neglect?[34]

Hume hoped that the bitterness and neglect felt by some Protestants could be harnessed to topple Jones. When a Liberal candidate chose to stand against the Attorney-General in the November Stormont election, Hume supported him. At a campaign meeting, Hume reportedly traced the origin of the 'plan' to 'destroy Derry' to 'fourteen years ago when the Unionist Party met to select ... Jones'.[35] The Liberals and Hume came away with a moral victory: the Unionist majority was cut to 1,014. As Jones left the count, he was greeted by 'a loud chorus of boohs'.[36]

This was what Jones had been dreading since the beginning of the year. On 11 February 1965, he had written to one of O'Neill's advisors about the danger of local Unionists being 'infected' by Hume's campaign.[37] An indication that the contagion had reached almost epidemic proportions came at the end of March 1965. The *Londonderry Sentinel* noted with approval that 'many of our correspondents have urged that the Unionist Party should select "new blood" – candidates who will oppose Government policy such as that presented to Parliament on the University question'.[38] Given that the editor was 'a member of the Council of the Londonderry and Foyle Unionist Association', Jones's appeals for Stormont to act grew more urgent.[39]

The Londonderry MP was not in fact orchestrating some deep-laid plot to deprive Derry of the second university; he was trying to undo some of the political damage done by a decision that had not been taken by Unionism. Coleraine was the choice of a committee whose dominant members came from British universities. They followed long-established British practices for selecting a location – and paid no attention to Northern Ireland's political fault lines. The authorities in Coleraine had discovered that the availability of seaside accommodation had been the deciding factor when it came to choosing where to build the new universities of Sussex and Essex. Lodging students in boarding houses was a more cost-effective option than constructing halls of residence. Coleraine's proximity to the resort towns of Portrush and Portstewart was therefore placed at the heart of its bid. By contrast, Londonderry's submissions to the committee made the mistake of assuming that the city's Magee University College was an asset rather than a liability. Magee had been founded in the nineteenth century to train Presbyterian ministers. Each time higher education had been reformed, the college had found itself ever more isolated. It was hamstrung by its Byzantine system of administration, the listlessness of the senior staff, and poor relations with Queen's University. The committee unsurprisingly concluded that Magee could not be used as the nucleus for the new university.[40]

Of all the committee's recommendations, the suggestion that Magee should be closed was the one that most alarmed the Stormont Cabinet. Having served on the 1949 enquiry into the college's affairs, O'Neill was painfully aware of the strength of the Magee lobby. Jones agreed with the Prime Minister that finding a future for Magee would pacify Derry.[41] He worked closely with the Education Minister to produce a compromise settlement that would be acceptable to Magee's trustees and staff.[42] This confidential campaign to save the college was aided by other leading figures in the local party: the 'nameless, faceless men'. On 19 February 1965, they begged O'Neill to give Magee one of the new university's faculties. Although this part of the meeting was less treacherous than Nixon later claimed, the conversation more closely resembled the conspiracy theory when it turned to the subject of industrial development. The overriding concern of everyone present was how to 'retain our position'. Even O'Neill contributed to the debate's sectarian tone, speculating about how 'to insure against a radical increase in R.C. papes'.[43]

Shortly before O'Neill met with the 'nameless, faceless men', the government had instructed the civil service to find ways to counter the claims that Derry was being deliberately neglected. The resulting memorandum placed the blame for the lack of industrial development at the feet of Londonderry Corporation: 'they give us no openings whatsoever'. The Wilson Report's assessment of Londonderry's economic problems was that 'A development plan is needed, and should be put in hand.'[44] But the civil service concluded that 'the internal stresses are so great and the attitude of the City to modern planning so completely obstructive that one cannot conscientiously advise this course at present – nor until there is a change of attitude on the part of the City Council'.[45]

Instead, it was a change of attitude on the part of Stormont that led to Londonderry Corporation embracing planning. Saving the college was simply not enough to satisfy Stormont's critics: houses and jobs were what was needed. In October 1965, Development Minister Bill Craig told the Corporation that he was 'anxious for the creation of a "masterplan" for the development of the north west'. This plan 'would be on the same lines as those envisaged for the creation of [the new city of] Craigavon'.[46] Other leading Unionists also made their way westwards to follow up on their colleague's initiative. In November 1965, the *Londonderry Sentinel* noted with approval that 'several Government Ministers ... have come into the lion's den'.[47]

O'Neillism rested on the assumption that economic and social modernisation was compatible with the Unionist Party's continued control of Northern Ireland. The plan to develop the Derry area was to provide further evidence that this was indeed possible. In a memorandum for the Cabinet, Craig noted that 'professional advice' highlighted the need to 'streamline and modernise' local government.[48] The maddening mixture of county councils, rural district councils, urban districts, and county boroughs was to be smoothed into seven local authorities – the six counties and Belfast. Given that Protestants made up most of the population of County Londonderry, the new council was almost guaranteed to have a Unionist majority.

Catholics could be given more homes and jobs, the gerrymander could be abandoned, and the second city could still be held.

This strategy, however, had one major flaw: it needed time to work. While the London-based consultants, the Ministry of Development, and local politicians were drawing up their plan, Derry's economic and social problems were worsening. In the past, the Nationalists had carried the complaints of the Catholic community to the Corporation. They had even resorted to direct action to register their protest at the injustices of Unionist rule. Eddie McAteer had withheld payment of his rates, declared the election of the Mayor invalid, and disrupted a reception for the Governor.[49] The author of *Irish Action*, however, had subsequently become the champion of the policy of conciliation. The Londonderry Area Plan was trumpeted by McAteer and other local Nationalists as a great success for their new approach. The party set itself the task of working with the authorities to transform the city.[50] By declining to confront the hated Corporation at a time of growing frustration, the Nationalists reluctantly created an opportunity for the Young Republicans and others on the radical Left. In a city of extremes, a tiny band of revolutionaries was able to have a political impact out of proportion to its size.

THE COMING TOGETHER OF ALL THE SECTIONS OF THE WORKING CLASS

In February 1968, four young mothers from Derry were waiting to be seen by the Housing Department. They fell into conversation with two English-born leftists and explained that they had come to complain about their landlord switching off their electricity supply. This encounter led to a series of meetings to organise the city's home-less. At each gathering, more people came on board: left-wing Republicans, Labour radicals, and individuals with no affiliation nor home of their own. These initial debates culminated on the St Patrick's Day weekend, when the Derry Housing Action Committee (DHAC) was launched. The new group decided to announce its arrival on the political stage with a protest at the March meeting of Londonderry Corporation.[51]

On 2 April 1968, the *Derry Journal* reported that a 'dozen men and girls' created 'uproar' in the Guildhall. A Nationalist councillor complained that they had 'come under the control of card-bearing members of the Communist Committee'.[52] 'One of the men in the gallery', according to the *Londonderry Sentinel*, 'called: "That's an old one! Every time we try to do something we are accused of being members of the Communist Party."'[53] This accusation, however, this time failed to prove fatal. As a June 1968 *Derry Journal* comment piece reasoned, 'I am no believer in extreme methods of protest but, knowing the conditions under which so many families are still condemned to live in this city, I find it difficult to censure those who feel themselves goaded into inordinate action.'[54]

The DHAC understood that many Catholics were no longer willing to wait for the area plan to see an improvement in their lives. The group's spokesman therefore demanded that the Corporation should extend the city boundary to make more space available to build homes and embark upon a crash house-building programme. There were few members of the Catholic community who would have disagreed with these remedies for the city's ills. By campaigning upon this reformist programme, the militants were hoping to gradually win support for their more radical goals. The DHAC statement read at the Corporation meeting made no secret of this:

> Finally we believe that the only long-term solution to the social concerns which beset Derry lies in the establishment of workers' power, and public ownership of all land, banks, and industries. The formation of this Committee marks the beginning of a mass movement away from the false political leaders and against the exploiting class.[55]

Despite the DHAC's claims to the contrary, this was not the beginning of the attempt to build a revolutionary movement. That had begun in January 1964 with an advertisement in the local press. It had asked the question 'Are you concerned about unemployment, emigration?' Someone signing himself 'Young Derryman' wanted to 'contact men of action prepared to do something concrete about these social evils'. He received only ten replies. Six months later, the *Derry Journal* published a letter from the 'Young Derryman' under his own name of Eamon Melaugh. The Republican radical complained about the apathy that had greeted his attempts to organise the city's 5,000 unemployed men and women. This indifference, however, had not weakened his conviction that 'Direct action must be taken now'.[56] Melaugh finally managed to set up his Derry Unemployed Action Committee (DUAC) at the beginning of 1965. But apathy continued to shackle his efforts. 'At the inaugural meeting last week,' a spokesman for the committee told the *Derry Journal*, 'members were critical of the non-attendance of people whom they thought would have taken advantage of the meeting.'[57] The DUAC opted to demonstrate its concern and stir the unemployed into action by undertaking something spectacular. When Londonderry Corporation held its January meeting, DUAC members packed the public gallery and poured scorn on the politicians who had failed to bring jobs to the city.[58] This was the first of many visits that Derry's radicals would make to the Guildhall.

The DUAC also marked the beginning of the political partnership of Melaugh, Finbar Doherty, and Eamonn McCann. These three men were behind most of the public protests that took place in Derry during the second half of the decade – including the 5 October 1968 march.[59] Doherty, another Republican, was a member of the DUAC's executive committee.[60] His older brother had been interned for three years during 'Operation Harvest' – simply for having Republican sympathies. Doherty volunteered for Goulding's IRA 'in the hope that non-violent action might obtain some remedies which their six year "war" had failed to achieve'.[61] In February 1966, a DUAC delegation headed by Doherty, who had come to London to find work, lobbied Westminster MPs.[62] The DUAC's activities in the capital continued into the next month with a picket of the Ulster Office. This was when McCann, another temporary exile, became involved.[63]

McCann was born into a Labour family. 'All my early memories of politics are of crowds of men ... in a room filled with smoke,' he told an American interviewer in 2000, 'because there were a lot of trade-union disputes ..., and my father was the secretary of the local branch of the electricians' union.' The Labour ministers who built the welfare state were his boyhood heroes, not the Easter martyrs who bled for the

Irish Republic. The Brooke government's post-war reforms provided the gifted McCann with the opportunity to study at the local grammar school and then at Queen's University. Soon after he arrived in Belfast, McCann joined the Labour Group – 'it was just natural for me'.[64]

McCann and some of his friends from Queen's formed the Working Committee on Civil Rights. In early 1964, they set out to compare conditions in Derry with those of Nationalist-controlled Newry.[65] Three years later, the Mayor of Londonderry received a letter that had been signed 'Eamonn McCann'. The letter-writer claimed that the committee had collected 'no evidence whatsoever to suggest that the Borough Council of Londonderry has at any time practiced [*sic*] discrimination'. The letter, however, was a fake. McCann made it publicly known that while extensive debts had forced the self-financing committee to abandon its work, the committee had by this stage come to a very different conclusion from that of the forger. The students had 'found that Derry Corporation had for many years been carrying out a policy of anti Roman Catholic discrimination in employment and rigid religious segregation in housing'.[66]

When McCann left Queen's University and moved to London, he also found himself moving further to the left. His old friend Kevin Boyle, who was studying criminology at Cambridge University in 1965–6, met up with him again in the metropolis. McCann and a few others from the Labour Group, Boyle later recalled, 'were in a kind of hazy organisation called the Irish Workers' Group (IWG)'.[67] As its newspaper, the *Irish Militant*, proudly proclaimed, the 'banner' of the 'Fourth International ... is carried in Ireland' by the IWG.[68] The group aimed to 'restore to rank-and-file members their control over the trade unions and the Labour Parties', to 'defeat ... the Tories in Ireland, North and South', and to build 'an Irish Workers Republic'.[69]

The international Communist movement and the reunited Fourth International were bound together by their shared allegiance to Lenin and by a blood feud that dated back to Stalin and Trotsky.[70] The leader of the IWG, the former IRA volunteer Géry Lawless, was C. Desmond Greaves's 'ultra-leftist "bête noire"'.[71] The *Irish Democrat* described the IWG as 'Children of enthusiasm if not of charity, in them dogmatism reaches its limit in self-contradiction, dedication in individualism'.[72] The *Irish Militant* returned the compliment: Greaves was a 'figure of fun'.[73] Leftist groups had on occasion gone beyond trading insults and invaded the London headquarters of the Connolly Association. Finbar Doherty, however, was welcomed into the offices of the *Irish Democrat*.[74] The *Irish Militant* regarded the 'cynical [Roy] Johnston faction' of the Republican movement as 'Stalinist fakers'.[75] Doherty, by contrast, 'worked closely' with '"Red Roy" Johnston'.[76]

Greaves was only too pleased to give over space in his newspaper to working-class Irishmen who had embraced Johnston and Coughlan's ideas. In the second of two articles published in 1968, Finbar Doherty argued that the 'solution to all the city's [Derry's] problems can only be achieved by the coming together of all the sections of the working class'. Greaves's three-pronged strategy had been adopted and adapted: 'The struggle of the homeless, the factory workers, the dockers, the unemployed and all those victims of social justice must become one struggle, with a united working-class bringing pressure to bear ... at local level [and] Stormont and Westminster level.'[77]

In London, the rival supporters of the Connolly Association and the IWG fought each other in the streets. On 26 September 1966, a brawl broke out after a charity football match organised by the Camden Town Irish Centre. The departing crowd was loudly 'advised' by two sixteen-year-old members of the IWG 'not to buy' the *Irish Democrat*. This criticism was silenced by the fists and feet of two members of the Connolly Association.[78]

Derrymen, however, preferred to work together rather than work each other over. Sectarianism was a luxury that could only be afforded by the radical Left of great cities like London and New York. In provincial cities such as Derry in Northern Ireland and Madison in Wisconsin, the radical Left was not so indulgent. A student who attended the University of Wisconsin in the early 1960s later remembered that

> We prided ourselves ... on our nonsectarianism ... We would hear about totally sectarian attitudes communists and Trotskyists had towards each other on the East and West coasts ... That seemed ridiculous. The Madison Left – that's the point, anyway. Even if people belonged on a national level to other organizations, those took second place.[79]

Equally, it was the Derry Left that mattered – not the Republican leadership in Dublin and not London's Trotskyist sects. McCann's memoirs describe an 'ad hoc alliance between the left of the Labour Party and the left of the Republican Club' that was 'frowned on by both local party establishments'.[80] Finbar Doherty later wrote that Republican activists were part of 'the broader, though still small, protest movement'. It was 'a complementary mix' of 'college-educated young radicals [and] working-class militants'.[81] This 'very disparate and incoherent group of people', McCann later explained, 'used to just decide to do things standing at the corner. Someone would say "let's do such and such" and we'd say "yeah, let's go!" And then we'd do it. *Immediately*.'[82]

POST H-BOMB

McCann met Lawless for the first time in 1965 when both men attended a march in Britain calling for nuclear disarmament.[83] Irishmen – from the North, the South, and the emigrant community – regularly participated in these British demonstrations. As early as April 1958, Irish peace activists had written to the press praising 'the protests being made in England' and urging their countrymen 'to give them every support'.[84] This call was largely answered by students.[85] The peace movement throughout the West was the gateway into political activism for many young people. Harriet Tanzman, a New Yorker who studied at the University of Wisconsin in the late 1950s and early 1960s, took part in '"Ban the Bomb" demonstrations at the UN' before she left for Madison. Tanzman went on to organise civil rights projects, trips to Cuba, and protests against the Vietnam War.[86] Claude Bourdet, who played a leading role in the French peace movement, later claimed that branches of his Movement against Atomic Armaments were the 'greenhouses' of '68.[87]

Radical pacifists had gone through difficult times during the Second World War and the first years of the Cold War. But they had endured in the prisons and the internment camps. When movements for civil rights in America and against nuclear weapons in the West as a whole began to take to the political stage, radical pacifists were waiting in the wings. They had kept alive a body of knowledge about how to protest and were eager to share it. In March 1956, America's leading pacifists – A.J. Muste, Bayard Rustin, and Dave Dellinger – put their names to a 'Tract for the Times'. Published in the first issue of the magazine *Liberation*, it advocated 'a post-Soviet, post-H-bomb expression of the needs of today': Gandhi's philosophy of non-violent direct action.[88] Satyagraha, 'soul force', required its adherents to oppose unjust laws and to accept the sacrifices that this would bring upon them. Whatever happened, the Satyagrahi had to stick to his or her stance of non-violence. Where violence was used to settle disputes, the different sides pushed themselves further and further apart. The lines of communication were closed down. The Satyagrahi, by contrast, aimed to demonstrate that coercion was pointless and that reconciliation was the best approach.[89]

Muste had taken a twisted path to the Mahatma's teachings. Despite a conservative and Calvinist upbringing, he became involved with the Quakers and pacifism after the start of the First World War. As the 1930s began, Muste discovered that his commitment to pacifism clashed with his commitment to the working class. He chose to embrace Marxism-Leninism and helped to set up the Trotskyist Workers Party of America. But his doubts persisted. In 1936, he visited Trotsky in Norway and returned to America as a Christian pacifist once again. During the early 1940s, he was involved in the attempt to adapt Gandhian principles to the African-American campaign for civil rights. The resulting Congress for Racial Equality (CORE) would not be about individual witnesses to conscience, but about building a mass movement for change. These hopes for the struggle, however, were not to be fulfilled until the middle of the 1950s.[90] The leader of this civil rights movement was Martin Luther King, and Muste was among those who had sparked his interest in Gandhi's ideas.[91]

The 1955–6 Montgomery bus boycott had initially followed the pattern of previous black protests. As the campaign dragged on, however, King was encouraged to develop a new strategy based upon Satyagraha. 'Christ furnished the spirit and the motivation,' he later wrote, 'while Gandhi furnished the method.'[92] King's efforts were supported by Rustin, who had spent six months studying Satyagraha in India and had been advised to head south by, among others, Muste. By the end of the boycott, Rustin had become King's closest advisor. The radical pacifist helped found the Southern Christian Leadership Conference and organise the 1963 March on Washington.[93]

Radical pacifists also acted as movement consultants for the Student Non-violent Co-ordinating Committee (SNCC). At the end of the 1950s, Muste's pacifist group, the Fellowship of Reconciliation, staged a series of non-violence workshops throughout the South. These training sessions were led by James Lawson, who had been imprisoned for resisting the Korean War draft and had studied Satyagraha while serving as a Methodist missionary in India. The workshop held at Nashville's Vanderbilt University was attended by SNCC's future leaders. When student activists came together to agree to form SNCC, Lawson was on hand to ensure that everyone felt that they were involved in the process and that their views mattered.[94] The workshop agreed a statement that affirmed 'the philosophical or religious ideal of non-violence as the foundation of our purpose, the presupposition of our faith, and the manner of our action'.[95]

Muste, Rustin, and associates had an international consultancy practice. When a group of British Quakers established the Direct Action Committee (DAC) in 1957 to protest against nuclear weapons, it was to their American friends that they turned for advice. Muste and Rustin exerted almost as great an influence over the development of the DAC as Gandhi did. Britain admittedly had its own tradition of direct action. However, the adoption and adaptation of Satyagraha radicalised pacifism. In November 1957, the DAC agreed with its supporters to organise a four-day Easter protest march from London to the Atomic Weapons Research Establishment at Aldermaston. The Campaign for Nuclear Disarmament (CND), an elitist pressure group that had been founded in the flat of Canon John Collins in January 1958, and the British New Left also contributed to this project.[96] E.P. Thompson later recalled that many of those who had left the Communist Party after Budapest had been involved in the Moscow-run peace campaigns of the early 1950s. They would now march for world peace rather than the greater glory of the Soviet Union.[97] Despite the involvement of these other bodies, the first Aldermaston march remained very much a DAC affair. It was a protest within the Gandhian tradition of non-violent direct action – but one that attracted thousands of participants and transformed the campaign into a mass movement.

Rustin had told the Trafalgar Square meeting which preceded the Aldermaston march of 1958 that protest movements had to look outside their own country for inspiration, that the 'leaders in Montgomery' 'got it because they had seen the tremendous thing done by Gandhi', and that his audience should derive its own from what King had accomplished.[98] But the teacher came to recognise that he could also learn from his students. As Rustin addressed the crowd at Aldermaston, the seeds of the March on Washington were sowed.[99] The Connolly Association also felt that there was something to learn from this new campaign and organised its own cross-country marches.[100]

The DAC prefigured many aspects of '68. As the minutes for its founding meeting show, the radical pacifists felt that 'Widespread material contentment and a feeling of impotence' 'made dramatic unorthodox means of spreading of ideas more and more necessary'.[101] Sit-down protests and publicity-seeking attempts to break into military bases were all part of the DAC's repertoire of civil disobedience. The ultimate goal of the DAC and the worldwide pacifist movement to which the activists believed they belonged was a non-violent society. This internationalism took the DAC to Africa for the Sahara Project. In conjunction with French and American pacifists, the DAC tried to disrupt the Fifth Republic's nuclear testing and take the message of non-violence to Ghana.[102]

The Third World was reluctant to learn from the British, but they found a more receptive audience in Western countries. In the Federal Republic of Germany, around 200 protesters marched to the Bergen nuclear missile base on Good Friday 1960. The Easter March movement adopted the Aldermaston march's slogans, songs, and symbols. The British influence was underscored by the presence of CND leaders Bertrand Russell and Canon Collins on the Easter March's board of trustees.[103] After some 50,000 people took part in 1962's marches, the West German government tried to break the ties that bound the movements together. In the spring of 1963, fifty-four British activists sought to challenge its ban on foreign participation in the Easter March. When they were refused entry at Düsseldorf airport, the British staged a sit-in and then stopped the plane from taking off for three days. Thousands of West German pacifists staged a solidarity demonstration at the airport.[104]

Such was the strength of the British model that the peace movements in Canada, Australia, New Zealand, and even Italy called themselves CND. The symbol of the first Aldermaston march – three lines representing an individual in despair with arms outstretched and palms facing downwards in the manner of Goya's peasant before the firing squad – became the symbol of the peace movement around the world.

The most dedicated follower of British fashion was the Southern Irish CND. Dubliners who went on the first Aldermaston march returned home to preach the good news. By the end of 1958, a group that included

Roy Johnston and Ciarán Mac an Áili had set up the Irish CND. Mac an Áili chaired the Irish Pacifist Movement – the Irish section of the War Resisters' International whose council members included Muste and Rustin.[105] Mac an Áili later delivered a lecture at the War Memorial Hall meeting that led to the creation of the Northern Ireland Civil Rights Association (NICRA).[106] Clinging to the coat-tails of the British peace movement, the Southern Irish campaign grew steadily.

In the November and December 1961 issues of the *Irish Democrat*, the campaign's Secretary looked back on its first three years. The President of the Irish CND was 'one of the country's leading geologists, its chairman, a former chairman of the Irish Trade Union Congress, and its honorary secretary, a former member of the Irish Anti-Partition League in Britain'. Its aims were 'to draw the attention of the Irish people to the menace of nuclear war and the dangers of nuclear testing … and to co-operate with similar movements elsewhere'.[107] Two marches had been held in Dublin to highlight 'the dangers to Ireland both of nuclear fallout and of political manoeuvres designed to involve Ireland in preparations for nuclear war'.[108]

However, the biggest marches that the Irish CND had taken part in between 1958 and 1961 were from Aldermaston to London. Anthony Coughlan went so far as to claim that this was 'the main public activity of the Irish CND each year'. The peace movement was an international movement, but one that was adapted to specific national and local contexts. Coughlan's concern was that the Irish aspect of the Irish CND was virtually non-existent. 'If one has to go outside Ireland to carry out one's main demonstration, why bother having an Irish CND at all?' The South was a neutral state, while the North was part of the United Kingdom and therefore the North Atlantic Treaty Organisation (NATO). 'A bomb on Belfast', Coughlan observed, 'would spread radioactivity over the whole of Ireland. If radioactivity fallout does not recognise a border, why should the Irish CND?'[109] The campaign took on board Coughlan's criticism. As the New Year began, members of the island's two CNDs marched from the centre of Derry to the American NATO base outside the city.[110] In the spring, young people from both sides of the border came together to form the Irish Students' CND. Coughlan was pleased to report in the March 1962 issue of the *Irish Democrat* that the Youth CND march from St Stephen's Green to the Parnell Monument had 'Defend Irish Neutrality' as its main slogan rather than 'Ban the Bomb'.[111]

Irish students were among the delegates at the June 1962 Camp Sunnybrook conference. Student peace groups were also invited to Pennsylvania from the United States, Canada, and Britain. The conference resolved to find ways to bind the international movement closer together.[112] On 5 October 1968, when Ireland's youth again found themselves part of an international movement, it was entirely appropriate that a CND banner was carried into the heart of Derry.[113] The Irish peace movement had been to a certain extent a dress rehearsal for the political drama of the civil rights movement.

A POLITICAL EDUCATION

Doris Lessing was one of the many literary figures who supported the British CND.[114] In her autobiographical novel *The Golden Notebook*, Anna Wulf watches a CND demonstration that 'was not at all like the orderly political demonstration of the Communist Party in the old days; or like a Labour Party meeting. No, it was fluid – experimental ...' Most of the sixty or so young Americans who attended the Port Huron conference in 1962 had just read, were reading, or would soon read Lessing's novel. The civil rights activists, pacifists, and campus reformers who met to draw up an 'agenda for a generation' identified with the older political generations depicted in *The Golden Notebook*. Like the young Saul Green, they were 'in the gang of idealist kids on the street corner, believing we could change everything'.[115] Green was a fictionalised version of the blacklisted Hollywood writer Clancy Sigal, Lessing's former lover. Some of those who came to Port Huron read his book *Going Away* – a dissident Communist pastiche of Jack Kerouac's *On the Road* – back to back with *The Golden Notebook*.[116]

The first issue of the *New Left Review* contained an 'open letter to the British Comrades of the New Left' from Sigal.[117] In the magazine's fifth issue, another American addressed a 'Letter to the New Left': C. Wright Mills.[118] This maverick sociologist was close to some of the British New Left's leading thinkers – who he felt were far ahead of their American counterparts. He had tried to find Thompson a job in Cuba and in 1957 had travelled around Eastern Europe with the Marxist intellectual Ralph Miliband. This tour of the Soviet bloc's failed revolutions was conducted on a motorcycle.[119] Mills was someone who aimed to make everything about his life and work big.[120] This American outsider's message to the

New Left was that 'Victorian Marxism's labour metaphysic' was out of date and that the 'young intelligentsia' was now the 'possible, immediate, radical agency of change'.[121] Indeed, Mills was convinced that the 'young intelligentsia' had made the Cuban Revolution.[122]

The young intellectuals like Tom Hayden who gathered at Port Huron two years later felt that Mills had 'anointed' them.[123] Hayden did not come from the conventional radical background: he was born into a conservative Irish-American family from the Midwest, not a left-wing Jewish one from New York. At the University of Michigan, he threw himself into student journalism. Gradually, Hayden went from reporting on the campaigns for civil rights, nuclear disarmament, and university reform to taking part. He joined the fledging Students for a Democrat Society (SDS) and agreed to draft its manifesto ahead of the Port Huron conference.[124] In search of inspiration, Hayden read Karl Marx's *Paris Manuscripts*, issues of *Liberation*, the British New Left's *Out of Apathy*, and many other texts. But it was Mills's take on G.D.H. Cole's ideas of radical democracy and Hayden's own experiences in the American South that exerted the greatest influence upon his thinking.[125]

'We are people of this generation,' the Port Huron Statement began, 'bred in at least modest comfort, housed now in universities, looking uncomfortably to the world we inherit.' Their 'complacency' had been shattered because they had become aware of two troubling facts:

> First, the permeating and victimizing fact of human degradation, symbolized by the Southern struggle against racial bigotry, compelled most of us from silence to activism. Second, the enclosing fact of the Cold War, symbolized by the presence of the Bomb, brought awareness that we ourselves, and our friends, and millions of abstract 'others' we knew more directly because of our common peril, might die at any time.

SDS believed that the 'contemporary social movements' for civil rights and for peace were connected. 'The fight for peace is one for a stable and racially integrated world'; 'The fight for civil rights is [one] for a reduction of the arms race which takes national attention and resources away from the problems of domestic injustice.' The 'fight for students, for internal democracy in the university,' was also related to these struggles.

Students were campaigning on campuses across America for the right to discuss the great issues of the day.[126]

The Port Huron Statement identified the universities as a 'potential base and agency in a movement of social change'. The universities were where the 'new left in America' would emerge. 'From its schools and colleges across the nation,' SDS imagined, 'a militant left might awaken its allies.' The small band of brothers and sisters who wrote the Port Huron Statement was aware that SDS could be accused of vaulting ambition. But they nevertheless felt that they had a responsibility to dream. 'If we appear to seek the unattainable,' the 'agenda for a generation' concluded, 'we do so to avoid the unimaginable.'[127]

SDS argued that the 'power of students and faculty united is not only potential; it has shown its actuality in the South'.[128] Indeed, the Port Huron conference was not the beginning of the student movement. The founding event had come almost two years before, on 1 February 1960. This was when four African-American students from Greensboro sat down at the whites-only lunch counter in their local Woolworth's store. The struggle for black equality, which had reached an impasse after the Montgomery bus boycott, was given new life. The Greensboro sit-in inspired other Southern college students to challenge the system of segregated lunch counters. The most impressive protest occurred in Nashville, where Lawson's workshop put into practice all that they had learned about non-violent direct action. By the time that sit-in leaders came together to form SNCC, 50,000 students had participated in the movement.[129]

SNCC was the cutting edge of the New Left. SDS's members in the North of the United States were in awe of the sit-in activists that they encountered at the National Student Association (NSA) congress in August 1960. Sandra Cason, who had organised the protests at the University of Texas, delivered a heartfelt speech explaining why she had got involved: 'I cannot say to a person who suffers injustice, "Wait"… And having decided that I cannot urge caution I must stand with him.' SDS resolved to stand with SNCC. This alliance was sealed by the sacrament of marriage: Hayden wed Cason in the autumn of 1961.[130]

At the wedding, passages of Albert Camus' work were read. Cason was one of the many students who found a way of reconciling two of the biggest youth trends of the 1950s: existentialism and religious revival. While she was at the University of Texas, Cason belonged to a residential religious study centre that promoted a form of Christian existentialism. Her desire to live an authentic life was turned outwards from spiritual contemplation into political action by the civil rights movement. As she told the NSA congress, 'I am thankful for the sit-ins [for] making a decision into action.' She hoped that 'all of us, Negro and white, [would] realize the possibility of becoming less inhuman humans through commitment and action'.[131]

This vision of black and white, Southern and Northern, students putting their bodies on the line for the sake of their own souls and that of America came to an end in Mississippi during the summer of 1964. SNCC's projects in the state were overseen by Bob Moses – a New York high school teacher who had been encouraged to head south by the sit-in movement and Rustin. Moses had a master's degree in philosophy from Harvard University and had taken Camus' motto 'I *rebel* – therefore we *exist*' as his own.[132] Indeed, he was a man of action as well as an intellectual; he wanted to do something in Mississippi. With state-sanctioned intimidation undermining attempts to register African-American voters, Moses arrived at a pragmatic solution to SNCC's problems. By bringing hundreds of white Northern students down to the Deep South, he knew that SNCC would attract the attention of the media and of Washington.[133]

Stuart Ewen, who was in his first year at the University of Wisconsin, was one of the volunteers. Soon after he had arrived at Madison, Ewen had 'got involved with a bunch of people who were marginally leftist, primarily into beat literature, existential acting-out'. These friends had taken part in a protest against a local chain store's racist employment practices. This was a revelation for Ewen: 'It mobilized a political sensibility and a love of political theatre.' So, he applied for the Mississippi Freedom Summer Project.[134]

At the training camp for the volunteers, Moses made frequent references to Camus' *The Plague*. The story of how the ordinary town of Oran was ravaged by the plague can be read as an allegory for France under the Nazi occupation. But Camus' novel transcends this specific time and place. Moses felt that the American South also had the plague. In Camus' tale of moral choices, a young Parisian journalist trapped in Oran and separated from his wife moves from private suffering to public struggle. The camp's volunteers were on the way to reaching the same conclusion as him: 'now that I have seen what I have seen, I know that

I came from here, whether I like it or not. This business concerns all of us.'[135] Indeed, they were discovering that the plague pervaded the whole of American society. The North's political and economic investment in the South mattered more to Washington than the civil rights of black Mississippians. A summer of liberal betrayals climaxed at the Democratic Convention. The regular segregationist party was seated instead of the integrated Mississippi Freedom Democratic Party that SNCC had helped to create.[136]

These were the lows, but there were also highs. One volunteer wrote to his parents, 'I feel like I've found something I've been looking for a long time.'[137] As was the case with many others who worked on the project, Ewen looked back on it as a major turning point in his life:

> It was a political education that changed who I was. It taught me how to be an organizer ... It was also a life of relative danger, not part of my suburban upbringing. I was in a war zone, a world of guns and shootings ... Being young, and without too many obligations, living such a life seems sensible and possible.[138]

Making the adjustment back to normal life became almost impossible. Another volunteer later recalled that 'coming down was so hard; you didn't want it to end'. The white Northern students returned to their campuses determined to recapture the highs of Mississippi. They also carried back with them into campus politics the radical worldview and organisational skills that they had picked up from the civil rights movement.[139]

When the authorities at Berkeley ended the practice of allowing 'off campus' groups to set up card tables, the Freedom Summer veterans applied what they had learnt to the struggle for free speech in the university. Friends of SNCC, CORE, SDS, and the Trotskyist Young Socialist Alliance as well as conservative societies such as Students for Goldwater joined together to form a united front. As the protest gathered momentum, the conventional forms of campus politics were supplemented by the new approaches acquired in the South. The united front became the Free Speech Movement; students who were not members of any group were elected by a mass meeting onto the executive committee. Negotiations with the authorities were backed up by acts of civil disobedience and sit-ins. This was a movement, not an organisation; it brought together the old and the new; it adopted ideas from elsewhere, but adapted them to the local situation.[140]

The 'Berkeley model', to quote a French '68er, was in turn adopted and adapted by Western European students.[141] Thanks to the student exchange programmes that had been set up by the Cold War allies, West German radicals were able to learn at first hand from their American counterparts. In the spring of 1965, West Berlin's Free University banned a journalist who had been critical of the institution from delivering a lecture. Students who had spent time at Ivy League universities were on hand to give advice on how to take direct action. The student government accordingly reacted to the ban by requesting the right 'to hear any person speak in any open area on campus at any time on any subject'. This was the same demand that the Free Speech Movement had made. Indeed, the West German students kept the slogan in its original English just to make sure that the reference was obvious.[142]

LOOKING FOR PUBLICITY

One of the leading figures in both the Queen's University Labour Group and the IWG was Michael Farrell. In the opinion of Kevin Boyle, Farrell was 'theological' – a 'priest' to McCann's 'leprechaun'.[143] Among the tracts that Farrell studied were pieces provided by the American Young Socialist Alliance. Farrell was 'heavily influenced' by the transcript of a speech given by George Breitman to the Chicago branch of the Young Socialist Alliance in January 1964.[144] Breitman, who began his long career in Trotskyist politics in Muste's Workers Party of America, looked at the civil rights movement and outlined 'How a Minority Can Change Society':

> 1. It can force serious concessions from the ruling class ... 2. A minority, properly oriented and led, can go much farther than it has thus far gone to make the present system unworkable and intolerable ... 3. A minority can, merely by carrying through its fight for democratic rights without compromise, help to educate and radicalize ... 4. A minority not only can educate other forces but can set them into motion too ... 5. A determined minority can also divide the majority, can actually split it up at decisive moments and junctures. [7.] ... while the Negro struggle is the struggle of

an oppressed minority for democratic rights, for equality, it tends, because the masters of this country are both unwilling and unable to grant equality, to become part of the general movement of the exploited and oppressed to abolish capitalism and proceed towards socialism.[145]

Farrell adopted these ideas and adapted them to Northern Ireland.

The mass media also helped to spread ideas around the globe. Even local newspapers like the *Derry Journal* carried agency reports on SNCC.[146] But the ideas were often in a fragmentary form removed from their original context.[147] In Paris, when barricades were built in the Latin Quarter during May 1968, the protesters were appealing to the public memory of France's revolutionary tradition as well as provoking the police.[148] Since 1795, the construction of barricades had been a collective ritual signalling that Paris was once again in revolt.[149] Foreign observers of the May events missed this historical allusion. For activists at New York's Columbia University, barricades were seen simply as a way of confronting the authorities. 'The Sorbonne thing,' an SDS activist later remembered, 'the thing that hadn't gone on in Columbia the first time [the campus had been occupied in April 1968], and had a visual impact, were the barricades.'[150]

Smoothing away national differences added to the impression that radicals around the world were part of the same struggle. The *Guardian*'s coverage of the April 1968 demonstrations in West Germany referred to the Easter March movement as CND.[151] The media allowed Western activists to conceive of themselves as belonging to the imagined community of global revolt.[152] Sixty-eight took place in the broadsheets as well as in the streets. The mainstream media, however, only covered those individuals, groups, movements and events that satisfied its need for spectacle.[153] In Derry, the *ad hoc* alliance of Labour leftists and Young Republicans spent the first half of 1968 chasing attention.[154] The DHAC protest at the March meeting of Londonderry Corporation was front-page news.[155] The radicals returned the following month, but on this occasion the report was tucked away in the inside pages.[156] The DHAC succeeded in forcing its way back into the headlines by blocking the main road of the Bogside with a caravan.[157] A week later, the DHAC dragged the caravan back into the middle of the street for a protest that was both longer and more militant than the first. When a policeman asked

Melaugh why he was stopping traffic, he was told: 'I hope that you will bring this matter to Court; then I will get the publicity I am looking for.'[158]

Activists in all Western countries found themselves caught up in this state of constant protest.[159] A British student radical later remembered being 'dazzled by the acceleration of events': 'Rushing from anti-Vietnam demonstrations to tenants' meetings, doing street theatre in Trafalgar Square, and occupying colleges, we gave little thought to the obstacles that faced us.'[160] Careful planning was almost impossible under such conditions. As McCann explained to an American interviewer, 'we became involved willy-nilly, just surfing along on it, and really making things up as we went along'.[161] There simply was not the time for '68ers to stop and think critically about what they were doing and why they were doing it.

TRANSNATIONAL NETWORKS

In February 1968, almost 4,000 activists gathered in West Berlin for the International Vietnam Congress. They came from the Federal Republic itself, the United States, France, Italy, Britain, Holland, Scandinavia, Africa, Latin America, and the Middle East. The Sozialistischer Deutscher Studentenbund (SDS) invited its guests to 'commence the coordinated battle against imperialism on European soil'.[162] Although the plan to link up with a mutiny of African- American militants at a local barracks had to be abandoned, an anti-war march still went ahead. Somewhere between 8,000 and 20,000 people paraded through the city. They carried red flags and giant portraits of Che Guevara, Mao Tse-tung, and Rosa Luxemburg.[163] They chanted 'Ho Ho Ho Chi Minh' and 'Weapons for the Viet Cong'.[164]

The Vietnam War had replaced the Bomb as the issue that could inspire mass protest around the world by the start of the second half of the decade. The Partial Test Ban Treaty of 1963 made it difficult to claim that the nuclear holocaust was fast approaching. The Vietnam War, however, was difficult to ignore. When the Northern Irish CND applied to march in late 1966, this was part of a campaign against British support for the American war effort rather than in favour of nuclear disarmament.[165] As America's military intervention expanded and grew more militant, so did the protest movements in every Western country.

Youthful leftists started to identify their cause with that of Vietnam's National Liberation Front.[166] This was the culmination of the radical Left's interest in the Third World's national liberation movements that stretched back to the Algerian War and the Cuban Revolution.

Fidel Castro's regime subscribed to the faith that any guerrilla campaign could generate the means to its own success. Che Guevara carried the word beyond Cuba that 'it is not always necessary to wait for all the conditions for revolution to exist – the insurrectionary focal point can at times create them'.[167] This contradicted the other main theorists of guerrilla war and Marxism in general. But it was the Cuban story that exercised the greatest fascination for the West's leftists.[168] The idea that revolution fundamentally depended on an act of will rather than on favourable conditions appealed to their existentialist instincts.[169] The main hall at the International Vietnam Congress was decorated with a huge North Vietnamese flag bearing Guevara's famous dictum: 'The duty of a revolutionary is to make a revolution.'[170]

SDS also provided delegates to the congress with translations of Guevara's *Message to Tricontinental Magazine*, in which he called for the creation of 'two, three, many Vietnams'.[171] Contrary to classical Marxism, West German radicals believed that revolution in the periphery provided the best chance of revolution in the centre. At a national congress entitled 'Vietnam – Analysis of an Example' held two years earlier, SDS had argued that the imperialist powers were inflicting exemplary punishment.[172] If the rest of the Third World could be cowed into abandoning hopes of liberation, then the capitalist system could be saved from serious disruption. The nightmares of America and its allies, however, mirrored SDS's dreams. If the Vietnamese continued their resistance and guerrilla wars were launched elsewhere, then the centre could not hold. Consumer culture had hidden the horrors of capitalism underneath an illusion of liberty and leisure. With revolutions in the Third World draining away the West's resources, the spell would start to shatter. At a time of unprecedented prosperity and freedom in the West, events in the periphery allowed leftists to dream of an unlikely revolution in the centre.[173]

In July 1967, the ageing critical theorist Herbert Marcuse told students at Berlin's Free University that he saw 'the possibility of an effective revolutionary force only in the combination of what is going on in the Third World with the explosive forces in the centres of the highly developed world'.[174] Leftists throughout the West believed that they had to open the second revolutionary front. McCann's *Irish Militant* declared that one of the 'duties to Vietnam' owed by 'socialists in Western Europe' was to provide a 'diversion of [American] attention'. The October 1967 March on the Pentagon and the solidarity demonstrations planned in Western Europe were a 'unique opportunity for this'. 'It will be the first occasion that the imperialists have been confronted in all countries of the world at the same time.' In Dublin, the IWG were going to raise a banner bearing the slogan 'US troops out of Vietnam now! Victory to the National Liberation Front!'[175] Taking into account relative population sizes, the Irish demonstration was one of the largest in Western Europe.[176] The regular protest marches organised by Belfast leftists, however, were poorly attended.[177]

SDS's understanding of what was happening in Southeast Asia was shaped by its grasp of what had happened when the Nazis had ruled Europe. The 'long '68' was the period during which West Germany came to terms with the appalling crime of the Holocaust. The trial of Adolf Eichmann in 1961 served as a series of lectures on the machinery of mass murder. The man who oversaw the transportation of millions to their deaths was a banal bureaucrat rather than a charismatic psychopath.[178] SDS felt that similar men were now planning the air war that was killing thousands each week in South-east Asia. West German radicals would not submit to what they regarded as the 'second silence' surrounding 'Auschwitz-Vietnam'.[179]

In their eyes the Federal Republic had failed to escape Germany's fascist past. 'Chancellor Democracy' continued the tradition of strong government, the social market economy built upon foundations laid by Albert Speer, and ordinary Germans still preferred prosperity to political participation.[180] Concerns about what was termed the 'fascism inside the structure' were heightened by the presence of ex-Nazis in the upper echelons of the state.[181] From December 1966, even the Chancellor was a former party member. He headed a Grand Coalition in the Bundestag and his government was close to passing the Emergency Laws that Christian Democrats had long been demanding. For SDS, this was conclusive proof that 'the postfascist system has become a prefascist system' and that an 'extra-parliamentary opposition' was needed.[182] By contrast, the political establishment believed that it was the disturbances in the streets rather than the deals in Parliament that recalled the last days of the Weimar

Republic. Activists and authorities became locked into an escalating cycle of violence that was driven in part by these conflicting interpretations of recent German history.[183]

SDS's development had been shaped by this specific cultural context. Nevertheless, the foreign delegations at the International Vietnam Congress chose to adopt and adapt much of what they had learnt in West Berlin. The French and the British even invited SDS activists to travel over to their countries and offer advice on their projects.[184] Less than a week after the congress ended, French leftists sought to replicate its militancy by occupying the heart of the Latin Quarter. A contemporary account of the 'Heroic Vietnam Quarter' demonstration highlighted how the marshals were 'particularly "well seasoned" since Berlin' and the chants were 'imported from Berlin'.[185]

In April 1968, the opportunity came for Berlin-style demonstrations to be staged across Western Europe: SDS leader Rudi Dutschke was the victim of an assassination attempt. As a conscientious objector on religious grounds, Dutschke had been barred from attending university in his native East Germany and therefore had to continue his education at the Free University. He read not only for his sociology course, but also to extend and deepen his understanding of revolutionary theory.[186] For Dutschke, the world was divided into North and South rather than East and West. With others in the West Berlin SDS, he argued that those in the North should support the Third World guerrilla fighters by becoming 'city guerrillas'. Such was Dutschke's respect for Guevara that he and his American wife named their son Che. Although Dutschke acknowledged that the situation in West Germany was not the same as in Vietnam or Bolivia, his attitude towards violence was at best ambivalent.[187] Indeed, he had developed links with the IRA.[188] When Johnston finally met Dutschke in Trinity College Dublin at the end of the decade, the two men found that they had little in common. The Irishman concluded that the German's dream of a 'workers council democracy' was hopelessly utopian.[189] Axel Springer, the West German newspaper baron, also thought Dutschke was hopeless, but not harmless. In January 1968, West Berlin's student radicals held an 'Anti-fascist Springer Tribunal' and found the media mogul guilty of trying to resurrect the ways of old Germany. The Springer empire threw the accusation back at SDS: *Das Bild* declared that it was 'the Start of the Thirties' and *Die Welt* drew subtle comparisons between Dutschke and Hitler.[190] On 11 April 1968, a young house-painter and avid reader of *Bild* travelled up to West Berlin from Munich and shot Dutschke in the head.[191]

West Germany's annual Easter peace marches became protests against Springer. *Bild* claimed that the SDS had promised that West Berlin would burn like the American ghettoes after Martin Luther King's assassination. Demonstrators reported that police had shouted 'communist pig' and 'go back to Vietnam'. The Easter weekend witnessed the most violent and destructive wave of protests since Kristallnacht. In Paris, around 2,000 people gathered in the Latin Quarter to show their solidarity with SDS. Nanterre's leftists issued a statement condemning 'those in Germany who for months have been carrying on a monstrous slander campaign against students fighting in support of the Vietnamese revolution'.[192] French Trotskyists called for 'two, three, many Berlins'.[193] In London, members of Britain's Vietnam Solidarity Campaign (VSC) broke off from a CND march and headed to the Federal Republic's embassy. They carried before them the SDS banner that a group of West German radicals had brought over for an anti-war demonstration held in Grosvenor Square on 17 March 1968.[194] The intelligence services informed the Cabinet that this 'strong arm delegation' were 'acknowledged experts in methods of riot against the police'.[195]

Although Britain sat on the sidelines of '68, the capital city was one of the focal points for the networks of rebellion. Special Branch noted with concern at the end of 1967 that 'leading members of The Resistance in the United States have visited London ... to urge the Americans here to increased efforts'. Dennis Sweeney, who was now applying what he had learnt during Freedom Summer to the draft resistance movement, inspired a group of students headed by Harry Pincus to set up a British chapter. The next day, Pinkus and CND's first General Secretary took out an advertisement in *The Times* urging everyone in Britain to give American draft resisters 'political support and practical assistance'. American students throughout Western Europe were staging similar protests. In early 1968, Pincus travelled to Paris along with other anti-war activists from across the continent to found American Opposition Abroad. A representative of the Paris Committee to Stop War came over to London, where Pincus's circle was involved with the VSC in planning the first Grosvenor Square march.[196]

McCann was active in the VSC before he came home from London in early 1968.[197] During his time in the metropolis, McCann attended the

1967 Congress on the Dialectics of Liberation at the Roundhouse – an event that brought together scholars and activists from both sides of the Atlantic. 'Groups all over the world are doing much the same as some of us are doing here in London,' declared the head of the planning committee, 'and we want to get this transnational network established.'[198] The speakers included Marcuse, the first editor of *Monthly Review*, a professor from the Sorbonne, the anti-psychiatrist R.D. Laing, the Beat poet Allen Ginsberg, and SNCC Chairman Stokely Carmichael.[199] McCann listened to the last proclaim that SNCC militants were 'going to extend our fight internationally and hook up with the Third World'. 'We are ... fighting to save the humanity of the world, which the West has failed miserably to preserve. And the fight must come from the Third World.'[200]

The Queen's University clique was also linked to the transnational networks through Farrell's involvement in student politics. As Chair of the Irish Association of Labour Student Organisations, he attended a host of foreign conferences. In 1966, he travelled to Vienna for the International Union of Socialist Youth (IUSY) congress. The IUSY could trace its origins back to Karl Leibknecht, who led the failed Spartakist uprising of 1919 with Rosa Luxemburg. Following the Second World War, French students had resurrected the IUSY. Although Western European student groups had initially dominated the IUSY, during the 1950s and 1960s a conscious effort was made to recruit members from the Third World. The IUSY was formally committed to the parliamentarian road to socialism, but no gathering of student activists in the late 1960s was free of leftists – as Farrell's presence demonstrated. He found considerable support for his resolutions calling for an end to discrimination in Northern Ireland and condemning the 'increasing anti-working class bias' of the Southern government.[201]

A younger set of Queen's University activists belonged to the Revolutionary Socialist Student Federation (RSSF). This was a British group committed to 'the revolutionary overthrow of capitalism and imperialism and its replacement by workers' power'.[202] The RSSF's inaugural conference was attended by leading foreign radicals from groups in France, Germany, and America, who had been invited to London by the BBC for a television programme on the global revolt.[203] Unsurprisingly, the RSSF's manifesto borrowed ideas and phrases from these 'fraternal ... organisations'. The group even described itself as an 'extra-parliamentary opposition'.[204] The Belfast branch of the RSSF was established by students who had come into contact with the organisation during a visit to the London School of Economics (LSE). The Queen's University students had crossed the Irish Sea to take part in the VSC's second Grosvenor Square march on 27 October 1968.[205] Northern Ireland was not under quarantine while the revolutionary contagion raged through the Western world.

PROVOCATION

On 2 August 1967, the bailiffs finally arrived at the McDonnell family's Derry home. The Young Republicans had left the house unguarded while they had a meeting with the Northern Ireland Civil Rights Association (NICRA). A crowd of several hundred watched and hurled insults as barricades were breached, furniture removed, and the distressed widow collapsed. Finbar Doherty, who had returned in time to call an ambulance for Mrs McDonnell, proposed a march to police headquarters but the Bogsiders preferred to return to their personal affairs than follow the Derry radicals.[206]

The working people of Derry behaved in accordance with the Leninist principle that through their own efforts they were only capable of developing a trade union consciousness. The tenants' association movement was started by ordinary citizens to find practical ways of improving their lives. It grew out of a few individuals acting as intermediaries between their neighbours and the authorities on issues such as road safety and playgrounds.[207] The tenants' associations were not an embryonic civil rights movement – even though the resources and opportunities were available for one to exist. Instead of turning away from Nationalism, the associations worked with the local party to redress grievances. The first and largest association, Foyle Hill II, almost immediately established links with the Nationalist Party. This was an arrangement that suited both sides: Nationalist politicians lobbied officials and the association gave the party its support.[208]

For the Derry radicals, the tenants' associations were not an independent social movement but another front for their activities. In July 1968, an association with McCann as its Chair was formed in Meenan Park to combat the NIHT's proposed rent increases.[209] The radicals attacked McAteer for failing to take a militant stand in the rent dispute and Foyle Hill II for supporting the Nationalist leader.[210] The Secretary of Foyle Hill II responded by praising the local MP for repeatedly taking 'the tenants' objections to the only people who could do anything about them'.[211] The radicals countered by denouncing 'McAteer's spineless policy, his puny solution to the grievances of the working class'.[212] But there were very few people who were prepared to embrace the radicals' revolutionary solution to these grievances.

By the summer of 1968, the Derry radicals had decided that they had to risk taking a short cut out of the political margins. As McCann wrote in his memoirs, 'our conscious, if unspoken, strategy was to provoke the police into overreaction and thus spark off a mass reaction against the authorities'.[213] Leftists elsewhere in the West had already resorted to provocation in the hope that they could reveal to the world what lay beneath the cloak of liberalism and in despair of making progress in any other way. In his instant history of May '68, the leading student radical Daniel Cohn-Bendit described how the tactic 'brought the latent authoritarianism of the bureaucracy into the open'. This 'opened the eyes of many previously uncommitted students' and inspired them 'to express their passive discontent'.[214]

Stokely Carmichael observed that 'once your enemy hits back then your revolution starts'.[215] This strategy, however, had an obvious weakness. As Harold Wilson explained to the Unionist leadership, 'The British constabulary had the answer as they proved at Grosvenor Square; they were not provoked.'[216] Following May '68, the United Kingdom's intelligence services were predicting a 'shallow but destructive explosion' as leftists were 'dead-set on violence'.[217] Fleet Street, too, was prophesying that there would be 'bloody chaos in London' – there were reports that activists 'were being prepared for the demonstration with a film of the Paris riots', that 'Eamonn McCann' had spoken to LSE students 'about methods of police control in Northern Ireland', and that Whitehall was worried about an IRA attack in the capital.[218] In the wake of 'The Revolution that Never Was', the press agreed with the Prime Minister that the 'British Bobby' – all 7,000 of them – was 'the hero of the hour'.[219] Fortunately for McCann, Cohn-Bendit, Carmichael, and other '68ers, most Western police forces failed to exercise similar restraint when provoked.

The Parisian police had acquired both personnel and practices from a military that had spent most of the post-war era fighting colonial wars. The West Berlin force had been built up since the 1950s to resist an invasion from the East. It packed more fire-power than an infantry division in the Wehrmacht. In both cities, the police believed that their duty was to combat opponents of the state. On 17 October 1961, close to 40,000 Algerian men, women, and children assembled in the French capital to protest against the curfew that had been imposed upon their community. The Prefect of Police had toured barracks in the weeks before the demonstration hinting to his men that brutality would be condoned. The police officers dutifully fired their weapons almost immediately, drew their clubs and charged the crowd. An estimated 200 people were killed.[220] West Berlin's Mayor agreed with his men that the only legitimate protests were those directed against East Germany and that student radicals were therefore a Communist 'fifth column'. In December 1966, the Free University's student government had written to him just before he took office to complain that the police were undermining the principles of democracy. The future Mayor returned the letter unread.[221]

The graduated scale of state violence in the West was topped by America, where the armed vehicles of the National Guard were brought on to city streets. Next were France and West Germany, whose police forces regularly used guns and gas. In the corporate state of Sweden, police officers waded into demonstrators armed only with clubs and whips.[222] At the very bottom of the scale was the British bobby.

The Royal Ulster Constabulary (RUC) ranked just above the Scandinavian police forces. When marchers in Northern Ireland violated the unwritten rule that each community should stay inside their own territory, the RUC could be relied upon to defend the status quo – especially if it was not an Orange march. As the *Derry Journal* reminded its readers in July 1968, '[during] the past twenty years several attempts have been made by the Nationalist Party ... to demonstrate in ... the main thoroughfares of the city. They were met by the imposition of the Special Powers Act and on two occasions police batons were out.'[223] Everyone in the city, McCann acknowledged in his memoirs, knew that the 'one certain way to ensure a head-on clash with the authorities was to organise a non-Unionist march through the city centre'.[224]

Although the strategy was simple in theory, it proved rather more difficult to put into practice. Compromise, not confrontation, was what generally characterised domestic politics in the Western world. Indeed, the first attempt to organise a march through Derry's walls was abandoned after opposition politicians joined with the RUC to object to the planned route. The Derry radicals had hoped, in July 1968, to exploit the centenary of James Connolly's in order to provoke a clash between protesters and police. But Gerry Fitt had advised Finbar Doherty against challenging the ban on marching into the city centre: 'the timing wasn't right, that too few might turn up, and that we didn't have the right "balance of forces" on our side as yet'.[225] The experienced professional, however, had outmanoeuvred the enthusiastic amateurs. Fitt used his speech at the commemoration to attack his rival McAteer and to announce that he was going to set up a branch of his Republican Labour Party in the city. To underscore his tough image, Fitt disingenuously expressed regret that the Derry radicals had chosen not to march.[226] Doherty and McCann were both stung by this betrayal.[227] For Doherty, 'the day of accepting bans had now passed, come hell, high water, or the dubious opinions of politicians'.[228] When NICRA's decision to adopt a marching strategy offered them a second chance, the Derry radicals were determined not to be fooled again.

STAGING THE MARCH

In February 1969, Frank Gogarty gave a Canadian friend 'a brief survey' of 'the revolution'. The NICRA Press Officer blamed the 'great reactionary bitch' Betty Sinclair for 'deserting the people of Derry' before the autumn of 1968. After NICRA consented to the DHAC's request to sponsor a march through the city on 5 October 1968, the responsibility for organising the event fell entirely upon the Derry radicals: thanks to NICRA, the 'people were left without leaders'.[229] The Belfast-based body had insisted that the DHAC should bring on board other local groups, but the Derry radicals had no difficulty circumnavigating this restriction as they operated under a variety of different guises. The march's planning committee therefore drew its membership from the Young Socialists, the Labour Party, the Republican Club, and the non-existent James Connolly Society.[230] The Derry radicals also exploited NICRA's relative ignorance of the city to extract its approval of a route that passed through Protestant territory.[231] McAteer, according to Fred Heatley, cautioned the NICRA executive about the 'company we were keeping'. But the outsiders chose to ignore the local MP's warning.[232] NICRA chose to ignore that it had lent its name to an attempt to provoke violence.

Unlike NICRA, the RUC was familiar with the provocative tactics of the Derry radicals and the city's sectarian geography. As the District Inspector later explained in court, 'the civil rights march route was unsuitable in light of his knowledge'. He therefore secured an order prohibiting the march from passing through Protestant districts.[232] The reasoning behind the ban was explained to the Home Office by the Ministry of Home Affairs: 'The Civil Rights Association is composed largely of persons opposed to the Constitution of Northern Ireland and, despite its title, is regarded by many – and rightly so – as having aims which are largely Nationalistic.' The Waterside and the old walled city had 'for long by custom been sectors ... where Nationalist organisations, or organisations with similar political views, do not parade'.[234]

An additional complication had been provided by the Apprentice Boys. This loyal order had served notice of an 'Annual Initiation Ceremony' for its Liverpool members that would parade along the same route on the same date. The *Derry Journal* accepted that the ceremony was genuine, but maintained that the new initiates were planning to travel by car to the city centre. The head of the order told the newspaper that he had 'no knowledge of a parade'. It was nothing more than a way of forcing Stormont to ban the civil rights march. Indeed, the Apprentice Boys agreed to abandon their parade after the march was prohibited in the Protestant parts of the city.[235] But Bill Craig did not need to have his mind made up for him: 'whether the Apprentice Boys were marching or not, we would have had to look at the public order aspect of a proposal that a nationalist element should go somewhere which would provoke extreme annoyance'.[236]

The Derry radicals had again succeeded in having a march banned from the Protestant citadel. It was at this stage, however, that their strategy once more began to unravel as their moderate collaborators backed away from defying the ministerial order. NICRA wanted to repeat the tactics that had been employed in Dungannon: withdraw from the police line when stopped and then hold a meeting. Gogarty, Heatley and Conn McCluskey were dispatched to Derry to inform the organisers of this decision. When they arrived on 4 October 1968 for a private meeting with the planning committee, the NICRA quartet was greeted by around seventy leftists. The Derry radicals were so anxious to avoid being outmanoeuvred again that reinforcements had been summoned from Belfast and Cork. After about two hours of lively debate, Gogarty embraced the arguments in favour of challenging the ban and thereby forced the other delegates to concede or split the campaign.[237] 'We greet this as a decision by the working class of Derry in all its organisations', the radicals told waiting reporters, 'to assert their rights come Hell, high water, or Herr William Craig.'[238]

A last, desperate attempt to convince Craig to reverse his order was launched by McAteer. In a lengthy telephone conversation, the Leader of the Opposition tried to persuade the Minister that such an action would be in both their interests.[239] As the independent commission of inquiry later concluded, the march would have been a 'very small and comparatively insignificant affair' that would have passed off 'without incident'.[240] Craig, however, remained stubborn – and not just because he was convinced that the march was a Republican/Communist plot. Earlier in the year, on Easter Sunday 1968, the police in Armagh had decided that order could be kept in the ecclesiastical capital only if a banned Republican parade was escorted through its streets. The RUC's common-sense approach ensured that both the parade and the loyalist counter-demonstration passed off peacefully. However, the failure to enforce the ministerial order proved controversial.[241] Allowing a non-Unionist parade to violate the sanctity of the Maiden City would have further incensed the Unionist Party's right wing. This was something that Craig was unwilling to risk as he was hoping that this constituency would eventually help him to depose O'Neill.[242]

Craig, the RUC, and NICRA were acting out the roles that the Derry radicals had scripted for them. Half a decade after the Homeless Citizens' League had adopted the African-American model of protest, a group of activists had finally succeeded in adapting it to Northern Ireland. Provoking the police into attacking seemingly peaceful protestors was the only certain way to wrest the political initiative from the government. Martin Luther King had been one of the first to follow a strategy of provocation, but other activists throughout the West had subsequently taken up the tactic. As one Unionist MP observed after the march, 'We have seen these sort of people at work lately … all over the globe and much nearer home, at Grosvenor Square in London, in Paris, Dublin, and now in Londonderry.'[243]

Chapter Six

The Derry Disturbances

THE DERRY YOUNG HOOLIGANS

As the afternoon of 5 October 1968 wore on, a small crowd assembled in the Diamond, Derry's main square, to greet the civil rights march. This gathering was alive with speculation about what had happened and a sinister rumour spread that a girl had been killed. Some marchers finally arrived and unfurled a Campaign for Nuclear Disarmament (CND) banner near the war memorial. When a couple of policemen attempted to seize the banner, the younger onlookers intervened. This rapidly degenerated into a full-scale riot that enveloped the Diamond and the streets on the edge of the Bogside. 'The sound of breaking glass and the scream of the crowd', the *Derry Journal* reported, 'echoed throughout the area until the crowd finally dispersed about 3:30 a.m. on Sunday.' In the afternoon, teenagers invaded the Diamond and began to smash the windows of a department store. Riot police succeeded in clearing the area and stationed cordons at the gates to the walled city. As night fell, in excess of 1,000 young people – many of them armed with steel rods and bricks – attempted to force their way back into the Diamond. When the police lines held, the rioters retreated behind hastily constructed barricades and began to hurl petrol bombs. The Royal Ulster Constabulary (RUC) used Land Rovers and the water wagon to demolish these barriers. Sworn testimony was later given that some officers had shouted sectarian insults. The crowd disappeared into the Bogside around midnight and soon only a small guard of police remained within the Diamond. Residents of the multi-storey flats on the edge of the Catholic district later claimed that these officers whiled away the nightwatch casting stones at their windows.

An *Irish Times* journalist was told by one of the participants that the city's Catholic youth were rioting 'Because we have nothing else to do'. The Londonderry Area Plan estimated that just over half the population was under twenty-five years of age.[8] Unemployment had started to fall, but in October 1968 it still stood at 12.5 per cent.[9] The 'large numbers of idle youth', to use the independent commission of inquiry's phrase, rather than the supposed expansion of the middle class was the demographic change that underlay the civil rights era.[10]

The 'Derry Young Hooligans' became locked into a self-sustaining cycle of confrontation with the security forces.[11] 'A Derry Teenager' claimed in a letter to the local newspaper that the image of the 'kindly policeman' had been replaced by 'a picture of a steel-helmeted truncheon wielder who uses it indiscriminately'.[12] This picture appeared in newspapers and on televisions throughout the West. Police brutality was one of the dominant images of '68. In France, the *curé* had been supplanted by the *flic* as a popular hate figure.[13] The forces of law and order, in turn, saw something sinister in their opponents. Bill Craig, relating to the Stormont Parliament the information he had received from the RUC, denounced the youths as 'something more than hooligans'.[14] Similarly, the FBI repeatedly warned those in power that the protests and riots of the 1960s were all part of a Communist conspiracy.[15] The cycle of confrontation in Derry, according to Eamonn McCann's memoirs, 'powered the civil rights campaign through its first frenetic months'.[16] With Derry in an almost constant state of disorder, the likelihood of bringing the crisis to a peaceful resolution was virtually non-existent.[17]

DERRY CITIZENS' ACTION COMMITTEE

Following the march and the ensuing weekend of riots, the middle classes and the middle-aged also began to express their opposition in the streets. Unemployment, lack of housing, discrimination and gerrymandering were perennial concerns, but only a tiny minority had ever sought their resolution outside the accepted political channels. Police brutality, however, was different. The Catholic community had an ambivalent attitude towards policing. 'Nationalists', noted the *Derry Journal* at the start of 1963, 'readily recognise the extreme efficiency of the RUC in carrying out the normal duties of a police force.' The newspaper was critical, though, when the force was used 'to protect coat-trailing Unionist processions [and] to assist in the suppression of Nationalist activities'.[18] Three months before the first Derry civil rights march, the Foyle Hill II tenants' association was campaigning for regular police patrols of the estate.[19] Six days after the march, over a hundred people gathered outside the Guildhall to protest against police brutality.[20] Around the Western world, this was the issue that mobilised the most people. It appealed at a gut level to their sense of right and wrong.

As Seamus Heaney observed, 'it seems now that the Catholic minority in Northern Ireland at large, if it is to retain any self-respect, will have to risk the charge of wrecking the new moderation and seek justice more vociferously'.[21] A mass movement had been born in Derry. The Catholic community's leaders were eager to exploit the situation to secure concessions from the Unionists. But they were also anxious to arrest what they regarded as the worrying drift towards the complete collapse of order in the city. Neither of these objectives, however, could be achieved while the Derry radicals remained the titular heads of the new movement. Indeed, they were trying to organise a second civil rights march for 12 October 1968. Fearing that another attempt to parade through the city walls would bring a repetition of the recent violence, Derry's moderates made their move.[22]

The 'origin' of the intrigue, as Finbar Doherty's memoirs acknowledge, 'is still shrouded in some mystery'.[23] What is clear is that moderates from 'the business, professional, religious, and trade union life of the city' held a meeting to discuss how to proceed. The Derry radicals were not invited, but turned up anyway after hearing rumours that they were being usurped. McCann took the chair and announced to the assembled moderates that the committee that had organised the first march was interested in canvassing their opinions. A proposal came from the floor that new members should be elected onto the committee at the meeting to make it more representative. McCann rejected this suggestion out of hand. The other radicals, however, reasoned that bringing the moderates on board would give the committee greater legitimacy while allowing them to keep the political initiative. In what he later characterised as 'a fit of either pique or principle', McCann surrendered the chair and walked out.[24] The new membership was headed by John Hume, Paddy Doherty, and Michael Canavan – the leading lights of the city's Credit Union. Prominent figures from the four main political parties were also elected: Nationalist Councillor James Doherty, former Unionist Alderman Campbell Austin, the Northern Ireland Labour Party's (NILP) Ivan Cooper, and Claude Wilton from the Liberal Party.[25] To show that the new committee was non-sectarian, the Protestant Cooper was appointed its Chair. Hume became the Vice-Chair and Canavan took the role of Secretary. 'There was general relief', Paddy Doherty recalled, 'that control of the campaign for civil rights had passed from Eamonn McCann and his followers to ... more solid, representative leaders.'[26] McCann, by contrast, told reporters that the new Derry Citizens' Action Committee (DCAC) was 'a disaster for the working class'. The new members were denounced as 'middle-aged, middle class, and middle of the road'.[27]

Hume and Canavan's template for the DCAC was the University for Derry Committee.[28] They hoped that an orderly, non-violent movement for civic change could replace the chaotic, bloody, and overtly political struggle launched by the Derry radicals. The DCAC therefore announced its arrival by cancelling the second civil rights march. In its place, a sit-down demonstration would be held in Guildhall Square on 19 October 1968, at which the DCAC's programme of action would be revealed.[29] Austin, however, regarded the committee as a means of bringing 'the two sides of the confrontation to the discussion table', not as a vehicle for protest. As he informed the local press, he 'was not prepared ... to be connected in any way with civil disobedience or criticism of the forces of order'.[30] Austin was a liberal Unionist who had attacked his former colleagues on the Council for 'murdering the city through party political bickering'.[31] His decision to resign was an early indication that civil rights would not bridge the two communities as the university issue had.

The DCAC was nevertheless still confident that it could mount 'a non-political, non-sectarian ... campaign to root out the causes of discontent and disharmony in the Derry area'.[32] At the sit-down protest, Hume presented to a crowd of around 5,000 people a self- consciously limited list of demands. All three related to the city's housing shortage: a 'crash programme' of house building; a 'fair points system' in the allocation of houses; and the 'Stormont Government to bring in some form of legal control in the renting of furnished accommodation'. Other committee members also emphasised the DCAC's moderate credentials. The Protestant Wilton called upon 'people of my religion' to 'stand together' with the Catholics to 'make our beloved city a place of which we shall all be proud'. Paddy Doherty provided the crowd with the opportunity to reject Craig's accusations. To shouts of 'No', Doherty asked whether the 'people of this city' were 'irresponsible' 'Communists', 'under the influence of any political organisation', or expecting 'bloodshed'.[33]

Although the DCAC was not anticipating any serious trouble at the rally, the stewarding system had been completely overhauled since the civil rights march. When a small group at the rally began singing the British national anthem, about twenty marshals immediately surrounded these loyalists and defused the potential flashpoint. The police also helped to ensure that the protest passed off peacefully by sealing off Guildhall Square from the threatened counter-demonstrations.[34] The RUC had made the pragmatic decision to put maintaining order above other concerns. 'Many congratulations', trumpeted the *Derry Journal*, 'have been extended to the Derry Citizens' Action Committee and to the police … on the dignified and orderly way in which [the] sit-down rally … was staged.'[35] This was in marked contrast to the violent polarisation of two weeks earlier and suggested that a peaceful resolution was possible.

In Paddy Doherty's opinion, a 'gesture of generosity from the government at this point would have stopped the civil rights campaign in its tracks'.[36] By taking the action that the DCAC was demanding on the city's housing problem, Stormont would perhaps have brought an end to Derry's massive civil rights demonstrations. This, in turn, would have removed the riot police, loyalist counter-demonstrators, and the Derry Young Hooligans from the streets. With the 'capital city of injustice' pacified, the civil rights movement in the rest of Northern Ireland would probably have lost all its momentum.

The DCAC's solution to the housing shortage, however, was not without political implications. A crash house-building programme and a fair points system would have fatally undermined the gerrymander – and Unionism's hold over the city. The Nationalists and the Derry Housing Action Committee (DHAC) had campaigned without success for similar measures to be adopted. They had discovered that the Unionist council valued power over improving people's lives.[27] Although Londonderry Corporation would never vote for change, Stormont was not so stubborn. The Development Ministry was planning to create a unitary authority for County Londonderry. So, the government's calculations were not dominated by the need to safeguard the gerrymander.[38] The new council would have a comfortable Unionist majority – regardless of whether or not the DCAC's proposals were introduced.[39]

Stormont, though, had committed itself to the Londonderry Area Plan.[40] Embracing the DCAC's approach would have been regarded as making concessions to the civil rights movement. The Cabinet was not yet willing to take such a controversial step.[41] There were also indications that early action on the housing issue would not succeed in satisfying even the moderates on the committee. The *Belfast Newsletter* noted that most speakers at the sit-down rally wanted the local government franchise to be reformed.[42] According to the *Derry Journal*, Hume had told the crowd that they had gathered to protest 'against what was the basic fundamental evil in [Derry] – minority rule – because out of that came every other evil'.[43] The DCAC's ambitions grew each day that Stormont remained silent about reform.

THE MARCHES

On 2 November 1968, the fifteen members of the DCAC set off to walk the route of the first civil rights march. They were watched by a crowd of almost 2,000 people. The first rank of marchers was made up of Hume, Canavan, and Cooper rather than members of the original committee. This was a clear indication of where power resided in the DCAC. Ronald Bunting, Ian Paisley's lieutenant, and a small band of loyalists tried to provoke violence. But the police and the stewards worked together to keep order. By the time the DCAC reached the Diamond, the crowd had doubled in size. A meeting was held at which Eamon Melaugh's eleven-year-old son read the United Nations Declaration of Human Rights. Cooper joined him on the platform to congratulate the people of Derry for the disciplined manner in which they had established their right to march through the city walls.[44]

This success encouraged the DCAC to announce that a full-scale march would be staged on 16 November 1968.[45] In this re-enactment of 5 October 1968, Craig reprised his role and proscribed the march from entering the city centre. The Home Affairs Minister believed that 'a blanket ban covering all processions in the neighbourhood of Londonderry' for the period of one month would bring calm to the city.[46] He was wrong. The DCAC issued a statement on 13 November 1968 denouncing Craig's action as inflammatory. Just as the original organising committee had done in October, the DCAC called upon 'all the people of Derry to resist the Minister'. The next day, Craig warned that the 'police will enforce the law ... in the last resort'.[47] This, however, was the point at which key roles started to be rewritten. The RUC's senior officers recognised that they lacked the men needed to stop thousands of marchers from breaching the city walls.[48] The DCAC's moderate leadership was also anxious to avoid a confrontation. To the frustration of the Derry radicals, the DCAC accepted the advice of the Society of Labour Lawyers to halt the march short of the police barricades.[49] This would be political theatre without the violent scenes.

The 15,000 or so people that gathered at the railway station on Saturday afternoon were instructed to hold a sit-down protest in front of the police barrier. Paddy Doherty again fired off a series of rhetorical questions: 'Are we going to throw the lie back in Craig's teeth?'; 'He wants us to climb through the police barricades. Are we going to do this?' As a further precaution against confrontation, a large group of stewards were stationed at the head of the march to restrain anyone who wanted to charge the police line. When the DCAC moved forward to negotiate with the RUC, the crowd was again told to 'accept what happens with peace, dignity, and self-discipline'. Hume asked the police – 'in the name of peace and non-violence and in the good name of your own force' – to 'let our people through'. The County Inspector replied that the ministerial order would be complied with in so far as the police were able to do so. The two sides, having discharged their respective duties, arrived at an acceptable compromise. Four committee members vaulted the first crash barrier, crossed the open space, and threw themselves at the RUC officers guarding the second one. As had been arranged in advance, no violence was used by those attacking the police barricades or by those defending them. Hume returned to the front of the march to report that the ban had been broken and reiterated the importance of proving to Craig that the 'people of Derry' were 'capable of peaceful protest'. DCAC members rushed backwards and forwards between the police lines and the marchers to negotiate an alternative route. As the crowd streamed into the Diamond, the RUC tactfully withdrew and left the city centre to the cheering demonstrators. 'We are within the walls,' Hume declared, 'and we will stay here.'[50]

THE SITUATION COULD GET OUT OF CONTROL

In the wake of the second civil rights march, Eddie McAteer observed that 'the law is going into disrepute'. 'The situation could get out of control.'[51] Stormont's grip on the city was undoubtedly weakening – but power was not passing seamlessly to the DCAC's moderate leadership.

Paddy Doherty recalled in his memoirs that the stewards were growing restless at the restraint being shown by the committee members. On the morning of the march, Doherty was forced to promise the stewards that he would defy the ban even if the DCAC as a whole decided against this. Doherty also felt that the marchers were determined to reach the city centre with or without the committee members at their head.[52] Indeed, the marshals were called upon on a number of occasions to prevent marchers surging towards the police barriers. The stewards, however, lacked both the numbers and the will to ensure that all the marchers took the diversion agreed by the DCAC and the RUC. A large group broke away from the main march and followed the original route to the city centre.[53]

When the rebel marchers neared the entrance to the walled city, they were confronted by a barrage of stones coming from a gang of loyalists. The RUC positioned officers in between the rival groups, but missiles still made it over the police cordon and marchers continued to pass through the walls. Within thirty minutes, sheer weight of numbers had compelled policemen and Paisleyites to retreat from the proscribed route.[54]

The interaction between protesters, counter-demonstrators, and police officers was one of the dynamics that propelled the events of '68. In Paris, during the first few of days of May 1968, Occident showed, by marching down boulevards ready for battle, that it would 'never … surrender the streets to the *chienlit*'. Student radicals at the Sorbonne prepared themselves for the expected onslaught. The intervention of the Parisian police, instead of restoring order, marked the beginning of the struggle for the Latin Quarter.[55]

The Derry radicals hoped that the weakness displayed by both the RUC and the DCAC moderates on the march could be exploited to their advantage. 'As far as the Left was concerned,' Finbar Doherty remembered, 'Craig's ban had been broken only by default.'[56] The Derry radicals were determined to smash it. Their opportunity arrived on 18 November 1968 with the first day of the court cases arising out of the first civil rights march. Members of the public arrived at the courthouse to attend the hearing, but found that the police were granting access only to journalists. After an attempt was made to break through the police lines, DCAC members and RUC officers agreed a deal to allow relatives into the public gallery. When Cooper and Gerry Fitt emerged from the courthouse, the waiting crowd carried the pair shoulder high through the walled city to Guildhall Square. Fearing that the Guildhall was going to be occupied, policemen closed the building's iron gates and drew their batons. A short brawl ensued before Cooper succeeded in persuading the crowd to resist the provocation. Following a further illegal parade through the city centre, the DCAC Chair eventually persuaded the marchers to disperse.[57]

This was only the start of a day of unplanned marches in defiance of the ministerial order, however. Rumours of police brutality had reached Derry's port and inspired some 400 dockworkers to undertake a protest march to the walled city. Hume was charged with defusing the situation. He promised the dockers that a telegram would be sent on their behalf to the British Prime Minister and asked them to return to their work. The DCAC Vice-Chair and hundreds of other people accompanied the dockworkers back through the city centre to the port – where he gave another speech praising their action.[58]

These spontaneous marches gave the Derry radicals the idea of bringing out other workers onto the streets. Finbar Doherty was despatched to the shirt factory near where he had grown up to win over the shop stewards. He received an enthusiastic response – the civil rights movement's foot soldiers were eager to overthrow Craig's blanket ban. Indeed, the idea proved so popular that the Derry radicals were arriving at factories to find that news had already reached the shop floor.[59] Close to 1,000 factory girls deserted their work benches to parade through the city centre.[60] The marchers were greeted in the Diamond by Hume and Cooper, who praised the spirit they had displayed and encouraged them to resume their abandoned work. McCann had a slightly different message from the DCAC moderates for the crowd. 'The factory girls of Derry', he declared 'have walked all over Craig's ban.' At the conclusion of the meeting, the marchers reformed and headed towards the city's main police station shouting 'SS RUC'.[61]

Similar chants were heard in other Western European cities during '68. In Paris, female students cried 'CRS = SS' as the police officers and the *gendarmes mobiles* arrested male protesters in the courtyard of the Sorbonne. The Compagnies Républicaines de Sécurité, the paramilitary riot police that had brutally restored order during the 1947 strikes and the

Algerian War, would soon afterwards be sent in to take on the students.[62] In Hamburg, young people demonstrating outsider the Springer offices taunted police officers with calls of 'Nazis' and 'SS'.[63] Police repression had supposedly revealed that behind the democratic façade the countries of Western Europe were still authoritarian states.

The Derry Young Hooligans were in close attendance as the factory girls paraded through the city centre. When the workers dispersed, the fifty or so teenagers that had been following the march embarked upon a circuit of the city walls. Once the perambulation had been completed, Hume was again called upon to address an impromptu meeting. The unemployed teenagers were his most difficult audience of the day, but they listened when he told them to 'go home'.[64] The DCAC possessed the moral authority to end the demonstrations after they had begun. However, committee members could not stop people coming onto the streets. The *Derry Journal* estimated that by nightfall over twenty marches through the banned area had taken place.[65] The movement was moving away from the DCAC's moderate leadership.

Finbar Doherty later remembered the day as 'a high point in the history of Derry's working class'.[66] The night, however, witnessed the city's proletariat fall into some of the worst sectarian violence since the Second World War. As the evening shift was leaving the Cerdic shirt factory on Abercorn Road, some forty teenagers from the Protestant Wapping Lane area began to throw stones and bottles. The Protestant boys were trying to put the Catholic girls back in their place. Cerdic was selected as the target because it was the nearest shirt factory to Wapping Lane and Cooper was its manager.[67]

On the following day, Derry's factory girls again took to the streets in one of the five spontaneous marches that took place within the old walls. Apart from a few minor clashes with policemen and loyalists, these afternoon parades passed off peacefully – but the trouble resumed at night. About 150 'civil rights sympathisers', as the *Derry Journal* described them, assembled at the Cerdic factory to protect the girls from the expected attack. As the loyalists again started to hurl missiles, the defenders returned the objects and a small group of RUC officers became caught in the middle of the skirmish. The riot police were summoned to the scene and inflicted a series of baton charges upon the rival gangs of streetfighters. DCAC stewards, who had arrived at the factory with the aim of keeping the peace, were among those knocked to the ground in the general mêlée. The marshals were nevertheless able to form a cordon that separated the two sides and secured their eventual dispersal.[68] Paddy Doherty, who was directing the stewards, was 'horrified' by the 'naked sectarianism'. He was even more shocked to find 'Catholics ... fighting Catholics'.[69] At the meeting held for the dockworkers, Hume had told a party of policemen standing nearby that they were not needed: 'We can control our own people.'[70] The violence outside the Cerdic factory's gates cast serious doubt upon this claim.

ONE OF THE TRAGEDIES OF IRELAND WAS SPLINTER GROUPS

The stewards had come from a huge DCAC meeting at the Guildhall – around 1,500 people inside the building and several thousand more outside.[71] One of the major themes running through the speeches delivered from the platform was the importance of halting the unofficial marches. Cooper pleaded with the audience to stop as Hume was 'dead on his feet' after having to 'police' so many marches. McAteer backed the DCAC's appeal for restraint. 'Derry people must keep their heads and use their heads,' he said, 'A rest for our marching feet would do no harm.'[73]

Another theme was the need for the movement to remain united. As had happened in France during the spring, police brutality had pulled together opponents of the regime. But in both countries the differences between reformers and revolutionaries began to pull the coalitions apart.[73] Hume announced to the Guildhall that they were trying to 'create a city in which Catholic, Protestant and Dissenter could work together'. Unfortunately, referencing Wolfe Tone's famous separatist slogan was more likely to alienate the unionist population than to bring them on board. Indeed, even reformers could sound like revolutionaries in a society that was divided along the lines of nationality. Hume had opened his speech by observing that Derry was 'the first colony of Britain [and] it looks like it might be the last'.[74]

The audience called for McCann to take the platform, he began by expressing 'regret' at the 'divide in our society'. McCann believed that loyalists would stop throwing stones and bottles 'if we can get the point over to these people that what we demand is in their interests – because many of them also suffer from a lack of civil rights in this city'. When people chanted one-man-one-vote, he told the meeting, they should 'remember that civil rights also meant one man, one job, one family, one house, and so on'. Matt O'Leary, the self-proclaimed 'Christian Communist' who had been the first Chair of the DHAC, was more explicit about how the Derry radicals viewed developments: 'This was a workers' revolution.'[75]

O'Leary was soon challenging the DCAC's call for a moratorium upon marches. On 20 November 1968, a crowd congregated outside the employment exchange for the start of a proposed Derry Unemployed Action Committee (DUAC) march. Hume and Cooper debated with O'Leary whether or not the march should proceed. Cooper asked the crowd to disperse for the 'sake of the people generally and particularly the workers of the factory in Abercorn Road'. Hume emphasised that the unemployed were part of a wider movement and should therefore abide by the will of the majority. 'One of the tragedies of Ireland was splinter groups,' he said. O'Leary countered that the unemployed were not under any obligation to adhere to the DCAC line and could decide upon their own approach. Elements within the crowd shouted O'Leary down before he finished his speech – Hume and Cooper's arguments had prevailed.[76] This episode exemplified how an activist's authority came from having their claim to speak for the civil rights movement accepted. Hume was not the leader of the Derry movement but, rather, had positioned himself at its head. His rhetoric, as McCann later conceded, 'perfectly matched the mood of the Catholic masses': 'reasonable, respectable, righteous [and] solid'.[77] But if the movement moved on, then its figurehead would be cast aside.

While Hume's views commanded the greatest support, other public figures were also able to justify their actions by reference to civil rights. At the Corporation's October meeting, the DHAC made its regular appearance in the public gallery. When the Unionist councillors adjourned for a short break, Melaugh entered the chamber and sat down in the empty mayoral chair. Addressing himself to the 'citizens of Derry', Melaugh proposed a crash programme of 2,000 houses and the extension of the boundary. As these mock motions received cries of affirmation, Melaugh declared 'This is democracy'.[78] In nineteenth-century France, the revolutionary crowd would take it in turns to sit on the throne or the president's chair. This was the fourth act of 'the revolutionary passion play' – the moment at which the people reclaimed their sovereignty.[79] The Derry radicals were giving the 'fascist clique' that ran the Corporation notice that its days were numbered.[80]

The DHAC and their supporters left the Guildhall to hold a teach-in on the city's housing problems.[81] The first ever teach-in was staged at the University of Michigan in March 1965. It was the idea of a sociology professor who had previously worked with the Congress of Racial Equality in Boston to organise a 'Freedom School' to teach black history during a city-wide schools boycott. He felt that this line of action should be adopted and adapted by the anti-war movement. The Michigan teach-in was a huge success and became the model for anti-war activists on other campuses.[82] At Berkeley, in June 1965, around 30,000 people attended a teach-in that ran for thirty-six hours. Representatives from the Student Non-violent Co-ordinating Committee, Students for a Democratic Society, the Young Socialist Alliance and CND all delivered lectures. Vietnam teach-ins also became popular on the other side of the Atlantic, with events at Oxford University and the Free University.[83]

The Derry radicals held another teach-in a week later – this time on the subject of unemployment. Melaugh again played a prominent role, but the jobless themselves also had the opportunity to speak during the seven-hour discussion. In a reference to the burning of draft cards by American activists, a couple of unemployed men made a miniature bonfire out of their signing-on cards.[84] Such enthusiasm encouraged the Derry radicals to resurrect the DUAC. The committee announced its return with a press statement denouncing the 'evil system' of capitalism and calling for 'a Workers' Council'. The DUAC hoped that the DCAC as a whole and the recently formed student action committee would support a mass teach-in on housing and unemployment.[85] Moderates, however, remained reluctant to involve themselves. Official DCAC participation was limited to the stewards, who blocked off a nearby loyalist counter-demonstration. Although the Derry radicals were left isolated, the teach-in was none the less a triumph. A crowd that varied in size from 200 to 500 people during the course of the afternoon listened to speeches on 'the struggle of the working classes'.[86]

After the proposed march of the city's unemployed was abandoned, the Derry radicals temporarily submitted to the DCAC's call for an end to marches that lacked its imprimatur. But the tensions between radicals and moderates continued to grow. When the DHAC picketed the Guildhall with placards calling for the Sanitary Officer to be dismissed, Hume's

Derry Housing Association issued a statement defending him.[87] Inside the Guildhall building, the Derry radicals were supporting the families squatting in protest against their housing plight. As time progressed, the squatting developed into a 'live-in': a permanent forum for the Derry radicals and their supporters.[88]

With the civil rights movement beginning to spread, the opportunity existed to take to another city's streets. The DHAC travelled to Armagh on 30 November 1968 to participate in the biggest civil rights march to be staged outside Derry.[89] Although the police retained their discipline, the loyalist counter-demonstrators provided the desired violence.[90] The radicals were waiting to escape the restraints imposed by the moderates and provoke similar trouble in Derry.

THE TAKEOVER

In the aftermath of the first march, the Nationalist leader left the Cabinet Secretary 'with the impression of being completely sick at heart'. McAteer told the prime ministerial aide that 'he had received absolutely nothing in return for securing the restraint and co- operation of the Nationalist Party'. He 'would now have to consider whether it was possible to continue on the present lines'.[91] Indeed, the pressure within Nationalism to abandon the policy of conciliation and adopt a civil disobedience strategy became irresistible.

Less than a fortnight later, the parliamentary party withdrew from its role as the Official Opposition.[92] At a special conference on 17 November 1968, 'non-violent civil disobedience' became party policy. A programme of 'minimum immediate demands' that endorsed the civil rights agenda was also agreed.[93] No agreement, however, was reached on how the new approach should be implemented: the initiative was left to the constituency parties. This compromise solution failed to address any of the problems facing the party. The Unionists were further antagonised, the divisions within Nationalism continued to deepen, and civil rights activists remained at the head of the movement.[94]

McAteer was beleaguered – but he was still the Catholic community's political leader and Derry's representative at Stormont. These offices granted him access to policy makers in London, Dublin, and Belfast. His strategy of fighting at 'the conference table instead of the barricades' had the potential to deliver better results than the DCAC's tactics. By the time the committee members presented their initial demands, McAteer had already informed O'Neill through go-betweens that a crash housing programme would probably end the street protests.[95] On 15 October 1968, the Leader of the Opposition took his concerns directly to the Prime Minister.[96] McAteer later admitted to the British government that this had been another disappointing meeting. O'Neill had conceded that McAteer's arguments were logical, yet he had stressed that his options were limited to what he could convince the Cabinet to accept.[97] The Nationalist leader recognised that the reforms required to halt the slide towards communal violence would only come with pressure from London.[98]

McAteer carried this message south to Dublin, where he had a meeting on 9 October 1968 with the Fianna Fáil Prime Minister.[99] Politicians from the Republic, however, failed to give the Nationalist leader the backing that he wanted. Fine Gael and the Irish Labour Party used the Derry disturbances to help them win the referendum on electoral reform. They claimed that the city's gerrymander was a good argument for keeping the system of proportional representation.[100] The interests of the wider nation were repeatedly sacrificed for party political advantage. Fianna Fáil's Neil Blaney tried to demonstrate his republican credentials by criticising the silence surrounding the issue of partition. 'I do wish', complained McAteer, 'that Dublin would avail themselves of my advice before launching these cross-border rockets.'[101] London, though, was prepared to listen. The information passed on by McAteer in person and over the telephone helped shape British strategy.[102]

McAteer's willingness to 'go anywhere, at any time, [to] obtain a political remedy' was matched by a similar flexibility over political principles.[103] Nationalists as well as Unionists would have to compromise to halt the drift towards sectarian conflict. Addressing the Derry party a month after the city's first civil rights march, he called on his fellow Nationalists to 'open our minds to the hurricanes of change which beat upon us all'. 'If indeed the ugly discrimination era is nearing its end,' McAteer mused, 'would it be treasonable to work towards rule from Belfast rather than Dublin' and 'a sort of little United-Nations-type grouping of these islands'.[104] This speech attracted the interest of the civil servants at the Home Office, who briefed Lord Stonham to press McAteer for further details when the two men met on 14 November 1968.[105] The Nationalist leader confessed to the British that 'he did not see any virtue in, nor did he desire, a unified Ireland'.[106]

McAteer clarified his position in a speech at London's Irish Club: an end to partition remained the party's ultimate aim but the resolution of the problem lay in the far future. Nationalists, he told his audience, were embarked upon a 'long journey to the Promised Land of a United Ireland' and he intended to lead his tribe 'along the middle of the road'. By defusing the partition question, McAteer hoped to silence the 'noise of heavy political artillery' and ensure that the 'smaller sounds of common sense' could be heard. The two communities, with the co-operation of Westminster and the Dáil, could then agree upon an 'honourable peace in the North'.[107]

In the absence of a comprehensive reform package, McAteer's constituents increasingly came to regard him as weak. Hume's blend of moderation and assertiveness was proving more attractive – but equally unsuccessful. As the seventh week of the Derry movement began, the reforms secured from Unionism were minimal. At a special meeting of Londonderry Corporation, a series of Nationalist motions on housing were passed unanimously. A fairer points system was introduced; responsibility for allocations was given to a representative committee; existing building projects were accelerated; and a detailed timetable for completion was agreed. The Unionist councillors, however, rejected a proposal to revise the ward boundaries.[108] Stormont seemed even more obstinate. It had failed to introduce any of the reforms demanded by the civil rights movement. Without a political settlement, the DCAC's main achievement – keeping order in the city – was ephemeral. As McAteer later observed, the indications were that all Hume and his allies would secure would be the 'efficient takeover of the work which has been carried on for many years by us'.[109]

DERRY AT THE CROSSROADS

The Derry movement, according to Paddy Doherty, 'lost its way, not in one afternoon, but over a number of weeks'. By the time the DCAC brought an end to the spontaneous marches, the 'marshals' role as peacekeepers was often ignored by the police and their stock had fallen among a section of the protesters'.[110] The moderate committee members were on the verge of complete exhaustion.[111] The constant succession of meetings, demonstrations, and media interviews were more demanding for men who had families and jobs than for radicals who lacked these responsibilities. Hume's wife was in the ninth month of her pregnancy, so his personal life was even more stressful than his political work.[112] The moderates were hoping that Stormont would soon grant serious concessions and give them the chance to bring the crisis to a peaceful resolution. Without the reforms that would enable them to claim victory, Hume and his allies would be cast aside by the movement that had swept them to prominence.

CHAPTER SEVEN

The Unionist Reaction

LYING IN PIECES IN THE GUTTER

On the evening of 5 October 1968, Terence O'Neill left Northern Ireland to attend an Ulster Week in the English Midlands. When he arrived at Leicester Town Hall, student radicals greeted the Unionist leader with catcalls. During the subsequent press conference, a female student mingled with the journalists and asked them to sign her petition. It read: 'We protest in the strongest possible terms at the oppression of the minorities in Northern Ireland and the use of religion to frustrate and castrate any opposition to the Unionist Party and the social forces that it represents.'[1]

Ulster Weeks exemplified O'Neillism, presenting a positive image of Northern Ireland and promoting the economic growth that was the basis for improving community relations. On this occasion, however, the media were interested in the Prime Minister's opinion of the violent scenes in Derry that weekend, not in Northern Irish goods. To quote O'Neill's autobiography, his policy was 'lying in pieces in the gutter'.[2] O'Neill's closest adviser, Deputy Cabinet Secretary Ken Bloomfield, found him extremely pessimistic about the longer-term consequences. The Stormont premier told Bloomfield that Westminster would undoubtedly increase the pressure for reform.[3] Indeed, the Labour leadership – Harold Wilson and Jim Callaghan – decided as early as 7 October 1968 that the situation could not be allowed to continue.[4] O'Neill also correctly predicted that if he were to appease Westminster he would first have to confront Unionist hardliners.[5]

This initial fatalism was dispelled by Bloomfield and other members of the Prime Minister's inner circle. From the beginning of his premiership, O'Neill had preferred to make policy with trusted civil servants rather than with his difficult Cabinet colleagues. The presidential aides had long been pressing for O'Neill to adopt a more liberal line – and they now saw their chance. Bloomfield remembered that: 'O'Neill was at length somewhat reluctantly persuaded that the pressures now so openly bearing upon the Northern Ireland administration could at least give him a once-for-all opportunity to sweep aside political resistance and win acceptance of major reform.'[6] O'Neill had decided that if there were to be a revolution it would be better to make it than to suffer it.

SELLING REFORM

Appropriately for a policy conceived by Stormont's mandarins, the struggle to reform Northern Ireland began with a memorandum. In this document, O'Neill urged the Cabinet to recognise that media coverage of the march and its aftermath had 'dramatically altered [the] situation to our great disadvantage'. For years, it had appeared to Westminster that Northern Ireland was 'calm' and that 'slow but steady progress was underway'. Wilson, observed O'Neill, had therefore 'fobbed off' backbench pressure for action and concentrated instead upon his 'many other headaches'. This was an accurate assessment of the Labour government's attitude – Callaghan himself later admitted that the policy was to use O'Neill to introduce reform and not to get involved.[7] However, as the memorandum explained, Northern Ireland had now become 'a focus of world opinion' and Westminster would 'no longer be able to stand aloof'. Returning to one of the main themes of his premiership, O'Neill proceeded to outline the array of sanctions available to the British government. Northern Ireland's total dependence on the Exchequer left it vulnerable. Westminster could squeeze Stormont into submission without having to do 'something openly spectacular'. Even if the Cabinet chose to endure losing millions of pounds worth of subsidies, Westminster still had the legal power to change Northern Ireland's constitution. Anyway, the Prime Minister was convinced that 'a U.D.I. [unilateral declaration of independence] attitude [was] wholly absurd in view of Ulster's geographical, military, and economic position'.[8]

The internal political situation had also been transformed – but this was something that Unionists were slow to grasp. In the words of the memorandum, 'the first reaction of our people to the antics of anti-partition agitators ... and the abuse of the world's Press is to retreat into hard-line attitudes'. The Prime Minister attempted to dissuade his Cabinet colleagues from this course by urging them to recognise past injustices and the likelihood of future violence. He noted that the multiple vote at local government elections could be ended and extra funding for the Mater Hospital granted without threatening the Unionist position. O'Neill even raised the possibility of sacrificing the Unionist shrine of Londonderry to protect the party's hold over the whole of Northern Ireland. These ideas would not be popular with Protestants. The Prime Minister therefore wanted a united Cabinet to 'undertake together – every one of us – the difficult task of selling [reform] to our supporters and to the country'.[9]

As O'Neill had expected, his rivals remained unconvinced. During the weekend of violence in Derry, Brian Faulkner and Bill Craig had both signalled their determination to stand firm. Faulkner had told the press that the cause of civil rights was 'a very convenient banner for a republican faction to hoist aloft'.[10] When the Cabinet met on 8 October 1968 the two ministers also registered their preference for a crackdown rather than concessions.[11] O'Neill had stressed in his memorandum that his rivals had personal experience of the attitude taken by the Labour government.[12] Faulkner and Craig, however, had reached a different assessment from their visit to Downing Street in January 1967. They 'thought it unlikely that Mr. Wilson would proceed to any extreme course which would be wholly unacceptable to majority opinion in Northern Ireland'. Craig was convinced that Westminster lacked the legal authority to intervene – even though the Attorney-General repeatedly told him that this was nonsense. Craig again displayed a lack of guile by refusing even to consider the issue of electoral reform. The end of the rate-payers' franchise was one of the civil rights movement's key demands. But Craig wanted a decision on the issue postponed until the restructuring of local government currently under way was completed. Faulkner, the more seasoned intriguer, maintained that he had 'no dogmatic views on the franchise', but was not prepared to institute changes 'under a threat of duress'.[13]

Faulkner and Craig's intransigence ensured that more than three weeks after the first Derry march the Cabinet remained divided. While Stormont had dithered, the crisis had deepened. The state was withering away in Derry and Wilson had requested a meeting with the Unionist leadership. The *Belfast Telegraph* thundered that the

Cabinet at Stormont is failing the greatest test of statesmanship on the highest level that Northern Ireland has yet faced. Since Derry it has said nothing ... that has been calming, constructive, or even diplomatic. All the rest has been bugle-calls sounding the retreat to the old trenches. The reason is plain, but all are trying to hide it. The Government and the Parliamentary Party are divided: the Prime Minister, who was the first to foresee the very challenge that Ulster has now to meet, and has striven to avert it, is unable to give the command that is needed.[14]

O'Neill tried again to give the command that was needed a few days before the Downing Street summit. The Prime Minister pleaded with the Cabinet to agree to at least some 'definite commitments'. He wanted the Stormont delegation to 'go into the conference chamber with some weapons in our own hands'. O'Neill suggested that a minimum consensus could be reached on a number of points: Londonderry's Unionist Corporation should be replaced by an appointed development commission; the Londonderry Area Plan's house-building programme should be speeded up; a specific date for local government restructuring should be set; and legislation to abolish the company vote should be introduced.[15] The Cabinet consented to the commission, broadly agreed that the reshaped local authorities should be in place by 1971 and accepted that the company vote should be abandoned at some point in the future. With Faulkner unwilling to assent to anything that would give the appearance of a concession, these commitments were all that O'Neill could secure.[16]

A DANGEROUS CONFRONTATION

At Downing Street, on 4 November 1968, the reforms agreed by the Stormont Cabinet were not enough to soothe a wrathful Wilson. Indeed, the reception given to O'Neill, Faulkner and Craig by the British Prime Minister exceeded even their most pessimistic predictions. Wilson declared that 'my government cannot tolerate a situation in which the liberalising trend was being retarded rather than accelerated and if this were to arise we would feel compelled to propose a radical course involving the complete liquidation of all financial agreements with Northern Ireland'. In an unconscious echo of O'Neill's first memorandum, the Labour leader stressed that the 'United Kingdom Government did not need to get involved in a constitutional crisis in order to exert its will on Northern Ireland'. Nevertheless, Wilson also raised the possibility of a change in the constitutional relationship. He mentioned his perennial bugbear: the eleven Ulster Unionist MPs, who took the Conservative whip at Westminster and voted against his domestic agenda.[17]

As well as showing the stick to the stubborn Stormont ministers, the British Prime Minister also dangled the carrot in front of them. Wilson explained that he would prefer to deal with the situation informally, as 'over the past four years he and his Government had taken the line that a great deal of liberalisation had been accomplished under Captain O'Neill despite the agitation of pressure groups'. Reform by proxy could continue if Stormont introduced the changes demanded by Westminster. These were: to hold an independent inquiry into the Derry disturbances; to revise the Special Powers Act; to implement a points system for public housing allocations; to abolish the company vote; to introduce universal adult suffrage for local elections; and to appoint a parliamentary ombudsman.[18]

Instead of presenting a united front, the Stormont ministers each mounted their own defence of the Unionist government's record. O'Neill stressed that community relations had been steadily improving; that local authorities had been instructed to accelerate their house-building programmes; that the recent Education Act had increased funding to Catholic schools; and that the process of electoral reform was proceeding. 'The events in Londonderry', he said, 'were … tragic at a time when community relations were improving and when a major breakthrough was about to be achieved on the industrial front in North-West Ulster.' Faulkner highlighted the Ministry of Commerce's successes in creating jobs despite the problems of attracting companies to the West of the country. He warned the British that: 'Unionist members were … inclined to look askance at concessions to the minority which they tended to interpret as undermining the constitution.' Craig argued that the Special Powers Act needed to stay on the statute book because 'some disquieting news about IRA policy had come to light which gave grounds for thinking that a new campaign of violence might be mounted'. 'In the long term,' the Home Affairs Minister continued, 'it seemed likely that Communist philosophies would dominate IRA thinking and that … the organisation would involve itself in trade disputes, evictions, etc. using such incidents to create unrest.' Craig also maintained that the franchise issue had to be considered in conjunction with the on- going investigation into the restructuring of local government.[19]

These arguments were brushed aside by Wilson and Callaghan. They were particularly unimpressed by the claim that one-man-one-vote could not be immediately introduced. Wilson lectured the Unionists that the 'onus must rest on those resisting the universal franchise to prove their case and he had not heard anything today which convinced him of its merits'. The British Prime Minister's frustration became increasingly obvious as the meeting drew to a close. He declared himself 'fed up' with the Short and Harland aircraft factory, which had become little better than a 'soup-kitchen'. Wilson drew unfavourable comparisons between the officers of the Royal Ulster Constabulary (RUC) and the British bobby. He proudly pointed out that the Grosvenor Square marchers 'included some of the best anti-barricades people from Europe ... and they were very tough indeed'.[20] There would be no British '68 and the crisis-racked Labour government felt entitled to gloat over this rare success. As riots were erupting across the Continent, British officials had blocked a Council of Europe proposal for summit talks with the '68ers and gleefully accused their opposite numbers of suffering from a 'crisis of nerve'.[21]

When the Stormont Cabinet met three days after the Downing Street meeting, it was suitably chastened. The minutes record that 'it was generally accepted that these discussions had brought about a most serious situation, in which clearly there would have to be some concessions on the part of Northern Ireland if a dangerous confrontation with the United Kingdom Government was to be avoided'. Although O'Neill discounted the possibility that Wilson was 'bluffing', his rivals were not prepared to fold. The two men had travelled to London convinced that Wilson would not risk provoking a 'massive loyalist uprising' and nothing had happened at the latest Downing Street meeting to make them change their minds.[22] Faulkner was confident that even if Wilson did resort to financial sanctions the responsibility for the resulting economic difficulties would 'clearly rest' with Westminster. O'Neill countered that in such circumstances the 'Ulster people' would 'lay their indignation at the door of their own Government'. The Attorney-General and the Chief Whip advised their colleagues to accept the Prime Minister's reasoning. But Faulkner and Craig would only commit to 'changes which they believed to be justifiable in themselves'.[23] Faulkner felt that redoubling efforts to build houses and attract overseas investment would be enough to isolate the extremists. As he told a rally in Armagh, 'Discrimination, gerrymandering, civil rights, Irish unity, may be the stuff that martyrs are made of, but they will not put butter on bread or one penny in the pay packet.'[24] The Cabinet remained deadlocked.

THE PACKAGE DEAL

At the next Cabinet meeting, O'Neill and his supporters launched a more co-ordinated attack upon the resistance being mounted by Faulkner and Craig. The Prime Minister opened by outlining how, as he had predicted, the failure to agree a programme of 'realistic' reform had increased the likelihood of a Westminster intervention. 'Since the entire future of Northern Ireland was at stake,' he pleaded, 'the Government must face up to their responsibilities and be prepared to take the action which they knew to be necessary, however unpopular.' O'Neill left it to his allies to make the specific proposals. He was concerned that the opposition of his rivals was in part motivated by personal animosity.[25]

The Chief Whip suggested that the Cabinet should 'consider a "package deal"'. He argued it would be better to offer 'not a grudging instalment of reform but the maximum possible concessions compatible with their vital political interests'. James Chichester- Clark, the Agriculture Minister and a loyal supporter of O'Neill's policies, then proceeded to detail the reforms that he envisaged making up this package. These were: a commission to investigate grievances; the early abolition of the company vote; a commitment to reach an accommodation with the Mater Hospital; measures to ensure fair allocation of public housing; a democratic decision – either a referendum or a general election – on the local government franchise; and the appointment of an ombudsman.[26]

The debate on the proposed package stretched over six Cabinet meetings. With each passing day, the O'Neillite faction's position was strengthened by further evidence of the internal and external pressures for reform. On 19 November 1968, Wilson informed Stormont that if his government had 'to resort to introducing legislation at Westminster, it would be wrong to conclude that legislation would necessarily be limited to reform of the local government franchise'.[27] The next day, senior police officers told ministers about the problems the RUC was facing in Derry. They claimed that 'unless the heat could be taken out of events by political means, the law-and-order situation could get completely out of control'. The Home Affairs Minister had previously admitted that he disagreed with how Derry was being policed. So, the presence of Northern Ireland's top policemen in the Cabinet Rooms showed how sharply his influence was declining. Indeed, Craig's colleagues agreed to abolish the company vote, even though it contradicted his 'consistent public position that local government reform must precede any examination of the franchise'.[28]

Craig was not alone in resisting the immediate introduction of universal adult suffrage, however. He was supported by not only Faulkner but also Chichester-Clark. Like O'Neill, to whom he was distantly related, Chichester-Clark came from an Ascendancy family, was educated at Eton, served in the Irish Guards, and was wounded during the Second World War.[29] His sense of duty had spurred him to stand by O'Neill, yet it also prevented him from supporting one-man-one-vote in the absence of an 'electoral mandate'.[30] Ambition may have played a role as well. With the backbench broadly against the reform, Chichester-Clark was perhaps reluctant to incur the party's wrath.[31] Frontier Unionists were especially hostile because the end of the property franchise threatened the party's position in Counties Fermanagh, Tyrone, Armagh, and Londonderry. According to the analysis prepared for the Cabinet, Catholics not Protestants would make up the majority of the local electorate in Fermanagh and Tyrone. But, as the memorandum noted, gerrymandering would mean that Unionism would only lose Armagh Urban District.[32] The vehemence with which the reform and in particular its timing were opposed arguably owed more to symbolism than to electoral calculations. Viscount Brookeborough's son announced that he would 'resist it to the very end ... because it could lead to interference on a much wider scale'.[33]

On 21 November the Stormont ministers approved a five-point reform programme: local councils would be encouraged to adopt a points system for public housing allocations; an ombudsman would be appointed on the British model; the powers that breached the European Convention on Human Rights would be withdrawn when the situation permitted it; the Londonderry Area Plan would be implemented by a commission; and the company vote would be abolished. This was as much change as there was unanimous support for in the Cabinet; it was also as much change as was acceptable to the Orange Order. In accordance with the deal made in March 1967, a delegation from the Grand Lodge of Ireland was consulted before final decisions were made on important issues.[34] The failure to end the rate-payers' franchise appeased Unionist hard-liners. O'Neill, however, confessed to his colleagues that he 'wondered' whether a reform package without one-man-one-vote 'would be sufficient … to satisfy the United Kingdom Government or to restrain the Civil Rights marchers'.[35]

Wilson appeared to react to Stormont's disobedience as O'Neill's rivals had predicted: he did not intervene. The Northern Irish Cabinet was merely informed by the British Prime Minister that he was 'disappointed that you have not so far felt able to announce a policy of early introduction of universal adult suffrage'.[36] However, Faulkner and Craig had not successfully called Wilson's bluff. Instead, they had forced the British government into finally accepting intervention as a serious option. Following the Downing Street summit, the civil service drafted a policy memorandum for the Prime Minister. The document's stated intention was to 'outline a new departure in our dealings with the Northern Ireland Government'. The Representation of the People Bill that was passing through the House of Commons was identified as a possible vehicle for imposing one-man-one-vote on Stormont. The paper acknowledged that this would provoke a 'grave constitutional crisis'. It would probably lead to an 'administration more reactionary in tone' and thus the need for 'direct rule'. Nevertheless, 'the time has come when Westminster must declare its willingness to act in this way whatever the consequences may be'. It was hoped that the most likely consequence of this 'great pressure' would be to bring the Stormont Cabinet and the wider Unionist Party to 'the point of agreeing reform'.[37]

Indeed, British civil servants and ministers were desperate for reform by proxy to succeed – they had no desire to be sucked into the Irish bog. London was therefore disturbed to learn from the Nationalist Party that the region's senior naval officer had publicly declared that he would be 'pleased to assist in the maintenance of law-and-order'.[38] The Attorney-General reported back to Wilson that British forces could theoretically be brought onto the streets of Northern Ireland by the unilateral action of Stormont. But, he added, '[while] the common law recognises that it is as much the duty of soldiers as it is of private citizens to assist the civil authorities in the maintenance of the peace, [the proviso is] that the commander should consult higher authority if there is time to do so'.[39]

The Ministry of Defence subsequently instructed the commander of the units based in Northern Ireland to contact London before he took such a momentous decision.[40] Callaghan tried to get O'Neill to put out of his mind any thought of calling for military aid by warning that Westminster would attach stringent conditions.[41]

The French army had helped Charles de Gaulle, the Supreme Commander-in-Chief, restore order during the summer of 1968. As millions went on strike, thousands of soldiers ensured that essential public services were kept going. But the military did more than stop the state from melting away; it dramatically raised the stakes in the struggle for power. With parachute regiments massing in the Paris *banlieue* and the General muttering about Communist subversion, the Left was scared and the Right was stirred.[42] Captain O'Neill could not call upon an army of his own to save his regime.

O'Neill's assessment of how the civil rights movement would react to the absence of one-man-one-vote from the reform package proved completely accurate. The Derry Citizens' Action Committee (DCAC) issued a statement in which it complained about 'the total failure of the Government to tackle what is the central and crucial issue – democratic representation in this city'. 'We regard this as being the root cause of the present difficulties and unrest in this area,' the media were told, 'and we pledge ourselves to the continuance of the struggle until this is achieved.'[43] The DCAC's moderate leadership was actually anxious to bring the crisis to a peaceful resolution but this was not a settlement that it could sell to the rank-and-file of the Derry movement. The other principal organiser of marches and protests was the radical student movement People's Democracy. It greeted the five points by publicly announcing that the movement's 'resources of pressure' had not been put into 'cold storage'.[44]

The failure to satisfy the two dominant civil rights groups meant that the movement continued to grow – spreading beyond the confines of Belfast and Derry. The first major demonstration after the reform programme took place in Armagh on 30 November. Loyalists were determined to prevent civil rights activists making 'Armagh another Londonderry' – to quote the posters that had been pasted up across the city. Ian Paisley had threatened to take 'appropriate' action if the local police decided not to stop the march. As the proposed route was that traditionally taken by Nationalist parades, the RUC saw no reason to impose a ban. Paisley responded by leading a hundred-strong band of armed loyalists into the city centre during the early hours of the morning. This illegal counter-demonstration eventually swelled to over ten times its original size. Despite repeated calls from the police to disperse, the loyalists held their ground. The RUC succeeded in avoiding a violent confrontation by persuading the leaders of the civil rights march to halt before they reached the Paisleyites. The 5,000 marchers stopped to listen to speeches from Michael Farrell and Ivan Cooper out of sight of the counter-demonstration. However, as the two sets of protesters began to head home, trouble flared. A stone-throwing crowd attacked two busloads of loyalists, sparking a minor riot. Before the incident could develop into a more serious disturbance, a police baton charge scattered the two sides.[45]

A week later, an 'extremely tired and depressed' O'Neill had a 'long talk' with the British Ambassador to Dublin. 'He repeated several times that five-and-a-half-years work had been ruined over night.' As O'Neill had feared, his rivals in the Cabinet had shown themselves 'inflexible' 'when asked to consider a programme of reform and pacification'. 'It seemed likely that within seven days, unless he could achieve a miracle, of which he no longer felt at all confident, the present Government of Northern Ireland would break up, with unforeseeable consequences.'[46]

The shock of '68 sent many other Western leaders into the depths of despair. De Gaulle and his family fled from France at the end of May 1968. When the presidential party reached Baden-Baden, the Commander-in-Chief of French forces in West Germany helped the General to regain his nerve. He returned to save France for the last time. De Gaulle confessed soon afterwards that his plan had been to go into exile in 'Ireland, the country of my maternal ancestors'. His troubles would have followed him into retirement.[47]

CROSSROADS

All the region's newspapers condemned the loyalist counter-demonstration in Armagh. The *Belfast Telegraph* branded 30 November 1968 'one of the blackest days in Northern Ireland's history'. The *Irish News* claimed that 'it will be a long time before the disgust and anger felt by the majority of people are erased'.[48] Further and more violent clashes between protesters and counter- demonstrators seemed likely. Armagh even succeeded in making the Northern Ireland Civil Rights Association (NICRA) more militant. 'We will march again,' NICRA proclaimed the next day, 'and not only in Armagh, but in every other town in Northern Ireland until our demands are met'.[49]

With the region on the verge of sliding back into sectarian conflict, the middle ground suddenly strengthened. The fiercely Unionist *Belfast Newsletter* observed that 'the vast majority of the people, of all the people, have had more than enough of civil strife and violence not far removed from anarchy in their streets'.[50] A *Belfast Telegraph* survey of the Unionist grassroots conducted at this time similarly concluded that 'if the Prime Minister is seen to be taking a firm stand and restoring the peace effectively many of the party faithful who have been hovering in the wings will rally to his banner'.[51]

O'Neill was receiving encouragement from across the communal divide to appeal to this supposed moderate majority for support. The *Belfast Telegraph*, which was more O'Neillite than O'Neill, had long been trying to establish a consensus of the centre.[52] In the aftermath of the initial Derry disturbances, the editorial claimed that accelerating the pace of reform would isolate the extremists. 'Otherwise Northern Ireland will be faced with more disturbance, followed by intervention by Westminster, and a new polarisation of Protestant and Roman Catholic.'[53] The *Belfast Telegraph*'s coverage adhered to this line throughout October and November.[54] Jack Sayers, the editor of the newspaper, was among a group of Protestant and Roman Catholic clergy and laymen who wrote to Cabinet Secretary Harold Black in late November. They 'pledged' themselves to 'what action they can take in the present crisis in community relations'.[55] The Presbyterian Church's Government Committee had a month before made known its 'appreciation of the rather lonely and difficult position' occupied by O'Neill.[56] Presbyterian ministers also operated as go-betweens for the presidential aides and the Nationalist leader. Through this and other informal channels, Eddie McAteer conveyed his party's 'willingness to contribute towards a lowering of the temperature'.[57]

Six months earlier, de Gaulle had faced a similar situation: a country apparently on the brink of violent upheaval and growing support for a restoration of order. The General had responded by addressing the nation on radio as he had from exile after the fall of France in June 1940. At a time when everything seemed to be in flux, the successful manipulation of the spoken word became an important source of power. De Gaulle blended fear with hope to create a potent message. He was confident that 'Progress, peace, and independence will triumph along with liberty', but he warned that 'the power that imposed itself at a time of national despair ... would be that of totalitarian Communism'.[58] Although its impact has been exaggerated, the 30 May 1968 broadcast marked the beginning of the Fifth Republic's revival.[59]

***

With the French example in mind, Northern Ireland's papier-mâché de Gaulle opted to make a televised presidential address on 9 December 1968. The script for this political drama was written by Bloomfield. The Deputy Cabinet Secretary had worked obsessively upon the text until the very last moment – dictating the script himself to the BBC staff who prepared the primitive autocue.[60] Another of O'Neill's aides later complained that he 'used to write in a particularly Churchillian manner for Terence's speeches'.[61] Winston Churchill's elevated rhetoric, which had seemed out of date in the 1930s, sounded timeless during the Second World War.[62] With Northern Ireland in crisis, O'Neill's mock-Churchillian style matched the level of events.

The so-called 'Crossroads' speech began with a question. Northern Ireland's Prime Minister asked his audience whether they wanted 'a happy and respected Province [or] a place torn apart by riots'. The text embraced the *Belfast Telegraph* line that the moderate majority had mostly been silent since the first Derry march.[63] O'Neill explained that matters were 'far too serious to be determined behind closed doors' or 'left to noisy minorities'. It was 'time ... for the people as a whole to speak in a clear voice'. Although O'Neill was reaching over the heads of political activists in some parts of the speech, in others he was speaking directly to civil rights protesters, loyalists, and Unionists.[64] The Prime Minister requested the first group to 'call [the] people off the streets and allow an atmosphere favourable to change to develop'. O'Neill had harsher words for the loyalists. He denounced them as 'disloyalists': 'disloyal to Britain, disloyal to the Constitution, disloyal to the Crown'. The majority of the broadcast resembled speeches he had previously given at Unionist meetings. The leader again told his party that dependence upon Britain meant that reform was inevitable. The only choice they had was whether it would be introduced by Stormont or by Westminster.[65] The *Sunday Telegraph*'s review of the performance praised the 'Prime Minister's show of near-Gaullist strength'.[66]

O'Neill's presidential appeal was followed by another Gaullist strategy: a plebiscite.[67] He had ended his address by calling upon the people to 'make your voice heard in whatever way you think best, so that we may know the views not of the few but of the many'.[68] They did. The *Belfast Telegraph* was the driving force behind the unofficial referendum on the Prime Minister and his policies. In the following day's editions, the newspaper printed coupons for its readers to sign that stated: 'I approve of Captain O'Neill's broadcast and support his efforts to heal the divisions in the community.'[69] Over 75,000 of these coupons were sent off and in total the Prime Minister received almost 150,000 messages of support in the week after his broadcast.[70] In the evening after de Gaulle's speech, more than 500,000 people gathered in the Place de la Concorde to chant 'Clean out the Sorbonne!', 'Down with the Communists!', and 'De Gaulle is not alone!' In France, the party of order had won.[71] In Northern Ireland, it now had a chance of victory.

On 13 December 1968, O'Neill praised the *Belfast Telegraph* for finding such 'a splendid way' 'to hear the voice of the people'. He also asked 'those who have made their voice known to continue to make their presence felt ... by getting involved in politics'.[72] The next day Unionist headquarters reported a huge number of applications from people wishing to join the party. The Party Secretary told the *Belfast Telegraph* that: 'Many business and professional people are now wanting to take an active part in supporting the Prime Minister from within the Party.'[73] The minority population was not as enthusiastic, but on the whole it was nonetheless prepared to offer O'Neill the breathing space he desired. The staff of Derry's Christian Brothers school sent a telegram to the Stormont premier conveying their support for his five-point reform package and the sentiments expressed in his speech. 'We believe, however, that this can only be the first step towards the granting of full civil rights.'[74]

With public opinion rallying behind him, O'Neill began to move against his internal opponents. The gambit of a televised appeal to the country was partly a reaction to Craig making an obvious bid for the leadership.[75] The Home Affairs Minister had delivered a series of speeches in which he presented himself as the defender of Ulster against the Republicans on the streets and the Labour Government at Westminster.[76] Craig told the Ulster Hall on 27 November that the 'traditional enemy' was exploiting the situation; that the minority population had not been denied basic human rights; that reform was unnecessary; that Catholic countries had a 'lower standard of democracy'; and that British 'interference' would be met with 'resolve'.[77] O'Neill publicly criticised the speech's 'tone' and made a reference to the Minister being under 'considerable strain'. Craig retaliated by repeating it word-for-word at his next speaking engagement.[78] The *Belfast Telegraph* – a newspaper that Craig believed had to be read 'with a big salt-cellar at your elbow' – commented that the 'hour of decision is at hand' for the power struggle.[79] Following the Prime Minister's television broadcast, Craig forcefully restated his own position.[80] This proved to be a fatal miscalculation.

Almost every party meeting since the first Derry march had passed a resolution backing Craig. But O'Neill was more popular with Unionist voters.[81] On 11 December 1968, the Prime Minister spent some of his newly acquired political capital: Craig was relieved of Cabinet office for harbouring ideas of a 'U.D.I. nature'.[82] O'Neill was in a triumphant mood after weeks of depression when Callaghan telephoned the next day to congratulate him. The Home Secretary, who was making the telephone call from his sick-bed, praised the Northern Irish Prime Minister's 'splendid' tactics. Callaghan was jubilant. The British government's continued commitment to the reform-by-proxy strategy seemed to have been justified. The Home Secretary also sent O'Neill his best wishes for the meeting of the parliamentary party. The experienced Labour politician reassured the Unionist leader that all parties had trouble with 'extremists'. He said that they 'tended to make the most noise even though they did not represent the bulk of the Party'.[83] In the aftermath of Craig being removed from office, however, O'Neill's other critics seem to have been reluctant to make much noise at the meeting. Faulkner merely questioned whether the television appearance had been necessary. The meeting was asked to endorse O'Neill's position as leader of both the party and the country. Twenty-eight MPs voted for the motion, none opposed it, only four abstained, and Craig walked out before the count.[84] A long-time opponent of O'Neill told a British journalist that: 'If you say a word against him now, people look at you as if you're attacking Christ on the Cross.'[85]

The principal civil rights groups also found themselves outmanoeuvred by O'Neill. Bowing to the popular mood, NICRA, the DCAC, and the People's Democracy submitted to the Prime Minister's request to suspend their street protests.[86] Civil rights marches and loyalist counter-demonstrations had been bringing law and order into contempt for both communities. Catholics believed that the Home Affairs Minister and the police were siding with the loyalists. Unionists felt that the RUC was caving in to the Republican movement. The temporary truce helped to replace the dynamic of polarisation that had been driving developments with one of moderation. O'Neill's success in halting marches where Craig had failed enabled him to sack the Minister with impunity. This served to further strengthen the centre ground and weaken extremism. Craig's departure from the Cabinet removed one of the major obstacles To Securing a peaceful resolution of the crisis. All that was left to do was to settle the issue of one-man-one-vote.[87]

O'Neill appears to have been planning to make another attempt to convince his party to concede universal adult suffrage at once. In his television broadcast, he had played down the significance of the reform by highlighting how Unionism would not lose a single seat at Stormont by accepting the change.[88] The *Belfast Telegraph* survey of the Unionist grassroots had found that the rank-and-file were largely ignorant of this fact. Their leader wanted to reassure them that Unionism was not conceding ground to its enemies. Three days later, in his statement on the unofficial plebiscite, O'Neill claimed that he had received 'new strength [to] pursue the path of reform [to] absolute victory'.[89] The Prime Minister had been granted a renewed mandate and the main opponent of one-man-one-vote was no longer in the Cabinet; Stormont seemed close to agreeing to what had become the central demand of both the civil rights movement and Westminster. Success, however, depended upon how long the uneasy peace on Northern Ireland's streets could last. 'O'Neill has not saved Ulster,' the *Observer* concluded, 'he has merely given her a breathing space'[90] – something the leftists wanted to take away.

CHAPTER EIGHT

People's Democracy

CAMPUS POLITICS

At Queen's University Belfast, a dress rehearsal of the events of 1968 had been staged in 1967. In the spring of that year, Bill Craig banned Northern Ireland's Republican Clubs. 'I am in no doubt', he told the press, 'that the clubs are a front organisation of the IRA [Irish Republican Army].'[1] This slowly stirred the student body out of its usual apathy. Although only a handful of Republicans were at the university, about sixty students decided to set up a club on 8 March 1967. In a further gesture of defiance against Craig's ban, the club applied to the Student Representative Council for official recognition. On 11 March 1967, the Young Socialists joined the protest and paraded through Belfast chanting 'Tories out – North and South', 'Craig must go', and 'No fascist laws – No fascist bans'. With a turnout of just eighty people, the march was disappointingly small. Eamonn McCann's *Irish Militant*, however, confidently predicted that 'the conflict between [the Academic Council] and the students will grow more acute in the near future'.[2]

In May 1967, the Republican Club was recognised as a university society by the Student Representative Council – but this ruling had to be ratified by the Academic Council. Acting on legal advice, the council announced in November 1967 that it had chosen to exercise its veto. As had happened in Berkeley and Berlin, Belfast's students were provoked into taking action by this decision to restrict freedom of expression. All the political societies except the Conservative and Unionist Association came together to co-ordinate the protest. The Joint Action Committee against the Suppression of Liberties (JAC) arranged a march on the Unionist Party's headquarters – although the inevitable loyalist counter-demonstration forced it to find an alternative route. So, on 15 November 1967, almost 2,000 people marched instead to Craig's house to protest against his ban.[3]

This huge demonstration was the high point of the campaign. After the march, it shrunk back to being something that only interested a small number of activists. Rory McShane, who had recently left the Irish Workers' Group (IWG), had an emergency resolution passed at the annual conference of the National Union of Students in April 1968.[4] A large majority condemned the harassment of students belonging to the Republican Club as 'worthy of the fascist Franco regime'. During the same month, the Republican Club organised a symposium in Belfast on 'The Special Powers Act and International Human Rights Year'. When the Chair of the National Council for Civil Liberties was giving his speech, police officers burst into the hall and asked everyone to leave as they had received a bomb threat.[5] This excitement, however, failed to revive the moribund campaign.

The Republican Club ban was just one of the many issues that leftists hoped would act as a 'bridge to involvement' for the university's 'coffee cup socialists'.[6] It was, however, a better failure than most of the others. As Michael Farrell later recalled, the leftists 'could never muster more than a dozen for an anti-apartheid picket or 50 for a CND march'.[7] As in universities throughout Western Europe, there were many more conservative students than student radicals at Queen's. The British journalists who descended upon Belfast in the autumn of 1968 found that 'the student body for the most part wear their hair short, their clothes square, and their views to match'.[8]

But Queen's University was nevertheless the place in Northern Ireland where sectarianism was weakest and progressive ideas strongest.[9] When C. Desmond Greaves visited in 1962, he met 'a member of the Tory Club (they don't call it Unionist since that sounds "too extremist") whose name was O'Kelly, believed a United Ireland was inevitable, but hoped it would be loyal to Britain, [and] wished that Lord Brookeborough would adopt the "Liberal Conservatism" of Mr R.A. Butler'. He was also surprised to discover that one-fifth of the membership of the New Ireland Society were Protestant. Greaves left Queen's with the impression that the university could 'form the centre of the strongest movement since the United Irishmen'.[10]

The Connolly Association's rival, the IWG, also recognised that Queen's University had potential and included it in the group's 'field of action'.[11] A branch was formed at Queen's – although only a tiny fraction of the university's 5,000 or so students joined it. The half-a-dozen members of the IWG also belonged to the Queen's University Labour Group.[12] Entryism was a classic Trotskyist strategy. In Britain, the student wing of the Labour Party, the Young Socialists, had been infiltrated by the Trotskyist Socialist Labour League. Some members of this group had been involved in the Connolly Association's rebel north London branch during the 1950s.[13] Once again, they fell foul of the parent organisation. In 1964, the Labour Party followed in the footsteps of West Germany's Social Democrats and abandoned its youth arm for being too radical.[14] Similar concerns led the Northern Ireland Labour Party (NILP) to reorganise its Young Socialist branches at the same time. The new body, however, was soon being infiltrated by IWG members. The speaker at the first major meeting of the South Belfast federation was John Palmer of the Trotskyist International Socialists. 'Talking on "The Crisis of the Labour Government",' the *Irish Militant* reported, 'Comrade Palmer stressed the link between the Government's imperialist foreign and defence policy and its anti-working-class domestic policy.' The newspaper praised the South Belfast federation for being 'the most active and politically developed branch'.[15]

By the end of 1967, Farrell, McCann, and their close comrades had become frustrated with the gradualist approach that the IWG's senior leadership advocated. Géry Lawless, in turn, criticised their belief that they could 'by-pass the struggle against British imperialism in Ireland' as an 'ultra-left ... impetuous mistake'.[16] Northern Ireland's leftists had decided to strike out on their own. When Farrell and Cyril Toman returned from post-graduate study in Britain, they founded their own political group. They named it the Young Socialist Alliance after the American group that had given Farrell many of his ideas. The alliance brought together radicals from the Young Socialists, Gerry Fitt's Republican Labour Party, and the National Democrats, as well as some independent socialists.[17] The emphasis was on practical politics rather than theoretical argument. As Farrell later admitted, he was 'never that clued up a Trotskyite'.[18] Similarly, a leading figure in the Jeunesse Communiste Révolutionnaire later claimed that it was 'more Guevarist than Trotskyist'.[19] Like the leftists on the continent, the Young Socialist Alliance therefore spent most of 1968 trying to provoke the police. Success finally came in the autumn – when the Belfast radicals helped their Derry counterparts spark an overreaction in the second city.[20] 'The events of 5th October', concluded the independent commission of inquiry, 'gave this group the opportunity to achieve major support at Queen's University.'[21]

STUDENT POWER

On the evening of 5 October 1968, Kevin Boyle was lying in bed listening to the radio. It was just over two years since he had taken up a lectureship at Queen's University. Boyle had turned down the chance to go to America as he 'really wanted to change things' in his homeland. Since his return, Boyle had campaigned for abortion to be legalised, joined the Homosexual Law Reform Society, supported the Republican Club protest, and attended the launch of the Northern Ireland Civil Rights Association (NICRA). But he had not take part in the Derry civil rights march – only a few hundred people had. However, he was aware that it had been taking place. When the music show on the radio was interrupted by an interview with Craig, Boyle therefore immediately realised that something 'serious' had happened.[22]

Another lecturer at Queen's, Seamus Heaney, noticed around the university 'embarrassed, indignant young Ulstermen and women whose deep-grained conservatism of behaviour was outweighed by a reluctant recognition of injustice'.[23] On 7 October 1968, some of these young men and women gathered in the student union to discuss how they should respond. The meeting decided to resurrect the JAC and organise a demonstration. An estimated 1,500 to 3,000 students assembled two days later to march on Belfast City Hall. The Royal Ulster Constabulary (RUC), however, wanted them to follow a different way to the centre. The students went as far as to fetch Boyle from his office to help them negotiate with the police, but they had little choice other than to submit to the diversion. Shortly after the march set off along this alternative route, the RUC had to bring it to a halt as loyalists were counter-demonstrating further down the road. Northern Ireland's police force yet again found itself standing between rival protesters. Except that on this occasion the marchers did something that the RUC officers were not expecting. Instead of trying to break through the police lines, the marchers staged a sit-down protest. As Boyle later recalled, they 'sat down because that is what students did. They had seen it happening around the world.' Deferring once more to their lecturer, the students invited Boyle to address the protest. The photograph of Boyle standing with his back to a crowd of puzzled policemen has taken on iconic status. The image also shows a man that Boyle remembered as a 'classic 1960s English anarchist' taunting the officers. The overwhelming majority of the students, though, wanted to avoid a violent confrontation and the sit-down protest passed off peacefully.[24]

On their return to Queen's, the frustrated marchers crowded into the university's MacMordie Hall to discuss the day's events. As the students struggled to hold a debate in chairs more suited to watching a film, Boyle headed back to his flat. He thought that what was happening was 'stimulating, exciting, and important', but ultimately 'a student thing'. 'I lay down in bed,' he later recalled, 'and started thinking, "No, you should be there, go back, you should get involved". I got up, got dressed, and got involved.'[25] The meeting decided to establish a permanent protest group to press for social and political change. Boyle made the 'existential choice' to stand for election to this new group's 'Faceless Committee'. By having a committee composed of people who had previously steered clear of politics and by making them delegates not representatives, the mass of the assembly had hoped to stop the experienced activists from taking over the movement. Boyle, however, was joined on the committee by members of the left-wing cliques and the university's political societies as well as by 'innocents'.[26] He also noticed that Farrell was present at the meeting.[27]

Farrell later recalled that during his time as a student Queen's University 'had been one of the most docile campuses in Western Europe'.[28] This was no longer the case. As the university's newspaper proclaimed, 'Student Power had come to Belfast'.[29] There was nothing unusual about this spectacular turnaround. Even as late as the start of spring 1968, only around 1 per cent of students attending the University of Paris at Nanterre were activists.[30] But, as Daniel Cohn-Bendit recalled, 'a minority of students' taking 'conscious advantage of their freedom to attack the established order' could become 'a catalyst activating a larger section of the student population'.[31] Nanterre's radicals had been forced to resort to extreme methods in an effort to provoke the liberal administration. In March 1968, four students were arrested for showing their solidarity with the guerrilla fighters of Vietnam by smashing the windows of the American Express offices. The different leftist groups chose to protest against this overreaction by occupying the administration building. This was the beginning of the 22 March movement – the name was a reference to Fidel Castro's 26 July movement.[32] The radicals set out to disrupt the normal workings of the university, but ultimately they brought the city to a standstill. Within the space of a few months, the cycle of provocation and repression initiated at Nanterre had brought tens of thousands of students onto the streets of Paris.

The anonymous, overcrowded, concrete and unfinished buildings of Nanterre were surrounded by *bidonvilles* into which were crammed thousands of North African immigrants. In the English Midlands, the University of Birmingham's mix of red-brick Victorian buildings and modernist architecture was set within hundreds of acres of parkland in the city's genteel Edgbaston ward. These contrasting campuses nevertheless experienced similar patterns of protest. In a report by the Registrar for the British government, the trouble at Birmingham was blamed upon a 'group of about fifty to one hundred students'. They derived their 'extremist attitudes ... from a knowledge of earlier student revolts in some French, German, American, and British Universities'. One member of the group had first-hand knowledge, having 'played a prominent part' in the London School of Economics (LSE) occupations. On Wednesday 27 November 1968, the extremists staged a sit-in inside the main building to protest against the lack of reform at the university. The following day, 'about 1,000 students' joined them. General assemblies were held and a 'Committee of Ten' was elected to co-ordinate the occupation. By the weekend, sophisticated metropolitans had become interested in what was happening in the provinces. The leader of the LSE movement arrived to praise the thousands of 'comrade students' for shutting down their university.[33]

Assembly meetings in Queen's University Belfast – no less than in Birmingham, the Paris *banlieue*, Berkeley and Berlin – served as a school of revolt. A National Democratic politician who attended a few of these meetings found: 'Enthusiasm was high, commitment was strong, and idealism pervasive.'[34] Intoxicated by this experience, many participants found themselves being swept in previously unimaginable directions. One undergraduate, Bernadette Devlin, later recalled that she and some of the other students 'educated ourselves into socialism'. This group found that 'the most effective solutions to the problems we discussed always turned out to be the solutions offered by the left'.[35] Throughout the Western world, new converts to the broad church of the New Left had not needed to study its sacred texts. The *Observer's* Berlin correspondent profiled a student radical who, 'Without reading the works of Marx and Marcuse', 'has come to the same conclusions as them'.[36] A large percentage of the protesters on the streets of Paris and London in 1968 subscribed to the basic principles of the global revolt. When *New Society* polled people at the second Grosvenor Square march, three-quarters of the respondents said they were against American imperialism, capitalism, and 'the general structure of present day British society'.[37] The central theme running through interviews conducted three decades later with participants in the May events was that '68 was an international struggle for a fairer political, social, and economic order.[38]

Northern Ireland's leading leftists taught at the school of revolt. Farrell drafted political programmes and press releases, Toman chaired debates and McCann gave a series of speeches at the university.[39] The Belfast branch of the Revolutionary Socialist Students' Federation (RSSF) was also represented on the faculty.[40] The group's news-sheet, *Defamator*, preached the same message as their 'comrades in France'. An issue from early December echoed Nanterre's radicals in claiming that 'relations of domination … are made apparent only when the bureaucracy is provoked into showing its true dictatorial nature'.[41] In keeping with this belief, the RSSF regularly tried to spark a reaction from the authorities. When Terence O'Neill visited Queen's on 13 November 1968, RSSF members chanted slogans and clashed with Special Branch detectives.[42]

Farrell and the RSSF both set out to educate the movement about the ways in which the problems facing Queen's students, police brutality in Derry and American imperialism were all connected to each other.[43] The strategy of showing the 'path from the examination room to the paddy fields of Vietnam' – to quote a British pamphlet in Boyle's possession – was one followed by many New Left groups.[44] The Columbia branch of Students for a Democratic Society (SDS) had exposed the close links that existed between the university and the military.[45] Similarly, the RSSF repeatedly alleged that the biochemistry department at Queen's was receiving funding from Porton Down and the CIA.[46] The Vice-Chancellor was so shaken by the rumours that he went as far as to reassure the annual meeting of graduates that 'we do not have any secret defence projects'.[47]

Although the RSSF won a few converts, a significant section of the student population remained hostile. One undergraduate wrote to the

Belfast Telegraph on behalf of the 'majority' to condemn the movement as 'a very small minority'.[48] *Defamator* replied to their criticism with a spoof letter from the 'decent hardworking subservient snivellers' on the role of the university: 'When we have been fed enough stuff for three or four years we regurgitate it to demonstrate our super memories and receive ... gaily coloured bits of paper. This is our admission ticket to our parents' grown-up world of Business and Politics. We can then tell all the less intelligent people e.g. workers what to do for their own good.'[49] Students were now 'suffer[ing] similar forms of alienation and lack of control' to those endured by the 'working classes'.[50] What had once been a community of scholars had become nothing more than a knowledge factory. In November 1967, the West German philosopher and sociologist Jürgen Habermas told an American audience that this was also one of the main criticisms levelled by the Federal Republic's student radicals against their universities.[51]

The problems facing students varied greatly across the Western world, but there were some common complaints. The RSSF was not alone in demanding greater freedom of expression, equal representation for students on governing bodies, the end of the concept of *in loco parentis*, and cheaper accommodation.[52] This was, though, only a 'transitional reform programme'. Echoing the American SDS's slogan 'A free university in a free society', the RSSF maintained that 'there cannot be a free university without a free society'.[53] As Habermas observed, the 'target' was not 'the university as such'.[54]

The students at Queen's, however, did not need to address their own problems before moving on to what was wrong with the world outside the walls of the academy. They were pushed out of apathy by the moral shock of what happened in Derry on 5 October 1968. In this way, the Queen's movement bore a closer resemblance to American student activism at the time of the sit-in protests than to the nine-day occupation of Birmingham University in late 1968. For a few short months, moments from across the 'long '68' were restaged in and out of their original order. The independent Algerian state was already in its seventh year, yet a recurring debate at Queen's was whether or not this colonial struggle had implications for Northern Ireland. Farrell argued that Protestants were the region's *pieds-noirs* – the settler population that had fled to France in their hundreds of thousands.[55] Farrell and the other leftists were plugged into the transnational networks of rebellion and had undergone a vicarious radicalisation. By contrast, the new activists were more like the Mississippi Freedom Summer volunteers at the beginning of that project than members of The Resistance after August 1968's 'Siege of Chicago'. Indeed, people at Queen's were even reading Camus and discussing non-violent direct action in the assemblies.[56] The liberal *Belfast Telegraph* had no doubt that most of the students could be classed as 'militant moderates'.[57] The newspaper shied away from their tactics, while sympathising with their agreed goals: one-man-one-vote, an end to gerrymandering, jobs to be appointed on merit, a points system for the allocation of public housing, the repeal of draconian public order legislation, the passage of the Liberal Party's Human Rights Bill and an impartial enquiry into events in Derry.[58] But some of these militants – the star pupils at the school of revolt – were starting to cast off this moderate stance. As happened to a number of the Mississippi Freedom Summer volunteers, a desire for reform gave way to dreams of revolution. For America's leading activists, this was a gradual transformation – a process of adapting to changing circumstances over the course of several years. In Northern Ireland, a similar shift occurred within a much shorter space of time as a few militants like Bernadette Devlin sprinted to catch up with the leftists.[59]

For the overwhelming majority of students who took part in the protests, the movement was not a way into radical politics but a way of enjoying themselves. 'A lot of it was just fun,' Boyle later remembered, 'and there were a lot of courtships.'[60] Mary Holland, the *Observer*'s elegant yet passionate Northern Irish correspondent, was delighted to discover that the undergraduates at Queen's shared her own wicked sense of humour. At one of the first assembly meetings, she heard a 'handsome bearded boy' suggest that, 'as they had been infiltrated by subversives, they might change the name of the university civil rights movement'. He proposed that they should 'call themselves the Civil Rights Action Infiltrated Group and "when we march we will just use the initials"'. The students got the joke immediately and began to shout out possible slogans: 'C.R.A.I.G. Says One-Man-One-Vote', 'C.R.A.I.G. Says End Gerrymandering', and 'C.R.A.I.G. Says Craig Must Go'.[61] The Queen's movement eventually opted to take the more serious name of People's Democracy.[62] This did not, however, mark a move away from the playfulness of the early protests. An agenda paper on 'Future Action' circulated in November suggested the '"Irrigation" of Mr Craig's garden' as well as a 'march in Trafalgar Square' and a 'Monster teach-in in the Ulster Hall'.[63] The political theatre staged by People's Democracy owed almost as much to the stunts of rag week as to the tactics of the global revolt.

The carnival atmosphere was encouraged during the protest movement's first few weeks by the most powerful men at Stormont. Conventional political and social relationships were briefly turned on their head. On 9 October 1968, two of Stormont's top civil servants patiently waited late into the night to meet a delegation carrying the movement's demands.[64] The university authorities later wrote to apologise for the failure of the students to 'follow the dictates of ordinary politeness'.[65] The Unionist government, however, was willing to tolerate ever more grievous breaches of etiquette. At one of the early assembly meetings, the Education Minister braved shouts of 'Heil Hitler' to speak to the students.[66] Around seventy People's Democracy activists were even let into Stormont on 24 October 1968 to listen to a parliamentary debate on civil liberties. When the Unionists voted to adjourn the House of Commons rather than discuss the Liberal Party's Human Rights Bill, the students filed into the central lobby. As the MPs had failed to address the biggest problem facing Northern Ireland, People's Democracy had usurped their role. The Speaker showed surprising restraint and refused to call in the police to remove the protesters. Instead, the Education Minister again volunteered to try to reason with the students. Although People's Democracy stated that the sit-in would continue until the MPs signed a declaration embodying basic civil rights, the demonstration ended peacefully and with only one Unionist agreeing to add his name. The students had had their fun for that day.[67]

As the demonstrations staged by People's Democracy and the loyalist reaction grew more militant, violent confrontations began and the carnival started to come to an end. Many Protestants were disgusted that their taxes were supporting students involved in protests.[68] Middle England shared their anger. Indeed, the Edgbaston Ratepayers' Association came close to marching on Birmingham University.[69] The Catholic community, on the other hand, was worried that the behaviour of the students was hurting the cause of civil rights.[70] Northern Ireland was losing patience with People's Democracy.

On 4 November 1968, concerns about a possible breach of the peace led the police to block a march from Queen's to city hall. The students therefore had to improvise – adapting tactics to suit the changing situation. Some marchers filtered past the police lines, provoking several RUC officers to break ranks and physically restrain them. When the police regrouped to form a stronger cordon, the marchers responded with a sit-down protest before voting to disperse and meet again at City Hall. When they reached the centre, a vote was taken to block traffic from entering or leaving Donegal Square. The RUC responded by beating and dragging protesters off the streets.[71]

The day's events were so momentous that the student newspaper decided to rush out a supplement with the main edition. Unnamed students of both sexes were quoted criticising the RUC: 'a policeman said to the demonstrators inside City Hall "We are not London policemen. Now you will get what you deserve."'; 'one of the policemen spat in my face'; 'I was grabbed by the throat and my head banged against the bonnet of a car by policemen'. For Protestant students in particular, this experience served to undermine long-standing convictions. One such 'staunch believer in the principles of Unionism' admitted that his 'faith in the RUC' was at 'a rather low ebb'.[72]

Although some People's Democracy members such as Devlin were moving 'inexorably left', most still shared Boyle's 'reformist' approach.[73] This tension between reformers and leftists was a feature of many other student movements. During the occupation of Birmingham University, the authorities tried to exploit this divide by offering to consider the 'four principles of the protest': no victimisation, administrative matters to be discussed in public, a student say in the government of the university, and a commission to look into the structure of the institution. The extremists argued for the struggle to continue; the majority of the students voted to 'end the sit-in and put a halt to direct action'.[74]

In Belfast, the tensions showed signs of developing into an open split as People's Democracy debated how to react to O'Neill's 'Crossroads' speech. The movement had responded to the five-point reform package by declaring that its 'resources of pressure' had 'not been put in cold storage'.[75] The leftists wanted to adhere to this uncompromising stance even after the Prime Minister's presidential address. McCann told the university debating society that 'radicals … should say to Terence O'Neill after his speech last night – "not nearly good enough. We want the lot, we want it now – and that's not fast enough."'[76] Someone who signed himself as a 'former support of PD' wrote to Boyle to condemn this 'abrupt' and 'irresponsible' 'rebuttal' of 'the appeal by the Prime Minister'.[77] Other students were also persuaded by O'Neill, but preferred to remain within People's Democracy and work to give him the breathing space that he desired. At a packed assembly meeting, the movement voted to abandon the march to City Hall that had been scheduled for 14 December 1968. The margin of victory was only small: the movement's polarisation was complete.[78]

THE LONG MARCH

On 21 December 1968, Frank Gogarty – the only member of the NICRA executive widely respected within People's Democracy – presented his proposals for a 'new programme'.[79] Stormont's 'sops', O'Neill's 'appeal for moderation', and the 'physical exhaustion' of activists had to be ignored because to 'do nothing' would be a 'betrayal of the people's trust'. Gogarty wanted to build on the success of civil rights marches by adopting another aspect of the 'Negro resistance in the United States', civil disobedience, and 'adapt[ing it] to the local scene'. The bus boycott in Montgomery, Alabama, and the alternative election that had been organised by the Freedom Summer volunteers were given as examples of what the Northern Irish movement could try. Some of the demonstrations that the region's leftists had put on, notably picketing and squatting, were also cited as possible models for the wider movement. Another set of ideas for Gogarty's civil disobedience campaign was taken from the Irish past: the boycott and hunger strikes.[80]

Gogarty felt that to 'continue a programme of marching' would 'be pushing luck too far' – 'an unfavourable public reaction is not unlikely'.[81] A violent confrontation, however, was exactly what Farrell wanted to provoke. 'I believed', he told an interviewer two decades later, 'that if you attacked on a number of fronts the whole thing would collapse … the state might dissolve – and then the demands you'd been making could be achieved.'[82] Before the 'Crossroads' speech, he had been organising a People's Democracy march from Belfast to Derry – the original idea for which had come from the floor of the assembly.[83] Although, after O'Neill's presidential address, a large meeting voted to abandon these plans, Farrell remained determined to lead a march to the Maiden City.[84]

On the seventh day of the Birmingham University occupation, the students voted by approximately 2,300 to 1,500 in favour of ending the protest. The extremists, though, were not prepared to accept this democratic decision. They exploited every procedure available to them to ensure that this vote was declared void and that a second one was scheduled for a later date.[85] At Queen's, Farrell was equally ruthless in the pursuit of what he believed to be the right result. The leftists reopened the question at a sparsely attended meeting held after the university had broken up for the Christmas vacation. The Young Socialist Alliance threatened to march under its own banner if People's Democracy voted to stand by the previous decision – a tactic that had also been used to pressure NICRA into marching on 5 October 1968. At the City Hotel meeting, the Belfast Young Socialists had supported the Derry radicals. This favour was now repaid: McCann and other members of the *ad hoc* alliance committed themselves to the Belfast–Derry march.[86] Boyle again found himself faced with a choice that would shape the rest of his life. Fearing that a breakaway action could mark the end of the movement, he decided that it would be better to support the leftist motion. Another influential member of the Faceless Committee, Devlin, reached the same conclusion. Their intervention proved decisive and the vote in favour of marching across Northern Ireland at the beginning of 1969 was carried.[87]

One of the cynical jokes that regularly did the rounds at assembly meetings was that the debate would be won by whoever had turned up with a draft press release. The statement that Farrell had prepared for the media drew parallels with the Selma–Montgomery march. Boyle tried without success to add an alternative reference to Martin Luther King's Poor People's Campaign – which had attempted to unite all disadvantaged Americans whatever their race in a struggle for social justice.[88] By contrast, the immediate goal of the Selma–Montgomery march was polarisation. It also differed from King's last campaign in that it was a success. By sparking racist violence, the march restarted the stalled American civil rights movement. The Federal government was compelled to despatch troops to Alabama and rush comprehensive voting rights legislation through Congress. Farrell hoped to provoke a similar reaction: 'Either the government would face up to the extreme right … and protect the march … or it would be exposed as impotent in the face of sectarian thuggery, and Westminster would be forced to intervene.'[89]

Farrell understood the thinking behind the Selma–Montgomery march. However, he got certain details wrong. Farrell regarded People's Democracy as a Northern Irish version of the Student Non-violent Co-ordinating Committee (SNCC). But the American group had wanted to build up a grassroots movement in Alabama and had initially opposed this publicity-seeking short cut. There was also a mix up over where the original march had started and finished, with People's Democracy incorrectly identifying Derry with Selma.[90]

Although Farrell was unfamiliar with the geography of Alabama, he was on home ground when selecting the itinerary for the four-day march across Northern Ireland. 'A lot of the route was through my home area of South Derry,' he later remembered, 'so I knew ... the likely reaction.'[91] Few others among the eighty or so people who gathered outside Belfast City Hall on 1 January 1969 were prepared for the reception awaiting them in the Protestant heartland.[92] As the independent commission of inquiry reported, 'they merely expected groups to come out and say "Boo" and "Go home"'.[93] Paul Bew, a Cambridge University undergraduate who gave up the last few days of his holiday to take part, later commented upon this naivety:

> If one had been more attuned to the society itself, one would have said, 'Well can one march between here and Derry 70 miles in these little Protestant villages, is this a wise thing to do?' In fact what we said was, 'We are socialists. We are progressive. Trying to stop us marching through your villages is ridiculous because we are carrying a banner of enlightenment.'[94]

The march would dispel these illusions about the significance of Northern Ireland's communal divide. The marchers were not only harried and hindered by a Paisleyite group led by Ronald Bunting. They were also met by counter-demonstrations from local loyalists along the route. Indeed, People's Democracy spent almost as much time in cars and police tenders being ferried away from trouble spots as they did on their feet marching along open roads.[95] On the Catholic side, there was an initial lack of enthusiasm that in some cases verged upon outright hostility. A senior figure in the Derry Nationalist Party denounced the plan as 'ill-advised' – and claimed that he was 'say[ing] publicly what many civil rights supporters are saying in private'.[96] However, as the youths struggled towards Derry, attitudes changed. Local Catholics turned out to support the marchers and offer them shelter for the night, Republicans guarded them as they slept, NICRA committee members provided help and even participated, and the Derry Citizens' Action Committee (DCAC) organised a reception in Guildhall Square.[97] For Boyle, the division was most starkly demonstrated when Dungiven's Catholic schoolchildren ran out to greet them while the Protestants remained in their classrooms.[98]

The RUC, which at times had one-sixth of its officers protecting the march, lacked the resources to bring People's Democracy safely from Belfast to Derry.[99] The police had to accept that there would be scuffles and stone-throwing incidents. Many members of the force even felt some sympathy for the counter-demonstrators. Consequently, as the marchers began the fourth and final day of the journey, the RUC was relatively unconcerned by reports that a small band of loyalists had assembled down the road. Farrell was told that a 'hostile crowd' had gathered ahead and there was a 'risk of stone- throwing', but People's Democracy chose to stick to the original route.[100] At Burntollet Bridge, however, an organised ambush rather than a rowdy counter-demonstration was waiting. Several hundred people wearing white armbands for identification and armed with cudgels fell upon the marchers.[101] Gogarty, who was carrying the civil rights banner, was surrounded and beaten unconscious as he attempted to cross the bridge.[102] A group of young girls were pursued by their attackers into the river and were then subjected to a hail of stones as they waded across to the opposite bank. Journalists and television crews were also targeted – an indication of how much the negative media coverage had angered the Protestant community.[103] One Unionist MP had gone as far as to describe the ladies and gentlemen of the press as 'roving vultures who follow the riot circuit around the world, whether it be in Grosvenor Square, Frankfurt, or Paris'.[104]

The commission of inquiry was usually critical of the RUC's conduct during the civil rights crisis. But on this occasion it found that 'a serious effort was made to protect the marchers'.[105] This is something of an exaggeration: photographs and eyewitness reports suggest that some policemen chose to stand on the sidelines.[106] Nevertheless, this constituted the extent of state collusion with the Burntollet ambushers. When Farrell and McCann's friends investigated, they concluded that the 'attack was organised locally'.[107] Although Unionist MPs had shown their usual willingness to appease loyalists during the first few days of the march, the ambush was strongly condemned.[108] The Attorney-General informed the Deputy Inspector-General that he felt 'those who took part' in the 'appalling affair' 'should be speedily brought to justice'.[109] Stormont, however, had by this stage surrendered the political initiative to the streets.

FREE DERRY

The night before the Burntollet ambush, Ian Paisley had led a prayer meeting in Derry's Guildhall. This was the second visit he had made to the second city during the civil rights crisis. On 9 November 1968, Paisley and his supporters had marched through Derry. One of the hooligans had told a *Sunday Times* journalist that they would not let 'that f-ing Paisley walk through the f-ing streets of f-ing Derry to curse the f-ing Pope'.[110] A gang of about a hundred teenagers had thrown stones and fireworks at the Paisleyites, waved an improvised Irish tricolour at them, and blocked their path with a sit-down protest. However, the overwhelming majority of the hooligans had dispersed when they were told to do so by the DCAC stewards – allowing Paisley to finish his march.[111] Two months later, the city's young were not so obedient. John Hume and Ivan Cooper once again addressed an angry crowd on the importance of remaining non-violent. But the hooligans no longer found this familiar argument convincing. When the Paisleyites emerged from the building brandishing improvised weaponry, the hooligans rushed towards them.[112] After the violence had died down, an emotional Hume journeyed out to Claudy, where the People's Democracy marchers had stopped for the night. Boyle found the DCAC's Vice-Chair 'in tears about the riot in Derry and why the march shouldn't have been begun, what he was going to do and so on'.[113] Hume's ability to influence developments in his city was waning. The following morning, People's Democracy spent an hour debating whether they should give up or continue on to Derry. They were told that people in the city were afraid that the march would bring communal violence in its train.[114] But, as Boyle later recalled, 'the people warning of the risks would always have grey hair. We couldn't be told, each generation cannot be told.' The riot in Guildhall Square was dismissed as nothing more than Paisley 'stirring it up' – and they were not going to 'bow to him'. The marchers therefore kept 'turning over the pages of history in ignorance'.[115] Farrell's mistake was that he believed that these were pages in a Marxist history book. At a meeting of leftists in December 1968, he had predicted that a serious loyalist attack on the march would provoke an uprising in Derry.[116] This was one of the reasons why Farrell had fought so strongly to stop the march from being abandoned. As the commission of inquiry concluded, he wanted 'martyrdom'.[117]

Following the Burntollet ambush, Derry was alive with rumours that some marchers had made the ultimate sacrifice for the cause of civil rights.[118] Paddy Doherty remembered Cooper screaming about murders as he burst into the room where the DCAC was meeting to finalise the details of the reception. Thoughts of how the committee and its stewards could maintain order were immediately forgotten.[119] The DCAC and the hooligans had previously been on opposing sides, but the city's Catholics were now united in anger. This rage deepened as the remaining marchers – as well as the hundreds of Derrymen and women who had turned out to support them – suffered two further attacks on their way to Guildhall Square. During the first of these stone-throwing incidents, Farrell was knocked unconscious and taken to hospital. Boyle was therefore 'left in control' of the 'shambles'.[120] With the police escort outnumbered and exhausted, the senior officer bluntly told Boyle that it was 'Up to you now'. Boyle chose to be taken by the safest route. Although the marchers were again subjected to a hail of missiles on the way to the square, the *Derry Journal* found nothing to criticise about the RUC's conduct on this final leg. Indeed, the riot police even launched a baton charge against the loyalists. This, however, did little to cool Catholic anger. 'No-one,' Paddy Doherty recalled, 'gave a damn about peace or marshals now.'[121]

Mary Holland was among the thousands of people who had gathered in Guildhall Square. She 'listened to civil rights leaders begging the people to go home, to refrain from violence, and to think of world opinion. The crowd said what they thought of world opinion in no uncertain terms, asked what it had ever done for the poor of Derry, and told their leaders that they were too late.'[122] When the reception came to an end, clashes between the hooligans and the police broke out in the side streets. Running battles were fought in the city centre until the early hours of the morning.[123] At some point that night, the RUC – while battling against fists, stones, petrol bombs, barricades, and fires – experienced a complete breakdown of discipline. After the riot ended, gangs of policemen seeking revenge penetrated into the Bogside. They shouted sectarian abuse, smashed windows, and even attacked people in their homes.[124]

The polarisation created by the Belfast–Derry march was demonstrated when O'Neill issued his first public statement. Ken Bloomfield had prepared a text that was a hollow echo of the 'Crossroads' speech. The Prime Minister declared that 'Ulster has had enough. We have heard sufficient for now about civil rights; let us hear a little about civic responsibility.' The *Derry Journal* countered with a 'plain speaking' editorial entitled 'Enough is Enough'. Catholics, argued the newspaper, 'from top to bottom of the social strata ... are no longer prepared to accept tamely the image the police have built up for themselves as a partisan body'. 'Are they really so foolish as to imagine that any police force can function, even in the ordinary day to day routine police activities not only without the co-operation but indeed against the opposition of the huge majority of people?'[125] The civil rights movement in Derry was starting to assume the form of a Catholic insurrection.

The morning after the attack the Bogside's men took to the streets armed with cudgels and iron bars. DCAC moderates eventually persuaded these vigilantes to abandon plans for an immediate march on police headquarters. Despite this success, Hume and Cooper recognised that concessions would have to be made to the more militant mood. At a public meeting, Cooper announced the end of the truce. The meeting also agreed to mount a march on the main police station, but one that was non-violent, marshalled by DCAC stewards and composed solely of women. Such protests, however, could no longer completely satisfy the Catholic community's anger. The appeal of defence and illegal activity was increasing at the expense of non- violence and direct action. Hume and Cooper were not prepared to lead – or, indeed, to follow – the Derry movement in this direction and their influence diminished accordingly. Traditionalist Republicans had no such qualms and seized the opportunity to escape from the political margins. When a 'Protection Association' was established to patrol the streets of the Bogside, the veteran Republican Seán Keenan became its Chair.[126] On 6 January 1969, the RUC informed Stormont 'that the police had temporarily withdrawn from an area of Londonderry, which was being controlled by an organised and armed force'.[127] The defiant message 'You are now entering Free Derry' – adopted and adapted from Berkeley – appeared on a gable end at the boundary of the Bogside.[128]

The Derry radicals and People's Democracy activists joined the traditionalist Republicans behind the barricades – but their moment had passed.[129] Like the 22 March movement, their strategy had assumed that 'Street fighting leads to political struggle'.[130] In Northern Ireland, however, the struggle that developed was between communities rather than classes. The leftists had acted like sorcerer's apprentices: they had unleashed powerful forces that they little understood and that ultimately mastered them. As the old conflict over national and communal identities started to come to the fore, hopes for a peaceful settlement also vanished. Although DCAC moderates convinced the community to bring the barricades down on 10 January 1969, the changes that had taken place while they had been up could not be dismantled.[131] Free Derry and the anti-RUC riot that spawned it were precursors of the more serious confrontations that were to come. Northern Ireland's '68 had ended.[132]

Conclusion

WE FAILED ABSOLUTELY

On the morning of the second Grosvenor Square march, the *Observer* attempted to explain the 'Student Revolt' to its readers. In a lengthy piece, the newspaper's Berlin correspondent reported on 'Where It All Started'. The revolutionaries that he had met in the city's squats were starting to lose their faith. 'At Easter,' one had told him, 'we thought anything, absolutely anything, could happen. Now everything is crumbling to pieces.'[1]

Six months later, it was Eamonn McCann's turn to lament the failure of '68 to a British journalist. 'All that we managed to get across', he confessed,

> was that we were more extreme than the Civil Rights people. We have never made it clear that this difference in militancy stemmed from a political difference ... and the reason for that, I believe, is that we have been frightened of scaring off our mass audience. We thought that we had to keep these people, bring them along, educate and radicalise them. It was a lot of pompous nonsense and we failed absolutely to change the consciousness of the people. The consciousness of the people who are fighting in the streets at the moment is sectarian and bigoted.[2]

As had happened during 1798, Ireland's secular revolutionaries found themselves saddled with sectarian followers. On the eve of the United Irishmen rising in Ulster, a Catholic deserter from the army allegedly declared, 'we'll pay the rascals this day for the battle of the Boyne'.[3] At the end of the 1960s, McCann sadly noted that 'the cry "get the Protestants" is still very much on the lips of the Catholic working class'.[4]

Northern Ireland was not alone in finding historic divisions asserting themselves as the decade drew to a close. In the United States, the malignant heritage of slavery lurked behind the ghetto riots and the 'white backlash'.[5] France was still riven by rivalries that had their roots in the Revolutionary era. As the party of order again rallied behind a strong leader, French leftists embarked upon an inquest into the *événements*. Key figures in the Trotskyist Jeunesse Communiste Révolutionnaire (JCR) came to regret having submerged their group within the May movement. The JCR, they now argued, should have acted as a strong vanguard party during 1968, instead of being 'more Guevarist than Trotskyist'.[6]

Tony Cliff, British Trotskyism's dominant figure, offered an identical assessment of where Northern Ireland's leftists had gone wrong. He was unable to persuade Farrell to accept this reading when the pair met in early 1969. Nevertheless, as Cliff later noted, Farrell and McCann eventually 'drew the right conclusion'.[7] In his 1974 memoir, McCann claimed that the 'left failed in Ireland' because it was 'not forearmed with a coherent class analysis of the situation and a clear programme based upon it'. 'In a phrase,' he concluded, 'we need to build a mass revolutionary Marxist party.'[8] C. Desmond Greaves, whom the '68ers saw as a Stalinist hack, believed that becoming a revolutionary required two decisions: the first was made in the innocence of youth, the second after bitter experience.[9] Farrell and McCann now made this second choice and embarked upon the thankless task of political organising on the radical Left.

At the same time as their influence in Northern Ireland was fading, the leftists were becoming international stars. With Western activists becoming increasingly militant, admiring glances were soon being cast at the violent scenes taking place on the streets of Belfast and Derry. French student radicals invited Bernadette Devlin and McCann to speak at the Sorbonne about 'la lutte populaire Irlandaise'. The posters for this meeting claimed the backing of the Palestine Liberation Organisation, the African National Congress, and America's Black Panther Party.[10] This last group hoped that under its tutelage race rioters could be transformed into guerrilla fighters.[11] Northern Ireland's leftists had similar aspirations. When civil rights delegations toured the United States during 1969 to raise money and awareness, the two sets of revolutionaries took advantage of the chance to meet each other. The Boston chapter even made one People's Democracy activist 'an honorary Black Panther sister'.[12] McCann returned the kindness shown to his comrade by giving the Black Panthers a present that Devlin had only recently received:a golden key to New York City.[13]

'The Black Panthers', McCann later recalled, 'were enormously popular in the Bogside.'[14] Conservative Irish Catholics on both sides of the Atlantic failed to share his enthusiasm. In Detroit, the organisers of a rally at which Devlin was the keynote speaker made sure that African-Americans were kept outside the hall. Devlin, though, refused to address a segregated audience – much to the annoyance of her Irish-American hosts. At the next stop on her itinerary, Chicago, Devlin further enraged the community by declining to meet the city's mayor.[15] Richard Daley was 'the most powerful Irish-American politician not called Kennedy', but Devlin would not shake hands with someone she felt was a racist.[16] She even had problems with Democrats from the left wing of the party. During their tour of the television newsrooms, Devlin and Kevin Boyle's babysitter was Paul O'Dwyer – an Irish-born New York lawyer who campaigned for civil rights and an end to the Vietnam War. On the 'Huntley-Brinkley Report', the pair began to explain that Protestants as well as Catholics lived in poor houses and that People's Democracy was trying to bring these two groups together. O'Dwyer was so appalled by what he was hearing that he got down on his hands and knees, crawled onto the set, came up behind Boyle and Devlin, and implored them to 'Talk about the fucking Catholics'.[17]

The British embassy reassured the Foreign Office that Devlin's 'diagnosis of Northern Irish problems as a matter more of class warfare than of religious conflict had not been generally shared'.[18] A small number of Irish-Americans, however, did share her diagnosis. The National Association for Irish Justice (NAIJ), which had been founded in reaction to the Troubles, believed that the Northern Irish struggle was part of the global revolt. The group's first national convention, which was attended by People's Democracy activists, recognised 'the similarity of the civil rights struggle in Northern Ireland with the struggle of the black civil rights movement'. It also passed resolutions that condemned the Vietnam War, and backed the 'people of Czechoslovakia in the struggle for self-determination'.[19] Conn McCluskey was furious at how the worldwide revolutionary struggle had come to take precedence over the campaign for Catholic equality. Citing the 'thousands of moderate Irish-Americans [who] now appear to be antagonised', McCluskey walked away from the civil rights movement.[20]

Devlin polarised people, but everyone could agree that she was one of the stars of '68. Ian Paisley crowned her 'International Socialist Playgirl of the Year'.[21] Devlin, however, discovered that the interest shown in her and the civil rights movement masked a lack of detailed knowledge about Northern Ireland. The leftists had adopted and adapted ideas that came from beyond the shores of Ireland without properly understanding their original context. This situation was now reversed. When Devlin began to suspect that elements within the NAIJ were channelling funds to the Irish Republican Army, she tried to take sole responsibility for getting American money back to Ireland. Devlin feared that the proceeds of her speaking tour in the United States would be used to purchase weapons rather than to help needy families.[22] In an interview with the *Observer*, Devlin remarked that inside the NAIJ 'the only qualification needed for being an expert on Northern Ireland was to have been involved in the California grape strike'.[23] During 'the Battle of the Bogside', foreign activists arrived at the then 'centre of revolutionary Europe' to learn at first hand.[24] While the nuances of Northern Irish politics proved difficult to master, they returned home with a new model for street fighting. As an Italian militant later observed of the ritualised battles he fought with the police, 'It was a Londonderry.'[25]

ENDINGS

At the end of his report from 'Where It All Started', the *Observer*'s Berlin correspondent began to consider how it would all finish. For guidance, he turned to one of the greatest students of revolution: Alexis de Tocqueville. But the writings of this nineteenth-century political thinker held little of comfort to twentieth-century leftists. 'In a rebellion, as in a novel,' he observed, 'the most difficult part to invent is the end.'[26]

The final paragraph of Albert Camus' *The Plague*, a book that had inspired thousands of activists, would have made for equally bleak reading at this time. The narrator knows that 'the plague bacillus never dies or vanishes entirely, that it waits patiently ..., and that perhaps the day will come when, for the instruction or misfortune of mankind, the plague will rouse its rats and send them to die in some well-contented city'.[27] Unthinking obedience to ideological dogma, moral cowardice, and political violence had not been banished from the world with the fall of the Third Reich. It was this realisation that had helped drive the radicalisation of the 1960s. However, like Jean Tarrou, the '68ers had been battling the plague while at the same time carrying the bacillus themselves. The struggle against imperialism, capitalism, and bureaucracy brought in its train Leninist sects and terrorist cells.

This, though, was only one of the ways that the stories of '68 ended. The January 1969 issue of *Ramparts*, the news-sheet of the Derry Labour Party, declared 'Come Back Mrs Pankhurst, We Have Not Yet Overcome'. As female activists throughout the Western world were discovering, some members of the movements against inequality were more equal than others. The article complained that women 'have been beaten and clubbed to the ground as viciously as male marchers yet only one female member of the C.R. movement has gained recognition'. With 'Organisations to demand equal rights for women … springing up all over', the time had come for a 'Feminist Movement [to] be formed in Derry'.[28] Although this proved to be a false start, the city's *ad ho*c alliance did help to launch second-wave feminism in Ireland. By the autumn of 1970, the Derry radical Nell McCafferty had joined a small Dublin-based group that met every Monday night to discuss the liberation of Irish women. The older political generation was represented by the likes of Maírín Johnston, 'Red' Roy's wife, and Maírín de Burca, the General Secretary of Official Sinn Féin. The New Lefts of '56 and '68 had wanted different revolutions, but neither of these would have solved the specific problems suffered by women. It was these issues that the Irishwomen's Liberation Movement now began to address.[29]

McCafferty was an outsider twice over as she was a lesbian. The Derry Labour Party and the civil rights movement had given her confidence and a set of beliefs. But they had also helped to make her feel 'lonely and alone'.[30] This contradiction pushed many homosexual '68ers into campaigning for gay liberation. Street politics had secured Northern Ireland's Catholics their civil rights, but it would be litigation that secured the region's gay men their rights. NICRA's half-hearted efforts to use the European Convention on Human Rights had ended in farce. The American lawyer engaged by the McCluskeys had indulged in one conspiracy theory too many for the European Court's liking.[31] The 1970s, however, witnessed a sea change in the legal culture. As the Marxist tide receded to reveal the older left-wing tradition of individual rights that it had submerged, Western European lawyers learned how to harness the full potential of the Convention.[32] Boyle was part of the legal team that took the case of Jeff Dudgeon to the European Court. Dudgeon was Secretary of the Northern Ireland Gay Rights Association. In January 1976, he was arrested for 'gross indecency between males'. Dudgeon complained that making sexual activity between consenting adults of the same gender a criminal offence interfered with his right to respect for a private life. On 22 October 1981, the Court ruled that there had been a breach of Article 8: male homosexuality had been decriminalised in Northern Ireland.[33]

Leninists, terrorists, feminists, gay liberation activists, human rights lawyers, celebrities, and conformers – these are familiar figures in the stories that are told of what happened after '68 had ended. For them, the global revolt was just part of a longer narrative. But there were others who could not so easily put the events of '68 behind them. They had been briefly freed from everyday life and given a glimpse of world in which the impossible could be made possible. After this, the prospect of having to return to the mundane pleasures and pains of normal life was unbearable. They started to grieve as if for a great lost love, succumbing to despair, mental illness, and even suicide.[34]

Stories of how political and personal disappointments can become entwined are more likely to be found in works of literature than of scholarship. In the first few years after *The Golden Notebook* was published, readers had written to Doris Lessing mainly about her novel's themes of left-wing politics and the sex war. Correspondence on the third theme of the breakdown had been rare. At the end of the 1960s, however, Lessing began to notice that she was receiving more and more letters on the subject of mental illness.[35] The Belfast-born playwright Anne Devlin also explores the personal tragedies that take place against the vast backdrop of political tragedies. As a teenager, Devlin had taken part in the People's Democracy movement. She drew upon these experiences in a series of plays screened by the BBC during the 1980s. In Devlin's *A Woman Calling*, the main character recalls 1968 as being 'the most exciting year of my life; inevitably I fell in love'.[36] *The Long March* features characters reminiscing about an early People's Democracy meeting and commenting about 'nothing in the present ever matching up to what there was in the past'. Helen Walsh's life in particular has drifted since the Belfast–Derry march. When she returns home after a decade's exile in England, Walsh struggles to fit back into a society that has been polarised by the hunger strikes. The play ends with Walsh contemplating the moon over Belfast and the hold of history over humanity:

> I still remember that time when we thought we were beginning a new journey: the long march. What we didn't see was that it had begun a long time before with someone else's journey; we were simply getting through the steps in our own time.[37]

Endnotes

PREFACE

1   *Belfast Telegraph*, 13 July 2018.
2   Richard Bourke, 'Historiography', in *The Princeton History of Modern Ireland*, eds. Richard Bourke and Ian McBride (Princeton, NJ, 2016), pp. 271–91.
3   *Derry Journal*, 3 October 2008.
4   Simon Prince, '"Do What the Afro-Americans Are Doing": Black Power and the Start of the Northern Ireland Troubles', *Journal of Contemporary History* 50, no. 3 (2015), pp. 516–35.
5   Rising Up Angry, Spring 1970, Public Record Office of Northern Ireland (hereafter PRONI), Belfast, D 3297/2; Poster advertising the event, [n.d.], PRONI, D 3253/5/14; *Irish Times*, 13 November 1970.
6   *Guardian*, 11 May 2018; *Belfast News-Letter*, 4 June 2018.
7   Martin McGuinness, Speech to the 40th Anniversary Civil Rights Commemoration Conference, Derry. 4 October 2008. http://cain.ulst.ac.uk/issues/politics/docs/sf/mmcg041008.htm (last accessed: 29 July 2018).
8   Mark Durkan, Speech to the 40th Anniversary Civil Rights Commemoration Conference, Derry, 4 October 2008. http://cain.ulst.ac.uk/issues/politics/docs/sdlp/md041008.htm (last accessed: 29 July 2018).
9   *Derry Journal*, 7 May 2008.
10 U. Neisser and L. Libby, 'Remembering Life Experiences', in *The Oxford Handbook of Memory* ed. E. Tulving and F. Craik (Oxford, 2000 edn.), pp. 315–32, p. 317; V. Reyna, F. Lloyd, and C. Brainerd, 'Memory, Development, and Rationality: An Integrative Theory of Judgment and Decision-Making' in *Emerging Perspectives on Judgment and Decision Research* ed. S. Schneider and J. Shanteau (Cambridge, 2003), pp. 201–45, pp. 234–9.
11 House of Commons, Northern Ireland Affairs Committee, *Ways of Dealing with Northern Ireland's Past: Interim Report -- Victims and Survivors* (London, 2005), Volume II, Ev 75.
12 Nancy Partner, 'Linguistic Turn along Post-Postmodern Borders Israeli/Palestinian Narrative Conflict', *New Literary History*, 39, no. 4 (autumn 2008), pp 823–45, pp. 830–41.
13 *Peace News*, September 1967; Jeremy Varon, *Bringing the War Home: The Weather Underground, the Red Army Faction, and Revolutionary Violence in the Sixties and Seventies* (Berkley, California, 2004), p. 44; D. Triesman, 'Essex', *New Left Review*, July–August 1968.
14 Martin Luther King, *Letter from Birmingham Jail*. http://www.stanford.edu/group/King/frequentdocs/birmingham.pdf (last accessed: 29 July 2018).
15 *Derry Journal*, 23 July 1968.

16 Thomas L. Haskell, 'Objectivity is not Neutrality: Rhetoric vs. Practice in Peter Novick's *That Noble Dream*', *History and Theory*, 29, no. 2 (1990), pp. 129–57, p. 132.

17 Mary Fulbrook, *Historical Theory* (London, 2002), p. 50.

18 Richard Bourke, 'Languages of Conflict and the Northern Ireland Troubles', *Journal of Modern History* 83, no. 3 (September 2011), pp. 544–78; Marianne Elliott, *Hearthlands: A Memoir of the White City Housing Estate in Belfast* (Belfast, 2017); Brian Hanley and Scott Millar, *The Lost Revolution: The Story of the Official IRA and the Workers' Party* (Dublin, 2009); Maggie Scull, 'Religion from Rome, Politics from Home? The Catholic Church and the Northern Irish Troubles, 1968–94' (PhD dissertation, King's College London, 2017).

INTRODUCTION

1 *Disturbances in Northern Ireland: Report of the Commission Appointed by the Governor of Northern Ireland (Cameron Report)* (Belfast: Her Majesty's Stationery Office, 1969), p. 27.

2 J. E. Greeves to Ivan Woods, 1968, Belfast, Public Record Office of Northern Ireland (PRONI), CAB/9B/205/7.

3 *Derry Journal*, 8 October 1968.

4 Roy Johnston, *Century of Endeavour: A Biographical and Autobiographical View of the 20th Century in Ireland* (Dublin: The Lilliput Press, 2004), pp. 152–6, 171–9, and 229–35.

5 *Derry Journal*, 25 June 1968.

6 Paddy Doherty, *Paddy Bogside* (Dublin: Mercier Press, 2001), p. 55; *Derry Journal*, 14 February 1961; *Derry Journal*, 17 February 1967.

7 Three eyewitnesses report on Londonderry, 8 October 1968, London, National Archives of the United Kingdom, PREM/13/2841.

8 Sean Redmond, *Desmond Greaves and the Origins of the Civil Rights Movement in Northern Ireland*, www.irishdemocrat.co.uk/bookshop/publications/greaves-and-civil- right, last visited 12 March 2006.

9 *National Guardian*, December 1967, quoted in Seymour Martin Lipset, *Rebellion in the University: A History of Student Activism in America* (London: Routledge, 1972), p. xxi.

10 Eamonn McCann, *War and an Irish Town* (London: Pluto, 1993 edn), p. 91.

11 Eamonn McCann, 'Preface', in Eamonn McCann, *McCann: War & Peace in Northern Ireland* (Dublin: Hot Press, 1998), p. 4.

12 *Derry Journal*, 10 September 1968.

13 *Irish Militant*, September 1967.

14 Civil Rights March from Coalisland to Dungannon, 29 August 1968, PRONI, CAB/9B/205/7.

15 Civil Rights March from Coalisland to Dungannon.

16 *Derry Journal*, 1 October 1968.

17 *Derry Journal*, 8 October 1968; Civil Rights March from Coalisland to Dungannon.

18 Mark Kurlansky, *1968: The Year that Rocked the World* (London: Jonathan Cape, 2004), p. 102.

19 *Derry Journal*, 1 October 1968; *Cameron Report*, p. 27; Rex Cathcart, *The Most Contrary Region: The BBC in Northern Ireland, 1924–84* (Belfast: Blackstaff, 1984), pp. 198–9 and 207–8.

20   John Hill to Harold Black, 20 February 1969, PRONI, CAB/9B/205/8.

21   Austin Currie, *All Hell Will Break Loose* (Dublin: O'Brien, 2004), pp. 110–11.

22   *Derry Journal*, 8 October 1968; *Derry Journal*, 6 December 1968; Three eyewitnesses report on Londonderry; *Cameron Report*, p. 28.

23   Anthony Peacocke to John Hill, 19 December 1968, PRONI, CAB/9B/205/8.

24   Police comments on the report submitted by the three British MPs; Three eyewitnesses report on Londonderry, PRONI, CAB/9B/205/8.

25   *Derry Journal*, 8 October 1968.

26   *Cameron Report*, p. 29.

27   *Derry Journal*, 6 December 1968.

28   Fionbarra Ó Dochartaigh, *Ulster's White Negroes: From Civil Rights to Insurrection* (Edinburgh: AK Press, 1994), p. 46.

29   Civil Rights March from Coalisland to Dungannon.

30   *Derry Journal*, 6 December 1968.

31   *Cameron Report*, p. 29.

32   Hill to Black, 20 February 1969.

33   *Cameron Report*, p. 29.

34   Police comments on the report submitted by the three British MPs.

35   *Derry Journal*, 8 October 1968; Three eyewitnesses report on Londonderry; Margie Bernhard, *Daughter of Derry: The Story of Brigid Sheils Makowski* (London: Pluto, 1989), p. 58.

36   *Derry Journal*, 8 October 1968; *Derry Journal*, 6 December 1968.

37   Jonathan Bardon, *Beyond the Studio: A History of BBC Northern Ireland* (Belfast: Blackstaff, 2000), p. 29.

38   Cathcart, *The Most Contrary Region*, pp. 207–8.

39   *House of Commons Debates*, vol. 770, 22 October 1968, cols. 1088–90.

40   Barry White, *John Hume: Statesman of the Troubles* (Belfast: Blackstaff, 1985), p. 41.

41   'Northern Ireland Forum: Humour in Northern Irish Politics', 15 February 2006, Cambridge.

42   Harold Marcuse, 'The Revival of Holocaust Awareness in West Germany, Israel and the United States', in Carole Fink, Philipp Gassert and Detlef Junker (eds), *1968: The World Transformed* (Cambridge: Cambridge University Press, 1998), p. 427; Donatella Della Porta, *Social Movements and Political Violence and the State: A Comparative Analysis of Italy and Germany* (Cambridge: Cambridge University Press, 1995), p. 58; Kristin Ross, *May '68 and Its Afterlives* (London: University Chicago Press, 2002), pp. 52–3.

43   Ross, *May '68 and Its Afterlives*, p. 204.

44   Alan Brinkley, '1968 and the Unraveling of Liberal America', in Carole Fink, Philipp Gassert and Detlef Junker, eds., *1968: The World Transformed* (Cambridge: Cambridge University Press, 1998), p. 222.

45   Pierre Nora, 'Generation', in Pierre Nora, ed., *Realms of Memory: Conflicts and Divisions*, trans. Arthur Goldhammer (New York: Columbia University Press, 1996), p. 500.

46   Roy Foster, *Modern Ireland, 1600–1972* (London: Penguin, 1989), p. 587.

47   David McKittrick and David McVea, *Making Sense of the Troubles* (Belfast: Blackstaff, 2000), p. 21.

48   See, for instance, Thomas Hennessey, *A History of Northern Ireland 1920–1996* (Dublin: Gill & Macmillan, 1997), p. 127.

49   See, for instance, Alvin Jackson, *Ireland 1778–1998* (Oxford: Blackwell, 1999), pp. 370–3.

50   Carole Fink, Philipp Gassert and Detlef Junker, 'Introduction', in Carole Fink, Philipp Gassert and Detlef Junker, eds, *1968: The World Transformed* (Cambridge: Cambridge University Press, 1998), pp.1 and 2.

51   Robert Tombs, *France 1814–1914* (London: Longman, 1996), p. 7.

52   *Guardian*, 22 July 2006.

53   Raymond Aron, *The Elusive Revolution: Anatomy of a Student Revolt*, trans. Gordon Clough (New York: Pall Mall, 1969).

54   Richard Rose, *Governing without Consensus: An Irish Perspective* (London: Faber, 1971), p. 5.

CHAPTER ONE

1   W.H. Van Voris, *Violence in Ulster: An Oral Documentary* (Amherst: University of Massachusetts Press, 1975), p. 5.

2   Brian Barton, *Brookeborough: The Making of a Prime Minister* (Belfast: Institute of Irish Studies, 1988), pp. 18, 21–6 and 31.

3   Circular in Brooke's private papers, 23 November 1920, quoted in Barton, *Brookeborough*, p. 40.

4   David Clay Large, *The Politics of Law and Order: A History of the Bavarian Einwohnerwehr, 1918–1921* (Philadelphia: American Philosophical Society, 1980), pp. 3, 8–9, 15–16, 39, 55 and 67.

5   Sir Basil Brooke to General Sir Nevil Macready, mid-July 1920, quoted in Barton, *Brookeborough*, p. 32.

6   Barton, *Brookeborough*, pp. 32 and 37.

7   Bryan A. Follis, *A State under Siege: The Establishment of Northern Ireland, 1920–1925* (Oxford: Oxford University Press, 1995), pp. 13, 17, 93, 95, 97, 102, 104, 108 and 121.

8   Follis, *A State Under Siege*, pp. 17, 24, 82 and 84.

9   Barton, *Brookeborough*, p. 44.

10   *House of Commons Debates*, vol. 123, 22 December 1919, col. 1202.

11   Memorandum by S. G. Tallents, quoted in Henry Patterson, *Ireland since 1939* (Oxford: Oxford University Press, 2002), p. 4.

12   Patrick Buckland, *The Factory of Grievances: Devolved Government in Northern Ireland* (Dublin: Gill & Macmillan, 1979), pp. 202 and 206.

13   Patrick Buckland, 'A Protestant State: Unionists in Government, 1921–39', in D. George Boyce and Alan O'Day (eds), *Defenders of the Union: A Survey of British and Irish Unionism since 1801* (London: Routledge, 2001), pp. 214–16.

14   Barton, *Brookeborough*, pp. 63–4.

15   Margaret MacMillan, *Peacemakers: The Paris Conference of 1919 and its Attempt to End War* (London: J. Murray, 2001), pp. 496–7.

16   The best account of the impact of conspiracy theories upon a political culture is found in Robert Tombs, *France 1814–1914* (London: Longman, 1996), pp. 89–95.

17   Ian Kershaw, *Hitler 1889–1936: Hubris* (London: Penguin, 1998), pp. 115–16.

18   Patrick Shea, *Voices and the Sound of Drums: An Irish Autobiography* (Belfast: Blackstaff, 1981), p. 113.

19   *Fermanagh Times*, 13 July 1933, quoted in Barton, *Brookeborough*, p. 78.

20 *Derry Journal*, 27 June 1967.

21 Barton, *Brookeborough*, pp. 84–9.

22 *Northern Ireland House of Commons Debates*, vol. 8, 25 October 1927, col. 2276, quoted in Buckland, *The Factory of Grievances*, p. 236.

23 Roy Foster, *Modern Ireland 1600–1972* (London: Penguin, 1989), p. 551.

24 Eamonn Collins, *Killing Rage* (London: Granta, 1997), p. 6.

25 John A. Oliver, *Working at Stormont* (Dublin: Institute of Public Administration, 1978), pp. 21–2, 25 and 45; Follis, *A State under Siege*, pp. 10–11 and 184.

26 Manuscript of speech delivered by Sir Ernest Clark at the first annual dinner of the Northern Ireland Civil Service, c. 1924, quoted in Follis, *A State under Siege*, p. 81.

27 John A. Oliver, 'The Stormont Administration 1921–72', in *Contemporary Record*, vol. 5, no. 1, 1991, pp. 71–104, p. 102.

28 Arthur J. Green, 'Bureaucracy for Belfast: A Hagiography', paper presented to the Belfast Literary Society, 10 January 2005.

29 Carl Schmitt, *Political Theology*, trans. George Schwab (Cambridge, MA: MIT Press, 1985), p. 15.

30 Carl Schmitt. *The Concept of the Political*, trans. George Schwab (Chicago: University of Chicago Press, 1996), p. 27.

31 *Northern Ireland House of Commons Debates*, vol. 16, 24 April 1934, col. 1095, quoted in Buckland, 'A Protestant state', p. 211.

32 *Fermanagh Times*, 14 July 1921, quoted in Barton, *Brookeborough*, p. 88.

33 *Northern Ireland House of Commons Debates*, vol. xvi, 24 April 1934, cols. 1117, 1118 and 1120, quoted in Barton, *Brookeborough*, p. 88.

34 Summary of the Civil Authorities (Special Powers) Act (Northern Ireland) 1922, in *Disturbances in Northern Ireland: Report of the Commission Appointed by the Governor of Northern Ireland (Cameron Report)* (Belfast: Her Majesty's Stationery Office, 1969), pp. 104–7.

35 Oliver, *Working at Stormont*, p. 134.

36 Kershaw, *Hitler*, p. 481.

37 Barton, *Brookeborough*, pp. 163 and 227.

38 Brian Moore, *The Emperor of Ice-Cream*, (London: Paladin, 1987), p. 204.

39 Brian Barton, *The Blitz: Belfast in the War Years* (Belfast: Blackstaff, 1989), pp. 108, 155–6 and 263–4.

40 Barton, *Brookeborough*, pp. 204 and 221.

41 Barton, *Brookeborough*, pp. 207 and 208.

42 Oliver, *Working at Stormont*, pp. 69–70 and 73–4.

43 Steven Fielding, Peter Thompson and Nick Tiratsoo, *'England Arise!' The Labour Party and Popular Politics in 1940s Britain* (Manchester: Manchester University Press, 1995), pp. 33–4.

44 Sir William Beveridge, *Social Insurance and Allied Services (Beveridge Report)* (London: His Majesty's Stationery Office, 1942), p. 6.

45 Tony Judt, *Postwar: A History of Europe since 1945* (London: William Heinemann, 2005), pp. 81–2; Patterson, *Ireland since 1939*, pp. 118–20.

46 *Belfast Newsletter*, 21 September 1947, quoted in Paul Bew, Peter Gibbon and Henry Patterson, *Northern Ireland, 1921–1994: Political Forces and Social Classes* (London: Serif, 1995 edn), p. 104.

47 Dehra Parker at an Orange Order rally. *Belfast Newsletter*, 13 July 1946, quoted in Henry Patterson, 'Party versus Order: Ulster Unionism and the Flags and Emblems Act', *Contemporary British History* 13 (1999), pp. 105–129, p. 111.

48 Patterson, *Ireland since 1939*, pp. 120 and 125–6.
49 Basil Brooke Diaries, 18 February, quoted in Patterson, 'Party versus Order', p. 113.
50 Patterson, *Ireland since 1939*, p. 128.
51 Memorandum by the Minister of Home Affairs on the Civil Authorities (Special Powers) Act, 22 February 1950, quoted in Patterson, 'Party versus Order', pp. 114–15.
52 Patterson, 'Party versus Order', 106, 109, 114–15, 117–18 and 120–6.
53 Michael Farrell, *Arming the Protestants* (London: Pluto Press, 1983), p. 269.
54 A.D. Moses, 'The State and the Student Movement in West Germany, 1967–77', in Gerard J. DeGroot (ed.), *Student Protest: The Sixties and After* (London: Longman, 1998), p. 141.
55 Eric D. Weitz, 'The Ever-Present Other: Communism in the Making of West Germany', in Hannah Schissler (ed.), *The Miracle Years: A Cultural History of West Germany, 1949–1968* (Oxford: Princeton University Press, 2001), p. 219.
56 Stuart J. Hilwig, 'The Revolt against the Establishment: Students versus the Press in West Germany and Italy', in Carole Fink, Philipp Gassert and Detlef Junker (eds), *1968: The World Transformed* (Cambridge: Cambridge University Press, 1998), p. 323.
57 Hanna Schissler, 'Rebels in Search of a Cause', in Hannah Schissler (ed.), *The Miracle Years: A Cultural History of West Germany, 1949–1968* (Oxford: Princeton University Press, 2001), p. 460.
58 Judt, *Postwar*, pp. 265–7.
59 Raymond Aron, *The Elusive Revolution: Anatomy of a Student Revolt*, trans. Gordon Clough (New York: Pall Mall, 1969), p. 117.
60 Sunil Khilnani, *Arguing Revolution: The Intellectual Left in Postwar France* (London: Yale University Press, 1993), pp. 17 and 24.
61 Tony Judt, *The Burden of Responsibility: Blum, Camus, Aron, and the French Twentieth Century* (Chicago: University of Chicago Press, 1998), p. 23.
62 *Derry Journal*, 25 June 1968.
63 *Irish Democrat*, September 1962.
64 Patterson, *Ireland since 1939*, pp. 139, 141–2 and 146–7.
65 Cabinet Conclusions, 11 July 1962, Belfast, Public Record Office of Northern Ireland (PRONI), CAB/4/1199.
66 *Derry Journal*, 26 October 1962.
67 A note by the Governor of Northern Ireland made for Government House records, 29 March 1963, London, National Archives, HO/284/57.
68 Sir Robert Matthew, *Belfast Regional Plan (Matthew Report)* (Belfast: Her Majesty's Stationery Office, 1964), pp. 24–5, 28 and 31.
69 Oliver, *Working at Stormont*, pp. 81–2.
70 Green, 'Bureaucracy for Belfast'.
71 *Derry Journal*, 8 May 1962.
72 *Matthew Report*, p. 22.
73 Ken Bloomfield, *Stormont in Crisis: A Memoir* (Belfast: Blackstaff, 1994), pp. 27 and 734–5.
74 Speech to Queen's University Unionist Association, 13 February 1964, in Terence O'Neill, *Ulster at the Crossroads* (London: Faber, 1969), p. 47.
75 A note by the Governor of Northern Ireland, 29 March 1963.

76   Terence O'Neill, *The Autobiography of Terence O'Neill* (London: Hart Davis, 1972), pp. 8–25.
77   A note by the Governor of Northern Ireland, 29 March 1963.
78   *Hibernia*, 28 August 1970.
79   Michael Farrell, *Northern Ireland: The Orange State* (London: Pluto Press, 1976), p. 222.
80   Brian Faulkner, *Memoirs of a Statesman* (London: Weidenfeld and Nicolson, 1978), pp. 14 and 28.
81   Bloomfield, *Stormont in Crisis*, p. 27.
82   Patterson, *Ireland since 1939* p. 146; David Bleakley, *Faulkner: Conflict and Consent in Irish Politics* (London: Mowbrays, 1974), p. 63; Cabinet Conclusions, 6 March 1962, PRONI, CAB/4/1189.
83   Bloomfield, *Stormont in Crisis*, p. 62.
84   Bloomfield, *Stormont in Crisis*, pp. 74–5.
85   Judt, *Postwar*, p. 290.
86   *Derry Journal*, 28 June 1963.
87   *Derry Journal*, 7 May 1963.
88   O'Neill, *Autobiography*, pp. 48–9, 53 and 57–8.
89   1962 Yale University Commencement Address, quoted in Kevin Mattson, *Intellectuals in Action: The Origins of the New Left and Radical Liberalism, 1945–1970* (University Park: Pennsylvania State University Press, 2002), p. 16.
90   *Derry Journal*, 11 June 1968.
91   *Sunday Express*, 20 October 1963.
92   Speech at Birmingham, 19 January 1964, quoted in Dominic Sandbrook, *Never Had It So Good: A History of Britain from Suez to the Beatles* (London: Little, Brown, 2005), p. 692.
93   Speech to the Annual Meeting of the Ulster Unionist Council, 5 April 1963, in Terence O'Neill, *Ulster at the Crossroads* (London: Faber, 1969), p. 41.
94   O'Neill, *Autobiography*, p. 52.
95   Green, 'Bureaucracy for Belfast'.
96   Cabinet Conclusions, no date given, PRONI, CAB/4/1239.
97   *The Times*, 24 April 1967.
98   *Derry Journal*, 2 November 1965.
99   O'Neill, *Autobiography*, p. 75.
100 Charles Brett, *Long Shadows Cast Before: Nine Lives in Ulster, 1625–1977* (Edinburgh: Bartholomew, 1978), p. 131.
101 *New Statesman*, 2 May 1969.
102 Weitz, 'The Ever-Present Other', p. 220.
103 Paul Bew at the Witness Seminar on British Policy in Northern Ireland 1964–1970, 14 January 1992, London, Institute of Contemporary British History.
104 Speech to the Annual Meeting of the Ulster Unionist Council, 5 April 1963, p. 41.
105 *Derry Journal*, 18 October 1963.
106 Speech to Queen's University Unionist Association, 13 February 1964, p. 48.
107 Jack Sayers, 'The First Year', Northern Ireland Home Service, 25 March 1964, in Andrew Gailey (ed.), *Crying in the Wilderness – Jack Sayers: A Liberal Editor in Ulster, 1939–69* (Belfast: Institute of Irish Studies, 1995), pp. 84–5.
108 Marc Mulholland, *Northern Ireland at the Crossroads: Ulster Unionism in the O'Neill Years 1960–9* (London: Macmillan, 2000), p. 199.

109 O'Neill, *Autobiography*, p. 59.

110 *Derry Journal*, 21 April 1964; *Derry Journal*, 9 October 1964.

111 Henry Patterson, 'Séan Lemass and the Ulster Question, 1959–65', *Journal of Contemporary British History*, 34 (1999), pp. 147–9.

112 Mulholland, *Northern Ireland*, pp. 79 and 82; Faulkner, *Memoirs of a Statesman*, p. 39.

113 *Derry Journal*, 15 January 1965.

114 O'Neill, *Autobiography*, pp. 70–2.

115 Ed Moloney and Andy Pollak, *Paisley* (Swords: Poolbeg Press, 1986), p. 119.

116 *Protestant Telegraph*, 5 October 1968; *Protestant Telegraph*, 19 April 1969; *Protestant Telegraph*, 2 August 1969.

117 *Northern Whig*, 25 July 1963, quoted in Steve Bruce, *God Save Ulster! The Religion and Politics of Paisleyism* (Oxford: Oxford University Press, 1986), p. 74.

118 *Protestant Telegraph*, 5 October 1968.

119 Moloney and Pollak, *Paisley*, p. 111.

120 Christopher Clark, 'The New Catholicism and the European Culture Wars', in Christopher Clark and Wolfram Kaiser (eds), *Culture Wars: Secular–Catholic Conflict in Nineteenth-Century Europe* (Cambridge: Cambridge University Press, 2003), pp. 44–6.

121 Henry Patterson, 'Border Unionism and the Stormont Regime 1945–72', paper delivered to the University of London Irish Studies Seminar, 3 December 2005.

122 *Derry Journal*, 13 July 1965.

123 *Derry Journal*, 12 July 1966.

124 *Derry Journal*, 2 October 1964.

125 O'Neill, *Autobiography*, pp. 63–4.

126 Moloney and Pollack, *Paisley*, pp. 116–17.

127 Minute from Sir Frank Soskice to the Prime Minister, 4 April 1966, London, National Archives of the United Kingdom (NAUK), PREM/13/980.

128 *Derry Journal*, 12 April 1966.

129 *Derry Journal*, 8 April 1966.

130 *Derry Journal*, 19 April 1966.

131 Seamus Heaney, 'Requiem for the Croppies', in *Door into the Dark* (London: Faber, 1969), p. 24.

132 Roy Garland, *Gusty Spence* (Belfast: Blackstaff, 2001), p. 57.

133 *Derry Journal*, 28 June 1966.

134 O'Neill, *Autobiography*, pp. 80–2; Cabinet Conclusions, 29 June 1966, PRONI, CAB/4/1335.

135 Garland, *Gusty Spence*, p. 67.

136 Margaret O'Callaghan and Catherine O'Donnell, 'The Northern Ireland Government, the "Paisleyite Movement", and Ulster Unionism in 1966', *Irish Political Studies*, 12, no. 2 (2006), pp. 203–22, pp. 209–10 and 215.

137 Bruce, *God save Ulster!*, p. 79.

138 Speech to the Northern Irish House of Commons, 15 June 1966, in Terence O'Neill, *Ulster at the Crossroads* (London: Faber, 1969), p. 117.

139 Moloney and Pollak, *Paisley*, pp. 131–5.

140 Cabinet Conclusions, 25 July 1966, PRONI, CAB/4/1336.

141 O'Neill, *Autobiography*, p. 82.

142 Harvard Sitkoff, *The Struggle for Black Equality, 1954–1992* (New York: Hill and Wang, 1992 edn), pp. 129–30 and 177.

143 Nick Thomas, *Protest Movements in 1960s West Germany: A Social History of Dissent and Democracy* (Oxford: Berg, 2003), p. 97.

144 Theodor W. Adorno, 'Education after Auschwitz', in Helmut Schreier and Matthais Heyl (eds), *Never Again! The Holocaust's Challenge for Educators* (Hamburg: Krämer, 1997), pp. 14 and 20.

145 Michael Seidman, *The Imaginary Revolution: Parisian Students and Workers in 1968* (Oxford: Berghahn, 2004), pp. 35–6.

146 O'Neill, *Autobiography*, p. 40.

147 Brooke to Macready, mid-July 1920, quoted in Barton, *Brookeborough*, p. 58.

148 Van Voris, *Violence in Ulster*, p. 45.

149 Van Voris, *Violence in Ulster*, p. 47.

150 Ron Wiener, *The Rape and Plunder of the Shankill in Belfast: People and Planning*, (Belfast: Nothems Press, 1976), pp. 37–8 and 130.

151 Mulholland, *Northern Ireland at the Crossroads*, pp. 35, 37, 39 and 110.

152 Mulholland, *Northern Ireland at the Crossroads*, pp. 108–9, 111 and 117.

153 Van Voris, *Violence in Ulster*, p. 45.

154 Bloomfield, *Stormont in Crisis*, p. 97.

155 Corrymeela Speech, 8 April 1966, in Terence O'Neill, *Ulster at the Crossroads* (London: Faber, 1969), p. 115.

156 Gailey, *Crying in the Wilderness*, pp. 92-3.

157 Speech to Belfast Ulster Week, January 1967, in Terence O'Neill, *Ulster at the Crossroads* (London: Faber, 1969), p. 152.

158 Speech to North Antrim Unionist Association, 25 January 1967, in Terence O'Neill, *Ulster at the Crossroads* (London: Faber, 1969), pp. 55 and 56.

159 Speech to Nottingham Chamber of Commerce, January 1967, in Terence O'Neill, *Ulster at the Crossroads* (London: Faber, 1969), p. 154.

160 Speech to Belfast Ulster Week, January 1967, p. 152.

161 Speech to Belfast Irish Association, 19 February 1968, in Terence O'Neill, *Ulster at the Crossroads* (London: Faber, 1969), p. 131.

162 Mulholland, *Northern Ireland at the Crossroads*, p. 129.

163 *Derry Journal*, 11 June 1968.

164 *Derry Journal*, 11 June 1968.

165 O'Neill, *Autobiography*, p. 101.

166 Walter Williams, Grand Secretary of the Grand Orange Lodge of Ireland, to Terence O'Neill, 12 November 1968, PRONI, CAB/9B/205/7.

167 *Derry Journal*, 24 May 1963.

168 *Derry Journal*, 25 November 1966.

169 *Belfast Telegraph*, 14 December 1967 quoted in Mulholland, *Northern Ireland at the Crossroads*, p. 149.

170 Mulholland, *Northern Ireland at the Crossroads*, pp. 149–50.

171 Memorandum by the Minister of Health and Social Services: Mater Hospital, 19 December 1968, PRONI, CAB/4/1424.

172 *Derry Journal*, 20 October 1967.

173 *Derry Journal*, 24 May 1968.

174 *Derry Journal*, 26 January 1968.

175 Cabinet Conclusions, 26 January 1967, PRONI, CAB/4/1354.

176 Joint Memorandum on Citizens' Rights to the Right Honorable Terence M. O'Neill, M.P., D.L., Prime Minister of Northern Ireland from the Parliamentary

Labour Party, the Northern Ireland Committee, Irish Congress of Trade Unions and the Northern Ireland Labour Party, 1966, PRONI, CAB/4/1347.

177 Patterson, *Ireland since 1939*, p. 130.
178 Citizens' Rights – Proposals by the Northern Ireland Labour Party: Memorandum by the Attorney-General, 28 October 1966, PRONI, CAB/4/1347.
179 Cabinet Conclusions, 10 November 1966, PRONI, CAB/4/1347.
180 Corrymeela Speech, 8 April 1966, p. 113.
181 Mulholland, *Northern Ireland at the Crossroads*, p. 132.
182 Peter Rose, *How the Troubles Came to Northern Ireland* (London: Macmillan, 2000), pp. 11–13.
183 'Northern Ireland – The Plain Truth', in Conn McCluskey, *Up off their Knees: A Commentary on the Civil Rights Movement in Northern Ireland* (Dublin: Conn McCluskey and Associates, 1989), p. 217; *Derry Journal*, 6 October 1964.
184 Buckland, 'A Protestant State', p. 225.
185 Speech to Queen's University Unionist Association, 13 February 1964, p. 48.
186 Speech to Mid Armagh Unionist Association, 19 November 1966, in Terence O'Neill, *Ulster at the Crossroads* (London: Faber, 1969), p. 54.
187 *The Unionist*, March 1967, quoted in Mulholland, *Northern Ireland at the Crossroads*, p. 153.
188 Speech by the Prime Minister, Captain Terence O'Neill D.L., M.P., at the annual confer- ence of the Ulster Unionist Conference, in the Ulster Hall, Belfast, on the evening of Friday, April 28 1967, quoted in Mulholland, *Northern Ireland at the Crossroads*, p. 154.
189 Philip Woodfield to G.J. Otton, 25 October 1964, PRONI, HO/5/186.
190 Covering note prepared by R.M. North, 1966, PRONI, HO/5/186.
191 R.T.G. to Charles Cunningham, 25 November 1964, PRONI, HO/5/186.
192 *Guardian* press clippings, PRONI, HO/5/186.
193 Labour Party Research Department – Northern Ireland: Matters for Discussion with Representatives of the Northern Ireland Labour Party, 1966, PRONI, HO/5/186.
194 Allegations of Religious Discrimination in Northern Ireland: The Position of the United Kingdom Government in respect of Matters Transferred to the Government of Northern Ireland, 1966, PRONI, HO/5/186.
195 Copy of Note by the Secretary of State, 15 November 1964, PRONI, HO/5/186.
196 Sir Frank Soskice to Harold Wilson, 26 November 1964, PRONI, HO/5/186.
197 Harold Wilson to Eugene O'Hare, 28 November 1964, PRONI, HO/5/186.
198 Roy Jenkins, *Asquith* (London: Collins, 1964).
199 Rose, *How the Troubles Came to Northern Ireland*, pp. 48 and 89; Peter Clarke, *Hope and Glory: Britain 1900–1990* (London: Penguin, 1996), pp. 298–300, 308 and 311–13.
200 Witness Seminar on British Policy in Northern Ireland.
201 Geoffrey Warner, 'Putting Pressure on O'Neill: the Wilson Government and Northern Ireland 1964–69', *Irish Studies Review*, 23, no. 1 (2005), pp. 12–31, pp. 12–13.
202 Harold Wilson, *The Labour Government 1964–1970: A Personal Record* (London: Weidenfeld and Nicolson), p. 99.
203 Burke Trend's Note for the Record of the Lunch between the Prime Minister, the Home Secretary and Terence O'Neill, 5 August 1966, London, National Archives of the United Kingdom (NAUK), CAB/164/574.

204 Discussions at Downing Street on 5 August 1966: Notes on the Main Points Raised, PRONI, CAB/4/1338.

205 Terence O'Neill to Sir Frank Soskice, 9 December 1965, quoted in Rose, *How the Troubles Came to Northern Ireland*, p. 18.

206 Minute from Sir Frank Soskice to the Prime Minister, 4 April 1966.

207 Memorandum, 27 July 1966, NAUK, CAB/164/574.

208 Cabinet Conclusions, 9 August 1966, PRONI, CAB/4/1338.

209 O'Neill, *Autobiography*, p. 88.

210 Meeting at Downing Street on 12 January 1967, PRONI, CAB/4/1353.

211 Cabinet Conclusions, 24 January 1967, PRONI, CAB/4/1353.

212 Burke Trend's Note for the Record of the Meeting between the Prime Minister, the Home Secretary, Terence O'Neill, Brian Faulkner and William Craig, 12 January 1967, NAUK, CAB/164/574.

213 Attorney-General to Harold Wilson, 5 April 1965, NAUK, CAB/164/574.

214 Cabinet Conclusions, 9 August 1966.

215 Cabinet Conclusions, 24 January 1967.

216 Harold Wilson, *The Labour Government* (London: Weidenfeld and Nicolson, 1971), p. 178.

217 Meeting at Downing Street on 12 January 1967.

218 Clarke, *Hope and Glory*, pp. 317–18.

219 Speaking Note, NAUK, CJ/3/81.

220 Minister of State: Visit to Northern Ireland, 31 May 1968, NAUK, CJ/3/81.

221 Report on discussion forum at Unionist Headquarters with rank and file members, September 1968, quoted in Patterson, *Ireland since 1939*, p. 207.

222 Corrymeela Speech, 8 April 1966, p. 113.

223 Speech to North Antrim Unionist Association, 25 January 1967, p. 56.

224 Speech to Unionist Party Conference, 29 April 1966, in Terence O'Neill, *Ulster at the Crossroads* (London: Faber, 1969), p. 52.

CHAPTER TWO

1 W.H. Van Voris, *Violence in Ulster: An Oral Documentary* (Amhurst: University of Massachusetts Press, 1974), pp. 61–2.

2 Richard Rose, *Governing without Consensus: An Irish Perspective* (London: Faber, 1971), p. 208.

3 See, for example, Niall Ó Dochartaigh, *From Civil Rights to Armalites: Derry and the Birth of the Irish Troubles* (Cork: Cork University Press, 1997), pp. 22 and 43; Paddy Devlin, *Straight Left: An Autobiography* (Belfast: Blackstaff, 1993), pp. 67 and 76.

4 *Derry Journal*, 31 August 1962.

5 Justin O'Brien, *The Arms Trial* (Dublin: Gill & Macmillan, 2000), pp. 9, 11–12 and 25; Roy Foster, *Modern Ireland 1600–1972* (London: Penguin, 1989), pp. 531, 538 and 544.

6 Enda Staunton, *The Nationalists of Northern Ireland 1918–1973* (Blackrock: Columba Press, 2001), pp. 171 and 181.

7 Conn McCluskey, *Up Off Their Knees: A Commentary on the Civil Rights Movement in Northern Ireland* (Dublin: Conn McCluskey and Associates, 1989), p. 16.

8   *Derry Journal*, 12 December 1967.
9   Robert Tombs, *France: 1814–1914* (London: Longman, 1996), pp. 51, 424 and 474.
10   Tony Judt, *Postwar: A History of Europe since 1945* (London: William Heinemann, 2005), p. 500.
11   *Dungannon Observer*, 4 January 1964.
12   Mary Harris, *The Catholic Church and the Foundation of the Northern Irish State* (Cork: Cork University Press, 1993), pp. 257–8 and 263–4.
13   J.P. Parry, 'Nonconformity, Clericalism and "Englishness: the United Kingdom', in Christopher Clark and Wolfram Kaiser (eds), *Culture Wars: Secular–Catholic Conflict in Nineteenth-Century Europe* (Cambridge: Cambridge University Press, 2003), p. 154.
14   Christopher Clark, 'The New Catholicism and the European Culture Wars', in Clark and Kaiser (eds), *Culture Wars*, pp. 35–6.
15   Wolfram Kaiser, 'Clericalism – That Is Our Enemy!: European Anticlericalism and the Culture Wars', in Clark and Kaiser (eds), *Culture Wars*, pp. 63 and 74.
16   Eugen Weber, *Peasants into Frenchmen: The Modernization of Rural France, 1870–1914* (London: Chatto and Windus, 1977); Tombs, *France 1814–1914*, pp. 302–11.
17   Clark, 'The New Catholicism', pp. 11, 13 and 43.
18   Christopher Clark and Wolfram Kaiser, 'Introduction: The European Culture Wars', in Clark and Kaiser (eds), *Culture Wars*, pp. 6–7.
19   Tombs, *France 1814–1914*, p. 481.
20   Clark and Kaiser, 'Introduction', p. 5.
21   Heidi Bossard-Borner, 'Village Quarrels and National Controversies: Switzerland', in Clark and Kaiser (eds), *Culture Wars*, pp. 264–5.
22   Henry Patterson, *Ireland since 1939* (Oxford: Oxford University Press, 2002), pp. 28–9.
23   Bernadette Devlin, *The Price of My Soul* (London: André Deutsch, 1969), pp. 62–70.
24   Rose, *Governing without Consensus*, pp. 336, 338 and 501.
25   Fionnula O'Connor, *In Search of a State: Catholics in Northern Ireland* (Belfast: Blackstaff, 1993), p. 311.
26   See, for example, *Derry Journal*, 18 August 1961; *Derry Journal*, 5 April 1963; *Derry Journal*, 4 June 1963.
27   Cabinet Conclusions, 26 January 1967, Belfast, Public Record Office of Northern Ireland (PRONI), CAB/4/1354; *Derry Journal*, 20 October 1967.
28   Judt, *Postwar*, pp. 8–9.
29   Frank Curran, *Derry: Countdown to Disaster* (Dublin: Gill & Macmillan, 1986), p. 14.
30   *Derry Journal*, 25 June 1968.
31   Seán Mac Entee speech, 15 April 1944, quoted in Patterson, *Ireland since 1939*, p. 35.
32   Brendan Lynn, *Holding the Ground: The Nationalist Party in Northern Ireland, 1945–72* (Aldershot: Ashgate, 1997), pp. 26–8.
33   Eddie McAteer, *Irish Action: New Thoughts on an Old Subject* (Belfast: Athol Books, 1979).
34   Lynn, *Holding the Ground*, pp. 11–13, 22, 31–3 and 52.

35   Staunton, *The Nationalists of Northern Ireland*, p. 163.

36   John Whyte, *Interpreting Northern Ireland* (Oxford: Oxford University Press, 1990), p. 117; Frank Gallagher, *The Indivisible Island: The History of the Partition of Ireland* (London: Victor Gollancz, 1957), pp. 88, 209 and 232.

37   McAteer, *Irish Action*.

38   *Derry Journal*, 8 October 1968; Brendan Lynn, 'Nationalist Politics in Derry 1945–1969', in Gerard O'Brien (ed.), *Derry and Londonderry – History and Society: Interdisciplinary Essays on the History of an Irish County* (Dublin: Geography Publications, 1999), pp. 605 and 606.

39   Staunton, *The Nationalists of Northern Ireland*, p. 184.

40   Peter Rose, *How the Troubles Came to Northern Ireland* (London: Macmillan, 2000), a. 2.

41   Herbert Morrison, 'Eire and Northern Ireland', 18 October 1968, London, National Archives of the United Kingdom (NAUK), CAB/129/13, quoted in Rose, *How the Troubles Came to Northern Ireland*, p. 2.

42   Bob Purdie, 'The Friends of Ireland', in Tom Gallagher and James O'Connell (eds), *Contemporary Irish Studies* (Manchester: Manchester University Press, 1983), pp. 86 and 88–9.

43   Patterson, *Ireland since 1939*, pp. 99 and 133–4; Lynn, 'Nationalist Politics in Derry 1945–1969', p. 605.

44   Staunton, *The Nationalists of Northern Ireland*, pp. 212–13.

45   Lynn, 'Nationalist Politics in Derry 1945–1969', pp. 608–9.

46   *Irish News*, 19 October 1953, quoted in Lynn, *Holding the Ground*, p. 110.

47   Staunton, *The Nationalists of Northern Ireland*, pp. 218 and 220–1.

48   *Sunday Independent*, 7 September 1958 quoted in Staunton, *The Nationalists of Northern Ireland*, p. 221. The Catholic Social Study Conference was held at St McNissis College, Garron Point.

49   *Derry Journal*, 29 May 1962.

50   Lynn, 'Nationalist Politics in Derry 1945–1969', p. 610.

51   Judt, *Postwar*, pp. 266–7 and 370; Nick Thomas, *Protest Movements in 1960s West Germany: A Social History of Dissent and Democracy* (Oxford: Berg, 2003), pp. 35–7.

52   Michael McKeown, *The Greening of a Nationalist* (Dublin: Murlough, 1986), pp. 17–18.

53   Report on National Unity Organisation, 21 January 1960, PRONI, HA/32/1/1361.

54   *Derry Journal*, 24 May 1963; James Scott to Eddie McAteer, 17 February 1963, quoted in Lynn, *Holding the Ground*, p. 165.

55   *Dungannon Observer*, 2 May 1964.

56   Lynn, *Holding the Ground*, pp. 173–6.

57   *Dungannon Observer*, 12 September 1964.

58   Lynn, 'Nationalist Politics in Derry 1945–1969', pp. 612–13.

59   *Derry Journal*, 17 August 1962.

60   *Derry Journal*, 15 March 1963.

61   *Derry Journal*, 20 July 1962.

62   *Derry Journal*, 24 July 1962.

63   *Derry Journal*, 17 August 1962.

64   *Derry Journal*, 2 October 1962; *Derry Journal*, 18 December 1962.

65   *Derry Journal*, 14 June 1962; *Derry Journal*, 18 June 1962; *Derry Journal*, 21 June 1962.

66   *Derry Journal*, 22 January 1965.
67   Curran, *Countdown to Disaster*, p. 38.
68   Michael Kennedy, *Division and Consensus: The Politics of Cross-Border Relations in Ireland* (Dublin: Institute of Public Administration, 2000), pp. 236–7.
69   Patterson, *Ireland since 1939*, pp. 159–61.
70   *Derry Journal*, 27 October 1967.
71   Frank Aiken to Séan Lemass, 27 January 1965, quoted in John Horgan, *Séan Lemass: The Enigmatic Patriot* (Dublin: Gill & Macmillan, 1997), pp. 158–9.
72   *Derry Journal*, 9 March 1962.
73   *Derry Journal*, 1 May 1962.
74   Curran, *Countdown to Disaster*, p. 38.
75   Gottfried Niedhart, 'Ostpolitik: The Role of the Federal Republic of Germany in the Process of Détente', in Carole Fink, Philipp Gassert and Detlef Junker (eds), *1968: The World Transformed* (Cambridge: Cambridge University Press, 1998), pp. 173–9.
76   Tralee speech, 29 July 1963, quoted in Horgan, *Séan Lemass: The Enigmatic Patriot*, p. 271.
77   J. J. Horgan to Séan Lemass, 24 October 1963, quoted in Henry Patterson, 'Séan Lemass and the Ulster Question, 1959–65', *Journal of Contemporary British History*, 34 (1999), pp. 145–159,154.
78   *Irish Democrat*, October 1965.
79   Patterson, 'Séan Lemass and the Ulster Question, 1959–65', pp. 153–9.
80   *Derry Journal*, 8 May 1962.
81   *Derry Journal*, 26 March 1963.
82   *Derry Journal*, 2 August 1963.
83   *Derry Journal*, 9 October 1964.
84   *Derry Journal*, 5 February 1965.
85   Judt, *Postwar*, p. 370.
86   Comments made by McAteer in a television interview, quoted in the *Derry Journal*, 3 January 1964.
87   *Derry Journal*, 17 January 1964; *Derry Journal*, 28 January 1964.
88   *Derry Journal*, 31 January 1964.
89   For example, *Derry Journal*, 12 August 1966; *Derry Journal*, 18 July 1967; *Derry Journal*, 12 September 1967; *Derry Journal*, 15 November 1968.
90   For example, *Derry Journal*, 10 June 1966.
91   *Derry Journal*, 28 September 1965.
92   *Derry Journal*, 23 May 1961.
93   *Derry Journal*, 17 July 1962; *Derry Journal*, 16 July 1968.
94   *Derry Journal*, 24 April 1967.
95   Eddie McAteer to Cahir Healy, 28 September 1964, PRONI, D/2991/B/21.
96   *Derry Journal*, 24 November 1964; *Derry Journal*, 28 September 1965; *Derry Journal*, 29 January 1965; *Derry Journal*, 3 November 1965.
97   Staunton, *The Nationalists of Northern Ireland*, p. 241.
98   Eddie McAteer to Cahir Healy, Harry Diamond, Charles Stewart, Frank Hanna and Gerry Fitt, 29 October 1964, PRONI, D/2991/B/21.
99   *Derry Journal*, 8 December 1964.
100   *Derry Journal*, 26 January 1968.
101   *Derry Journal*, 27 December 1968.
102   *Derry Journal*, 7 December 1965.

103 *Derry Journal*, 25 June 1968; Cabinet Conclusions, 2 July 1968, PRONI, CAB/4/1400.

104 *Derry Journal*, 25 June 1968.

105 *Derry Journal*, 25 June 1968.

106 Judt, *Postwar*, p. 269.

107 *Dungannon Observer*, 27 April 1963; *Dungannon Observer*, 21 September 1963.

108 Rose, *Governing without Consensus*, pp. 292–4.

109 John Whyte, 'How Much Discrimination Was There under the Unionist Regime, 1921–68?', in Tom Gallagher and James O'Connell (eds), *Contemporary Irish Studies* (Manchester: Manchester University Press, 1983), p. 19.

110 Rose, *Governing without Consensus*, pp. 29–34; Christopher Hewitt, 'Discrimination in Northern Ireland: A Rejoinder', *British Journal of Sociology*, 34 (1983), pp. 446–51, 447.

111 Graham Gudgin, 'Discrimination in Housing and Employment under the Stormont Administration', in P. Roche and B. Barton (eds), *The Northern Ireland Question: Nationalism, Unionism and Partition* (Aldershot: Ashgate, 1999), pp. 101–2.

112 Dennis P. Barritt and Charles F. Carter, *The Northern Ireland Problem: A Study in Group Relations* (Oxford: Oxford University Press, 1962), p. 113.

113 Whyte, 'How Much Discrimination Was There under the Unionist Regime, 1921–68?', pp. 20–1.

114 *Disturbances in Northern Ireland: Report of the Commission Appointed by the Governor of Northern Ireland (Cameron Report)* (Belfast: Her Majesty's Stationery Office, 1969), p. 61.

115 Rose, *Governing without Consensus*, pp. 294–5.

116 McCluskey, *Up Off Their Knees*, p. 10.

117 Jonathan Bardon, *A History of Ulster* (Belfast: Blackstaff, 1992), pp. 642–3.

118 *Dungannon Observer*, 11 May 1963.

119 *Dungannon Observer*, 18 May 1963.

120 *Dungannon Observer*, 18 May 1963.

121 Brian Dooley, *Black and Green: The Fight for Civil Rights in Northern Ireland and Black America* (London: Pluto, 1998), p. 30; Harvard Sitkoff, *The Struggle for Black Equality, 1954–1992* (New York: Hill and Wang, 1993 edn), pp. 127 and 130.

122 Sean Chabot and Jan Willem Duyvendak, 'Globalization and the Transnational Diffusion between Social Movements: Reconceptualizing the Dissemination of the Gandhian Repertoire and the "Coming Out" Routine', *Theory and Society*, 31 (2002), pp. 697–740, 699, 701, 706 and 727–8.

123 Paul Arthur, *Government and Politics of Northern Ireland* (Harlow: Longman, 1980), p. 50; *Irish Times*, 5 October 1968.

124 *Dungannon Observer*, 7 September 1963.

125 *Dungannon Observer*, 25 May 1963.

126 *Tyrone Courier and Dungannon News*, 6 June 1963.

127 McKeown, *The Greening of a Nationalist*, p. 20.

128 *Dungannon Observer*, 1 June 1963.

129 For example, *Dungannon Observer*, 8 June 1963; *Dungannon Observer*, 17 August 1963; *Dungannon Observer*, 31 August 1963.

130 For example, *Dungannon Observer*, 15 June 1963.

131 *Dungannon Observer*, 31 August 1963; *Dungannon Observer*, 7 September 1963.

132 *Dungannon Observer*, 15 June 1963.

133 *Dungannon Observer*, 31 August 1963.

134 McCluskey, *Up Off Their Knees*, pp. 11 and 12.

135 *Dungannon Observer*, 7 September 1963.

136 The Campaign for Social Justice, 'Northern Ireland – The Plain Truth' (2nd edn), in McCluskey, *Up Off Their Knees*, p. 217.

137 *Belfast Telegraph*, 4 September 1963.

138 *Dungannon Observer*, 7 September 1963; McCluskey, *Up Off Their Knees*, pp. 12–13; Conn McCluskey to Minister of Health and Local Government, 14 December 1964, PRONI, D/2993.

139 Memorandum to the Minister of Health and Local Government, PRONI, D/2993.

140 McCluskey to Minister of Health and Local Government, 14 December 1964.

141 *Dungannon Observer*, 28 September 1963.

142 *Dungannon Observer*, 18 January 1964.

143 *Dungannon Observer*, 11 April 1964.

144 *Tyrone Courier and Dungannon News*, 30 April 1964.

145 *Dunganon Observer*, 23 May 1964.

146 *Tyrone Courier and Dungannon News*, 23 January 1964.

147 Henry Patterson, 'Party versus Order: Ulster Unionism and the Flags and Emblems Act', *Contemporary British History*, 13 (1999), pp. 105–29, p. 114.

148 *Dungannon Observer*, 18 January 1964.

149 McCluskey, *Up Off Their Knees*, pp. 10–12 and 129.

150 Judt, *Postwar*, pp. 484–7; Thomas, *Protest Movements in 1960s West Germany*, pp. 240–1.

151 Conn McCluskey to Paul Rose, 6 December 1965, PRONI, D/2993; McCluskey, *Up Off Their Knees*, p. 5.

152 Campaign for Social Justice to United Nations Ambassadors, 15 August 1967, PRONI, D/2993; Campaign for Social Justice to Harold Wilson, 30 August 1968, PRONI, D/2993.

153 Memorandum to the Minister of Health and Local Government.

154 McCluskey, *Up Off Their Knees*, pp. 16 and 17.

155 The Campaign for Social Justice, 'Why Justice Cannot Be Done', in McCluskey, *Up Off Their Knees*, p. 227; The Campaign for Social Justice, 'Northern Ireland – The Plain Truth', p. 190.

156 Campaign for Social Justice to Harold Wilson, 19 October 1967, PRONI, D/2993.

157 Campaign for Social Justice to Roy Jenkins, 25 January 1966, PRONI, D/2993.

158 Campaign for Social Justice to Roy Jenkins, 5 September 1966, PRONI, D/2993.

159 Harold Wilson's Personal Secretary to Campaign for Social Justice, 17 October 1966, PRONI, D/2993.

160 J.A. Chilcot to Campaign for Social Justice, 21 November 1966, PRONI, D/2993.

161 William Wade and Christopher Forsyth, *Administrative Law* (Oxford: Oxford University Press, 2000), pp. 25–6 and 142.

162 Campaign for Social Justice, 'Why Justice Cannot Be Done', p. 229.

163 Harry Calvert, *Constitutional Law in Northern Ireland: A Study in Regional Government* (London: Steven & Sons, 1968), pp. 32–3, 251, 253, 267, 334–5 and 343.

164 Conn McCluskey to Pat Byrne, 8 August 1968, PRONI, D/3026/1.

165 Cabinet Conclusions, 21 May 1965, PRONI, CAB/4/1306.

166 Brief on Statutory Safeguards against Discrimination on Religious Grounds, 29 October 1968, PRONI, CAB/4/1411.

167 Campaign for Social Justice, 'Why Justice Cannot Be Done', pp. 229–34.

168 Kevin Boyle, Tom Hadden and Paddy Hillyard, *Law and State* (Belfast: Robertson, 1972), pp. 22–3.

169 Campaign for Social Justice, 'Why Justice Cannot Be Done', p. 229.

170 Wade and Forsyth, *Administrative Law*, pp. 35, 256–7, 365, 377 and 448–9; Campaign for Social Justice, 'Northern Ireland – The Plain Truth', pp. 217–19.

171 Campaign for Social Justice to Jenkins, 5 September 1966.

172 Boyle, Hadden and Hillyard, *Law and State*, p. 23.

173 Wade and Forsyth, *Administrative Law*, pp. 637, 640 and 667.

174 Arthur, *Government and Politics of Northern Ireland*, p. 82.

175 Campaign for Social Justice to Jenkins, 5 September 1966.

176 Brief on Statutory Safeguards against Discrimination on Religious Grounds.

177 Campaign for Social Justice to Jenkins, 5 September 1966.

178 Campaign for Social Justice, 'Northern Ireland – The Plain Truth', pp. 206–7.

179 McCluskey, *Up Off Their Knees*, pp. 27 and 44.

180 Van Voris, *Violence in Ulster*, p. 51.

181 *Tyrone Courier and Dungannon News*, 23 January 1964.

182 Campaign for Social Justice, 'What the Papers Say', quoted in Bob Purdie, *Politics in the Streets: The Origins of the Civil Rights Movement in Northern Ireland* (Belfast: Blackstaff, 1990), p. 98.

183 Gallagher, *The Indivisible Island*, p. 209.

184 McCluskey, *Up Off Their Knees*, pp. 17–19; Campaign for Social Justice, 'Northern Ireland – The Plain Truth', pp. 193, 195, 197–8, 209, 211 and 218.

185 McCluskey, *Up Off Their Knees*, p. 18.

186 Purdie, *Politics in the Streets*, pp. 101–2.

187 Campaign for Social Justice, 'Northern Ireland – The Plain Truth', pp. 211–12.

188 Gudgin, 'Discrimination in Housing and Employment under the Stormont Administration', p. 105.

189 Barritt and Carter, *The Northern Ireland Problem*, pp. 96–8.

190 Hewitt, 'Discrimination in Northern Ireland', p. 449; Rose, *Governing without Consensus*, p. 336.

191 Hewitt, 'Discrimination in Northern Ireland', 368–9.

192 Patrick Shea, *Voices and the Sound of Drums: An Irish Autobiography* (Belfast: Blackstaff, 1981), pp. 101–2 and 112–13.

193 Whyte, 'How Much Discrimination Was There under the Unionist Regime, 1921–68?', pp. 10–12.

194 Gudgin, 'Discrimination in Housing and Employment under the Stormont Administration', pp. 110–11.

195 Comments by B. Gallagher on Proposed Discrimination Pamphlet, 12 August 1964, quoted in Patterson, 'Séan Lemass and the Ulster Question, 1959–65', p. 150.

196 Campaign for Social Justice, 'Northern Ireland – The Plain Truth', p. 190.

197 Paul Bew, Peter Gibbon, and Henry Patterson, *Northern Ireland, 1921–1994: Political Forces and Social Classes* (London: Serif, 1995 edn), pp. 163–4.

198 Cal McCrystal to Campaign for Social Justice, 6 July 1966, PRONI, D/2993.

199 *Sunday Times*, 3 July 1966.

200 Cal McCrystal, *Reflections on a Quiet Rebel* (London: Penguin, 1997), pp. 14 and 252.

201   McCluskey, *Up Off Our Knees*, pp. 26–7.

202   Paul Rose, *Backbencher's Dilemma* (London: Muller, 1981), p. 178.

203   Introduction to the Files of the Campaign for Democracy in Ulster, 8 April 1974, PRONI, D/3026/1.

204   Conn McCluskey to Patrick Byrne, 26 August 1967, PRONI, D/3026/1; Patrick Byrne to Stan Orme, 11 February 1968, PRONI, D/3026/1; Patrick Byrne to C. Desmond Greaves, 10 March 1968, PRONI, D/3026/1.

205   *Derry Journal*, 18 April 1967.

206   *C.D.U. Newsletter*, October 1967, PRONI, D/3026/1.

207   Note on Meeting with Northern Ireland Labour Party National Executive, 2 August 1967, PRONI, D/3026/1.

208   Patrick Byrne to Conn and Patricia McCluskey, 13 August 1967, PRONI, D/3026/1.

209   *House of Commons Debates*, vol. 729, 27 May 1966, cols. 923–951, quoted in Rose, *How the Troubles Came to Northern Ireland*, p. 37.

210   Merlyn Rees at the Witness Seminar on British Policy in Northern Ireland 1964–1970, 14 January 1992, London, Institute of Contemporary British History.

211   *The Times*, 27 August 2005; *Daily Telegraph*, 27 August 2005.

212   *House of Commons Debates*, vol. 727, 25 April 1966, cols. 437–46.

213   Interview with Paul Rose, 14 August 1992, quoted in Rose, *How the Troubles Came to Northern Ireland*, p. 68.

214   Witness Seminar on British Policy in Northern Ireland.

215   Prime Minister's Personal Secretary to Miss Patricia Byrne, PRONI, D/3026/1.

216   Memorandum to the Central Committee of the Campaign for Democracy in Ulster, Kevin McNamara Papers, quoted in Rose, *How the Troubles Came to Northern Ireland*,   p. 103.

217   Eddie McAteer to Cahir Healy, 11 December 1967, PRONI, D/2991/B/21.

218   Staunton, *The Nationalists of Northern Ireland*, p. 248.

219   *The Times*, 25 April 1967; *Times*, 24 April 1967.

220   Marc Mulholland, *Northern Ireland at the Crossroads: Ulster Unionism in the O'Neill Years 1960–9* (London: Macmillan, 2000), p. 154; McCluskey, *Up Off Their Knees*, pp. 17–20.

221   Conn McCluskey to Pat Byrne, 8 August 1968, PRONI, D/3026/1.

222   Eddie McAteer to Conn McCluskey, 19 August 1964, Derry, Eddie McAteer Papers, quoted in Staunton, *The Nationalists of Northern Ireland*, p. 237.

223   Discussions at Downing Street on 5 August 1966: Notes on the Main Points Raised, PRONI, CAB/4/1338.

224   Patterson, *Ireland since 1939*, pp. 240–1.

225   Witness Seminar on British Policy in Northern Ireland.

226   Campaign for Social Justice, 'Northern Ireland – The Plain Truth', NAUK, HO/221/223.

227   Lord Stonham to Campaign for Social Justice, 4 September 1969, PRONI, D/2993.

228   Rose, *How the Troubles Came to Northern Ireland*, pp. 110–13.

229   McCluskey, *Up Off Their Knees*, p. 19.

CHAPTER THREE

1   George Thayer, *The British Political Fringe: A Profile* (London: Anthony Blond, 1965), pp. 225 and 229–35.

2 Philip Williamson, *Stanley Baldwin: Conservative Leadership and National Values* (Cambridge: Cambridge University Press, 1999), p. 256.

3 W.K. Anderson, *James Connolly and the Irish Left* (Blackrock: Irish Academic Press, 1994), p. 47.

4 Anthony Coughlan, 'C. Desmond Greaves, 1913–1988: An Obituary Essay', *Saothar*, 14 (1989), pp. 5–15, pp. 5–6 and 8.

5 Anthony Coughlan, *Draft Connolly Association History* (unpublished manuscript); *Irish Democrat*, October 1958.

6 Coughlan, 'C. Desmond Greaves, 1913–1988', p. 6.

7 Doris Lessing, *The Golden Notebook* (London: Michael Joseph, 1972 edn), p. 67.

8 C. Desmond Greaves, *Journals*, 19 October 1956, extract from the Century of Endeavour electronic archive (contact Roy Johnston at www.*rjtechne@iol.ie* about access).

9 Michael Kenny, *The First New Left: British Intellectuals after Stalin* (London: Lawrence & Wishart, 1995), pp. 16–19.

10 Lessing, *The Golden Notebook*, p. 177.

11 Coughlan, 'C. Desmond Greaves, 1913–1988', pp. 6 and 12.

12 Roy Johnston, *Century of Endeavour: A Biographical and Autobiographical View of the 20th Century in Ireland* (Dublin: The Lilliput Press, 2002), pp. 123, 167 and 170.

13 Willie Thompson, 'British Communists in the Cold War, 1947–52', *Contemporary British History*, vol. 15, no. 3 (2001), pp. 105–32, 118–9 and 122.

14 Greaves, *Journals*, 19 February 1949, extract from the Century of Endeavour electronic archive.

15 Anthony Coughlan (ed.), 'Insight, Ideas, Politics: The Table Talk of C. Desmond Greaves, 1960–1988' (unpublished manuscript).

16 Coughlan (ed.), *Insight, Ideas, Politics*.

17 *Irish Democrat*, July 1960; *Irish Democrat*, July 1964.

18 *Irish Democrat*, August 1968.

19 *Irish Democrat*, August 1968.

20 *Irish Democrat*, June 1962.

21 *Irish Democrat*, January 1965.

22 *Irish Democrat*, July 1964.

23 *Irish Democrat*, July 1961.

24 *Irish Democrat*, April 1961.

25 *Irish Democrat*, June 1962.

26 *Irish Democrat*, February 1960.

27 *Irish Democrat*, July 1961.

28 *Irish Democrat*, July 1960.

29 *Irish Democrat*, July 1961.

30 John Hostettler, *Torture Trial in Belfast* (London: Connolly Association, 1958).

31 Coughlan, *Draft History of the Connolly Association*.

32 *Irish Democrat*, August 1958.

33 *Irish Democrat*, March 1959.

34 *Irish Democrat*, July 1960.

35 *Irish Democrat*, May 1961.

36 *Irish Democrat*, March 1962.

37 *Irish Democrat*, February 1962.

38 *Irish Democrat*, April 1965.

39 *Irish Democrat*, October 1965.

40 *Irish Democrat*, June 1969; *Irish Democrat*, July 1963; *Irish Democrat*, July 1965; *Irish Democrat*, July 1966.

41 *Irish Democrat*, May 1961; *Irish Democrat*, July 1961; *Irish Democrat*, May 1962; C. Desmond Greaves, *Reminiscences of the Connolly Association* (London: Connolly Association, 1978), p. 31.

42 Coughlan, 'C. Desmond Greaves, 1913–1988', p. 8.

43 *Irish Democrat*, April 1962.

44 *Irish Democrat*, April 1962; Greaves, *Reminiscences of the Connolly Association*, p. 31.

45 C. Desmond Greaves to Cahir Healy, 16 February 1960, Belfast, Public Record Office of Northern Ireland (PRONI), D/2991/B/72.

46 *Irish Democrat*, March 1964; C. Desmond Greaves, *The Irish Crisis* (London: Lawrence & Wishart, 1972), p. 129.

47 *Irish Democrat*, June 1965; Greaves, *Reminiscences of the Connolly Association*, pp. 32–3.

48 *Irish Democrat*, April 1966; *Irish Democrat*, November 1967.

49 *Irish Democrat*, May Special 1966.

50 *Irish Democrat*, April 1964; *Irish Democrat*, December 1966.

51 *Irish Democrat*, July 1963; *Irish Democrat*, July 1965; *Irish Democrat*, July 1966; *Irish Democrat*, July 1967.

52 *Irish Democrat*, June 1965.

53 Introduction to the Files of the Campaign for Democracy in Ulster.

54 Paul Rose, *Backbencher's Dilemma* (London: Muller, 1981), p. 178.

55 *Irish Democrat*, May 1962; e-mail correspondence with Anthony Coughlan, 5 August 2006.

56 *Irish Democrat*, March 1965; *Irish Democrat*, April 1965; Greaves, *The Irish Crisis*, p. 130.

57 For example, *Irish Democrat*, September 1965.

58 *Irish Democrat*, April 1967.

59 *Irish Democrat*, February 1968.

60 *Irish Democrat*, March 1968.

61 Byrne to Greaves, 10 March 1968.

62 Sean Redmond to Paddy Byrne, 20 March 1969, PRONI, D/3026/1; *Irish Democrat*, May 1968.

63 *Irish Democrat*, May Special 1966.

64 Bob Purdie, *Politics in the Streets: The Origins of the Civil Rights Movement in Northern Ireland* (Belfast: Blackstaff, 1990), p. 106.

65 *Irish Democrat*, March 1965.

66 C. Desmond Greaves to Cahir Healy, 10 June 1962, PRONI, D/2991/B/72; *Irish Democrat*, June 1960; *Irish Democrat*, July 1960; *Irish Democrat*, May 1962; *Irish Democrat*, August 1962; Greaves, *The Irish Crisis*, p. 133.

67 *Derry Journal*, 14 September 1962.

68 *Irish Democrat*, February 1960; *Irish Democrat*, January 1961; Purdie, *Politics in the Streets*, pp. 121 and 122.

69 *Irish Democrat*, December 1962.

70 Greaves, *Journals*, 19 April 1964, extract from the Century of Endeavour electronic archive.

71 National Council for Civil Liberties Northern Ireland Conference, 13 March 1965, PRONI, D/2993.

72 *Irish Democrat*, April 1965.
73 *Irish Democrat*, November 1967.
74 *Irish Democrat*, November 1967.
75 *Irish Democrat*, July 1964.
76 Greaves to Healy, 6 July 1961.
77 *Irish Democrat*, September 1965.
78 *Irish Democrat*, November 1962.
79 *Irish Democrat*, July 1964.
80 John Hewitt, *A Northern Light*, quoted in Edna Longley, 'Bookmen: Left-wing Politics and Ulster Protestant Writers', in Eve Patten (ed.), *Returning to Ourselves: Second Volume of Papers from the John Hewitt International Summer School* (Belfast: Lagan Press, 1995), p. 23.
81 Robert Tombs, *France 1814–1914* (London: Longman, 1996), pp. 9 and 18.
82 Karl Marx, *Economic and Philosophical Manuscripts*, trans. David McLellan, in David McLellan (ed.), *Karl Marx: Selected Writings* (Oxford: Oxford University Press, 1977), p. 89.
83 Albert Camus, *The Plague*, trans. Robin Buss (London: Penguin, 2006), p. 195.
84 Albert Camus, *The Rebel*, trans. Anthony Bower (London: Penguin, 2000), p. 195.
85 Tony Judt, *The Burden of Responsibility: Blum, Camus, Aron, and the French Twentieth- Century* (London: The University of Chicago Press, 1998), p. 26.
86 Sunil Khilnani, *Arguing Revolution: The Intellectual Left in Postwar France* (London: Yale University Press, 1993), pp. 50–1, 67–8 and 129.
87 Mark Poster, *Existential Marxism in Postwar France: From Sartre to Althusser* (Princeton: Princeton University Press, 1975), pp. 211–17.
88 Poster, *Existential Marxism in Postwar France*, pp. 42 and 51.
89 Marx, *Economic and Philosophical Manuscripts*, pp. 96–109.
90 Marx, *Economic and Philosophical Manuscripts*, pp. 77–87.
91 Karl Marx, *The Holy Family*, trans. David McLellan, in David McLellan (ed.), *Karl Marx: Selected Writings* (Oxford: Oxford University Press, 1977), pp. 134–5.
92 Poster, *Existential Marxism in Postwar France*, p. 216.
93 Stuart Hall, 'The "First" New Left: Life and Times', in Robin Archer, Diemut Bubeck, Hanjo Glock, Lesley Jacobs, Seth Moglen, Adam Steinhouse and Daniel Weinstock (eds), *Out of Apathy: Voices of the New Left Thirty Years on* (London: Verso, 1989), pp. 14–15 and 23–4.
94 Kenny, *The First New Left*, p. 54.
95 E-mail correspondence with Roy Johnston, 21 April 2006.
96 Roy Johnston, 1940s political module of the hypertext political thread, Century of Endeavour electronic archive.
97 *The Harp*, March 1908, quoted in Anderson, *James Connolly and the Irish Left*, p. 42.
98 Johnston, 1940s political module; Roy Johnston, 1950s political module of the hypertext political thread, Century of Endeavour electronic archive.
99 Johnston, *Century of Endeavour*, pp. 152, 156–8 and 167.
100 Greaves, *Journals*, 1 August 1963, extract from the Century of Endeavour electronic archive.
101 Johnston, *Century of Endeavour*, p. 171.
102 E-mail correspondence with Roy Johnston, 21 April 2006.
103 *Guardian*, 4 March 2004.
104 Johnston, *Century of Endeavour*, p. 171.

105 Van Gosse, *Where the Boys Are: Cuba, Cold War America and the Making of a New Left* (London: Verso, 1993), p. 50.
106 Lessing, *The Golden Notebook*, p. 601.
107 Draft of 'A Republican Programme for the 1960s', November 1963, Century of Endeavour electronic archive.
108 Frantz Fanon, *The Wretched of the Earth*, trans. Constance Farrington (London: Penguin, 2001), pp. 53 and 251–4; *United Irishman*, October 1964, Century of Endeavour electronic archive.
109 Greaves, *Journals*, 13 July 1968, extract from the Century of Endeavour electronic archive.
110 Johnston, *Century of Endeavour*, p. 235.
111 Séan Mac Stíofáin, *Memoirs of a Revolutionary* (London: Gordon Cremonesi, 1975), pp. 1–55.
112 Henry Patterson, *The Politics of Illusion: A Political History of the IRA* (London: Serif, 1997 edn), pp. 96–7.
113 Henry Patterson, *Ireland since 1939* (Oxford: Oxford University Press, 2002), pp. 136–8.
114 Roy Johnston, political work in the early 1960s module of the hypertext political thread, Century of Endeavour electronic archive.
115 Richard English, *Radicals and the Republic: Socialist Republicanism in the Irish Free State, 1925–1937* (Oxford: Oxford University Press, 1994), pp. 255 and 270.
116 Richard English, *Armed Struggle: The History of the IRA* (London: Macmillan, 2003), p. 87.
117 Programme of the Wolfe Tone Directories, quoted in Johnston, *Century of Endeavour*, p. 175
118 *Fortnight*, 22 March 1974.
119 Belfast Wolfe Tone Society Memorandum, 21 February 1968, PRONI, D/3253/4.
120 Johnston, *Century of Endeavour*, pp. 176 and 180.
121 *Irish Democrat*, April 1965.
122 Johnston, *Century of Endeavour*, p. 185.
123 Interview with Séan Mac Stíofáin, quoted in O'Brien, *The Arms Trial*, pp. 19–20.
124 Mac Stíofáin, *Memoirs of a Revolutionary*, pp. 93–7.
125 Sinn Féin Ard Comhairle minutes, 4 December 1965, Century of Endeavour electronic archive.
126 Johnston, political work in the early 1960s module.
127 Greaves, *Journals*, 6 July 1968, extract from the Century of Endeavour electronic archive.
128 *Guardian*, 2 November 2000.
129 Roy Johnston, Notes on Memoirs of Séan Mac Stíofáin, Century of Endeavour electronic archive.
130 English, *Armed Struggle*, pp. 84, 87 and 90.
131 Johnston, *Century of Endeavour*, pp. 192–3; Mac Stíofáin, *Memoirs of a Revolutionary*, pp. 75–9.
132 Greaves, *Journals*, 10 December 1965, extract from the Century of Endeavour electronic archive.
133 Report on 'Paisleyite Movement', 20 June 1966, PRONI, CAB/9B/300/1, quoted in Margaret O'Callaghan and Catherine O'Donnell, 'The Northern Ireland Government, the "Paisleyite Movement", and Ulster Unionism in 1966', *Irish Political Studies,* vol. 21 (2006), pp. 203–22, 213.

134 Johnston, *Century of Endeavour*, pp. 219-20 and 229.
135 *Tuairisc*, August 1966.
136 *Tuairisc*, August 1966.
137 *Tuairisc*, August 1966.
138 *Tuairisc*, August 1966.
139 *Tuairisc*, August 1966.
140 Johnston, *Century of Endeavour*, p. 198.
141 E-mail correspondence with Anthony Coughlan, 4 August 2006.
142 Johnston, *Century of Endeavour*, p. 231.
143 *Tuairisc*, August 1966.

CHAPTER FOUR

1 *Irish Democrat*, April 1965; *Irish Democrat*, June 1965.
2 Mike Milotte, *Communism in Modern Ireland: The Pursuit of the Workers' Republic since 1916* (Dublin: Gill & Macmillan, 1984), pp. 237–8 and 253–5.
3 *Irish Democrat*, April 1965.
4 Roy Johnston, *Century of Endeavour: A Biographical and Autobiographical View of the 20th Century in Ireland* (Dublin: The Lilliput Press, 2002), pp. 187 and 197–201.
5 *Irish Democrat*, January 1967.
6 Northern Ireland Civil Rights Association, *We Shall Overcome ... The History of the Struggle for Civil Rights in Northern Ireland, 1968–78* (Belfast: NICRA, 1978), pp. 7–8; Conn McCluskey, *Up Off Their Knees: A Commentary on the Civil Rights Movement in Northern Ireland* (Dublin: Conn McCluskey and Associates, 1989), pp. 104–5; *Fortnight*, 22 March 1974.
7 *Irish Democrat*, March 1967; Anthony Coughlan, 'Draft History of the Connolly Association' (unpublished manuscript).
8 Milotte, *Communism in Modern Ireland*, pp. 253, 257 and 264; National Council for Civil Liberties Report to the Home Secretary, 31 March 1967, London, National Archives, CAB/164/574.
9 C. Desmond Greaves, *Journals*, 20 April 1967, extract from the Century of Endeavour electronic archive.
10 *United Irishman*, Special Bicentenary Issue, Century of Endeavour electronic archive.
11 Paul Dixon, *Northern Ireland: The Politics of War and Peace* (Basingstoke: Palgrave, 2001), p. 75.
12 *Irish Democrat*, January 1968.
13 Johnston, *Century of Endeavour*, p. 222.
14 *Irish Democrat*, February 1968.
15 Johnston, *Century of Endeavour*, pp. 217–18.
16 *Disturbances in Northern Ireland: Report of the Commission Appointed by the Governor of Northern Ireland (Cameron Report)* (Belfast: Her Majesty's Stationery Office, 1969), p. 22.
17 Northern Ireland Civil Rights Association, *We Shall Overcome*, p. 11.
18 Civil Rights March from Coalisland to Dungannon, 29 August 1968, Belfast, Public Record Office of Northern Ireland (PRONI), CAB/9B/205/7; Austin Currie, *All Hell Will Break Loose* (Dublin: O'Brien, 2004), pp. 96–8.

19 Interview with Austin Currie, quoted in Brian Dooley, *Black and Green: The Fight for Civil Rights in Northern Ireland and Black America* (London: Pluto Press, 1998), p. 47.

20 *Cameron Report*, p. 21; Graham Gudgin, 'Discrimination in Housing and Employment under the Stormont Administration', in P. Roche and B. Barton (eds), *The Northern Ireland Question: Nationalism, Unionism and Partition* (Aldershot: Ashgate, 1999), p. 100.

21 *Dungannon Observer*, 25 May 1968.

22 Dooley, *Black and Green*, pp. 45–6.

23 *Derry Journal*, 27 October 1967.

24 Civil Rights March from Coalisland to Dungannon.

25 Northern Ireland Civil Rights Association, *We Shall Overcome*, p. 9.

26 *Dungannon Observer*, 29 June 1968.

27 Interview with Currie, quoted in Dooley, *Black and Green*, p. 49.

28 *Cameron Report*, pp. 21–2; McCluskey, *Up Off Their Knees*, pp. 106 and 107; *Fortnight*, 5 April 1974; Currie, *All Hell Will Break Loose*, pp. 100–1.

29 Introduction to the Frank Gogarty Papers, PRONI, D/3253/1.

30 Henry Hampton and Steve Fayer (eds), *Voices of Freedom: An Oral History of the Civil Rights Movement from the 1950s through the 1980s* (London: Vintage, 1995), p. 480.

31 *Fortnight*, 5 April 1974.

32 *Dungannon Observer*, 3 August 1968.

33 *Cameron Report*, pp. 14, 22 and 26.

34 Civil Rights March from Coalisland to Dungannon.

35 Currie, *All Hell Will Break Loose*, pp. 102–3.

36 McCluskey, *Up Off Their Knees*, pp. 107–8.

37 Bernadette Devlin, *The Price of My Soul* (London: André Deutsch, 1969), pp. 91–4.

38 Civil Rights March from Coalisland to Dungannon.

39 Johnston, *Century of Endeavour*, pp. 232–3.

40 Northern Ireland Civil Rights Association, *We Shall Overcome*, p. 11.

41 Civil Rights March from Coalisland to Dungannon.

42 Tony Judt, *Postwar: A History of Europe since 1945* (London: William Heinemann, 2005), pp. 443–4.

43 Currie, *All Hell Will Break Loose*, p. 103.

44 Civil Rights March from Coalisland to Dungannon.

45 Currie, *All Hell Will Break Loose*, pp. 101–2.

46 Civil Rights March from Coalisland to Dungannon.

47 *Dungannon Observer*, 24 August 1968.

48 Terence O'Neill, *The Autobiography of Terence O'Neill* (London: Faber, 1972), p. 102.

49 *Belfast Telegraph*, 3 October 1968.

50 Henry Patterson, *Ireland since 1939* (Oxford: Oxford University Press, 2002), p. 200; Dixon, *Northern Ireland*, pp. 89–90.

51 Harvard Sitkoff, *The Struggle for Black Equality, 1954–1992* (New York: Hill and Wang, 1992 edn), pp. 126–8.

52 *Derry Journal*, 25 June 1968; *Cameron Report*, pp. 22–3.

53 Currie, *All Hell Will Break Loose*, p. 107.

54 Civil Rights March from Coalisland to Dungannon.

55 Milotte, *Communism in Modern Ireland*, pp. 136 and 164; Patterson, *Ireland since 1939*, pp. 10 and 13.

56 Civil Rights March from Coalisland to Dungannon; Fionbarra Ó Dochartaigh, *Ulster's White Negroes: From Civil Rights to Insurrection* (Edinburgh: AK Press, 1994), p. 45.

57 Interview with Tomás Mac Giolla quoted in Dooley, *Black and Green*, p. 51.

58 Currie, *All Hell Will Break Loose*, p. 150.

59 Eamonn McCann, *War and an Irish Town* (London: Pluto, 1993 edn), pp. 91–2.

60 Currie, *All Hell Will Break Loose*, p. 106.

61 Civil Rights March from Coalisland to Dungannon.

62 *Cameron Report*, p. 24.

CHAPTER FIVE

1 *Derry Journal*, 11 October 1966.

2 *Derry Journal*, 4 August 1967.

3 Fionbarra Ó Dochartaigh, *Ulster's White Negroes: From Civil Rights to Insurrection* (Edinburgh: AK Press, 1994), p. 34.

4 Bernadette Devlin, *The Price of My Soul* (London: André Deutsch, 1969), p. 143.

5 *Derry Journal*, 29 November 1963; *Derry Journal*, 3 June 1966.

6 *Disturbances in Northern Ireland: Report of the Commission Appointed by the Governor of Northern Ireland (Cameron Report)* (Belfast: Her Majesty's Stationery Office, 1969), pp. 24 and 60.

7 *The Listener*, 24 October 1968.

8 Edmund Warnock to Terence O'Neill, 13 November 1968, Belfast, Public Record Office of Northern Ireland (PRONI), CAB/4/1414.

9 *Derry Journal*, 8 September 1961.

10 Frank Gallagher, *The Indivisible Island: The History of the Partition of Ireland* (London: Victor Gollancz, 1957), p. 243.

11 *Derry Journal*, 8 September 1961.

12 Niall Ó Dochartaigh, 'Housing and Conflict: Social Change and Collective Action in Derry in the 1960s', in Gerard O'Brien (ed.), *Derry and Londonderry – History and Society: Interdisciplinary Essays on the History of an Irish County* (Dublin: Geography Publications, 1999), pp. 625–7.

13 *Derry Journal*, 20 September 1966.

14 Richard I.D. Harris, *Regional Economic Policy in Northern Ireland, 1945–88* (Aldershot: Avebury, 1991), p. 19.

15 Frank Curran, *Derry: Countdown to Disaster* (Dublin: Gill & Macmillan, 1986), p. 23.

16 *Derry Journal*, 11 October 1966.

17 Henry Patterson, *Ireland since 1939* (Oxford: Oxford University Press, 2002), pp. 128 and 130–1.

18 Sir Basil Brooke, *Diaries*, 24 February 1956, quoted in Patterson, *Ireland since 1939*, p. 131.

19 Speech to the Annual Meeting of the Ulster Unionist Council, 5 April 1963, in Terence O'Neill, *Ulster at the Crossroads* (London: Faber, 1969), p. 41.

20 *Derry Journal*, 7 February 1964.

21 *Derry Journal*, 18 August 1964.

22   *Derry Journal*, 21 August 1964.
23   *Derry Journal*, 1 January 1965.
24   *Derry Journal*, 2 February 1965.
25   *Derry Journal*, 9 February 1965.
26   *Derry Journal*, 19 February 1965.
27   *Derry Journal*, 2 March 1965.
28   *Derry Journal*, 5 March 1965; *Londonderry Sentinel*, 3 March 1965.
29   *Derry Journal*, 11 May 1965; *Londonderry Sentinel*, 12 May 1965.
30   Paddy Doherty, *Paddy Bogside* (Dublin: Mercier Press, 2001), pp. 26–30 and 32.
31   *Derry Journal*, 14 February 1961.
32   *Derry Journal*, 6 December 1968.
33   *Derry Journal*, 14 February 1961.
34   *Derry Journal*, 22 October 1965.
35   *Derry Journal*, 10 December 1965.
36   *Derry Journal*, 26 November 1965.
37   E.W. Jones to C.J. Bateman, 11 February 1965, PRONI, CAB/9D/31/2.
38   *Londonderry Sentinel*, 31 March 1965.
39   E.W. Jones to H. Black, 2 April 1965, PRONI, CAB/9D/31/2.
40   Gerard O'Brien, '"Our Magee Problem": Stormont and the Second University', in O'Brien, G. (ed.), *Derry and Londonderry – History and Society: Interdisciplinary Essays on the History of an Irish County* (Dublin: Geography Publications, 1999), pp. 647–8, 661–8 and 685.
41   O'Brien, ' "Our Magee Problem" ', pp. 677–9 and 683.
42   E.W. Jones to Herbert Kirk, 2 April 1965, PRONI, CAB/9D/31/2.
43   'Handwritten Note of Discussion between the Prime Minister, Education Minister, and Representatives of Londonderry Unionism', 19 February 1965, PRONI, CAB/9D/31/2; *Londonderry Sentinel*, 2 June 1965.
44   Thomas Wilson, *Economic Development in Northern Ireland (Wilson Report)* (Belfast: Her Majesty's Stationery Office, 1964), p. 135.
45   Memorandum from John Oliver to Harold Black, 17 February 1965, quoted in O'Brien, '"Our Magee problem"', pp.682–3.
46   *Derry Journal*, 19 October 1965.
47   *Londonderry Sentinel*, 3 November 1965.
48   Memorandum on Local Government Reorganisation, 15 October 1968, PRONI, CAB/4/1316.
49   Brendan Lynn, 'Nationalist Politics in Derry 1945–1969', in Gerard O'Brien (ed.), *Derry and Londonderry – History and Society: Interdisciplinary Essays on the History of an Irish County* (Dublin: Geography Publications, 1999), p. 607.
50   *Derry Journal*, 5 March 1968.
51   *Reality*, Anniversary Edition 1968-9, PRONI, D/2560/4/2.
52   *Derry Journal*, 2 April 1968.
53   *Londonderry Sentinel*, 3 April 1968.
54   *Derry Journal*, 25 June 1968.
55   *Derry Journal*, 2 April 1968.
56   *Derry Journal*, 2 June 1964.
57   *Derry Journal*, 26 January 1965.
58   *Derry Journal*, 29 January 1965; *Londonderry Sentinel*, 27 January 1965.
59   *Derry Journal*, 5 July 1968; *Derry Journal*, 16 August 1968; *Derry Journal*, 10 September 1968; Eamonn McCann, *War and an Irish Town* (London: Pluto, 1993 edn), pp. 91–4.

60 *Derry Journal*, 5 February 1965.

61 Ó Dochartaigh, *Ulster's White Negroes*, pp. 15 and 20.

62 *Derry Journal*, 15 February 1966.

63 *Derry Journal*, 29 March 1966.

64 Margot Gayle Backus, '"Not Quite Philadelphia, Is It?": An Interview with Eamonn McCann', *Éire-Ireland*, 36, 3 & 4 (2001), pp. 178–91, 176–7.

65 *Derry Journal*, 6 March 1964.

66 *Irish Militant*, April 1967; *Derry Journal*, 2 May 1967.

67 W. H. Van Voris, *Violence in Ulster: An Oral Documentary* (Amherst: University of Massachusetts Press, 1975), pp. 60–1.

68 *Irish Militant*, September 1967.

69 *Irish Militant*, April 1967.

70 Tony Judt, *Postwar: A History of Europe since 1945* (London: William Heinemann, 2005), p. 402.

71 Comment made by Roy Johnston on C. Desmond Greaves, *Journals*, 7 September 1965, extract from the Century of Endeavour electronic archive.

72 *Irish Democrat*, May 1967.

73 *Irish Militant*, May 1967.

74 Ó Dochartaigh, *Ulster's White Negroes*, p. 19.

75 *Irish Militant*, September 1967.

76 Ó Dochartaigh, *Ulster's White Negroes*, p. 32; e-mail correspondence with Roy Johnston, 21 April 2006.

77 *Irish Democrat*, February 1968.

78 *Irish Militant*, November 1966.

79 Elizabeth Ewen, 'A Way of Seeing', in Paul Buhle (ed.), *History and the New Left: Madison, Wisconsin, 1950–1970s* (Philadelphia: Temple University, 1990), p. 151.

80 *Derry Journal*, 2 July 1968; McCann, *War and an Irish Town*, p. 86.

81 Ó Dochartaigh, *Ulster's White Negroes*, pp. 15 and 19.

82 Backus, '"Not Quite Philadelphia, Is It?"', p. 183.

83 Bob Purdie, *Politics in the Streets: The Origins of the Civil Rights Movement in Northern Ireland* (Belfast: Blackstaff, 1990), p. 229.

84 Lawrence S. Wittner, *Resisting the Bomb: A History of the World Nuclear Disarmament Movement, 1954–1970* (Stanford: Stanford University Press, 1997), p. 85.

85 *Irish Democrat*, May 1960.

86 Harriet Tanzman, 'Civil Rights and History', in Paul Buhle (ed.), *History and the New Left: Madison, Wisconsin, 1950–1970s* (Philadelphia: Temple University, 1990), pp. 142–7.

87 Wittner, *Resisting the Bomb*, p. 461.

88 Gregory Nevala Calvert, *Democracy from the Heart: Spiritual Values, Decentralism and Democratic Idealism in the Movement of the 1960s* (Eugene: Communitas, 1991), pp. 43 and 46.

89 Jonathan Schell, *The Unconquerable World: Power, Non-violence, and the Will of the People* (London: Allen Lane, 2004), pp.117–19; Maurice Isserman, *If I Had a Hammer: The Death of the Old Left and the Birth of the New Left* (New York: University of Illinois Press, 1987), pp. 129 and 195.

90 Francesca Polletta, *Freedom is an Endless Meeting: Democracy in American Social Movements* (London: The University of Chicago Press, 2002), pp. 35–6 and 39–40; Jo

Ann Ooiman Robinson, *Abraham Went Out: A Biography of A.J. Muste* (Philadelphia: Temple University Press, 1981).

91 James Farmer, 'The March on Washington: The Zenith of the Southern Movement', in Armstead L. Robinson and Patricia Sullivan (eds), *New Directions in Civil Rights Studies* (London: University of Virginia Press, 1991), pp. 30–1.

92 Charles Marsh, 'The Civil Rights Movement as a Theological Drama', in Ted Ownby (ed.), *The Role of Ideas in the Civil Rights South* (Jackson: University of Mississippi Press, 2002), p. 31.

93 Calvert, *Democracy from the Heart*, pp. 43, 61 and 64; Sean Chabot and Jan Willem Duyvendak, 'Globalization and the Transnational Diffusion between Social Movements: Reconceptualizing the Dissemination of the Gandhian Repertoire and the "Coming Out" Routine', *Theory and Society*, 31, 6 (December 2002), pp. 697–740, 715 and 719–24.

94 Clayborne Carson, *In Struggle: SNCC. and the Black Awakening of the 1960s* (Cambridge, MA: Harvard University Press, 1995 edn), pp. 18–24; Polletta, *Freedom is an Endless Meeting*, pp. 44–8; Robinson, *Abraham Went Out*, pp. 118–19; Chabot and Duyvendak, 'Globalization and the Transnational Diffusion between Social Movements', p. 725.

95 Student Non-violent Co-ordinating Committee Founding Statement, in Alexander Bloom and Wini Breines (eds), *"Takin' It to the Streets": A Sixties Reader* (Oxford: Oxford University Press, 1995), pp. 24–5.

96 Richard Taylor, *Against the Bomb: The British Peace Movement 1958–1965* (Oxford: Oxford University Press, 1988), pp. 23, 121–3, 167–8, 178 and 188.

97 Wittner, *Resisting the Bomb*, p. 95.

98 'Transcription of shorthand notes taken by P.S. Westgate at a demonstration in Trafalgar Square on Friday 4.4.1958', London, National Archives of the United Kingdom (NAUK), HO/325/149.

99 Wittner, *Resisting the Bomb*, p. 49.

100 Anthony Coughlan, 'Draft History of the Connolly Association' (unpublished manu- script).

101 1957 Committee foundation meeting, quoted in Taylor, *Against the Bomb*, p. 121.

102 Taylor, *Against the Bomb*, pp. 167 and 174.

103 Rob Burns and Wilfried van der Will, *Protest and Democracy in West Germany: Extra- Parliamentary Opposition and the Democratic Agenda* (Basingstoke: Macmillan, 1988), pp.89 and 92–3.

104 Wittner, *Resisting the Bomb*, pp. 220 and 360.

105 Wittner, *Resisting the Bomb*, pp. 74, 77, 203, 220 and 298; e-mail correspondence with Roy Johnston, 21 April 2006.

106 Roy Johnston, *Century of Endeavour: A Biographical and Autobiographical View of the 20th Century in Ireland* (Dublin: The Lilliput Press, 2004), p. 201.

107 *Irish Democrat*, November 1961.

108 *Irish Democrat*, December 1961.

109 *Irish Democrat*, November 1961.

110 *Irish Democrat*, January 1962.

111 *Irish Democrat*, March 1962.

112 Wittner, *Resisting the Bomb*, p. 298.

113 *Cameron Report*, p. 29; J. Quinn, 'No Surrender! History of the Early PD', *Anarchy*, 1, 6 (1971), p. 15.

114 Wittner, *Resisting the Bomb*, p. 192.

115 Doris Lessing, *The Golden Notebook* (London: Michael Joseph, 1963), pp. 495 and 601.

116 Tom Hayden, 'The Way We Were and the Future of the Port Huron Statement', in Students for a Democratic Society, *The Port Huron Statement: The Visionary Call of the 1960s Revolution* (New York: Thunder's Mouth Press, 2005), pp. 1–40, p. 8.

117 Clancy Sigal, 'Open Letter to the Left', *New Left Review* (January–February 1960).

118 C. Wright Mills, 'Letter to the New Left', *New Left Review* (September–October 1960).

119 Kathryn Mills and Pamela Mills (eds), *C. Wright Mills: Letters and Autobiographical Writings* (Berkeley: University of California Press, 2000), pp. 241, 243 and 316.

120 *New York Times*, 9 July 2000.

121 Mills, 'Letter to the New Left'.

122 Kevin Mattson, *Intellectuals in Action: The Origins of the New Left and Radical Liberalism, 1945–1970* (University Park: The Pennsylvania State University Press, 2002), pp. 83 and 85.

123 Interview with Tom Hayden, quoted in James Miller, *Democracy is in the Streets: From Port Huron to the Siege of Chicago* (London: Simon & Schuster, 1987), p. 86.

124 Hayden, 'The Way We Were and the Future of the Port Huron Statement', pp. 3–8.

125 Miller, *Democracy is in the Streets*, pp. 44–54 and 78–9; Polletta, *Freedom is an Endless Meeting*, pp. 24–6; Mattson, *Intellectuals in Action*, p. 70.

126 SDS, *The Port Huron Statement*.

127 SDS, *The Port Huron Statement*.

128 SDS, *The Port Huron Statement*.

129 Harvard Sitkoff, *The Struggle for Black Equality, 1954–1992* (New York: Hill & Wang), 1993 edn), pp. 94–5; Polletta, *Freedom is an Endless Meeting*, pp. 44–7.

130 Doug Rossinow, *The Politics of Authenticity: Liberalism, Christianity, and the New Left in America* (New York: Columbia University Press, 1998), pp. 104 and 135.

131 Rossinow, *The Politics of Authenticity*, pp. 5–7, 54, 75, 83, 104 and 135.

132 Albert Camus, *The Rebel*, trans. Anthony Bower (London: Penguin, 2000), p. 28.

133 Carson, *In Struggle*, pp. 96–8; Polletta, *Freedom is an Endless Meeting*, pp. 58–61 and 70.

134 Stuart Ewen, 'The Intellectual New Left', in Paul Buhle (ed.), *History and the New Left: Madison, Wisconsin, 1950–1970s* (Philadelphia: Temple University, 1990), pp. 179–80.

135 Albert Camus, *The Plague*, trans. Robin Buss (London: Penguin, 2001), p. 162; Tom Hayden, *Reunion: A Memoir* (London: Hamish Hamilton, 1989), pp. 76–7 and 117.

136 Carson, *In Struggle*, 108, 126–8, 236 and 241–2.

137 Doug McAdam, *Freedom Summer* (Oxford: Oxford University Press, 1988), p. 68.

138 Ewen, 'The Intellectual New Left', p. 180.

139 McAdam, *Freedom Summer*, pp. 67, 111, 117, 132, 137 and 163–9.

140 David Lance Goines, *The Free Speech Movement: Coming of Age in the 1960s* (Berkeley: Ten Speed, 1993), pp. 97–8, 105, 116–17 and 142.

141 Gabriel Cohn-Bendit and Daniel Cohn-Bendit, *Obsolete Communism: The Left-Wing Alternative*, trans. Arnold Pomerans (Penguin: London, 1969), p. 24.

142 James F. Tent, *The Free University of Berlin: A Political History* (Indianapolis: Indiana University Press, 1988), pp. 292–3.

143 Van Voris, *Violence in Ulster*, pp. 61–2.

144 Brian Dooley, *Black and Green: The Fight for Civil Rights in Northern Ireland and Black America* (London: Pluto, 1998), pp. 50 and 55; Purdie, *Politics in the Streets*, pp. 227 and 230–2.

145 George Breitman, 'How a Minority Can Change Society', *International Socialist Review* (Spring 1964).

146 *Derry Journal*, 5 April 1960; *Derry Journal*, 30 May 1961; *Derry Journal*, 23 July 1968.

147 Wilfried Mausbach, 'Historicising "1968"', *Contemporary European History*, 2, 1 (2002), pp. 177–88, p. 181.

148 Keith A. Reader and Khursheed Wadia, *The May 1968 Events in France: Reproductions and Interpretations* (Basingstoke: Macmillan, 1993), p. 11.

149 Robert Tombs, *France 1814–1914* (London: Longman, 1996), p. 22.

150 Todd Gitlin, *The Whole World Is Watching: Mass Media in the Making and Unmaking of the New Left* (London: University of California Press, 1980), pp. 194–5.

151 *Guardian*, 15 April 1968.

152 Carole Fink, Philipp Gassert and Detlef Junker, 'Introduction', in Carole Fink, Philipp Gassert and Detlef Junker (eds), *1968: The World Transformed* (Cambridge: Cambridge University Press, 1998), pp. 2, 3, 9 and 10.

153 Gitlin, *The Whole World Is Watching*, p. 235.

154 *Derry Journal*, 2 July 1968; McCann, *War and an Irish Town*, p. 86.

155 *Derry Journal*, 2 April 1968.

156 *Derry Journal*, 3 May 1968.

157 *Derry Journal*, 25 June 1968.

158 *Derry Journal*, 5 July 1968.

159 Gitlin, *The Whole World Is Watching*, p. 234.

160 *New Statesman*, December 1987.

161 Backus, ' "Not Quite Philadelphia, Is It?"', pp. 184–5.

162 Wilfried Mausbach, 'Auschwitz and Vietnam: West Germany's Protest Against America's War During the 1960s', in Andreas W. Daum, Lloyd C. Gardner and Wilfried Mausbach eds), *America, the Vietnam War, and the World: Comparative and International Perspectives* (Cambridge: Cambridge University Press, 2003), p. 297.

163 *Avant-Garde Jeunesse*, Special No. 10–11 (February-March 1968), in Alain Schnapp and Pierre Vidal-Naquet (eds), *The French Student Uprising November 1967–June 1968: An Analytical Record* (Boston: Beacon, 1971), pp. 74–9.

164 Nick Thomas, *Protest Movements in 1960s West Germany: A Social History of Dissent and Democracy* (Oxford: Berg, 2003), p. 159; Gretchen Dutschke, *Wir hatten ein barbarisches, schönes Leben – Rudi Dutschke: Eine Biographie von Gretchen Dutschke* (Cologne: Kiepenheuer & Witsch, 1996), pp. 180–7.

165 *Irish Democrat*, November 1966.

166 Ingo Juchler, *Die Studentenbewegungen in den Vereinigten Staaten und der Bundesrepublik Deutschland der sechziger Jahre: Eine Untersuchung hinsichtlich ihrer Beeinflussung durch Befreiungsbewegungen und -theorien aus der Dritten Welt* (Berlin: Duncker & Humblot, 1996), pp. 16–17, 391–2.

167 Che Guevara, 'Guerrilla Warfare: A method', in Jay Mallin (ed.), *Che Guevara on Revolution* (Coral Gables: University of Miami Press, 1969), p. 89.

168 Jay Mallin, 'Introduction', in Mallin (ed.), *Che Guevara on Revolution*, pp. 19–46, pp. 22–3, 30–1 and 41–3.

169 Juchler, *Die Studentenbewegungen in den Vereinigten Staaten und der Bundesrepublik Deutschland der sechziger Jahre*, p. 398.

170 Dutschke, *Wir hatten ein barbarisches, schönes Leben*, p. 184.

171 Ingo Cornils, '"The Struggle Continues": Rudi Dutschke's Long March', in Gerard J. DeGroot (ed.), *Student Protest: The Sixties and After* (London: Longman, 1998), p. 106.

172 Thomas, *Protest Movements in 1960s West Germany*, p. 76.

173 Mausbach, 'Auschwitz and Vietnam', pp. 288 and 289; Wilfried Mausbach, '"Burn, Ware-House, Burn!" Modernity, Counterculture, and the Vietnam War in West Germany', in Axel Schildt and Detlef Siegfried (eds), *Between Marx and Coca-Cola: Youth Cultures in Changing European Societies, 1960–1980* (Oxford: Berghahn Books, 2006), pp. 185 and 189.

174 Herbert Marcuse, 'The Problem of Violence and the Radical Opposition,' in Herbert Marcuse, *Five Lectures: Psychoanalysis, Politics, and Utopia*, trans. Jeremy J. Shapiro and Shierry M. Weber (London: Penguin, 1970), pp. 83–108, 95.

175 *Irish Militant*, October 1967.

176 *Irish Democrat*, November 1967.

177 *Derry Journal*, 27 September 1968.

178 Harold Marcuse, 'The Revival of Holocaust Awareness in West Germany, Israel, and the United States', in Fink, Gassert and Junker (eds), *1968: The World Transformed*, pp. 422–4.

179 Mausbach, 'Auschwitz and Vietnam', pp. 287–8 and 295.

180 Judt, *Postwar*, pp. 277, 355 and 416–17.

181 Claus Leggewie, 'A Laboratory of Postindustrial Society: Reassessing the 1960s in Germany', in Fink, Gassert and Junker (eds), *1968: The World Transformed*, p. 286.

182 Mausbach, 'Auschwitz and Vietnam', p. 294.

183 Kay Schiller, 'Political Militancy and Generation Conflict in West Germany during the "Red Decade"', *Debatte*, 11, 1 (2003), pp. 19–38, 23, 28–9, and 34.

184 Tariq Ali, *Street Fighting Years: An Autobiography of the Sixties* (Glasgow: Fontana, 1987), p. 171.

185 *Avant-Garde Jeunesse*, Special No. 10–11 (February–March 1968), pp. 74–9.

186 *Der Spiegel*, 26 June 1967.

187 Juchler, *Die Studentenbewegungen in den Vereinigten Staaten und der Bundesrepublik Deutschland der sechziger Jahre*, pp. 75, 89 and 391–2.

188 Dutschke, *Wir hatten ein barbarisches, schönes Leben*, pp. 18, 30, 40, 172 and 178.

189 E-mail correspondence with Roy Johnston, 23 June 2006.

190 Stuart J. Hilwig, 'The Revolt against the Establishment: Students versus the Press in West Germany and Italy', in Fink, Gassert and Junker (eds), *1968: The World Transformed*, pp. 327 and 331.

191 Thomas, *Protest Movements in 1960s West Germany*, p. 168–70.

192 Cohn-Bendit and Cohn-Bendit, *Obsolete Communism*, p. 52.

193 *Avant-Garde Jeunesse*, Special No. 12 (May 1968), quoted in Alain Schnapp and Pierre Vidal-Naquet (eds), *The French Student Uprising November 1967–June 1968: An Analytical Record* (Boston: Beacon, 1971), p. 74.

194 Ali, *Street Fighting Years*, pp. 180–9.

195 *Guardian*, 31 May 2000.

196 Special Branch report on American political activity in London, 24 November 1967, NAUK, HO/325/104; Special Branch report on American political activity in London, 26 February 1968, NAUK, HO/325/104.

197 Backus, ' "Not Quite Philadelphia, is it?"', p. 185.
198 David Cooper, 'Beyond Words', in David Cooper (ed.), *The Dialectics of Liberation* (London: Penguin, 1967), pp. 201–2.
199 David Cooper, 'Introduction', in Cooper (ed.), *The Dialectics of Liberation* pp. 7 and 9.
200 Stokely Carmichael, 'Black Power', in Cooper (ed.), *The Dialectics of Liberation*, p. 168; Dooley, *Black and Green*, p. 46.
201 Paul Arthur, *The People's Democracy* (Belfast: Blackstaff, 1974), pp. 23–4; *Irish Democrat*, July 1966.
202 *New Left Review*, January–February 1969.
203 Colin Crouch, *The Student Revolt* (London: the Bodley Head, 1970), pp. 70 and 116.
204 *New Left Review*, January–February 1969.
205 Jean-François Lévy, 'La People's Democracy', *Les Temps Modernes*, 20, 311 (1972), pp. 2009–47, 2011; Purdie, *Politics in the Streets*, pp. 211, 228–31 and 233–6.
206 *Derry Journal*, 4 August 1968.
207 Interview with Mary Nelis, www.tallgirlshorts.net/marymary/sli_arch_frameset.html, last accessed 26 April 2005.
208 *Derry Journal*, 4 August 1967; 16 August 1968.
209 *Derry Journal*, 19 July 1968.
210 *Londonderry Sentinel*, 7 August 1968.
211 *Derry Journal*, 16 August 1968.
212 *Derry Journal*, 27 August 1968.
213 McCann, *War and an Irish Town*, p. 91.
214 Cohn-Bendit and Cohn-Bendit, *Obsolete Communism*, pp. 54–5.
215 Seymour Martin Lipset, *Rebellion in the University: A History of Student Activism in America* (London: Routledge, 1972), p. xxi.
216 Meeting at 10 Downing Street on 4 November 1968, PRONI, CAB/4/1413.
217 *Guardian*, 31 May 2000.
218 *Sunday Telegraph*, 20 October 1968; *Sunday Telegraph*, 27 October 1968.
219 *Sunday Telegraph*, 3 November 1968.
220 Kristin Ross, *May '68 and its Afterlives* (London: University of Chicago Press, 2002), pp. 42–4 and 48–53.
221 Thomas, *Protest Movements in 1960s West Germany*, pp. 74–5 and 80–1
222 Thomas Etzemüller, 'A Struggle for Radical Change? Swedish Students in the 1960s', in Schildt and Siegfried (eds), *Between Marx and Coca-Cola*, pp. 248 and 250.
223 *Derry Journal*, 23 July 1968.
224 McCann, *War and an Irish Town*, p. 91.
225 Ó Dochartaigh, *Ulster's White Negroes*, p. 25.
226 *Derry Journal*, 23 July 1968.
227 McCann, *War and an Irish Town*, p. 92.
228 Ó Dochartaigh, *Ulster's White Negroes*, p. 25.
229 Frank Gogarty to George, 18 February 1969, PRONI, D/3253/1.
230 McCann, *War and an Irish Town*, p. 94.
231 *Derry Journal*, 10 September 1968.
232 *Fortnight*, 5 April 1974.
233 *Derry Journal*, 13 December 1968.
234 J.E. Greeves to Ivan Woods, 1968, PRONI, CAB/9B/205/7.

235 *Derry Journal*, 4 October 1968.

236 *Belfast Telegraph*, 4 October 1968.

237 *Cameron Report*, p. 26; *Fortnight*, 5 April 1974; Conn McCluskey, *Up Off Their Knees*, pp. 110–11; Northern Ireland Civil Rights Association, *We Shall Overcome ... The History of the Struggle for Civil Rights in Northern Ireland, 1968–78* (Belfast: NICRA, 1978), p. 13; McCann, *War and an Irish Town*, pp. 96–7; Ó Dochartaigh, *Ulster's White Negroes*, p. 48.

238 *Derry Journal*, 8 October 1968.

239 *Derry Journal*, 4 October 1968; Curran, *Derry*, p. 79.

240 *Cameron Report*, p. 69.

241 *Derry Journal*, 16 April 1968.

242 Van Voris, *Violence in Ulster*, pp. 45 and 71–2.

243 *Northern Ireland House of Commons Debates*, vol. 170, 16 October 1968, cols. 1014–1022 and 1025.

CHAPTER SIX

1 Niall Ó Dochartaigh, *From Civil Rights to Armalites: Derry and the Birth of the Irish Troubles* (Cork: Cork University Press, 1997), p. 20.

2 *Disturbances in Northern Ireland: Report of the Commission Appointed by the Governor of Northern Ireland (Cameron Report)* (Belfast: Her Majesty's Stationery Office, 1969), pp. 29–30; Paddy Doherty, *Paddy Bogside* (Dublin: Mercier Press, 2001), p. 58.

3 *Derry Journal*, 8 October 1968.

4 *Derry Journal*, 25 October 1968.

5 *Derry Journal*, 17 December 1968.

6 *Derry Journal*, 8 October 1968; Frank Curran, *Derry: Countdown to Disaster* (Dublin: Gill & Macmillan, 1986), pp.??4.

7 *Irish Times*, 7 October 1968.

8 *Derry Journal*, 5 March 1968.

9 *Derry Journal*, 25 October 1968.

10 *Cameron Report*, p. 90; Paul Bew, Peter Gibbon and Henry Patterson, *Northern Ireland, 1921–1994: Political Forces and Social Classes* (London: Serif, 1995), pp. 150–1.

11 This was the name that the British army later gave the city's disaffected young people. Henry Patterson, *Ireland since 1939* (Oxford: Oxford University Press, 2002), p. 223. The commission of inquiry and Eamonn McCann also referred to them as 'hooligans'. *Cameron Report*, p. 227; Eamonn McCann, *War and an Irish Town* (London: Pluto, 1993 edn), p. 114.

12 *Derry Journal*, 15 October 1968.

13 Michael Seidman, *The Imaginary Revolution: Parisian Students and Workers in 1968* (Oxford: Berghahn, 2004), p. 110.

14 *Northern Ireland House of Commons Debates*, vol. 170, 16 October 1968, col. 1022.

15 David Farber, *Chicago '68* (London: The University of Chicago Press, 1988), p. 249.

16 McCann, *War and an Irish Town*, p. 113.

17 Ó Dochartaigh, *From Civil Rights to Armalites*, p. 47.

18   *Derry Journal*, 18 January 1968.

19   *Derry Journal*, 28 June 1968.

20   *Derry Journal*, 15 October 1968.

21   *The Listener*, 24 October 1968.

22   *Derry Journal*, 11 October 1968; *Cameron Report*, p. 84.

23   Fionbarra Ó Dochartaigh, *Ulster's White Negroes: From Civil Rights to Insurrection* (Edinburgh: AK Press, 1994), p. 58.

24   McCann, *War and an Irish Town*, pp. 100–1.

25   *Derry Journal*, 11 October 1968.

26   Doherty, *Paddy Bogside*, p. 62.

27   *Londonderry Sentinel*, 16 October 1968.

28   Barry White, *John Hume: Statesman of the Troubles* (Belfast: Blackstaff, 1984), p. 64; Ó Dochartaigh, *From Civil Rights to Armalites*, p. 23.

29   *Derry Journal*, 15 October 1968.

30   *Derry Journal*, 15 October 1968.

31   *Derry Journal*, 16 May 1967.

32   *Derry Journal*, 18 October 1968.

33   *Derry Journal*, 22 October 1968; *Londonderry Sentinel*, 23 October 1968.

34   *Londonderry Sentinel*, 23 October 1968; Ó Dochartaigh, *Ulster's White Negroes*, p. 60.

35   *Derry Journal*, 22 October 1968.

36   Doherty, *Paddy Bogside*, p. 63.

37   *Derry Journal*, 28 July 1968; *Derry Journal*, 2 April 1968.

38   Memorandum on Local Government Reorganisation, 15 October 1968, Belfast, Public Record Office of Northern Ireland (PRONI), CAB/4/1316.

39   Memorandum on the Franchise, PRONI, CAB/4/1411.

40   *Northern Ireland House of Commons Debates*, vol. 170, 16 October 1968, cols. 1031–58.

41   Cabinet Conclusions, 23 October 1968, PRONI, CAB/4/1409.

42   *Belfast Newsletter*, 20 October 1968.

43   *Derry Journal*, 22 October 1968.

44   *Derry Journal*, 5 November 1968; *Londonderry Sentinel*, 6 November 1968.

45   *Derry Journal*, 8 November 1968.

46   Cabinet Conclusions, 31 October 1968, PRONI, CAB/4/1412.

47   *Derry Journal*, 15 November 1968.

48   Cabinet Conclusions, 19 November 1968, PRONI, CAB/4/1417.

49   Doherty, *Paddy Bogside*, p. 65.

50   *Derry Journal*, 19 November 1968.

51   *Derry Journal*, 19 November 1968.

52   Doherty, *Paddy Bogside*, pp. 68–72.

53   *Derry Journal*, 19 November 1968; *Londonderry Sentinel*, 20 November 1968; Ó Dochartaigh, *Ulster's White Negroes*, p. 66.

54   *Derry Journal*, 19 November 1968; *Londonderry Sentinel*, 20 November 1968; Ó Dochartaigh, *Ulster's White Negroes*, p. 66.

55   Seidman, *The Imaginary Revolution*, pp. 92–5.

56   Ó Dochartaigh, *Ulster's White Negroes*, p. 66.

57   *Derry Journal*, 19 November 1968; *Londonderry Sentinel*, 20 November 1968.

58   *Derry Journal*, 19 November 1968; *Londonderry Sentinel*, 20 November 1968.

59   Ó Dochartaigh, *Ulster's White Negroes*, pp. 69–70.

60 *Londonderry Sentinel*, 20 November 1968.
61 *Derry Journal*, 22 November 1968.
62 Seidman, *The Imaginary Revolution*, pp. 34, 94–5 and 164.
63 Stuart J. Hilwig, 'The Revolt against the Establishment: Students versus the Press in West Germany and Italy', in Carole Fink, Philipp Gassert and Detlef Junker (eds), *1968: The World Transformed* (Cambridge: Cambridge University Press, 1998), p. 328.
64 *Derry Journal*, 19 November 1968; Curran, *Derry*, p. 100.
65 *Derry Journal*, 22 November 1968.
66 Ó Dochartaigh, *Ulster's White Negroes*, p. 67.
67 *Londonderry Sentinel*, 20 November 1968.
68 *Derry Journal*, 22 November 1968.
69 Doherty, *Paddy Bogside*, p. 82.
70 *Derry Journal*, 19 November 1968.
71 Doherty, *Paddy Bogside*, p. 82.
72 *Derry Journal*, 22 November 1968.
73 Seidman, *The Imaginary Revolution*, pp. 97–8.
74 *Derry Journal*, 22 November 1968.
75 *Derry Journal*, 19 November 1968; *Derry Journal*, 22 November 1968.
76 *Derry Journal*, 22 November 1968.
77 McCann, *War and an Irish Town*, p. 103.
78 *Londonderry Sentinel*, 30 October 1968; Ó Dochartaigh, *Ulster's White Negroes*, pp. 62–3.
79 Robert Tombs, *France 1814–1914* (London: Longman, 1996), p. 24.
80 *Derry Journal*, 1 November 1968.
81 *Londonderry Sentinel*, 30 October 1968; *Derry Journal*, 1 November 1968.
82 Doug McAdam, *Freedom Summer* (Oxford: Oxford University Press, 1988), p. 174.
83 Sylvia Ellis, ' "A Demonstration of British Good Sense?" British Student Protest during the Vietnam War', in Gerard J. DeGroot (ed.), *Student Protest: The Sixties and After* (London: Longman, 1998), p. 62; James F. Tent, *The Free University of Berlin: A Political History* (Indianapolis: Indiana University Press, 1988), p. 330.
84 Mark Kurlansky, *1968: The Year that Rocked the World* (London: Jonathan Cape, 2004), p. 55; *Derry Journal*, 1 November 1968.
85 *Derry Journal*, 8 November 1968.
86 *Derry Journal*, 12 November 1968; *Londonderry Sentinel*, 13 November 1968.
87 *Derry Journal*, 17 December 1968.
88 Ó Dochartaigh, *Ulster's White Negroes*, pp. 71 and 75–7; *Derry Journal*, 6 December 1968; *Derry Journal*, 10 December 1968; *Derry Journal*, 3 January 1969.
89 *Derry Journal*, 26 November 1968.
90 *Cameron Report*, pp. 41–3.
91 Note by Harold Black, no date, PRONI, CAB/9B/205/7.
92 *Belfast Telegraph*, 16 October 1968.
93 *Derry Journal*, 19 November 1968.
94 *Belfast Newsletter*, 18 November 1968; *Derry Journal*, 22 November 1968; Brendan Lynn, *Holding the Ground: The Nationalist Party in Northern Ireland, 1945–72* (Aldershot: Ashgate, 1997), pp. 213–14.
95 Note by Harold Black, 15 October 1968, PRONI, CAB/9B/205/7.
96 *Belfast Telegraph*, 15 October 1968.

97 Note for the Record of the Lord Stonham–Eddie McAteer Meeting, no date, London, National Archives of the United Kingdom (NAUK), CJ/3/30.

98 *Derry Journal*, 15 November 1968.

99 *Derry Journal*, 11 October 1968.

100 Curran, *Derry*, p. 84–7.

101 *Derry Journal*, 12 November 1968.

102 Stonham–McAteer meeting; Telephone Conversation between Eddie McAteer and Lord Stonham's Private Secretary, NAUK, CJ/3/30; Military Aid to the Civil Authority in Northern Ireland, 13 December 1968, NAUK, PREM/13/2841.

103 *Derry Journal*, 11 October 1968.

104 *Derry Journal*, 8 November 1968.

105 Note for the Minister of State, no date, NAUK, CJ/3/30.

106 Stonham–McAteer meeting; Telephone conversation between McAteer and Private Secretary.

107 *Derry Journal*, 15 November 1968; Curran, *Derry*, pp. 92–3.

108 *Derry Journal*, 12 November 1968.

109 Eddie McAteer to Corinne Philpott, 24 March 1969, quoted in Enda Staunton, *The Nationalists of Northern Ireland 1918–1973* (Blackrock: Columba Press 2001), p. 260.

110 Doherty, *Paddy Bogside*, p. 84.

111 *Derry Journal*, 19 November 1968.

112 *Belfast Telegraph*, 11 December 1968.

CHAPTER SEVEN

1 *Belfast Telegraph*, 7 October 1968.

2 Terence O'Neill, *The Autobiography of Terence O'Neill* (London: Faber, 1972), pp. 102–3.

3 Ken Bloomfield, *Stormont in Crisis: A Memoir* (Belfast: Blackstaff, 1994), p. 98.

4 B.C. Cubbon Note, 7 October 1968, London, National Archives of the United Kingdom (NAUK), PREM/13/2841.

5 Bloomfield, *Stormont in Crisis*, p. 98; Cabinet Conclusions, 8 October 1968, Belfast, Public Record Office of Northern Ireland (PRONI), CAB/4/1405.

6 Bloomfield, *Stormont in Crisis*, pp. 74–5 and 98–9.

7 Witness Seminar on British Policy in Northern Ireland 1964-1970, 14 January 1992, London, Institute of Contemporary British History.

8 Memorandum by the Prime Minister, 14 October 1968, PRONI, CAB/4/1406.

9 Memorandum by the Prime Minister, 14 October 1968.

10 *Belfast Telegraph*, 5 October 1968.

11 Cabinet Conclusions, 8 October 1968.

12 Memorandum by the Prime Minister, 14 October 1968.

13 Cabinet Conclusions, 23 October 1968, PRONI, CAB/4/1409.

14 *Belfast Telegraph*, 23 October 1968.

15 Memorandum by the Prime Minister, 28 October 1968, PRONI, CAB/4/1411.

16 Cabinet Conclusions, 31 October 1968, PRONI, CAB/4/1412.

17 Meeting at 10 Downing Street on 4th November 1968, PRONI, CAB/4/1413; Extract from a Meeting Held at 10 Downing Street on 4th November 1968, NAUK, PREM/13/2841; Meeting on 4th November 1968, NAUK, CAB/164/334.

18 Meeting at 10 Downing Street on 4th November 1968; Extract from a Meeting Held at 10 Downing Street on 4th November 1968; Meeting on 4th November 1968.

19 Meeting at 10 Downing Street on 4th November 1968; Extract from a Meeting Held at 10 Downing Street on 4th November 1968; Meeting on 4th November 1968.

20 Meeting at 10 Downing Street on 4th November 1968; Extract from a Meeting Held at 10 Downing Street on 4th November 1968; Meeting on 4th November 1968.

21 *Guardian*, 31 May 2000.

22 Cabinet Conclusions, 23 October 1968.

23 Cabinet Conclusions, 7 November 1968, PRONI, CAB/4/1413.

24 *Belfast Newsletter*, 6 November 1968.

25 Cabinet Conclusions, 14 November 1968, PRONI, CAB/4/1414; Marc Mulholland, *Northern Ireland at the Crossroads: Ulster Unionism in the O'Neill Years 1960–9* (London: Macmillan, 2000), p. 164.

26 Cabinet Conclusions, 14 November 1968; Clive Scoular, *James Chichester-Clark* (Killyleogh: Clive Scoular, 2000), pp. 29–30, 52, 56 and 63.

27 Harold Wilson to Terence O'Neill, 19 November 1968, NAUK, PREM/13/2841.

28 Cabinet Conclusions, 23 October 1968; Cabinet Conclusions, 20 November 1968, PRONI, CAB/4/1418.

29 *Guardian*, 20 May 2002.

30 Cabinet Conclusions, 20 November 1968; O'Neill, *Autobiography*, p. 106.

31 *Belfast Telegraph*, 30 October 1968.

32 Memorandum on the Franchise, PRONI, CAB/4/1411.

33 *Belfast Telegraph*, 31 October 1968.

34 Walter Williams, General Secretary Grand Orange Lodge of Ireland, to Terence O'Neill, 12 November 1968, PRONI, CAB/9B/205/7.

35 Cabinet Conclusions, 21 November 1968, PRONI, CAB/4/1420.

36 Harold Wilson to Terence O'Neill, 23 December 1968, NAUK, PREM/13/2841.

37 Memorandum by the Prime Minister, NAUK, CJ/3/30.

38 *Londonderry Sentinel*, 23 October 1968; Note for the Record of the Lord Stonham–Eddie McAteer Meeting, NAUK, CJ/3/30.

39 Military Aid to the Civil Authority in Northern Ireland, 13 December 1968, NAUK, PREM/13/2841.

40 Chief of the General Staff to General Officer Commanding, 6 December 1968, NAUK, PREM/13/2841; Northern Ireland – Internal Security/Higher Chain of Command/Draft Note by the Defence Operations Staff, 4 December 1968, NAUK, CJ/3/31.

41 Witness Seminar on British Policy in Northern Ireland.

42 Michael Seidman, *The Imaginary Revolution: Parisian Students and Workers in 1968* (Oxford: Berghahn, 2004), pp. 215–21.

43 *Derry Journal*, 26 November 1968.

44 Observations on the Stormont Package, 25 November 1968, PRONI, D/3297/1.

45 *Disturbances in Northern Ireland: Report of the Commission Appointed by the Governor of Northern Ireland (Cameron Report)* (Belfast: Her Majesty's Stationery Office, 1969), pp. 36–43; Cabinet Conclusions, 2 December 1968, PRONI, CAB/4/1422; *Belfast Telegraph*, 2 December 1968; *Belfast Newsletter*, 2 December 1968; *Irish News*, 2 December 1968.

46 A. Gilchrist to the Western European Department of the Foreign Office, 9 December 1968, NAUK, CJ/3/30.

47 Jean Lacouture, *De Gaulle: The Ruler 1945–1970*, trans. Alan Sheridan (London: HarperCollins, 1991), pp. 557–8.

48 *Belfast Telegraph*, 2 December 1968; *Irish News*, 2 December 1968.

49 *Derry Journal*, 3 December 1968.

50 *Belfast Newsletter*, 2 December 1968.

51 *Belfast Telegraph*, 11 December 1968.

52 Andrew Gailey (ed.), *Crying in the Wilderness – Jack Sayers: A Liberal Editor in Ulster, 1939–69* (Belfast: Institute of Irish Studies, 1995), pp. 92–3.

53 *Belfast Telegraph*, 7 October 1968.

54 *Belfast Telegraph*, 14 October 1968; *Belfast Telegraph*, 22 October 1968; *Belfast Telegraph*, 26 October 1968; *Belfast Telegraph*, 1 November 1968; *Belfast Telegraph*, 4 November 1968; *Belfast Telegraph*, 12 November 1968; *Belfast Telegraph*, 23 November 1968.

55 James Scott, Louis Boyle, Rev. William Boland, James and Miriam Daly, Rev. R.D. Eric Gallagher, Rev. J.W. Henderson, Rev. J.L.M. Haire, Rev Alfred Martin, John and Marie F. Mee, B. Mick McGuigan, Rev. Desmond Mack, Ven J. Mercer, G.B. Newe, Norman and Monica Patterson, Rev. T. Carlisle Patterson, John E. Sayers, A.S. Worral, Rev. Desmond Wilson and Rev. D.H.A. Watson to Harold Black, 21 November 1968, PRONI, CAB/9B/205/8.

56 A. J. Weir, Clerk of Assembly and General Secretary of the Presbyterian Church in Ireland, to Terence O'Neill, 16 October 1968, PRONI, CAB/9B/205/7; *Belfast Telegraph*, 17 October 1968.

57 Note by Harold Black, 14 October 1968, PRONI, CAB/9B/205/7; Cabinet Conclusions, 15 November 1968, PRONI, CAB/4/1415.

58 Keith A. Reader and Khursheed Wadia, *The May 1968 Events in France: Reproductions and Interpretations* (Basingstoke: Macmillan, 1993), pp. 17–18.

59 Raymond Aron, *The Elusive Revolution: Anatomy of a Student Revolt*, trans. Gordon Clough (New York: Pall Mall, 1969), p. 25.

60 Bloomfield, *Stormont in Crisis*, pp. 75 and 101.

61 W.H. Van Voris, *Violence in Ulster: An Oral Documentary* (Amherst: University of Massachusetts Press, 1975), p. 45.

62 Peter Clarke, *Hope and Glory: Britain 1900–1990* (London: Penguin, 1996), p. 195.

63 Bloomfield, *Stormont in Crisis*, p. 101; *Belfast Telegraph*, 22 October 1968.

64 Mulholland, *Northern Ireland at the Crossroads*, p. 171.

65 Crossroads Speech, 9 December 1968, in Terence O'Neill, *The Autobiography of Terence O'Neill* (London: Faber, 1972), pp. 145–8.

66 *Sunday Telegraph*, 15 December 1968.

67 Ingrid Gilcher-Holtey, 'May 1968 in France', in Carole Fink, Philipp Gassert and Detlef Junker (eds), *1968: The World Transformed* (Cambridge: Cambridge University Press, 1998), p. 267.

68 Crossroads Speech, 9 December 1968, p. 149.

69 *Belfast Telegraph*, 10 December 1968.

70 *Belfast Telegraph*, 16 December 1968.

71 Jean Lacouture, *De Gaulle*, pp. 557–8.

72 *Belfast Telegraph*, 13 December 1968.

73 *Belfast Telegraph*, 14 December 1968.

74   *Derry Journal*, 13 December 1968.
75   Mulholland, *Northern Ireland at the Crossroads*, pp. 167–70.
76   O'Neill, *Autobiography*, p. 107. For example: Speech by Bill Craig to the Executive Committee of the Larne Constituency Unionist Association, 6 November 1968, PRONI, CAB/9B/205/7; *Belfast Newsletter*, 15 November 1968; *Belfast Telegraph*, 20 November 1968.
77   *Derry Journal*, 3 December 1968.
78   *Belfast Telegraph*, 5 December 1968.
79   *Belfast Telegraph*, 6 December 1968.
80   *Belfast Telegraph*, 11 December 1968.
81   *Belfast Telegraph*, 4 December 1968.
82   *Belfast Telegraph*, 11 December 1968.
83   I.M. Burns to Cairncross, 12 December 1968, NAUK, CJ/3/30.
84   *Belfast Telegraph*, 12 December 1968; *Belfast Telegraph*, 13 December 1968; *Derry Journal*, 13 December 1968.
85   *Observer*, 15 December 1968.
86   *Belfast Telegraph*, 10 December 1968; *Cameron Report*, p. 44; 'A former supporter of P.D.' to Kevin Boyle, 10 December 1968, PRONI, D/3297/1; *QUBIST*, 12 December 1968, Belfast, Public Record Office of Northern Ireland, D/3297/3; Paul Arthur, *The People's Democracy* (Belfast: Blackstaff, 1974), p. 38.
87   *Derry Journal*, 10 December 1968.
88   Henry Patterson, *Ireland since 1939* (Oxford: Oxford University Press, 2002), p. 208.
89   *Belfast Telegraph*, 13 December 1968.
90   *Observer*, 15 December 1968.

CHAPTER EIGHT

1   *Derry Journal*, 21 March 1967.
2   *Irish Militant*, April 1967.
3   Paul Arthur, *The People's Democracy* (Belfast: Blackstaff, 1974), p. 26; *Irish Democrat*, December 1967.
4   *Observer*, 20 October 1968.
5   *Irish Democrat*, May 1968.
6   *Irish Militant*, October 1967.
7   Michael Farrell, 'Introduction', in Michael Farrell (ed.), *Twenty Years on* (Dingle: Brandon, 1988), p. 14.
8   *Observer*, 20 October 1968.
9   *Irish Democrat*, March 1962.
10   *Irish Democrat*, March 1962.
11   *Irish Militant*, October 1967.
12   *Observer*, 20 October 1968.
13   *Guardian*, 5 November 2002; Anthony Coughlan, 'Draft Connolly Association History' (unpublished manuscript).
14   Nick Thomas, *Protest Movements in 1960s West Germany: A Social History of Dissent and Democracy* (Oxford: Berg, 2003), p. 59; John Callaghan, *British Trotskyism: Theory and Practice* (London: Blackwell, 1984), p. 127.
15   *Irish Militant*, November 1966.

16 Bob Purdie, *Politics in the Streets: The Origins of the Civil Rights Movement in Northern Ireland* (Belfast: Blackstaff, 1990), pp. 230–2.

17 Arthur, *The People's Democracy*, p. 24; Purdie, *Politics in the Streets*, pp. 230–2.

18 Ronald Fraser, *1968: A Student Generation in Revolt* (New York: Random House, 1988), p. 211.

19 A. Belden Fields, *Trotskyism and Maoism: Theory and Practice in France and the United States* (New York: Autonomedia, 1988), p 50.

20 *Derry Journal*, 4 October 1968.

21 Cameron Report, p. 32.

22 Kevin Boyle interview, 28 October 2006.

23 *The Listener*, 24 October 1968.

24 Boyle interview; *Belfast Telegraph*, 9 October 1968.

25 Boyle interview.

26 W.H. Van Voris, *Violence in Ulster: An Oral Documentary* (Amhurst: University of Massachusetts Press, 1975), pp. 73–5.

27 Boyle interview.

28 Farrell, 'Introduction', p. 14.

29 *Gown*, 22 October 1968.

30 Michael Seidman, *The Imaginary Revolution: Parisian Students and Workers in 1968* (Oxford: Berghahn, 2004), p. 23.

31 Gabriel Cohn-Bendit and Daniel Cohn-Bendit, *Obsolete Communism: The Left-Wing Alternative*, trans. Arnold Pomerans (London: Penguin, 1969), p. 47.

32 'Resolution adopted by 142 students occupying the Nanterre administrative buildings at night 22 March 1968', in Vladimir Fis˘era (ed.), *Writing on the Wall – May 1968: A Documentary Anthology* (London: Allison & Busby, 1978), pp. 76–7; Kristin Ross, *May '68 and its Afterlives* (London: University of Chicago Press, 2002), p. 91.

33 An account by the Registrar of a one-week demonstration by students and the events that led up to it, London, National Archives of the United Kingdom, CAB/151/67.

34 Michael McKeown, *The Greening of a Nationalist* (Lucan: Murlough, 1986), pp. 47–8.

35 Bernadette Devlin, *The Price of My Soul* (London: André Deutsch, 1969), p. 117.

36 *Observer*, 27 October 1968.

37 *New Society*, 31 October 1968.

38 Bertram Gordon, 'The Eyes of the Marcher: Paris, May 1968 – Theory and Its Consequences', in Gerard J. DeGroot (ed.), *Student Protest: The Sixties and After* (London: Longman, 1998), p. 42.

39 *Derry Journal*, 15 November 1968; *Derry Journal*, 13 December 1968; Voris, *Violence in Ulster*, p. 75.

40 *Disturbances in Northern Ireland: Report of the Commission Appointed by the Governor of Northern Ireland (Cameron Report)* (Belfast: Her Majesty's Stationery Office, 1969), p. 81.

41 *Defamator*, no. 3, Belfast, Public Record Office of Northern Ireland (PRONI), D/3219/3.

42 *Defamator*, no. 2, PRONI, D/3219/3.

43 Boyle interview.

44 Tom Fawthrop, *Education or Examination*, PRONI, D/3297/8. 45 Fraser, *1968*, p. 20.

46　*Defamator*, no. 4, PRONI, D/3219/3.

47　*Belfast Telegraph*, 1 November 1968.

48　*Belfast Telegraph*, 16 November 1968.

49　*Defamator*, no. 2.

50　*Defamator*, no. 3.

51　Jürgen Habermas, 'Student Protest in the Federal Republic of Germany', in Jürgen Habermas, *Toward a Rational Society*, trans. Jeremy J. Shapiro (London: Heinemann, 1971), pp. 13–30, 15.

52　*Defamator*, no. 1, PRONI, D/3219/3.

53　*Defamator*, no. 3; Columbia Strike Co-ordinating Committee statement, in Alexander Bloom and Wini Breines (eds), *"Takin' It to the Streets": A Sixties Reader* (Oxford: Oxford University Press, 1995), pp. 388–90.

54　Habermas, 'Student Protest in the Federal Republic of Germany', p. 20.

55　Boyle interview.

56　Albert Camus, *Neither Victims nor Executioners*, PRONI, D/3219/3; *Billy Liar*, November 1968, PRONI, D/3219/3; Boyle interview.

57　*Belfast Telegraph*, 20 November 1968.

58　J.E. Greeves to Harold Black, 10 October 1968, PRONI, CAB/9B/205/7.

59　Robbie Lieberman and David Cochran, '"It Seemed a Very Local Affair": The Student Movement at Southern Illinois University at Carbondale', in John McMillian and Paul Buhle (eds), *The New Left Revisited* (Philadelphia, Temple University Press, 2003), p. 112.

60　Boyle interview.

61　*Observer*, 20 October 1968.

62　*Belfast Telegraph*, 14 October 1968.

63　People's Democracy Agenda, PRONI, D/3297/1.

64　Greaves to Black, 10 October 1968.

65　Cornelius O'Leary to Harold Black, 18 October 1968, PRONI, CAB/9B/205/7.

66　*Belfast Telegraph*, 11 October 1968.

67　*Belfast Telegraph*, 25 October 1968; Devlin, *The Price of My Soul*, pp. 108–9.

68　*Belfast Telegraph*, 29 October 1968; *Newsletter*, 31 October 1968.

69　An account by the Registrar.

70　Arthur, *The People's Democracy*, pp. 33–4.

71　*Gown – March Supplement*, 5 November 1968, PRONI, D/3219/3.

72　*Gown – March Supplement*, 5 November 1968.

73　Devlin, *The Price of My Soul*, p. 117; Boyle interview.

74　An account by the Registrar.

75　Observations on the Stormont Package, 25 November 1968, PRONI, D/3297/1.

76　*Derry Journal*, 13 December 1968.

77　'A Former Supporter of PD' to Kevin Boyle, 10 December 1968, PRONI, D/3297/1.

78　*QUBIST*, 12 December 1968, PRONI, D/3297/3; *Cameron Report*, p. 44; Arthur, *The People's Democracy*, pp. 36–7.

79　*Defamator*, no. 4; Frank Gogarty to George, 18 February 1969, PRONI, D/3253/1.

80　Frank Gogarty, Towards a Programme of Campaign for 1969, December 1968, Belfast, Linen Hall Library Political Collection, P1063.

81　Gogarty, Towards a Programme of Campaign for 1969. 82 Fraser, *1968*, p. 210.

83　*Derry Journal*, 3 December 1968.

84　Boyle interview.

85　An account by the Registrar.

86 Fionbarra Ó Dochartaigh, *Ulster's White Negroes: From Civil Rights to Insurrection* (Edinburgh: AK Press, 1994), p. 78.

87 *Cameron Report*, pp. 44 and 82; Arthur, *The People's Democracy*, p. 39; Boyle interview.

88 Boyle interview.

89 Michael Farrell, *Northern Ireland: The Orange State* (London: Pluto, 1975), p. 249.

90 Brian Dooley, *Black and Green: The Fight for Civil Rights in Northern Ireland and Black America* (London: Pluto, 1998), pp. 55 and 57; Harvard Sitkoff, *The Struggle for Black Equality, 1954–1992* (New York: Hill and Wang, 1993 edn), pp. 189 and 200; Voris, *Violence in Ulster*, p. 86.

91 Michael Farrell, 'Long March to Freedom', in Michael Farrell (ed.), *Twenty Years On* (Dingle: Brandon, 1988), p. 57.

92 *Belfast Telegraph*, 1 January 1969.

93 *Cameron Report*, p. 44.

94 Witness Seminar on British Policy in Northern Ireland 1964–1970, 14 January 1992, London, Institute of Contemporary British History.

95 *Belfast Telegraph*, 1 January 1969; *Belfast Telegraph*, 2 January 1969; *Belfast Telegraph*, 3 January 1969.

96 *Derry Journal*, 27 December 1968.

97 Hand-written note, PRONI, D/3253/3/8/1, Frank Gogarty Papers; *Derry Journal*, 3 January 1969; *Fortnight*, 26 April 1974; Bowes Egan and Vincent McCormack, *Burntollet* (London: LRS, 1969), pp. 2–3, 11 and 48.

98 Voris, *Violence in Ulster*, p. 85.

99 Northern Ireland Information Service press release, 5 January 1969, PRONI, CAB/9B/205/8.

100 *Cameron Report*, p. 46.

101 Egan and McCormack, *Burntollet*, pp. 26–40; Boyle interview.

102 Frank Gogarty to Michael Farrell, 6 January 1969, PRONI, D/3253/3/8/3; *Fortnight*, 26 April 1974.

103 *Derry Journal*, 7 January 1969.

104 *Belfast Telegraph*, 18 October 1968.

105 *Cameron Report*, pp. 45–6.

106 *Derry Journal*, 7 January 1969; Voris, *Violence in Ulster*, pp. 87–9; Devlin, *The Price of My Soul*, pp. 139–41.

107 Egan and McCormack, *Burntollet*, pp. 12–14, 26–40 and 56.

108 *Belfast Telegraph*, 3 January 1969; *Belfast Telegraph*, 6 January 1969.

109 Basil Kelly to J.A. Peacocke, 14 January 1969, PRONI, CAB/9B/205/8.

110 *Sunday Times*, 1 December 1968.

111 *Derry Journal*, 12 November 1968.

112 *Derry Journal*, 7 January 1969; *Cameron Report*, p. 46; D.I. McGimpsey Report, 14 January 1969, PRONI, CAB/9B/312/5.

113 Voris, *Violence in Ulster*, p. 89.

114 *Cameron Report*, p. 46.

115 Boyle interview.

116 Henry Patterson, *Ireland since 1939* (Oxford: Oxford University Press, 2002), p. 209.

117 *Cameron Report*, p. 47.

118 Frank Curran, *Derry: Countdown to Disaster* (Dublin: Gill & Macmillan, 1986), p. 107.

119 Paddy Doherty, *Paddy Bogside* (Dublin: Mercier, 2001), pp. 87–8.

120 Voris, *Violence in Ulster*, pp. 92–3 and 97.

121 Doherty, *Paddy Bogside*, p. 88.

122 *Observer*, 5 January 1969.

123 *Derry Journal*, 7 January 1969; Egan and McCormack, *Burntollet*, pp. 46–8 and 57–8; Voris, *Violence in Ulster*, pp. 92–3 and 97.

124 *Cameron Report*, p. 73; Eamonn McCann, *War and an Irish Town* (London: Pluto, 1993 edn), p. 108; Voris, *Violence in Ulster*, p. 97.

125 *Derry Journal*, 7 January 1969.

126 *Derry Journal*, 7 January 1969.

127 Cabinet Conclusions, 6 January 1969, PRONI, CAB/4/1425.

128 Eamonn McCann, 'You Are Now Re-Entering Free Derry', in Eamonn McCann, *McCann: War & Peace in Northern Ireland* (Dublin: Hot Press, 1998), pp. 151–2.

129 *Cameron Report*, p. 83.

130 'Daniel Cohn-Bendit and Jean Pierre Duteuil', in Hervé Bourges (ed.), *The Student Revolt: The Activists Speak*, trans. B.R. Brewster (London: Panther, 1968), p. 69.

131 McCann, *War and an Irish Town*, pp. 109–10.

132 Patterson, *Ireland since 1939*, pp. 209–11.

CONCLUSION

1 *Observer*, 27 October 1968.

2 *New Left Review*, May–June 1969.

3 Brendan Simms, 'Continental Analogies with 1798: Revolution or Counter-Revolution?', in Thomas Bartlett, David Dickson, Dáire Keogh, and Kevin Whelan (eds), *1798: A Bicentenary Perspective* (Dublin: Four Courts, 2003), pp. 588–9.

4 *New Left Review*, May–June 1969.

5 Manfred Berg, '1968: A Turning Point in American Race Relations?', in Carole Fink, Philipp Gassert, and Detlef Junker (eds), *1968: The World Transformed* (Cambridge: Cambridge University Press, 1998), pp. 399–400.

6 Keith A. Reader and Khursheed Wadia, *The May 1968 Events in France: Reproductions and Interpretations* (London: Palgrave Macmillan, 1995), pp. 56–7; A. Belden Fields, *Trotskyism and Maoism: Theory and Practice in France and the United States* (New York: Praeger, 1988), p. 50.

7 Tony Cliff, *A World to Win*, www.marists.org/archive/cliff/works/2000/wtw/ch04.htm, last visited 26 April 2005.

8 Eamonn McCann, *War and an Irish Town* (London: Pluto, 1993 edn), pp. 311–12; Margot Gayle Backus, '"Not Quite Philadelphia, is it?": an Interview with Eamonn McCann', *Éire-Ireland*, 36, 3 & 4 (2001), p. 188.

9 *Irish Militant*, May 1967; Anthony Coughlan, 'C. Desmond Greaves, 1913–1988: An Obituary Essay', *Saothar*, 14 (1989), pp. 5–15, p. 6.

10 Poster advertising the meeting, Belfast, Public Record Office of Northern Ireland (PRONI), D/3253/5/14.

11 Berg, '1968', p. 406.

12 Eilis McDermott, 'Law and Disorder', in Michael Farrell (ed.), *Twenty Years on* (Dingle: Brandon, 1988), pp. 151–2.

13 Bernadette Devlin, 'A Peasant in the Halls of the Great', in Michael Farrell (ed.), *Twenty Years On* (Dingle: Brandon, 1988), p. 87.

14 Backus, '"Not Quite Philadelphia, is it?" ', p. 185.

15 Devlin, 'A Peasant in the Halls of the Great', p. 87.

16 Eamonn McCann, 'Preface', in Eamonn McCann, *McCann: War & Peace in Northern Ireland* (Dublin: Hot Press, 1998), p. 4.

17 Kevin Boyle interview, 28 October 2006.

18 The British Embassy to the Foreign Office, 15 September 1969, London, National Archives of the United Kingdom, CAB/164/573.

19 Andrew J. Wilson, *Irish America and the Ulster Conflict* (Belfast: Blackstaff, 1995), pp. 30–1; National Association for Irish Justice Conference, PRONI, D3297/4.

20 Appendix one to the secretary's report to Northern Ireland Civil Rights Association third annual general meeting – accusation of the resigned members, February 1970, PRONI, D3297/4.

21 Bernadette Devlin, *The Price of My Soul* (London: André Deutsch, 1969), p. 187.

22 Wilson, *Irish American and the Ulster Conflict*, pp. 35–6; National Association for Irish Justice to Kevin Boyle, 17 December 1969, PRONI, D/3297/8.

23 *Observer*, 7 September 1969.

24 Devlin, *The Price of My Soul*, p. 205; *Violence and Civil Disturbances in Northern Ireland in 1969: Report of the Tribunal Inquiry* (*Scarman Report*) (Belfast: Her Majesty's Stationery Office, 1972), p. 78.

25 Donatella Della Porta, *Social Movements, Political Violence, and the State: A Comparative Analysis of Italy and Germany*, (Cambridge: Cambridge University Press, 1995), p. 159.

26 *Observer*, 27 October 1968.

27 Albert Camus, *The Plague*, trans. Robin Buss (London: Penguin, 2001), pp. 237–8.

28 *Ramparts*, no. 2, PRONI, D/2464.

29 Nell McCafferty, *Nell* (Dublin: Penguin Ireland, 2005), pp. 200–1.

30 McCafferty, *Nell*, pp. 126 and 143.

31 Ciarán Mac an Áili to Frank Gogarty, 1 January 1970, PRONI, D/3297/2.

32 Tony Judt, *Postwar: A History of Europe since 1945* (London: William Heinemann, 2005), p. 565.

33 Boyle interview.

34 Kristin Ross, *May '68 and its Afterlives* (London: The University of Chicago Press, 2002), pp. 141–2 and 198–9.

35 Doris Lessing, *The Golden Notebook* (London: Michael Joseph, 1971), 'Preface'.

36 Anne Devlin, 'A Woman Calling', in Anne Devlin, *Ourselves Alone, with A Woman Calling and The Long March* (London: Faber, 1986), pp. 157–91, p. 180.

37 Anne Devlin, 'The Long March', in Anne Devlin, *Ourselves Alone, with A Woman Calling and The Long March* (London: Faber, 1986), pp. 91–155, pp. 111 and 155.

Index